THE EMPIRE THAT
WOULD NOT DIE

Based on the Carl Newell Jackson Lectures

THE EMPIRE THAT WOULD NOT DIE

The Paradox of Eastern

Roman Survival, 640–740

JOHN HALDON

Harvard University Press

Cambridge, Massachusetts

London, England

2016

Second printing

Library of Congress Cataloging-in-Publication Data

Haldon, John F., author.
The empire that would not die : the paradox of eastern Roman
survival, 640–740 / John Haldon.
pages cm
"Based on the Carl Newell Jackson Lectures"—Half title page.
Includes bibliographical references and index.
ISBN 978-0-674-08877-1 (alk. paper)
1. Byzantine Empire—History—527–1081. 2. Byzantine Empire—
Foreign relations—Islamic Empire. 3. Byzantine Empire—Politics and
government—527–1081. 4. War and society—Byzantine Empire.
5. Human ecology—Byzantine Empire. I. Title.
DF571.H354 2016
949.5'013—dc23   2015033363

Contents

Illustrations and Tables

Note on Names

I have used standard English forms for personal names, where they exist; and where not, Latinized versions. Transliterations of Arabic names and terms are according to a slightly simplified version of that employed in the *Encyclopaedia of Islam*. I have left Greek place names and Greek titles, ranks, and offices in their transliterated Greek form.

Greek, Latin and other technical terms, ranks, and titles are elucidated in a glossary at the end of the volume.

Acknowledgments

The present volume represents a considerably expanded version of the four Carl Newell Jackson lectures that I had the honor to deliver at Harvard University in April 2014. I am grateful to the founder of the lectures for the opportunity it gave me to outline some new ideas, and to the Department of the Classics for the invitation; and I thank the members of that department who showed me such kindness and hospitality during my stay there, as well as all those who attended the lectures and asked such incisive questions. The lectures began as a relatively brief comment on the state of our understanding of the seventh-century east Roman world and more especially about the mechanics and details of the survival of an east Roman Empire at all. But I soon discovered that the material pulled me in so many exciting and challenging directions that I found myself writing a much longer book than I had envisaged. The writing and research took place across two and a half years: in Princeton, where I owe a debt of gratitude to my colleagues in the Departments of History, Art History and Archaeology, Classics and Near Eastern Studies as well as in the Seeger Center for Hellenic Studies for their forbearance, interest, and support during the writing; in Vienna and Frankfurt, where colleagues were likewise generous with comments and time; and in the field in Turkey, where I was able to visit several key sites and continue to expand my understanding of the relationship between land, people, and environment. Many colleagues and friends have contributed, in various ways and often unwittingly, to the development of this book and to deepening my understanding of the period, its sources, and its problems, and I would like to thank Wolfram Brandes, Peter Brown, Michael Cook, Molly Green, Robert Hoyland,

Eric Ivison, William Chester Jordan, Walter Pohl, Petra Sijpesteijn, Yannis Stouraitis, and Jack Tannous, in particular. I want also to express my special gratitude to my colleagues and friends Helmut Reimitz, Meaghan McEvoy, Adam Izdebski, and Zachary Chitwood, and to my graduate students Cecilia Palombo and Lorenzo Bondioli, all of whom read and offered helpful and critical comments on the manuscript; and to the anonymous reviewers for Harvard University Press, whose helpful and constructive remarks and insights encouraged me to sharpen and clarify a number of ideas as well as ways of expressing them. Any failings in the final product are, of course, entirely my own.

THE EMPIRE THAT

WOULD NOT DIE

Introduction

Goldilocks in Byzantium

In this year [740], in the month of May, indiction 8, Souleiman invaded the Roman country with 90,000 men under four commanders. One of these, Gamer [Ghamr b. Yazid], led the van with 10,000 scouts and set up ambushes in the region of Asia. He was followed by Melich [Malik b. Shu'aib] and Batal ['Abdallah al-Battal] with 20,000 cavalry as far as the area of Akroinos and, after them, Souleiman with 60,000 men advanced to the area of Tyana in Cappadocia. Those in Asia and Cappadocia captured many men, women and animals and returned home unharmed, whereas the contingents of Melich and Batal were fought and defeated by Leo and Constantine at Akroinos. Most of them, including the two commanders, perished by the sword.[1]

Akroinos in Phrygia is modern Afyonkarahisar, and the battle described in the opening passage from the early-ninth-century *Chronographia* of the monk Theophanes is often assigned special significance as the point at which the almost constant Arab raids and attacks into Anatolia was finally stopped. In fact, they continued for a while thereafter, but it is true that this was the first battle for almost a century in which eastern Roman rulers (Leo III and Constantine V) at the head of their army had defeated an invader so decisively. And yet only forty years earlier it had seemed as though the Roman Empire was doomed to extinction. The purpose of this book is to explain how this situation had been transformed.

Déjà Vu?

It is now twenty-five years since the first edition of *Byzantium in the Seventh Century: the Transformation of a Culture* was published, and in that time a substantial amount of important and often exciting work on this complex and transformative period has been done. But while I think that the basic picture painted in that book remains, in its broad outlines, more or less valid, scholarship on many single aspects of many different problems has moved ahead. Our knowledge of the archaeology of the late Roman world in the east is now vastly greater than it was in the 1980s, even if there is still much work to be done and even though there are still fundamental gaps in our knowledge and in the data at our disposal. Our understanding of the religious conflicts, in particular the issues surrounding the so-called monothelete conflict, is now very much clearer than it was, both in respect of the theological as well as the political aspects. More scholars than ever are actively engaged in elucidating specific details of the period, ranging from hagiographical and homiletic studies, through the study and history of both canon and secular law, to administrative and sigillographic research and to questions of environmental history.

It is a great pleasure to be able to look back over this material and to be able to evaluate it, to build upon it, and to attempt to generate a new synthesis of some of it in an effort to understand how the east Roman state survived the seventh century. Syntheses always run the risk of being seen as premature, of course. Yet, as has often been pointed out, we will never have "enough" data to offer satisfactory and persuasive answers to all the questions we want to ask, and since each generation of historians has its own questions as well as those it shares with previous generations, waiting until the time is right is perhaps a fruitless enterprise.[2] Given how much new research has now been made available, it seemed an appropriate moment to consider pulling some of this material together, not in order to update an older work but, on the contrary, to approach the subject of large-scale historical transformation with some slightly different questions in mind. For in spite of all this recent work, I still do not think that we have fully grasped the mechanics of east Roman survival. That the empire did survive in a somewhat altered form is clear, and we can trace and describe many of the aspects that composed part of that process. But the specific interconnections, the articulation of the various dynamic elements that facilitated the emergence of a "medieval" state from a late ancient eastern Roman one, are still not entirely clear. In attempting to synthesize as well as to offer new material, new approaches, and new questions for discussion, it will be necessary in places to go over old ground. But I have tried not to repeat in detail arguments made elsewhere. I have also tried to put those arguments into a different context and to refocus our attention toward a balanced appreciation of all the different elements at issue and a qualitatively different sort of answer to the question of how and why the empire survived. I hope very much, therefore, that this will not be felt to be a case of déjà vu.

An End to the "Dark Ages"

No longer can we dub this era a "dark age"—a term first coined by Petrarch in the fifteenth century, intended to describe the difference between the classical civilization of Rome and the ensuing centuries of "barbarism." Reaching from the seventh to the ninth century in Byzantium as elsewhere in Europe, the period from the middle of the seventh through into the ninth century was thought of as an era during which literary culture almost ceased to exist, in which traditional forms of historical writing fell into abeyance—in short, a time in which the civilizing influence and hegemony of Rome was shattered. Indeed, only with Petrarch's own era, the Renaissance, was it thought that some of the sophistication of the ancient world in both culture and intellectual affairs had returned. Even today it is an appealing notion to think that we are finally able to overcome a barbarous past and recover the values of learning and aesthetics that are assumed to have been possessed by the intellectuals and even the politicians of the classical world or of late Republican Rome. Of course, color symbolism, the symbolism of light and darkness, has a very powerful hold on our imagination. We speak of golden ages or silver ages, but nothing is quite as effective as the notion of a dark age in invoking something gloomy, impenetrable, something problematic, even mysterious—and something from which societies and cultures have to recover.

But the historiography of the twentieth and twenty-first centuries has come to see the Dark Ages from a somewhat different angle: they are dark not because they were barbarous but because there are so few documentary or written sources, or at least that is the reasoning. Yet these supposed Dark Ages are dark only because we are still wearing our Rome-tinted spectacles, and if we look for different sorts of literature and different sorts of evidence, we discover that there is a good deal of information but that we need to handle it with different sorts of questions and with a different historical agenda from the way in which we might deal with a different period, better documented from the point of view of narrative sources. This is a point now well established and frequently repeated, and we need not pursue it further.[3] But it is worth reminding ourselves that the period from the late seventh until the later ninth century witnessed the birth and formation of the characteristic features of middle Byzantine state and culture. The transformations that took place during the seventh century, especially after the first Arab-Islamic conquests, were accompanied by broad shifts in the direction of both secular and ecclesiastical culture; in the organization of government and the administration of finance, of the army; in the administration of justice and the transmission of the law; and in many other areas. Such changes reflected changed priorities and concerns as the empire struggled against apparently overwhelming odds.

The Byzantine Empire[4]—better described, in fact, as the medieval Eastern Roman Empire—has been characterized as many things: as a bulwark against expanding Islam, as a bridge between east and west, as the transmitter or at least as a conserver of Classical literature and learning, as the last ancient state. Depending on one's perspective, none of these is totally incorrect—but it does depend on one's perspective. Perhaps the most dramatic claim, widely accepted for many years, is that the Byzantine Empire and Byzantine civilization held back "the tide of Islam" for over six centuries. This permitted the medieval west to mature into the shape and evolve the institutions that are the basis for the modern European world. Such teleologies hardly aid us in understanding how the medieval Eastern Roman Empire evolved and came to occupy the position in later views of its history that it did. Neither does such a Eurocentric and determinist view help us get beneath the surface of east Roman society, culture, and economy, nor does it help to understand how the Romans of the eastern empire in the sixth–ninth centuries saw themselves or understood their role in the world as they perceived it.[5]

But it is many years now since the Eastern Roman Empire was seen through the eyes of Enlightenment thinkers such as Edward Gibbon as a corrupt and reactionary culture. Gibbon remarked of Byzantium that "in the revolution of ten centuries, not a single discovery was made to exalt the dignity or promote the happiness of mankind." Yet however reluctantly, perhaps grudgingly, he was forced to admit that what he perceived as the abject failure of the Byzantines to sustain civilization was in itself the cause of the rise "of new colonies and kingdoms." Byzantium was at least "passively connected with the most splendid and important revolutions which have changed the state of the world" as well as stopping the early expansion of Islam—from his perspective, of course, something to be avoided at all costs.[6] East Roman survival is, perhaps with greater justification in some respects at least, also held to have set the seal on the direction and form of eastern European and Russian history, with implications for the nature of political authority, ideology, and the exercise of power that are still with us today in the lands that once formed what Dimitri Obolensky famously dubbed the "Byzantine commonwealth."[7]

That some people in the Eastern Roman Empire in the seventh century understood their struggle to survive as a clash of civilizations—between the values and culture of the traditional Roman world, on the one hand, and what the patriarch of Jerusalem could only describe in the 630s as "the abomination of the desert," on the other—would not be entirely incorrect.[8] But this reflects neither the nature of east Roman perceptions of the challenge nor the different levels of understanding and awareness that were present in eastern Roman society, nor again does it do justice to the ways in which east Roman society thought or functioned. Already by the year 700, a short sixty years after the initial conquests in the east, a hagiographer could refer to Palestine and Greater Syria as "the land of our enemies."[9] Yet this was not yet a clash between Christianity and Islam. Even if some Christian thinkers as early as Anastasius of Sinai in the later seventh century saw Islam as a distinct religion,[10] from the Roman point of view the conflict was a confrontation between a civilized state and society and uncivilized barbarians. They were the "godless Saracens," as the patriarch of Constantinople, Thomas, called them in a letter written at some point between April 667 and November 669,[11] and this view predominated throughout the first century of the conflict. In contrast, it is no surprise to learn that interest in Islam as such evolved far more rapidly and was far better informed in the conquered provinces of the east, provoking Christian apologetic writings as well as lively debate and discussion between Christians and Muslims.[12] Within the Eastern Roman Empire, indeed, only from the later eighth and early ninth century did a more nuanced understanding of Islam evolve, and only in the last decades of the ninth century did Islam begin to be seen as an existential challenge to the eastern Roman state and the Christianity through which it represented itself to the world. By the same token, we should recall that recent studies of early Islam have suggested that a fully Islamic identity was still in many respects a work in progress at the end of the seventh century.[13]

We still do not fully understand how the eastern Roman state managed to live through this initial conflict and get past the year 700—indeed, how it managed to overcome what look today like quite overwhelming odds. As I noted, there has been a good deal of attention paid to the seventh century in recent years, with a substantial literature on its many and various aspects. The political events of the period as viewed through the complex written source material, the religious history and conflicts of those years, and the archaeology of the city and of rural settlement have all received scrutiny. In reflecting this interest and the scholarship invested in the period and its problems, the present volume goes into the details, the mechanics of survival, to see how exactly it was possible.

Some Issues for Comparison: Collapse, Survival, and Agency

One of the most fascinating questions asked by historians and social scientists alike is, why do social systems collapse? What conditions arise that bring about the breakdown of a great empire? The concomitant questions are, obviously enough, why do some systems not collapse, and what permits a society or state to survive the sorts of traumatic structural and conjunctural damage inflicted upon it of the sort experienced by the eastern Roman state in the second half of the seventh century? There are almost as many answers to such questions as there have been states and empires themselves. Just as importantly, there is little agreement among historians or social scientists about how best to describe "transformation" or change in a way that is heuristically open and does not fall into teleology or foreclose the discussion by assuming the out-comes.[14] The study of states and especially of empires or imperial sys-tems has become especially active in the last three decades, in part a reflection of contemporary discussions and concerns about the nature of imperialism in the modern world; the degree to which states on the one hand and empires on the other represent separate or similar sets of structures; the extent to which they benefit, exploit, or do both; and the reasons for the evolution and growth of states as well as empires in the first place.

Comparative social historians exploit both political science as well as historical perspectives on state systems and state formation, and they have been especially productive of questions and frameworks for analysis and discussion. Most historians have tended to deal with just one or per-haps two empires or states, comparing and contrasting their different features and characteristics, or, alternatively, to focus on one particular state and society, in the study of which they are specialized, while some—the minority—tackle the question through the elaboration of metahistorical models into which a range of historical exempla are fitted and explained on the basis of a common causal logic. Depending on one's perspective, all of these can be useful and have an explanatory value. And while this book will not address these issues directly, it is important to bear in mind that there exists a long-standing and rami-fied debate among historians and social and political scientists about the dynamics of state and imperial systems within which discussion of the history of the Eastern Roman Empire should be situated.[15]

A key motive for reexamining the business of eastern Roman sur-vival, therefore, will be in respect of the nature of recent comparative work on imperial systems and empires, and especially premodern em-pires. Several studies have appeared in recent years that take up issues of imperial collapse or of systems collapse or, to take the words of one well-known popular writer, of "how societies choose to fail or succeed." Some of this is sophisticated, some of it less so, but nearly all of it de-pends on zooming out of the detailed level of source-based analysis and construction of evidence-based arguments to that of broad comparisons between "systems" in order to arrive at generalizable conclusions.[16] There is nothing wrong with this; indeed, it is something to be welcomed by specialist scholars of particular areas or periods because it compels us to look above the parapet of our own disciplines and think about big

issues that make the study of the past relevant to contemporary concerns
and questions. But there is also a tendency to take the societies examined in this way out of their own sociocultural and material context, to
dehistoricize them to a degree, and this is regrettable because we lose
sight of what is culturally specific in the process of causation. In looking
once again at what happens to the late Roman Empire and state in the
east in the period from the fifth to the ninth or tenth century, one of
the aims of my own work has been to rehistoricize the story, but without
losing sight of this larger picture.

So why do states "fail?" Indeed, is this even the right question? It
might be helpful to offer a few general observations about the nature of
the discussion mentioned above. From a historian's perspective, the
"failure" of a state or the "collapse" of a social formation has, in fact,
much more to do with processes of transformation and their complex
and interrelated causes than it has with any notion of failure. This is not
to deny that catastrophic change occurs, nor that when it happens it
does not bring with it the collapse of traditional modes of social organization and the breakdown of material cultural systems and technologies. Indeed, the whole question of "late Antiquity" and where and at
what levels of sociocultural organization continuity and gradual transformation as opposed to discontinuity and collapse are to be located is a
classic case.[17] "Failure," however, is a political science concept replete
with teleology (think of "failed states," for example): failure is the result of malfunction in a system, and while it is often helpful to speak of
a social or economic or political system, it is important to keep in view
the fundamentally unpredictable nature of human responses to change
and the fundamentally dynamic and shifting nature of human social
organization, even in intensely conservative sociopolitical cultures.
"System" itself implies, even if unintentionally, a certain stability and
the fixed relationships of the parts of the system to one another that thus
generate a particular whole.

This is useful in some analytical and comparative contexts, as the
rich literature on comparative social and political evolution demonstrates, and it would be unduly negative to avoid the term. Indeed, it is
essential to be able to generalize if we are to make comparisons that help
understand elements that were held in common by very different formations. Examining systems as dynamic and evolving makes more
sense, and several scholars have looked for the reasons behind sys-

temic collapse from the perspective of their increasing complexity and sophistication—the more complex they become, the finer the balance between the mutually interdependent parts of which they consist and the greater the potential for disequilibrium to set in when one feature becomes unstable, generating a domino-effect breakdown of the whole.[18] This approach has been useful in thinking about large-scale systemic breakdown in, for example, patterns of trade and exchange, as well as in respect of international political systems.[19] The difficulty with this assumption is that complex systems may also demonstrate great flexibility, and resilience is another key feature for which we need to be on the lookout. Resilience is, in fact, a much better way to think about non-collapse and collapse, and whether we apply this to a single cultural entity or to an international system, it is a useful way to think about both aspects.[20] Of course, with hindsight and from such a comparativist, complex systemic perspective, states and political systems as well as social formations do indeed change and disappear, to be replaced by other, often different arrangements. So to speak of systems failing or being replaced offers some advantages in respect of descriptive convenience as well as analytical simplicity. Since, at this level of analysis, the pressures and stresses that generated these changes were not unique to any single "system," the fact that they had different potentialities and effects in different contexts means that comparative analysis is essential to grasping how these were worked out in actual empirical cases. Another, complementary way of approaching this question has been summed up in recent years through "complexity theory," the aim of which is to explain the result of the interaction of systems and sub-systems over a specific period of time and in a specific context. This approach can also be described as the science of "non-linear dynamics." Drawn originally from mathematics (for example, chaos theory), computer science and the physical sciences, complexity theory challenges the principles of linear explanation and causation. It emphasizes the randomness of causation, in which the interplay of multiple human actors with one another, within behavior-determining social and institutional contexts, and with the physical environment, generates "emergent" social praxis. Societies and state systems can be seen as complex adaptive systems, and emphasis is placed on the unpredictability of possible outcomes (or, in historical terms, of knowing all the causal elements leading to a particular outcome).[21] To some extent, of course, this describes what historians have always done when working at this level of causal explanation, but the introduction of the term and the ideas it embodies is a useful reminder of the complex nature of causal dynamics in a historical context. And it should also be noted that this randomness is not actually chaotic or entirely random—all human social action is constrained by certain physical and spatial conditions as well as by pre-existing cultural limitations and norms—indeed if this were not the case, the writing of history as causal analysis would be impossible.

The counterpart to system has to be "conjuncture," that is to say, the processual moments experienced by the set of relationships described by the term "system," moments that impose the pressures that promote change or shifts. Here we may invoke theoretical models such as resilience theory, for example, developed by prehistorians and archaeologists of preliterate cultural systems to account for the transformative processes that bring about change. This approach takes as its starting point the nature of the adaptive cycles that the evidence reflects in terms of strategies of risk minimization (in periods of insecurity or stress, whether environmental or anthropogenic) or maximization (in times of stability and demand for increased gains from production processes and relations of exploitation). This is of interest because it theorizes the ways in which different types of political organism, from small-scale lineage structures to imperial systems, respond to challenges with greater or less success and offers a set of paradigms within which historians and archaeologists might try to understand their often highly problematic and patchy data. To be heuristically useful it needs to take into account as much as can be known about *mentalités,* about attitudes and beliefs, about the "world view" of the cultures in question. This is always a very problematic area, but it is essential insofar as social practice, and the ability to react effectively to changes in circumstances are also built into the thought-world, the conceptual environment inhabited by people in the society under study.[22]

I mention just one set of potentially helpful ways of asking questions about how we can valorize and make sense of the varied types of evidence at our disposal. The discussion around state formation and around the growth and decline or collapse of both imperial and simple state systems is complex and substantial. Many different models of such developments, based on many different typologies of social and political systems, have been developed. But in most theorizations there are a number of constants, key features that all agree can lead to the break-down of states, although with differently configured roles according to the type of state formation at issue. Thus the tensions and contradictions thrown up by increasingly complex administrative and functional requirements,[23] the issues associated with demographic pressure or changes, factionalism and competition within dominant elites over access to resources,[24] imbalances in the relationship between production and environment or between these and the demands of the state and/or a landlord elite, and "external" factors such as the impact of warfare and consequent economic, social, and demographic disruption have all been singled out as potential causal triggers, usually in various combinations.[25] As we have just said, their impact depends then upon the type of political-economic organization in question since clearly different levels of flexibility can be expected from states and societies according to their internal articulation as well as their geography, ecology, and relationship to other formations—whether, for example, they are "marcher" polities, peripheral to one or more interior systems and thus with greater room for maneuver in times of stress, or "interior" states, elements of a congeries of political formations that in effect block one another's expansion.[26]

Quite apart from issues of system and conjuncture are questions of the relationship between agency and structure—questions of belief, of ideological cohesion, of the impact and penetration of sets of ideas and concepts held by different social-economic groups within a social formation, and the social practices that accompany these. At the level of the grand narratives and comparative historical work just described, such aspects often get pushed into the background or generalized, and thus trivialized in terms of their causal importance. Of course there are exceptions, such as Michael Mann's discussion of the role of the monotheistic soteriological world religions from the first century CE onward.[27] The degree to which certain key ideas are held across a society as a whole, or the extent to which the beliefs and ideology of the dominant political elite are irrelevant for the day-to-day interests and identities of the mass of the population, have a crucial impact on social cohesion, whether in times of stress or not, and must be a significant factor in how a given state system organizes its control of resources or whether it has the internal strength or flexibility to weather particular political, social, or economic moments or longer periods of pressure. The extent to which

a religious ideology or a political theology of rule and rulership pene-
trates to the roots of a society affects both the way in which people perceive and respond to the challenges they face, or even whether they
perceive them at all, as well as the means through which a cultural
system hangs together under stress. Part of this is also tied into notions
of the law, of rights, responsibilities, and the sources of judicial, moral,
and spiritual authority. All these are important elements in the fabric
of the social whole, and it is only by taking them all into account and
seeing how they overlap, interlink, and act upon one another that we
can hope to glimpse something of the social mechanisms behind people's
actions as both individuals and as members of one or more groups.[28]

Individual, Agency, and Belief

This brings us to a number of questions. First, how can we appreciate the
role of the individual and of groups in their social and cultural context
as agents in a way that accounts for both the irrational as well as the
intentional (regardless of whether such intentions can be known or
not) in individual choice, and that likewise accepts that what may seem
irrational or illogical to us may not be understood as such from the perspective of the culture that we study? How can we take into account
the ambiguities of daily life and the multiple roles and contested situations or moments in which individuals as well as groups of people so
often find themselves? Second, how do we understand the play between
the social and economic structures or contexts into which individuals
are born (to the maintenance or not of which they come to contribute)
on the one hand, and, on the other, the broader sets of "economic"
relationships—production relations—within which all these factors are
inscribed but which they in turn affect. Social "structures"—relational
and institutional—determine the access people have to resources, both
material as well as cultural/spiritual, and, hence, the range of possibilities open to people to act in particular ways: they determine the
structural capacities open to human beings in their social context.[29] But
an adequate understanding of human action must also take human
beings as possessing intentions, beliefs, and desires in their activity
(even if for many cultural systems we generally cannot know what these
were), hence reconciling both the constitutive and constituted aspects
of human personality and self-perception. Understanding how the

"symbolic universe" of the culture (the "Weltanschauung," the shared world of knowledge and concepts, tacit and voiced, implicit and explicit, that inform people's lives and understanding of their universe) determines and informs social action and how such action reacts back upon that ideational space is one important aspect of this, and in thinking about historical change it is important not to push it to the side if we are to avoid a mechanistic view of medieval society and properly take into consideration the conjunctural, emotional and "lived" experience of the individuals and groups who populate the historical landscape. By the same token, understanding how a political ideology, a more-or-less rational system that legitimates and explains power-relationships within a given political culture, is grounded in the symbolic universe is just as important.[30]

This serves, importantly, to emphasize that what people believe as the expression of human perceptions of their world and their effectiveness in it can also be a material force and can provide an account of the world based in one set of structural relationships, which can promote practices that transcend or transform those relationships. Asserting the relevance of intentions as a fundamental element in human consciousness and practice is not to assume thereby either that intentions can ever be identified or located, or—more importantly—that the intentions ascribed to actions by the actors or by other commentators are necessarily true. It is simply to underline the point that we cannot take structures as objects for analysis without also taking the agents who both constitute and are in turn constituted by them as part of the same equation.

Now I do not wish to give the impression that what people believe is a fixed quantity, nor that where we have some idea of those beliefs, at any period of human history, we can explain actions and responses through assuming a direct relationship. What is believed and how that fits into the complex set of ideas, concepts, and tacit knowledge that people have of their world certainly sets limits to how they respond and react to their environment, as I have already observed. Beliefs respond to perceptions of the world as much as they represent a narrative about the world and therefore imply conjuncture and contingency. Yet, at the same time, how people respond to changes they see or events that concern them does permit us to limit the range of motives underlying those actions and responses. While we cannot know much, if anything at all, about the beliefs of most of the individuals who populate the history of the seventh- and eighth-century east Roman world, we may still deduce something of their views and of the issues that concerned them from their reactions to events as described in chronicles and histories, in letters and in sermons, in the acts of church councils, in the writings of hagiographers and theologians and, sometimes, in the writings of the individuals themselves.

One of the enduring myths about the Byzantine world is that it was somehow more pious, more observant than the societies with which most of us are familiar—the secularizing cultures of the industrial and postindustrial "west." Similar attitudes prevail in regard to medieval and, indeed, premodern cultures more generally, certainly among those who are not familiar with their history and with the world of medieval beliefs and ideas. Yet such a perspective renders it almost impossible to grasp the cultural logic of the medieval world. "Byzantines" were every bit as pragmatic as modern people, but their pragmatism, just like ours, was determined in its expression and in its possibilities by their own symbolic and moral universe. For "average" medieval people—whether in the west or in the Byzantine world—what we might deem the supernatural (a miracle, a vision, a prophecy, or a dream) was taken as entirely real, as a natural element of the everyday world. It is perfectly possible to believe in demons and evil spirits, in the power of an amulet or of prayer to ward off evil, in the strength of one's faith to preserve one's kin or city or army from disaster, and at the same time to act in an entirely pragmatic way in order to achieve certain ends—as we see in every account of east Roman strategic politics and military activity. This should not be taken to mean, incidentally, that some individuals may not have harbored extreme doubts about some elements of the world-view of their fellows, nor that medieval people could not also be deeply cynical about certain ideas or practices, as we will see in Chapter 2 of this volume. Choices made by individuals and under some circumstances then adopted by groups reflect perceptions of self as well as awareness of the likely results of certain actions. Historically, individuals have pursued courses that they knew would lead to suffering, torture, pain, or death in order to affirm belief in a particular understanding of the world and/or to affirm membership of a particular group or community and its aims, whether this be religious or political, for example. Others avoided such courses, for exactly the same reasons. Such choices

[handwritten marginalia: We have not become smarter, just differently informed]

should be understood for what they were—rational decisions grounded in a particular identity, value system, and perception of causality, regardless of their knowing precisely what the consequences might be. The medieval real or imaginary was not necessarily the same as our own perceptions of reality or the imagined, but this does not mean that choices were irrational, nor that people were somehow unaware of the consequences of their actions and utterances.[31] But it does mean that the logic of another culture's symbolic universe will mean that its assumed causal relationships may be invisible to us as outsiders, or that actions will be based on a causal logic that makes no sense for us. This means neither that people were acting illogically or foolishly, nor that their logic did not seem to work perfectly well. Most importantly, that logic must be understood as the basis from which actions were derived and reactions were motivated, and as historians we need to build that into our explanations of the ways in which people worked on their world and conducted their affairs.[32] To see properly into the logic and rationale of such a different *mentalité* requires an approach informed both by careful historical and cognitive anthropological analysis of texts and cultural production, something we cannot begin to address here.[33] But we should have constantly in mind the fact that this cultural logic is the backdrop to the events and actions that we will be examining.

The Medieval East Roman Paradigm

How does the Eastern Roman Empire fit into this? As has been remarked before, the history of the medieval Eastern Roman "Empire" is largely one of contraction, although it also remains remarkable for the fact that it was one of the longest-lived state formations in historical times of which we are reasonably well-informed, with an unbroken succession of rulers, institutional and sociocultural continuity, and territorial cohesion lasting over a millennium.[34] Indeed, it should be taken as an uninterrupted continuation, in the Balkans and Anatolia, of the Roman Empire—dramatic changes in its physical shape there may have been, yet there was no political rupture and no break in the traditions of imperial rule. Of course, there were fundamental changes and transformations across its history. The outer provinces of the eastern part of the later Roman Empire were peeled away during the course of the later sixth and seventh centuries, but Anatolia and the Aegean basin remained (along with Sicily, parts of Italy and North Africa for a while) to become the heartland of a medieval, Christian "Roman" state, with a powerful centralizing ideology—a 'political theology'—based in a Christian eschatology that predicted that its emperor, God's vicegerent on earth, would eventually prevail against all enemies, establish the world dominion of orthodox Christianity, and lead into the Second Coming, the end of time, and the last judgment.[35]

Byzantine rulers struggled across the centuries to preserve this system in practical terms, chiefly through diplomatic means and the erection and maintenance of a complex system of political interdependencies between the empire and its immediate neighbors, and between the latter and those beyond them. Diplomacy was largely defensive. Offensive wars were undertaken occasionally, generally justified or understood as attempts to restore the world empire rather than expand it.[36] And whereas strands of continuity ran through Roman political and military institutions into the late Roman period and then beyond into the medieval period, they were to a large extent completely transformed in respect of religion and culture. The fundamental assumptions of autocratic rule and the emperor's absolute authority—thought to be granted by God—were, as a formally sanctioned (although never set out in detail) theoretical exposition of the ruler's position, unchallenged. But the situation was complicated in practical respects by a division of responsibilities, always contested, between the secular and religious spheres, between emperor and patriarch, between the notion of the emperor's God-granted authority and the authority he received through popular sanction of senate, army and people. Such tensions were embodied in the reality of potential opposition to a particular emperor from a variety of sources—the military, members of the elite, provincial populations, or the church, or any combination of these—opposition that could be justified or at least explained post factum by invoking the will of God, the needs of the state or its inhabitants (or a section of them), or other salient factors picked out by the medieval commentators.[37] It is, of course, undeniable that many members of the cultural elite were at the same time familiar with classical literature, philosophy and historiography in which the absolute power of the ruler or rulers was constrained by an antique tradition about the right of citizens to determine who ruled them and to intervene if that rule was perceived to have gone awry. From one perspective, the traditional groups of senate, people and

Dichotomy: a traditional & "new, christianity" understanding of the role of the emperor [handwritten annotation]

army always retained a "constitutional" right to rebel or to depose an emperor, for example.[38] On the basis of these traditions and the knowledge of them among members of the elite, an argument has been made that the autocratic aspect of the imperial system should be set aside as fundamentally misleading: it was not the emperor, but the people as a conscious political body, that held sovereign power. The East Roman state should thus be understood as a "republican monarchy," in which the ruler's authority was tempered by "the people," and in which the Christianity of the imperial ideological system, what I would refer to as the political theology of the empire, has been given far too great a weight by modern historians.[39] But while the fact remains that much of the Greco-Roman heritage survived, albeit often in a transformed and reconfigured framework, most obviously in the literature and cultural self-image of the (numerically very small) elite, Christianity entirely replaced the older pantheon for the majority. Imperial authority could rarely be challenged effectively, and certainly not by "the people," whoever this term is meant to represent—even if it is the case that at Constantinople emperors had to be aware of and take into account the dangers of alienating a large urban populace that could at times readily be manipulated by a variety of oppositional interests as well as breaking into spontaneous demonstrations of discontent or hostility.[40] What is important is how these relationships evolved along quite different trajectories in the former western lands of the Roman Empire and in the regions that become the medieval eastern Roman state. I shall have more to say about this in Chapter 3 in particular.

Socially, culturally, and economically, the eastern half of the Roman Empire before the middle of the seventh century had been polycentric, with major urban foci of culture located in Egypt, Syria, and Palestine as well as the Balkans, even if it is also the case that the imperial court at Constantinople became the major trans-Mediterranean focus for social advancement.[41] But in the course of the sixth century and much more clearly during the seventh century, with the loss of much territory, it became a metropolitanocentric empire, focused on its capital, Constantinople. This can be seen in the extraordinary power of its emperor as well as in art and architecture, which for the most part, with important exceptions at times, radiated to the periphery. The impregnability of Constantinople was one factor among many—and certainly a very important one—in keeping the empire alive for more than a millennium against pressures from Goths, Huns, Avars, Persians, Arabs, Bulgars, and later the Ottomans, even when, during its last century, it was reduced to a tiny rump territorially. Yet already in the fifth and sixth centuries the strategic focus of the eastern half of the empire had been concentrated on the east, in Syria and Mesopotamia, in the Caucasus, and in the Balkans (and on the Ukrainian steppe). It was in this sense very much a Middle Eastern and Balkan state, even if vested interests, tradition, and politics also meant a continued regard for western affairs.

For the student of early medieval history observing the explosive dynamism of the early Islamic expansion the survival of the eastern Roman state may seem like something of a miracle. From the standpoint of the later Roman Empire of the fourth and fifth centuries, or even that of the expansionist age of Justinian in the middle of the sixth century, the institutional, ideological, and fiscal solidity of the eastern Roman state are impressive. At first sight it seems easy enough to claim that, in spite of territorial loss, plague, military defeat, religious conflict, and an enormous collapse in fiscal revenue, the empire was sound enough to resist even the most determined of onslaughts. On the other hand, if we look at the empire in the 620s and 630s, then its considerably weakened situation after the exhaustion of the Persian war under Heraclius (the "last great war of Antiquity," as it has been appropriately dubbed), the religious dissent within the eastern provinces, the fervent opposition to imperial policy led by such brilliant theologians as Maximus the Confessor, the depleted state of the imperial armies and the beginnings of substantial economic change, including demographic decline—all this would surely suggest a very fragile edifice that ought to have come tumbling down, as indeed the opening phases of Arab-Islamic expansion would seem to indicate.

There has been plenty of research to show that Justinian's achievement was already substantially jeopardized by the end of his reign, overstretched both financially and militarily, his successors inheriting a poisoned chalice in many respects. By the same token the parlous state of the empire by the time the Persian war ended in 628 is widely recognized, as is the fact that civil war in the Caliphate in the second half of the seventh century gave the empire a breathing space, or breathing spaces, just when it most needed them and permitted some stabilization of the situation. And so we return to the question of societal or political

collapse—or noncollapse. The way a political system or a social formation or an economy respond to stresses and pressures of varying degrees
depends, as well as on the factors noted earlier, upon their origins—how
and under what conditions did the Eastern Roman Empire evolve, what
were the parameters within which it could prosper, and how flexible
were Roman social and economic relations and structures in the face of
stress?

And so what Byzantines believed and how those beliefs affected how
they acted is an essential aspect of how their society worked: beliefs and
the symbolic and moral universe that people, all people, inhabit are absolutely crucial elements in the functioning of any culture. The following chapters consider the ways in which what people thought about
their world affected the way they acted on a day-to-day basis as well as
their response to perceived problems or worries. I do not mean to suggest that belief determines action in any absolute or mechanistic sense—
on the contrary, what and how individuals believe represents their
contingent reaction to the world they see around them as well as a means
of representing themselves to themselves and to others, depending upon
social/cultural context. Yet, while a specific set of ideas or beliefs should
not be characterized as fixed or essential, it is also the case that the group
and cultural narratives generated to explain the world do provide the
framework within which social action can be thought of and thus offer
a way into the cultural logic of a specific historical moment. How did
people in the eastern Roman world respond to the events of the seventh
and early eighth centuries? How did they construct their world in their
own minds, and what did that set of ideas entail in terms of the way
they understood what was happening to that world? And how did all
this affect how they understood themselves as members of a community, where they saw themselves in this light at all? Issues of leadership
are just as important here—that is to say, the role of emperors and their
advisers as well as of the cultural and political elite, in the survival of
the eastern Roman state. These are difficult questions with complex
answers, but I will try to show how these factors played a key role both
in the survival of the empire and in how we understand the Byzantine response to the developments of the period with which we are
concerned.

Whether people invest in civic infrastructure and amenities, as in
the Hellenistic and Roman world up to the third century; whether they

invest in church- or temple-building or the endowment of religious foundations, artwork and decoration, or charity; or whether they invest in court offices, tax farms, or commercial ventures, or a combination of all of these, such activities obviously reflect prevailing values and assumptions about what is important in their world. Beliefs can be seen to directly affect patterns of wealth investment and, consequently, the ways in which elites, for example, appropriate and consume wealth as well as the ways in which political regimes are able to maintain themselves, or not. Since what people believed certainly affected political action and thus, potentially (depending on context), economic relations, it seems obvious that if we want to understand the processes of change, we need to build beliefs and their contingent social effects into our model of causal relationships. Indeed, the effect of what people believed about a situation upon their reactions or responses is a key element of social action. Social practice is predetermined by a range of limiting and qualifying conditions into which people are born and that circumscribe both their field of action and the possibilities open to them intellectually. But the cumulative effects of social praxis have unforeseen outcomes, so intentions are rarely matched by results. Karl Marx's famous comment at the beginning of his *The Eighteenth Brumaire of Louis Bonaparte* is a useful reminder of all this: "Men make their own history, but they do not make it just as they please; they do not make it under circumstances chosen by themselves, but under circumstances directly encountered, given and transmitted from the past." So, as I have already suggested, it is important to remember that politics and cultural practice—ideology—are not secondary but are rather the expression of sets of relationships between people, and between people and their cultural environment, in a multitude of different contexts.[42]

There is another important aspect in this story that I want to underline. Largely ignored, taken for granted, or glossed over in historical scholarship of the period is the simple fact that eastern Roman society was stratified, highly exploitative, and, in socioeconomic terms, deeply divided. It was a society divided not just by regional differences and identities, by linguistic variation, by status markers, by vertical as well as horizontal associations of kinship and patronage, and by gender. It was divided by strongly-marked socio-economic differences, in which a few controlled and had access to the resources generated by the many. Awareness of such distinctions existed, of course, most especially and obviously in Christian ethical discourse about wealth and poverty, and action to address aspects of them, through charitable activities, for example, can also be found—indeed imperial charitable institutions and the help they offered to the indigent or dispossessed were an important aspect of the philanthropy expected of the ruler.[43] Put another way, and from a purely economic perspective, this was a class society, like all the surrounding socio-cultural formations, even if the people who comprised those classes had no awareness of this—there simply was no suitable vocabulary—in such modern terms.[44]

It is easy to see the imperial court and those who made up the social elite of the empire in our written sources, and it is not so hard to see the middling and upper levels of urban populations also. But the vast mass of the subjects of the eastern Roman emperors are less obvious, present but silent in legislation and histories and other types of text, objects of the views, prejudices, and often hostility (although occasionally also the sympathy) of those who were literate. These were the working populace of the cities, great and small, and the rural populations of the provinces, the great majority farmers and herdsmen, along with the craftsmen, artisans, and others of similar status and occupations in small rural towns or in villages. Most farmers and herdsmen were peasant tenants of varying legal status, some semifree, some free, but all subject to the coercive power of the state fiscal apparatus, a landlord, or both.[45] The differences in wealth between the ordinary rural population of the empire and the social elite were massive, and such dramatic disparities could only be overcome through a constantly fluctuating combination—varying by region and situation—of physical force, ideological constraint (secular law as well as ecclesiastical; custom and tradition; inherited and timeless "ways of doing"), and patronage.

The army was the only coercive force at the disposal of the state, and social tension and violent conflict—between taxpayers and fiscal authorities, between brigands and bands of robbers or runaway peasant tenants and slaves and the authorities, for example—was not unusual. The wealthy, especially in the provinces and on the estates from which their wealth was derived deployed substantial bands of armed retainers to enforce their own authority, even though the government frequently tried to ban or control such bodies. And imperial legislation had to take these conditions into account, as we will see in Chapters 3 and 4. Such tension and conflict is regularly written out of the modern history of the Byzantine Empire, and while it is the case that we learn very little about it because our sources either choose not to mention it or because we have no sources that refer to it, we should not forget that it lies under the surface of the historical events that we can see and that it informed the beliefs and actions of all the individuals and groups with whom we shall be concerned. Yet, by looking more carefully at the archaeological data, where we have it, we can sometimes glimpse aspects of the lives of ordinary people in town and country with regard, for example, to changes in the spatial organization of dwellings or public spaces, sources of water and arrangements for managing water supplies, and so forth.[46] And by taking all these varied and multifaceted questions and placing them in their broader environmental context—shifts in patterns of seasonal rainfall, the nature of land use and agriculture, or more general changes in climatic conditions—we can begin to sketch out some possible answers to questions about the processes and underlying causes of change.

Recent historical study of the seventh century has focused on the politics of the period, both secular and imperial as well as religious and ecclesiastical, on the one hand, and on the archaeology, patterns of exchange, and economic history of the period, on the other. As a result of this excellent work we now have a much better understanding of the origins, evolution, and course of the so-called monothelete controversy,[47] a better and fuller picture of the political events of the period and of the various and complexly-interrelated written sources,[48] a greater understanding of the administrative and institutional evolution of the states that inherited the Roman world,[49] and a more rounded picture of the fate of urbanism, of settlement patterns, and of exchange relationships both within the east Roman world and across the broader east Mediterranean basin.[50] We know a great deal more today than we did twenty or thirty years ago about the origins, development, and political as well as social, cultural, and economic history of the early Islamic world and of the early post-Roman Balkans and Italy.[51] In particular, scholarship has seen that conflict and confrontation was but one aspect of the relationship between the young world of Islam and the old world of Rome, and that behind the political struggle there was a great deal of interaction, of overlapping social and cultural practice, of interchange of ideas and concepts, and of shared traditions.[52] It is also generally recognized that many of the key developments of the seventh century have their origins long before as the social, economic, and political-ideological changes that were generated within the later Roman world ran their course. The changes and transformations in urban life and civic culture; shifts in the nature of the ruling elite across the empire and in the relationship its members held with the imperial court and administration both at Constantinople and in the provinces; shifts in attitudes to the emperor, to imperial rule, to the relationship between ruler and church; changes in the way the empire was managed fiscally and militarily—all had their roots in the fifth and sixth centuries as the creaking structure of the late Roman state evolved in new directions under new pressures and in the face of inbuilt systemic contradictions and stresses.[53]

There is, as ever, a great deal more to be done, and as new archaeological material comes to light and new technologies help us understand that material, as old sources are subject to reappraisal and reassessment, so our conclusions must by definition remain provisional. To offer answers to the questions I have outlined, I will deal with them by looking at three key areas representing three intersecting and interdependent fields of social being: "ideas" (mostly Chapters 2 and 3 with parts of Chapter 4), "spaces" (mostly Chapters 5 and 6), and "praxis" (Chapters 4, 5, and 7, but in fact some aspects of all the chapters). The ideational—beliefs, ideas, and ideologies—played a fundamental role in informing people's actions on a day-to-day basis as well as reflecting and being constituted by the social context within which they evolved and were maintained and reproduced; the spatial—the geography, ecology, and environment of the eastern Roman world, its resources, and communications—all impacted and inflected the physical as well as the metaphysical or imaginary spaces within which people lived out their lives, within which they imagined themselves and their world, within which also the state functioned, and from which it, as well as private persons, derived their livelihoods; and the practical—social being in the widest sense, praxis—comprised the managerial and administrative arrangements of state and church, of family and household, of soldier and cleric and farmer as well as the ideas and beliefs that went along with these and many other roles. The Eastern Roman Empire in fact offers a good opportunity to ask the question of collapse from the other side, about a collapse that we might think should have taken place but did not: how did the much-reduced rump state of east Rome deal with its

mammoth eastern neighbor, a neighbor that outnumbered and out-
gunned it on virtually every count? How could such a political-military
David have resisted the onslaught of this Goliath of the Near and Middle
East? What were the key factors that permitted it to withstand the systemic and structural stresses to which it was subjected during those
years? What sort of society was it that was able to resist what might
seem like the inevitable for so long, and how did it evolve and transform over the centuries? Questions of resilience and adaptation clearly
lie at the heart of all this. But to a large extent scholarship has been
content to describe what happens in the seventh and eighth century (in
itself a complex and substantial undertaking), note that this demonstrates the resilience and adaptability of "Byzantine society" or state,
and leave things there. In fact, this does not get us very far. What we
need to know is how exactly this resilience and adaptability actually
worked—how does resilience express itself in social action and beliefs,
for example? How does adaptation appear in the institutional arrangements, economic and political relationships we can observe in our
sources? These are the big questions underlying this book. Readers will
judge whether a sufficiently persuasive answer has been offered.

Some years ago natural scientists coined the term "the Goldilocks
Principle" to describe the very specific sets of conditions that make a
particular phenomenon possible, a term that has now begun to be used
in engineering and economics as well as psychology and other social sciences. Simply put, this states that something must fall within certain
margins, as opposed to reaching extremes, in order to survive or to be
effective. When the effects of the principle are observed, it is known
as the Goldilocks effect. It is, of course, based on the story of Goldilocks
and the Three Bears, in which the little girl of the same name happens
upon a cottage owned by three bears. Each bear has its own preference
of food, beds, chairs, and so forth. After testing each of the three items,
Goldilocks determines that one of them is always too much at one
extreme (too hot, too large, etc.), one is too much in the opposite extreme
(too cold, too small, etc.), and one is "just right." Thus, in economics, a
Goldilocks economy sustains moderate economic growth and low infla-
tion; and a Goldilocks market is when the price of goods falls between
a bear market and a bull market; in medicine it can refer to the ideal
dosage of a medication, for example, between the extremes that might
result in the demise of a patient.[54] In our terms, the question is: what

were the mechanisms, the context, and the forms of social and cultural practice that together represented the "Goldilocks conditions" for Byzantium? It hardly needs pointing out that, as soon as one thinks about it, it becomes apparent that absolutely everything has its "Goldilocks parameters," so I want to stress that the term is deployed here merely in a figurative rather than any formal analytical way. But it is a useful way to ask precisely what conditions were necessary for the continued existence of the eastern Roman state and society, culture, and religion?

1

The Challenge

A Framework for Collapse

On account of the frequent assumptions of imperial power and the prevalence of usurpation, the affairs of the empire and of the City were being neglected and declined . . . As a result, the enemy were able to overrun the Roman state with impunity and cause much slaughter, abduction and the capture of cities. For this reason also the Saracens advanced on the imperial City itself, sending forth by land an innumerable host of horse and foot from the various peoples subject to them, as well as a great fleet.[1]

In 565, the last year of the reign of Justinian I, the Eastern Roman Empire stretched from southern Spain and North Africa across to the Syrian desert and included Italy and Sicily, Sardinia and Corsica, the Balearic islands and the Balkans up to the Danube. Yet by 650 this picture had changed in ways that a century earlier would have been unimaginable. A glance at the map will help: on the one side, instead of the Sasanian Persian state, the enormous caliphate now dominates, stretching from the Atlantic to northern India and the central Asian steppe, and including the rich provinces of Syria, Iraq, and Egypt. On the other side, the little Eastern Roman Empire, after the collapse of Roman power following the Arab attacks and conquests of the years 634–650, reduced to a rump of its former self. By the year 700, all its Middle Eastern, North African, and western Mediterranean provinces had been lost, with the possible exception of a tenuous Roman presence in the Balearics into the second half of the eighth century and, of course, Sicily, southern

Italy, and the exarchate of Ravenna in the north. The regions that remained were among the least wealthy of its former provinces, among
which Egypt had contributed as the most productive, the main source
of grain for Constantinople, and a major source of the state's tax income.
We get some idea of the enormity of the change when we look at the
differences in income to the state from the middle of the sixth to the
end of the seventh century.

Although reliable statistical data from the late Roman world is relatively sparse, at least in terms of the global sums with which we are
interested here, it is possible to arrive at some generally agreed figures
that give some idea of the relative proportions of the state's fiscal income
(in both grain and gold) derived from its various provinces and regions.
Thus, from figures given by a range of sources, it has been calculated
that in the later fifth and sixth centuries Egypt contributed revenues of
something between 1.4 and 2.6 million gold *solidi* (Gr. *nomismata*);[2] that
the Justinianic prefecture of Africa could contribute some 390,000–
400,000 solidi,[3] or between about 25 percent and 16 percent that of
Egypt (depending on which of the figures suggested for Egypt is taken);[4]
and that Sicily may have contributed at the very least 150,000 and possibly as much as 400,000 solidi, the same as Africa.[5] At an absolute minimum, Egypt provided something like 35 percent to 40 percent of the
total fiscal income of the eastern prefecture (including Thrace),[6] which
amounted to some 4 million solidi yearly, with the remaining eastern
dioceses of Asiana, Pontica, and Oriens together contributing 2.5 million
solidi. The Anatolian regions of Pontica and Asiana were not significantly wealthy, certainly not as wealthy as the Syrian regions, although
the exact relation between the two can only be guessed at—perhaps
1:2 on the basis of later sixteenth-century Ottoman revenue figures, so
that Syria generated 1 million of the total of 1.5 million solidi.[7] The Balkan
provinces, although in theory quite wealthy, generated only minimal
revenues after the middle of the fifth century, in view of their relatively
dislocated economies; indeed, by the middle of the sixth century the
combined revenues from Africa, Italy, and Illyricum (the Balkan provinces outside greater Thrace: the provinces of Thracia, Haemimontus,
Rhodope, and Europa) amounted to only about 25 percent of those of
the eastern prefecture.[8]

These proportions can be corroborated to a degree by anecdotal references in early Islamic sources, and by comparing these figures with

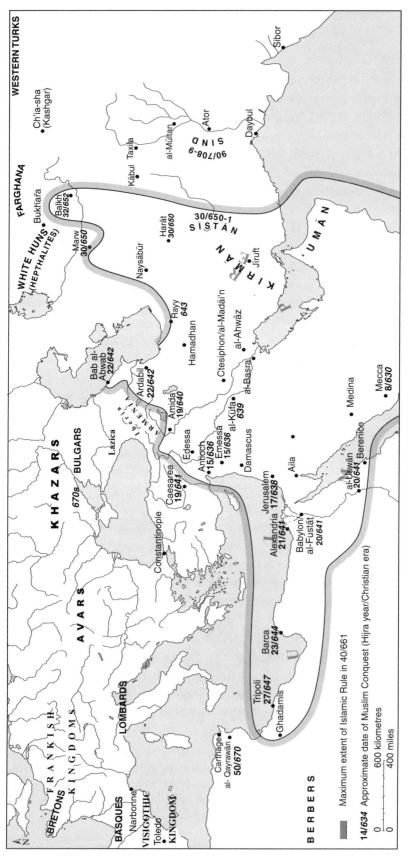

Map 1.1. The Umayyad caliphate, ca. 720. (Reprinted from *The Palgrave Atlas of Byzantine History* by John Haldon, Map 2.8 with minor omissions. Basingstoke and New York: Palgrave Macmillan. © 2005 by John Haldon.)

more detailed budgetary accounts from sixteenth-century Ottoman records. In the Ottoman case, the income of the Balkan region up to the Danube and that of Ottoman Anatolia were very approximately equal, although there are some obvious disparities in coverage between these regions in their late Roman and Ottoman forms, not least because the relative stability of the region under Ottoman rule as well as the clearance of some woodland, the extension of arable farming, and a flourishing international market in bulk agricultural commodities such as grain along with improved mining technology meant a generally greater productive output and thus higher fiscal revenue. But this nevertheless gives a crude idea of the relative economic value of the two regions.[9] In the late Roman period, however, the bulk of the state's income outside of Egypt had been derived from the rich provinces of Syria, Mesopotamia, Euphratensis, Osrhoene, Phoenicia, Palestine, and Cilicia, all lost after the 640s (although there was a partial recovery of some northern districts during the tenth century).

All this means that, with the loss of Egypt and greater Syria, the empire retained a much-reduced fiscal income. On the basis of the above crude calculations, with effective control over all but the coastal periphery of much of the southern Balkans lost during the later sixth and first half of the seventh century but before the loss of Africa and after the early 640s, gross revenues may have been reduced to some 1.5 million *solidi* from a Justinianic maximum calculated at between 5 and 6 million. With the loss of Africa—finally in 698, but probably effectively some time before that date—this total annual revenue was cut to a mere 1 million, thus something in the order of 20 percent of the income before the Arab-Islamic invasions began. This was a truly dramatic collapse of fiscal income.[10] By the early ninth century, a rough calculation—albeit based on even more problematic data—would suggest that, with the stabilization of the economy achieved under Constantine V and his immediate successors, the overall fiscal revenue of the empire had risen to about 1.5 million *nomismata*.[11]

While statistical comparisons arc both difficult to make and problematic, it is certain that the Umayyad caliph in Damascus had, in theory at least, many times more resources available to him than had the Byzantine ruler in Constantinople—the income from Egypt and Syria alone probably amounted to more than three times the total revenue available to the eastern Roman emperor. (See Map 1.1.) Of course, this does not mean that it could all be thrown into war with the Byzantines—on the contrary, warfare in the northeast, in Transoxiana, and in North Africa or Spain; the costs of maintaining internal peace and political control; and the vast expenses entailed in maintaining the *dīwān*, the list of pensions owed to families associated with the Prophet's original campaigns, were a substantial drain on caliphal income, and the devolved nature of both taxation and provincial government meant that the caliphs had a constant struggle on their hands to secure their share of the revenues from more distant provinces. Indeed, it has been noted that access to these resources, especially those from Egypt, would not have been straightforward, and was on occasion probably quite limited.[12] Nevertheless, the disparity was massive, and the investment both in large-scale expeditions as well as constant independent raids and attacks deep into east Roman lands throughout the period ca. 660–780 can be shown to have had a dramatic impact on economy and society. Both textual and, more importantly, paleo-environmental evidence can be adduced to demonstrate just how this affected the Byzantine landscape and Byzantine society.

Apart from the archaeological and survey evidence for the shrinkage and fortification of many minor as well as larger urban settlements, along with a high degree of localization of exchange and commerce, the government at Constantinople undertook the compulsory transplanting of captive populations from the Balkans into devastated regions of Asia Minor in order to make good the loss of manpower through captivity and death.[13] By the middle of the eighth century, even Constantinople itself had to be repopulated, and for the first time in a century the major aqueduct bringing water into the city from outside was repaired and brought back into use.[14] There is also written and archaeological evidence for the flight of populations as well as the movement of settlements to more defensible locations, especially in the Aegean islands, the object of the attention of raids and attacks from the later seventh into the ninth and tenth centuries. Hagiographies of a slightly later period, the ninth, tenth, and eleventh centuries, all make reference to the devastation caused by such warfare; indeed, in some cases it seems that areas in Asia Minor first attacked in the seventh century, and regularly thereafter, were still only at the beginning of recovery in the later tenth century, a point nicely confirmed by palynological data for land use at this time, which I'll discuss later. And this is, of course, apart from the narrative evidence of the chronicles and histories of the period.[15] In one seventh-century account, the population of the beleaguered fortress town of Euchaïta, much further north than the area under consideration here, considered abandoning their homes in an effort to locate a less hazardous environment (as did indeed happen in one or two documented cases), and the text speaks almost mechanically in terms of "when the yearly raid of the Saracens came."[16]

I mention but one set of examples to illustrate the general point: that the Byzantine economy in the frontier districts and behind was radically affected by this constant warfare; that urbanism declined; that populations shrank; that the empire was, compared with its Islamic neighbor, deeply impoverished. Of course, neither should we exaggerate—some towns survived with minimal effects, and clearly the population of the countryside was able to continue producing enough surplus for the government to extract resources. Indeed, it is important to bear in mind that, first, a general demographic downturn had already set in after the great plague of the middle of the sixth century, but that, second, the rate of change in urbanism reflected also preexisting contexts. Thus, while the number of urban settlements in some regions appears to have undergone a sometimes drastic reduction in the seventh and eighth centuries, the population probably declined less dramatically, and rural population density may in places have increased, while the rate of urban "decline" reflected the pre-seventh-century context—less marked in relatively underurbanized districts than in those with a high level of urban settlement, for example.[17]

The Story

In order to provide a structure or framework within which to locate the various topics I will address in the chapters that follow as well as to underline the dramatic nature of the challenges faced by rulers and their administration at Constantinople, it will be worth briefly reviewing, very summarily, the course of events from the 640s to the reign of Leo III (717–741).[18] There have been several such surveys in recent years, and while some issues remain contentious, either in respect of dating or in terms of the balance between different and often contradictory accounts, the general picture is agreed by most historians who have written on the period, whatever their particular angle of approach.

Constans II was eleven years old when he became sole ruler on November 9, 641.[19] His first years were dominated by senior members of the senatorial elite, a group that, as we will see in Chapter 4, experienced a substantial increase in influence in the seventh century, certainly in comparison with its role and fortunes through much of the sixth century. In the circumstances, the issue of a copper coin with a radically different design and bearing the words *"en toutō nika"* ("conquer in this" [i.e., the cross]) on the obverse and *"ananeōsis"* ("renewal") on the reverse sent a clear ideological message about the intentions of the new regime.[20] Political uncertainty offered the senate opportunities, something that can be seen from its new assertiveness during the reigns of Phocas and of Heraklonas and Constantine III (Heraclius's eldest son) as well as during the first years of Constans II. The political difficulties inherited from the reign of his half-uncle Heraklonas and his step-grandmother, Martina, who had made the Armenian general Valentinus *komēs* of the *excubitores* (a small palatine guards unit), continued to be a source of concern.[21] Valentinus, who, it has been suggested, reflected the interests of a more hawkish group at court and in the senior military, already commanded a substantial army based near Constantinople and seems to have been in charge of operations on the eastern front. He was one of the key movers in deposing Martina and had himself proclaimed co-emperor or Caesar (or tried to do so). But in attempting to impose his will through his troops in the capital, a popular riot was set in motion, which resulted in the defeat of the soldiers and his own lynching, probably in 644 or 645.[22]

The external situation of the empire was precarious. Martina had favored peaceful negotiations with the Arabs where possible, and as a result and in accordance with an agreement reached by the patriarch Cyrus, Byzantine troops evacuated Alexandria in September 642. The Arab leader 'Amr ibn al-'As entered the city on September 29. There then followed a slow expansion of Islamic power along the coastal provinces of North Africa—the Pentapolis, then in 643 Tripolis. A temporary Byzantine reoccupation of Alexandria took place in 645, when 'Amr was called back to Mecca, but the imperial forces were expelled permanently in 646. From the early 640s, Arab forces started raiding Anatolia and Armenia as well, and although some Roman successes were registered under the commander of the forces in Armenia, Theodore Rštuni, one of the foremost Armenian princes, there were also some major defeats, notably in the year 642/643 under the Roman general Procopius. In 647 Muʿāwiya raided Cappadocia, besieged Caesarea, raided into Phrygia, and attacked Amorium. No permanent bases were established, but an enormous booty was taken back to Damascus. Until this point Byzantine control of the sea had been unchallenged, as the reoccupation of Alexandria, for example, demonstrated, but the Arab leadership soon grasped the need for naval presence in order to meet and preempt Byzantine attacks on coastal regions, especially in Syria, as well as to extend their conquests. Muʿāwiya seems to have been the first to act on this. In 649 the first Arab naval expedition took place, directed against Cyprus. Constantia, the island's capital, was taken by storm. A second attack took place in 650, at the outset of which the reinforced defenders simply abandoned the island and withdrew. Both raids netted a large booty and tens of thousands of captives. Whether these attacks were intended as diversions or not, the Arab fleet then laid siege to the imperial base on the island of Aradus (Arwad) off the Syrian coast. With no clear hope of relief, the garrison came to terms and surrendered. Another raid into Asia Minor targeted the province of Isauria, and in response a truce was agreed for three years.[23]

In 648 or 649 the imperial government had decreed that the Armenian Church should be subordinate to the see of Constantinople and the Chalcedonian creed. At the synod of Dvin, held in 649, the Armenian clergy and a number of princes, including the Byzantine governor, Theodore Rštuni, rejected and condemned the imperial decree. Meanwhile, in 653 and following the breakdown of a Roman-Arab truce in the region agreed in 650, Theodore transferred his allegiance to the Arabs, a move that led to the defeat of a substantial Roman force on the Euphrates, brought about in part at least by the betrayal of the Roman troops by Theodore's son, Vard, who commanded an Armenian contingent that went over to the Arabs during the engagement. This forced Constans to assemble his forces and march east to deal with the situation. Most of the Armenian and imperial forces in the region abandoned Theodore. Although the expedition was successful, as far as it went, Muʿāwiya was meanwhile preparing a much more significant move, this time against Constantinople itself, which he launched in 653, thus compelling Constans's return to defend the capital, upon which the Armenian situation reverted to its former state. The emperor was also faced with a plot involving members of the senate and of the Armenian military

internal + external conflicts

aristocracy, some of whom held commands in the forces then in Thrace. While the plot was betrayed and the emperor was able to arrest the conspirators, it may represent both senatorial hostility to the emperor who was now beginning to assert his independence from the advisors who had hitherto dominated as well as a more general discontent among the Armenian elite, who were later also to prove difficult and who may eventually have been key players in his downfall. Constans left the general Marianus in charge in the east, but he was subsequently defeated by a combined force of Armenian rebels with Arab reinforcements. Armenia remained under Muslim domination until the murder of the caliph 'Uthmān in 656, when the prince Hamazasp Mamikonian returned to the Byzantine fold.[24]

Arab naval construction had proceeded apace and, as noted, hostilities resumed at the end of the truce in 653. Preparatory to the major attack against the capital, Rhodes was attacked and ravaged in 654 (the fallen Colossus was sold off to an Edessan merchant), Cos was taken, and Crete was pillaged. In 655, taking personal command of the imperial fleet, Constans confronted the Arab forces at sea off the coast of Lycia but was crushingly defeated and barely escaped with his life. The campaign against Constantinople now picked up pace. Another fleet sailed from Egypt accompanying transport vessels, while two substantial forces had marched into Anatolia, one establishing a base in Cappadocia in 654, and the other, under Mu'āwiya's personal command, marching across the plateau to the Bosphorus Strait. But aided by a storm that inflicted substantial damage on the Arab fleet, Roman naval power was reasserted and the attack defeated. Without adequate naval support, the land forces could do nothing and were withdrawn. The Cappadocian force was also defeated and driven out of Roman territory, and Roman field forces were again active in Armenia.[25]

These defeats, combined with a number of other setbacks and rebellions in the Caucasus and in Khorasan, as well as discontent about the leadership of the caliph 'Uthmān, led to disputes in Mecca and the murder of the caliph in 656. The resulting civil strife (*fitna*) between those who wanted a caliph chosen by council through debate and those who believed leadership should stay within the Prophet's family led, first, to the proclamation of 'Ali as caliph and then to outright civil war. The conflict that now developed offered an important breathing space for the empire, since in order to focus on defeating 'Ali and his supporters Muʿāwiya agreed to a truce in 659, which lasted until 661/662 and his final victory.[26] In the fall of 659 Constans had again marched to Armenia in order to bolster the system of client princes on the eastern front that he had been building up through gifts, titles, and other imperial endowments to the Armenian and Caucasian elites more broadly. Among these were Juansher, prince of Caucasian Albania, but within a year of Constans's departure Juansher and most of the other lords of the region had returned to their allegiance to Muʿāwiya.[27] In Anatolia, raids and attacks on fortresses and settlements continued from 662/663; indeed, the intensity of the attacks increased as Muʿāwiya built up his resources and softened up Byzantine resistance in Anatolia once again as a preliminary to a second major attack on Constantinople.[28]

Power struggle — allegiances

But the short pause in the warfare had important consequence, since it permitted Constans to turn his attention to the Balkans. Here imperial troops had been more or less constantly on the defensive. In 658, while civil war in the caliphate relieved the pressure on Anatolia, Constans launched an expedition into the Sklaviniai, the regions of the Slavs, where he reportedly defeated many tribes and took many prisoners. Several thousands of prisoners with their families were resettled in devastated or deserted areas of Anatolia, while some of the prisoners were probably enrolled as soldiers in the provincial armies—a policy that was pursued by later emperors including both Constantine IV and Justinian II. Some have argued that it was at this time that Constans and his advisors reorganized imperial defenses and the armies, creating what the later sources refer to as *themata*, or military provinces. Suffice to say here that there is not a shred of evidence to support such an idea, although the armies were certainly redistributed across the Anatolian provinces and there were likely administrative consequences of these changes. We will return to this question in Chapter 7.[29]

Constans's reign was dogged by problems inherited from Heraclius associated with the doctrines of monoenergism and monotheletism, and I will look in more detail at some of these issues in Chapters 2 and 4. Already in the years preceding the first Arab attacks Heraclius and the patriarch Sergius had struggled to find a formula that would facilitate the reunification of the miaphysite and dyophysite communities. Monoenergism was the doctrine of the "single energy" or "operation" of Christ. Elaborated at Constantinople during the later 620s, the issues it addressed had been under discussion in some ecclesiastical circles for several decades and a developed doctrine, as presented by Sergius, was by no means an absolute novelty. But in the 620s and 630s it had the added value of presenting an opportunity to reconcile the miaphysite and dyophysite churches, and was probably introduced as the official position of the imperial church with this in mind. It was at first well received by some elements of the eastern churches and formed the basis upon which the Armenian and Chaldean churches accepted communion with Constantinople shortly thereafter.[30] Although the patriarch of Alexandria also accepted it, as did the pope, Honorius (although with his own reservations), along with a number of others in the eastern provinces, the patriarch Sophronius of Jerusalem was not persuaded, and it was in part his opposition that led after a short time to the rethinking of the doctrine.[31] We have no information about the response of the provinces of Greater Syria to this rejection of an imperially sponsored theology except that it is clear that Sophronius was not alone, and that among those who formed the heart of the opposition a few years later was the abbot Maximus the Confessor (even if it also seems clear that Maximus took some time to clarify his own thinking on the subject).[32] In light of later developments in Africa, as we shall see, it is not impossible that in the Syrian provinces this conflict over dogma damaged the willingness of many of those who understood the issue to support imperial policy in resisting the invader.

In response to the opposition from Sophronius and others, and following on from a council held on Cyprus in 636 at which Sergius, his close ally Cyrus of Alexandria, as well as Sophronius were all present, Heraclius had issued the so-called *Ekthesis* in 636 or 638 (the date is contested), although the text of this document was likely the work of the patriarch Sergius. Discussion of the issue of operations was prohibited, and at the same time a further compromise was attempted based around the concept of a single will of Christ, transcending both his human and divine natures. While this "monothelete" approach was clearly intended to silence discussion and dissent within the neo-Chalcedonian church as well as to normalize the situation as it had been before Sophronius's opposition, the *Ekthesis* had the opposite effect—indeed, it appears that it was this document that inflamed opinion and ultimately led to rebellion. And while it was unlikely to have had the specific aim of maintaining the loyalty of the miaphysite communities in the eastern provinces, this was still a central concern of the government, since at this stage it was assumed that the empire would at some point defeat the invader and recover its control in the region.[33] The patriarchate of Jerusalem seems to have been at the heart of opposition, but as monks and clergy from Palestine moved westward and away from the new Islamic domination of their province, they brought their hostility to the imperial position with them.[34] Maximus the Confessor became a prominent figure among these migrants, a man with a widespread network of correspondents, including senior churchmen and monastics as well as leading officials of the state, both military and civilian. It is possible that he also had a connection with the family of Heraclius himself, a connection made during a stay in Africa during the Persian occupation of Palestine in the period 618–628.[35]

But while opposition to imperial policy grew in the west, in North Syria and Palestine later evidence would suggest that at some point, and certainly from the time of the council of 681–682 (see below) the neo-Chalcedonian communities espoused the formula of monotheletism with some enthusiasm in spite of Sophronius's position. The same may indeed also have been true of much of the remaining imperial territory in Anatolia, and this fact in itself may have been a significant factor in persuading Constans and his advisors to maintain the policy as the official line. It certainly implies that the doctrine of the single will was not merely an artifice or tool of imperial politics but had a genuine hold in society more broadly, at least in certain regions.[36] Meanwhile, in North Africa several local synods took place across the first months of 646, most likely a result of Maximus's campaign against monotheletism. The result was a condemnation of imperial religious policy. The exiled monothelete patriarch of Constantinople, Pyrrhus, lost a public debate with Maximus, presided over by the exarch (military governor) himself, Gregory; and it was probably the solidarity of the North African bishops in opposing imperial policy that encouraged the exarch to declare his opposition to Constans's rule in 646/647 and have himself proclaimed emperor. His short-lived usurpation met with failure when in the following year Gregory was killed fighting Arab raiders near Sufetula, after which a truce seems to have been arranged. When the raiders withdrew, imperial authority was rapidly reestablished, marked by a special issue of silver by the mint at Carthage. In an effort to reassert imperial authority, the patriarch Paul issued another decree in Constans's name, the so-called *Typos,* in 648. This ordered that the *Ekthesis* be removed from the narthex of Hagia Sophia, but no further discussion was to be permitted. The issue of a single will or operation of Christ was not to be debated. But this was unlikely to produce agreement, and at the Lateran council held in Rome in 649, under the newly elected Pope Martin, the 105 western bishops who were present condemned both *Ekthesis* and *Typos*, together with the patriarchs Sergius and Pyrrhus as well as the then incumbent Paul.[37] The decisions of the synod were circulated in both eastern and western sees and copies sent to Constantinople. However politely the pope may have expressed himself in his letter to the emperor, the challenge to imperial authority could not be mistaken:

> To the most pious and serene master and triumphant victor, [our] son who loves God and our Lord Jesus Christ, Constantine Augustus, from bishop Martin, servant of the servants of God . . . We therefore inform your pious and serene authority that, assembling together in this your Christ-loving and God-serving city of Rome, all of us . . . have confirmed synodically the pious definition of the orthodox faith, and fitly annulled the discordant teachings of the heretics, both past and present [including the patriarchs of Constantinople Sergius, Pyrrhus and Paul] who in the perversity of their reasoning separated themselves from the truth.
>
> They lawlessly seduced the ears of your serenity, as also those of your serenity's blessed grandfather of blessed memory [Heraclius], so that they might criminally inflict their own guilt on others . . . For not only have the pious congregations been scandalized, but the godless barbarians are now mocking the great mystery of our confession . . .
>
> In order, therefore, to show clearly to your authority the difference between the two—that is, the fathers of piety and their definitions, and the impious men and their doctrines—we . . . have sent our synodical proceedings, together with their translation into the Greek language, beseeching and exhorting your serenity, wise in the things of God, to deign to give them a fitting reading, and to condemn by laws of piety the said heretics together with their heresy . . . For when your serenity has a correct faith in the Lord, who arms his creation to ward off the enemy, he will deservedly give aid to your authority in conquering your enemies.[38]

Recent research has made it clear that the council itself was orchestrated and dominated by Maximus and his allies and aimed at achieving the greatest possible propaganda effect.[39]

Such a response, a public corrective to imperial policy, could not be ignored. At issue in such a rejection of imperial policy was the orthodoxy and fitness to sit on the imperial throne of Constans himself. The government ordered Olympius, the exarch of Ravenna, to arrest Martin and to compel western episcopal confirmation of the *Typos*. Like Gregory in Africa, however, Olympius seems to have found it more acceptable to rebel and to have himself proclaimed emperor. The government could do nothing in light of the difficulties it faced in the east (attacks against Cyprus and a growing threat to Constantinople itself). Whether Olympius intended eventually to move on Constantinople itself, as some have suggested, remains unknown since the sources make no reference to this. He initially seems to have aimed to seize Sicily, whether because it was at that point the target of a major Arab raid or because of its wealth, or both, is again unknown.[40] In either case, his independence was short-lived since he died of an infection in 652, and by June 653 the new exarch was in command and had been able to arrest the pope. Martin arrived in Constantinople in December. His trial was conducted entirely on the basis of the political case against him, including supporting the usurpation of Olympius, and he was predictably enough found guilty. Initially sentenced to death, this was quickly commuted to exile in Cherson in the Crimea. He died in 656. The trial and interrogations of Maximus went no differently—he was accused, quite justifiably in the eyes of the imperial authorities, of high treason and the betrayal of the empire, although it is clear that the government invested much effort in trying to persuade him to take communion with the imperial church and recognize that the emperor's authority was absolute. At a synod convened at Constantinople in 662 the results of the trial and interrogations were confirmed. Maximus was punished by mutilation and died in exile in 662 in the fortress of Schemarion in Lazica, in the Caucasus. The government response to what, from the imperial point of view, could only, and quite legitimately be understood as treason was in the context entirely predictable.[41]

As we might expect, while the see of Constantinople, along with that of Antioch, conformed to imperial policy, Roman sentiment remained hostile; however, the clergy did accept the new pope, Eugenius, imposed by Constantinople. Shortly before his death in exile in 655, Martin also recognized him, thus permitting the imperial government to inform Maximus during his own trial that the whole church was united and that he alone was now out of step (although reports from Constantinople had reached first Sardinia and then Rome about the nature of

Maximus' trial. In the face of popular anger, Eugenius was forced to reject the synodical letters of the new patriarch, Peter).[42] And although
Maximus would not give in to this pressure, the government was thus
able to enforce its policy, and resistance seems to have been very limited.[43] But the whole long, drawn-out episode raised a host of questions
about imperial authority and about the relationship between belief,
dogma, and the secular empire and its rulers. The emperor's role and
his function as God's vicegerent had been placed under scrutiny, while
the insistence of the Constantinopolitan regime that imperial monotheletism must be enforced reflected its own anxieties about the imperial
authority. It may be true that many of the lands at whose miaphysite
populations monotheletism had been aimed were by the 640s lost to
the empire, but there is good reason to believe that the government
assumed that their loss was temporary and could be reversed, at least
until the 680s.

There was clearly some doubt at court and among senior military officers about imperial policy. Constans's brother Theodosius may have
been involved in a plot of antimonothelete groups to depose Constans,
although the evidence is not clear. But in 654 Constans crowned his son
Constantine co-emperor and in 659 his two younger sons, Heraclius and
Tiberius, were also raised to the imperial dignity. In thus passing over
his younger brother Theodosius, Constans clearly aimed to exclude him
altogether, and in 660 Theodosius was tonsured, effectively excluding
him from the imperial succession, and shortly thereafter he was mur-
dered. The synod of 662 in Constantinople at which Maximus the
Confessor was condemned and exiled is very likely connected with Theodosius' plot and his execution. Although these events caused considerable
disquiet in Constantinople, the threat cannot have been too obvious or
serious, for otherwise the emperor would not have left the capital.[44]

Following the monothelete synod of 662, Constans set out on a major
expedition to the west, a move that more likely reflects concerns connected with grain supplies and the other resources of Sicily and North
Africa than a response to his apparent unpopularity. Constans likely
viewed the western provinces as both strategically and politically key
to imperial survival, for despite the Islamic naval challenge, the empire
was still united by the Mediterranean. The risks were considerable, especially as far as Anatolia was concerned, for it is hardly a coincidence
that as soon as the emperor had marched west the yearly attacks from

North Syria, including the first overwintering raids, commenced. Whether he really wished to make Rome the capital of the empire once more as reported by a later source is a moot point.[45] His aim seems to have been to defeat the Lombards and incorporate them into his rule as well as to reorganize the defense and administration of Africa. He marched via Thessaloniki, Athens, Corinth, and Patras, where he embarked for Otranto. His campaign in Italy was less successful than planned, for he was unable to take Beneventum, although a peace treaty was agreed. Retiring with his forces to Naples, he then visited Rome and was involved in celebrations and prayer for twelve days, having been welcomed by Pope Vitalian (monotheletism does not appear to have hindered a friendly reception). Thereafter he returned to Naples and then to Sicily, where he established his headquarters at Syracuse.[46]

Whatever his longer-term strategic plan, his presence on the island soon became unpopular, given the burdens it imposed. Financial difficulties forced him to borrow funds from the Church of Ravenna and to seize quantities of bronze and other metals from Rome. In return for its support, the see of Ravenna was granted autocephaly, much to the annoyance of the papacy. But the unpopularity of his presence, with his army and court, is very clear in the sources:

> He stayed in Rome twelve days; he dismantled all the city's bronze decorations; he removed the bronze tiles from the roof of the church of St Mary *ad martyres,* and sent them to the imperial city . . . He imposed such afflictions on the people, inhabitants and proprietors of the provinces of Calabria, Sicily, Africa and Sardinia for many years by tributes, poll-taxes and ship-money, such as had never been seen, so that wives were even separated from their husbands and sons from their parents . . . They took away all the sacred vessels and equipment from God's holy churches, leaving nothing behind.[47]

The empress and their three sons were not permitted to join him, detained by senior officers of state and by members of the demes. Finally, in 669 he became the victim of an assassination plot at the hand of a certain *cubicularius,* Andreas, son of the senior courtier Troilus, and shortly thereafter the Armenian general Mzez Gnouni, or Mizizius, probably commander of the imperial field army, the Opsikion, was acclaimed emperor.[48] One theory has it that this plot was engineered or at least supported by Mu'āwiya; another that it was hatched by a group of

senior members of the court in Constantinople who, along with certain
Armenian princes, were keen on a long-term peace plan with the Arabs
and whose plot merely coincided with the launch of Muʿāwiya's more aggressive strategy in the central and western Mediterranean; while a third
view, perhaps the most sober and plausible, sees the plot as a response
on the part of the senior commanders and members of the imperial
elite at Constantinople to the emperor's inaction and preoccupation in
Italy and in the northwest Balkan regions in the face of the clear evidence for the major Arab assault on the capital city of the empire.[49]

In either case, Constans's assassination occurred at a most unfavorable moment. Muʿāwiya's commanders launched attacks by land into
Roman Byzacena in North Africa and by sea against coastal settlements
and islands. The commander of the Armeniakon forces, an Armenian
named Saborius (Shapur), rebelled with Muʿāwiya's support in 668,
intending to join forces with the caliph's troops in their march on
Constantinople;[50] and while the untimely death of the rebel ended the
revolt—the troops of the region reaffirmed their loyalty to the empire—
the event is symptomatic of the difficulties with which the government
had to contend where the complex interrelationship between state
policy, local identities, and religious questions were concerned. And in
667/668, probably coordinated with all these developments, Muʿāwiya
launched a second major assault on Constantinople, with Cyprus,
Rhodes, Cos, and Cyzicus all occupied by Arab naval forces.[51] In Sicily,
Mizizius was apparently acclaimed against his will and in any case
seems to have had little support. The forces of the exarch, reinforced by
units from Africa and possibly with the arrival of a naval force under
the new emperor, Constantine IV himself, after the defeat of the Arab
attack on Constantinople, put an end to the usurpation, probably in 671
or 672. The exact length of the rebellion and whether or not Mzez's son
John also raised an independent revolt remain open. Shortly thereafter,
though, the Arabs mounted another substantial raid on Sicily, possibly
a reflection of the departure of the troops that had been based there
under Constans.[52]

It is difficult to assess Constans's achievement. His was a fiercely
aggressive policy toward the caliphate, no doubt based upon the assumption that the situation could, in due course, be made good. The
precedent set by Heraclius in recovering the empire's lost territories
and humbling its enemies by doggedly pursuing the war for as long as

it took—in Heraclius's case, a good eighteen years—cannot have been forgotten; indeed, many of those involved in Constans's government in the 640s must have been directly involved in that struggle, and it would have been relatively fresh in their collective memory. But Constans's attempts to maintain the established imperial state in the east through building up clients and allies in the Caucasus was not a success, no more than was his effort to reorient imperial defenses in the west and North Africa by his move to Sicily. His and his advisors' adherence to imperial monotheletism—again perhaps indicating too much determination to adhere to the policy aims of Heraclius—alienated the papacy and caused the emperor some difficulties at court and within his own immediate family. The issue during his "regency" period of the copper coinage with the "renewal" motif and its continuation under his personal rule is an indication of his approach—an approach that in effect *unwilling to change* refused to recognize that any of the dramatic political changes that had occurred were permanent, but rather required merely time, patience, and effort to reverse. He has been attributed with the foundation of the so-called theme system, but there is no more evidence to support this than there is to support the older contention that the emperor Heraclius was responsible. Whether or not he created a Byzantine war fleet, as opposed to expanded and reorganized it, also remains an open question.[53]

The blockade and siege of 667–669 had been defeated partly by the deployment at sea of the new terror weapon of liquid fire and partly by disease that broke out in the Arab camp.[54] Thereafter, the Romans were able to conduct more offensive operations, defeating Arab columns in Anatolia in 674 and at sea in the same year. By 677–678, after several months of rebellion in the Amanus highlands of northwest Syria involving both locals and the Mardaites,[55] and faced by increasing internal opposition that would shortly thereafter break out into civil war (the second *fitna*), Muʿāwiya had to sue for a cessation of hostilities. A thirty-year peace was brokered, to be accompanied by a yearly payment of three thousand gold pieces, fifty Byzantine prisoners, and fifty stallions. This was a signal success for Constantine IV, immediately reestablishing Roman prestige: both the khagan of the Avars and the chieftains of the various Balkan peoples recognized imperial supremacy. Dissension within the caliphate after Muʿāwiya's death and the accession of Yazīd I in 680 seemed to offer new opportunities to the empire,

both in terms of consolidation as well as in respect of a hope for the recovery of lost provinces.[56]

Constantine used the breathing space thus achieved to convoke an
ecumenical council, the sixth, which was held at Constantinople in
680–681, at which papal representatives were present and at which imperial monotheletism was abandoned and "orthodoxy" reestablished.[57]
Either a few months beforehand (more likely), or in the course of the
council, however, the emperor left to deal with the arrival of the Bulgars on the Danube. In practical terms this whole region was no longer
under imperial authority at all: effective control was restricted to coastal
settlements and fortresses in Greece, the Peloponnese and Dalmatia.
There were frequent attacks against Byzantine fortresses and towns,
and Thessaloniki in particular led a precarious existence, besieged in
675–676 and again in 677, for example. Slav raiders attacked imperially-
held islands by sea in 678–679; and while imperial expeditions undertaken to reassert imperial authority after the 660s had only a very limited
impact, both Constans and Constantine IV were able to seize numbers
of captives and transport them to Anatolia where they were resettled to
compensate for the losses incurred through Arab raiding activity.[58] The
appearance of the Bulgars changed this situation completely.

The confederation of Onogur-Bulgar clans that made up the khanate
of old Great Bulgaria had had friendly relations with the empire since
the time of Heraclius and had freed themselves from Avar domination
with Roman support. The arrival of the Khazars resulted in the collapse
of this grouping, with some Bulgars joining the Khazars and others
fleeing west. One such group arrived north of the Danube delta during
the 670s, hoping to settle on "Roman" land south of the river and gain
access to its fertile pasture. Unwilling to admit them, the emperor
marched against them, supported by a fleet, in the late spring of 680,
once troops from the eastern front could be released. Unfortunately, and
after only a few months of campaigning, Constantine left the army and
returned to the capital. The reasons remain unclear: the traditional story
is that he suffered from gout and was forced to withdraw, leaving the
army without direction. The alternative, and more plausible, interpretation is that, underestimating an enemy that had occupied a secure defensive position in the marshlands of the northern delta of the Danube, and
assuming his forces could safely be left to deal with a campaign that was
dragging on longer than anticipated, he had to return to the capital to

deal with the preparations for the upcoming ecumenical council. But at some point the troops panicked, and the Bulgars were able to defeat the imperial forces, establishing themselves in the marsh and fenlands of the delta. Constantine was forced quickly to conclude a treaty that recognized Bulgar occupation of the districts they now held and additionally agreed to an annual subsidy. A number of Slav groups transferred their nominal allegiance to the Bulgar ruler, who established a capital at Pliska—a location that permitted the Bulgars to control the road from the Danube via Anchialus to Constantinople as well as the approaches to the Dobrudja. The empire was now confronted for the first time with an independent, organized, and potentially hostile power in the Balkans.[59]

The main task of the council of 680–681 was to revoke monoenergism and monotheletism and reestablish ecclesiastical and political unity. There can be no doubt that Constantine's main aim was to end the empire's relative ideological and political isolation and reestablish good relations with the papacy in particular. The price paid was heavy: the former patriarchs of Constantinople, Sergius, Pyrrhus, and Paul, along with Cyrus of Alexandria and the still living Macarius of Antioch, together with Pope Honorius I—who collectively were held responsible—were condemned and anathematized.[60] Eighteen sessions were held, presided over by the emperor himself for the first eleven and the during the final meeting. And while the council certainly reflects Constantine's recognition that the split in the Church, promoted by his father, was injurious to his own position as orthodox ruler and defender of the faith and to his authority in theoretical and theological terms, there was certainly opposition at court and in the army to the change, indeed the emperor's absence from sessions twelve to seventeen may be directly associated with the complex negotiations that these issues required and the need to determine the degree of potential support or opposition within the church for the emperor's new policy. The deposition and mutilation of his brothers Heraclius and Tiberius seem to be connected with public opposition from both soldiers and senior commanders—perhaps also directly connected with the recent and unexpected defeat at the hands of the Bulgars. The leaders of the protesting troops (apparently from the Anatolikon division) were arrested and executed. The troops were returned to their bases. Monotheletism continued to have its adherents—much of northern Syria appears to have remained loyal to it (see Chapters 2 and 3), as did a number of individuals, many of them military.[61]

While the reconciliation with Rome also facilitated a peace arranged with the Lombards, it was achieved at the cost of the autonomy of the see of Ravenna, since in 683 Constantine placed it once again under Roman authority.[62] In Africa, despite the successful Arab raids deep into the Roman provinces, key fortresses and cities in the exarchate held out, and during Constantine's final years and in alliance with indigenous tribes a major victory was achieved over the renowned Arab leader 'Uqba, whose expeditions were launched from the Libyan Pentapolis, which had been in Muslim hands since the 640s. In spite of such occasional successes, the Roman forces contributed little to Arab difficulties, for the most part operating an entirely defensive posture. As the indigenous Berber clans were converted to Islam, so the isolated Byzantine settlements and fortified centers fell. Carthage was taken in 697 and, although briefly recovered in 698, fell permanently later in the same year.[63]

The relatively stable situation that had prevailed lasted until 683, but, taking advantage of the civil war in the caliphate that had broken out in that year over the caliphal succession, Constantine led a successful expedition into Cilicia, taking Mopsuestia, destroying the Arab fortress at Germanikeia and recovering Antioch, while the imperial fleet attacked a number of coastal towns, including Askalon, Caesarea, Acre, and Tyre. Together with the activities of the Mardaites, these operations forced the caliph to open peace negotiations.[64] While the Arab leadership sued for another truce, Constantine died in either July or September and was succeeded by his son Justinian II, who launched an expedition under the general Leontius to the Caucasus, where a number of regions and their rulers were brought back for a while to their earlier allegiance with the empire. The new caliph, 'Abd al-Malik, who succeeded his father, Marwān, in April 685, thus inherited an extremely precarious situation, exacerbated by a Khazar invasion of the Caucasus in which his Armenian allies were soundly defeated and urgently needed a settlement with the Romans. The treaty made by Mu'āwiya and Constantine IV was renewed, as it was extremely advantageously for Justinian: 'Abd al-Malik undertook to pay a tribute of one thousand *nomismata* per day, together with a symbolic horse and a slave, in return for the Byzantines halting their advance. It was agreed also to share the income from the island of Cyprus as well as that from Armenia and Iberia. In return, the Mardaites, a major problem for the caliph in North Syria, were transferred to western Asia Minor.[65]

With pressure on the eastern front reduced, Justinian could turn his attention to the Balkans, and in 687/688 he led an expedition against the Sklaviniai, the regions occupied or controlled by various Slavic and other indigenous groups, pushing through to Thessaloniki and in the process reestablishing imperial authority in the region. The fact that he had to fight his way through to Macedonia reflects the practical realities, however. But he was able to take a large number of captives and transfer them to Anatolia, specifically to the depopulated regions of Bithynia and Cappadocia that appear to have suffered most from the presence of hostile forces. Some of these were later drafted into the provincial armies, although many subsequently deserted. The emperor also transferred part of the population of Cyprus to the Cyzicus region, also badly affected during the Arab blockade of Constantinople, while the Mardaites were moved to the Peloponnese and the southwest coastal region of Asia Minor. The policy of transferring captives to repopulate devastated areas was in itself not new—such transfers had been carried out during the reigns of Justinian I and Maurice, for example, and the policy was continued under Constantine V and Basil I. Justinian also continued to pursue a policy of maintaining client-principalities in the Caucasus and in 689/690 traveled to Armenia himself to reinforce his policies. But in general the success or failure of imperial policy in this regard in the Caucasus depended on the success or failure of Byzantine diplomatic or military action in respect of the caliphate more generally. As soon as the Romans were defeated in battle, the Armenian and other princes of the region tended to revert to their allegiance to the caliphate.[66]

Whether or not the transfer of the Cypriots was a breach of the agreement with ʿAbd al-Malik remains unclear.[67] But in 692/693 the truce was broken, and at a major battle at Sebastopolis the imperial forces were decisively defeated, partly because the recently conscripted Slav troops deserted. In the following year a second Roman thrust was thrown back. The consequence was, first, that the Armenian princes transferred their allegiance once more to the caliphate,[68] while ʿAbd al-Malik launched a new series of regular raids into Anatolia, the provinces of which had only just begun their recovery from the previous decades of devastation. To what extent the chroniclers were correct to attribute this to Justinian's desire for glory and his rash political actions remains debated. In any case, the east Roman state was once again plunged into a very one-sided conflict. The early-ninth-century chronicler Theophanes reports that Justinian avenged himself by massacring the Slavs who remained within the empire, although the veracity of this account, derived from later sources, is dubious. The deserters were settled in Syria.[69]

Justinian was keen to consolidate the religious policies of his father and to cement a positive relationship with the papacy. In 687 he issued a statement, witnessed and confirmed by the Church and the army units at Constantinople, underlining his acceptance of the results of the sixth council of 680–681 and stressing his function as God's representative and chosen guardian of orthodoxy. In placing the motto *servus Christi* on his coins, together with a bust of Christ, he stressed the divine source of his authority. That 'Abd al-Malik's reformed coinage was a response to this or Justinian's reformed *nomisma* was a response to 'Abd al-Malik's coinage seems unlikely, however, although we should not deny absolutely the element of propaganda warfare involved, even if it may well have been incidental, for this tension then developed into a breach of the treaty between the two rulers and led to the battle at Sebastopolis and the Roman defeat in 693.[70]

But in the year 691/692, in confirmation of his ideological program, Justinian had convoked the so-called Quinisext or Trullan Council (so-called because it confirmed the matters treated at the fifth and sixth ecumenical councils, in 553 and 680–681) and met in the Trullos or domed hall of the imperial palace. And this was the context, it has been argued, for which Justinian's reformed coinage was devised—a specifically Roman context, in which the imperial coinage could be understood to reinforce and further add authority through iconographic means to the decisions of the council.[71] A number of "Western" traditions in respect of clerical discipline were rejected, while canon 82 prohibited the representation of Christ as a lamb—increasingly common in the West—insisting that he be presented in human form, while canon 36 (following canon 3 of the council of Constantinople of 381 and canon 28 of the council of Chalcedon of 451) emphasized the parity of the sees of Rome and Constantinople in their precedence over the sees of Jerusalem, Antioch, and Alexandria.[72]

Papal opposition brought Constantinople and Rome once more into conflict, of course. The papacy challenged the ecumenical validity of the council, and Justinian, following imperial precedent, ordered the pope's arrest. The troops in both Rome and Ravenna were opposed to this, and the *prōtospatharios* Zacharias, who had been delegated with this task, escaped violence only by throwing himself on the pope's mercy. But the emperor's fiscal policies had already made him deeply unpopular both at Constantinople and in the provinces. He seems to have aroused substantial opposition in the leading circles and the senate in particular. In 695 he was overthrown in a coup, in the course of which the general Leontius, recently appointed to command the military forces in Hellas, was acclaimed emperor. With support from leading members of the senate and the palatine troops, Justinian and his hated subordinates were seized. The emperor had his nose and tongue slit and was banished to Cherson.[73]

Leontius, who appears to have been a popular choice, was emperor for a mere three years. In his second year he was faced with a rebellion in Lazica in the Caucasus, and it was likewise during his reign that east Roman power in Africa was finally extinguished. Carthage fell to an Arab attack in 697, upon receiving news of which Leontius dispatched a fleet and troops to retake it. They were successful, but a strong Arab counterattack forced their withdrawal. This was the last outpost of the exarchate in Africa, and its loss meant an end to Roman North Africa.[74] The fleet, under its commander, John, withdrew to Crete to await orders, but the soldiers mutinied and proclaimed as emperor their own commander, the *drouggarios* Apsimar. Sailing to Constantinople, the army landed at the port of Sykai on the Golden Horn and besieged the city, which was suffering from a plague epidemic at the time, yet held out for some six months until some of the garrison opened the gates. Leontius was mutilated to disqualify him from the imperial throne and confined to a monastery in Constantinople. Apsimar adopted the imperial name of Tiberius, thus associating himself with the family of Heraclius and legitimating his rule.[75]

Tiberius Apsimar, as he is generally known, held the throne until 705. During his reign the pace of Arab incursions and raids in Anatolia increased and the frontier was progressively pushed north and west. North Africa received no attention at all, all efforts being concentrated

on Anatolia. Here the emperor's brother Heraclius commanded the
provincial cavalry forces and was able to achieve moderate success, although this did not affect the fundamental strategic situation. The fick-
leness of the princes and rulers of the Armenian highlands certainly
affected imperial strategy and the ability of the empire to defend its core
regions. Having accepted Muslim authority in 703, the *nakharars* rebelled once again the following year and called on Roman support in
their fight.[76] There is some evidence of military action in the southern
Balkans; and some of the Cypriots who had removed to the Cyzicus region under Justinian II returned to Cyprus. Tiberius also carried out
repairs to the sea defenses of Constantinople, which had been allowed
to decay and in places collapse. He reigned only seven years, however,
for in 705 Justinian was able to return with the help of the Bulgar khan
Tervel. Supported by a Bulgar force, he was able to gain access through
one of the viaducts into the city and with the help of his supporters
there was quickly able to seize control. Leontius and Tiberius Apsimar
were both executed, and Justinian had his son Tiberius crowned
coemperor.[77]

Tervel was granted the title of Caesar, and Justinian then proceeded
to hunt down and have those who had opposed him executed or otherwise punished before embarking on a vengeful reign of terror. He seems
to have been especially keen to restore friendly relations with the
papacy. Soon after his recovery of the throne, two metropolitan bishops
were sent to Rome with imperial letters in which the emperor offered
to convene an ecumenical council at which he would confirm whichever of the canons of the council of 691/692 the pope wished. Whatever the reason, Pope John VII refused to act and simply returned the
bishops and the imperial sacra to the emperor, a surprising response
given the substantial concessions offered by Justinian—even the author
of John's biographical notice in the *Liber pontificalis* found this difficult
to understand.[78] Justinian did not give up, however, and in 710 invited
the pope, by then Constantine I, to visit Constantinople. The pope was
received in the capital by the young emperor Tiberius accompanied by
the senate, before proceeding to Nikomedeia, where he met with the
emperor, who performed *proskynēsis* before him. The privileges of the
Roman see were confirmed, agreement was reached on the various
canons of the Quinisext that had caused offense in Rome, an unwritten
accord was agreed, and the pope returned to Rome in the fall of 711.[79]

In the course of the preparations for Constantine's visit, however, Justinian had to deal with a rebellion in Ravenna which was hostile to the papacy and the fact that Constantine IV had rescinded its autonomy vis-à-vis Rome. A naval force was sent to deal with this, although in later tradition the expedition was ascribed to Justinian's exacting revenge for Ravennate support for his deposition in 695.[80]

Justinian did send a punitive expedition to Cherson, however, ostensibly to reestablish imperial authority in the region against Khazar encroachment. After another revolt against Justinian in the city, a second expedition was dispatched. In the ensuing confusion the fleet mutinied; proclaimed an exiled officer, Bardanes, emperor; and sailed to Constantinople. Justinian left to raise troops in the Opsikion and Armeniakon regions, but his allies abandoned him to his fate. Bardanes, who had adopted the imperial name Philippicus, sought Justinian and his son out and both were killed. Justinian's death ended the dynasty of Heraclius, and a period of political instability followed. The deacon Agathon, an eyewitness of the events, described it as a time during which imperial authority was treated with contempt and the empire was humbled. Tyranny, usurpation, and violent changes of power characterized the period. In an attempt to restore imperial authority, to recall past victories and successes, and to consolidate his own position, the new emperor issued an edict condemning the acts of the sixth ecumenical council of 680–681 and reestablishing monotheletism as the official creed. As Theophanes put it, "Philippicus was not ashamed to make a furious attack on the holy sixth ecumenical council, hastening to subvert the divine doctrines that had been confirmed by it."[81]

How much support this move had remains unclear—the clergy seem largely to have accepted it (including the later patriarch Germanus as well as the homilist Andrew of Crete), although the evidence is sparse and fear of imperial reprisals would have discouraged open opposition. Opposition from Rome was inevitable and the papacy returned Philippicus's portrait, sent to Rome by the new emperor, as was the custom, along with his monothelete declaration of orthodoxy.[82]

We should recall that, in the midst of this internal political turmoil, hostile activity along the empire's frontiers continued unabated. In the Balkans there prevailed a relatively peaceful situation following Justinian's agreement with Khan Tervel, but that emperor's deposition gave Tervel an excuse to invade, and his forces devastated southern

Thrace as far as the walls of Constantinople. Arab raids on Anatolia continued on an annual basis, and the Roman defenses continued to lose ground. The fortress town of Tyana fell in 707/708 after a Roman relief force was defeated; the frontier town of Sision was abandoned in 711; Amaseia, Misthia, and Antioch in Pisidia were sacked in 712–713; and Roman forces had to abandon a series of fortified strongholds around Melitene.[83] Philippicus undertook preparations to counter these raids, but in early summer 713 the soldiers of the Opsikion division mutinied. The emperor was deposed and blinded in June, and the *prōtoasēkrētis* Artemius, a palatine clerical official, became emperor as Anastasius II.[84]

Anastasius's first move was to restore Chalcedonian orthodoxy and to rehabilitate the sixth council. Measures were set in train for the strengthening of the defenses of Constantinople in the face of an impending attack. A naval force was fitted out in an attempt to preempt the blockade of the city by attacking the Arab ships in their ports.[85] But once again the Opsikion forces mutinied, this time while in Rhodes, where the expedition was assembling. They returned to the mainland and with other units acclaimed as emperor a hitherto unknown fiscal official named Theodosius. Although he attempted to avoid this dubious honor, he was prevented from leaving and was compelled to receive the troops' acclamation. The rebellious units marched on Constantinople, which capitulated after a short siege. Anastasius had left the city and taken refuge in Nicaea, although not before sending an appeal to the caliph via the commander of the invading armies, Maslama, for military help against the usurper.[86] But he quickly abdicated and retired as a monk to Thessaloniki.

His successor, Theodosius III, occupied the throne for just over twelve months.[87] His only lasting achievement was a peace agreement and the arrangement of a formal and recognized frontier between Roman and Bulgar territory in Thrace.[88] Given that this stretched from the Gulf of Burgas on the Black Sea coast through northern Thrace to the Maritsa on the Aegean, it illustrates the extent of Bulgar power and the inability of the Romans effectively to reassert imperial authority in the region. But Theodosius had to face rebellion almost as soon as he had sat upon the throne—indeed, the major Arab assault on the capital of the empire for which his predecessor had been preparing had already begun when the commander of the Anatolikon forces, Leo, together with the commander of the Armeniakon division, Artavasdus (soon to marry Leo's daughter) rebelled. Both appear to have remained loyal to Anastasius II, or at least that was the formal justification for their rebellion. The Opsikion division, based around Constantinople and in Bithynia, remained loyal to Theodosius, but his son was captured at Nicomedia as Leo marched on the capital. Theodosius very quickly abandoned the struggle and, armed with a guarantee of personal safety, entered a monastery at Ephesus. In March 717 Leo was crowned emperor by the patriarch, Germanus, in the church of the Holy Wisdom. Within weeks the capital of the east Roman state was once more blockaded and under siege.[89]

Leo seems to have been an effective military commander as well as an accomplished politician and diplomat. He outmaneuvered the Arab commanders, won time for the Roman military both to organize a defense of the capital and to dog the Arab columns as they marched through Anatolia, and employed the Roman war fleet and its terror weapon, "liquid fire," to great effect. In 716 he succeeded in convincing Suleymān, the Arab commander of the column that entered Anatolia from Cilicia, that Amorium would be handed over to the invaders. But instead he was able to garrison the hitherto defenseless fortress town and thus compel the invaders to withdraw. The Arab attack had several components, and while Leo was dealing with Suleymān, a fleet attacked and devastated several regions along the Aegean coast, at the same time as the main invasion column under the caliph's brother, Maslama, waited to hear of Suleymān's success. In spite of Suleymān's withdrawal, Maslama entered Roman territory through Cappadocia, and, having understood Leo's cunning deception, seized both Sardis and Pergamum, where he established winter quarters. The fleet wintered in Cilicia. The following year the combined forces invested Constantinople by land and by sea. Yet, thanks to the defensive measures taken under Anastasius II, a stout defense, the use once again of liquid fire, and the additional support of the Bulgars, the city survived. The onset of the winter of 717–718, the constant harrying of the besieging forces by the Bulgars, the defeat of Arab units in Bithynia, and finally the outbreak of disease in the Arab camp meant that the invaders could make no headway. Eventually, in August 718 and following the death of the caliph Suleymān, his successor ʿUmar II ordered the withdrawal of Maslama's armies and fleet. In the course of the withdrawal, bad weather combined with Byzantine naval attacks caused huge losses; indeed, in

the medieval Islamic tradition this was one of the greatest catastrophes
to befall an Islamic army. The caliphate had to accept that the eastern
Roman state could not be eradicated.[90]

Regardless of this major disaster, attacks along the whole frontier
region and deep into Roman territory continued with yearly raids or
expeditions well into the 740s. The border regions, increasingly devastated yet never entirely depopulated,[91] saw settlements moved to defensible high ground, forts and fortresses lost, retaken and lost again,
in a grinding and monotonous pattern in which each side attempted to
wear the other down. A Roman victory near Akroinos over one of three
invading columns in 740 was significant more for its impact on both
Byzantine and Arab morale than for its strategic worth, but it is presented
in the sources as an encouraging sign for the Romans. Within a few
years the civil war that led to the collapse of the Umayyad caliphate and
the beginnings of Abbasid rule further shifted the balance in favor of
the empire.[92] With the transfer of power and authority to Baghdad, the
pressure on the empire lessened but did not disappear. But the changed
situation permitted Constantine V, Leo's son and successor, to take a
more aggressive strategic stance, and from the 750s the changed character of the conflict between empire and caliphate gradually produced
a more balanced, if still not even, contest.

With hindsight we can see that Leo's usurpation and successful defense of Constantinople mark a change in both the internal as well as
the external situation of the east Roman state. Even within a year of
the ending of the great siege, an imperial fleet attacked the coastal town
of Laodikeia (Latakia) in North Syria and carried off the population
while imperial forces were active on land. There were, inevitably, some
initial difficulties. Sergius, the commander of forces in Sicily, proclaimed
as emperor a certain Tiberius in 717/718, very probably on the grounds
that Constantinople would fall and that an emperor was needed. But
when the troops learned of Leo's accession and of the victory over the
Arab forces, the leading rebels were placed in the custody of the *chartoularios* Paul, Leo's envoy to Sicily, and his soldiers. Another attempted
coup was engineered by a senior palatine officer, the *magistros* Nicetas
Xylinites, who plotted with the deposed emperor Anastasius, supported
by the Bulgar khan Tervel. But the rebels failed to obtain support in the
city, Tervel decided to abandon the plotters, and Leo was able to crush
the attempt.[93]

The stability that Leo was able to achieve marked a significant change in internal politics, although there were other oppositional movements later on in southern Greece among the officers and soldiers of the Helladic military division and in Italy. Both were associated at least to some degree with Leo's fiscal policies, although for the papacy this became entangled from the year 730 with Leo's religious politics and the introduction of his particular form of imperial iconoclasm, and it proved to be a more long-lasting bone of contention.[94] But that is less relevant to our immediate purpose, which is to sketch in, however summarily, the political fortunes of the east Roman state from the time of Heraclius into the early eighth century in order to give some body and shape to the period and to underline the complex interweaving of issues and challenges faced by the empire in its struggle for survival against almost overwhelming odds. What should perhaps be emphasized is the ongoing stream of official communications between emperors and caliphs from the very beginning, and persisting through periods of open hostilities as well as during times of peace—caliphal requests for technical aid and resources in constructing mosques in Damascus and in Mecca, for example, as well as on other issues, quite apart from Roman diplomatic efforts to end or limit the fighting or arrange for exchanges of captives. Assuming the substantial body of evidence to support this correspondence can be believed, at least in its general outlines and tendency, then it seems clear that, regardless of any expressed strategic aim to eradicate the Roman state, the caliphate had in fact also come to deal with it as a foe to be treated with respect, and as a neighbor who was not about to disappear.[95]

The Questions

From the early 640s onward, then, the empire was at no time free of substantial military challenges. Regardless of fluctuating strategic patterns evident in the pace and direction of Arab attacks,[96] of its remaining core provinces in Anatolia, those in the south and southwest suffered unremitting economic and social disruption at the hands of raiding forces on an almost annual basis apart from those few years in the late 670s and early 690s when a truce was operating. Even provinces not constantly affected, such as the Pontic region, did not escape occasional raiding and the sacking of settlements. The empire's limited remaining

Balkan territories were similarly affected by raids and disruption from
Slav groups and then from the 680s from the more organized forces of
the Bulgar khans. Beyond this, raiding and seaborne invasions of both
Cyprus and Sicily meant that there were no safe havens—every Roman
province was a potential target. North Africa suffered from both seaborne and land attacks from the 640s, increasing in intensity from
the 660s, although perhaps less unrelenting than the activity directed
at Anatolia. In all this it seems reasonable to see that, certainly under
Mu'āwiya and probably under later caliphs, a coherent strategic plan existed aimed at achieving specific ends—the knock-out blow would have
been the capture of Constantinople, and Mu'āwiya's strategic thinking
in the 650s and 660s certainly seems to point in this direction. Failure
to achieve that aim entailed a return to a policy of wearing the empire
down by a combination of long-distance penetrative attacks on major
fortresses and cities, on the one hand, and constant harassment of the
provinces nearest Islamic territory in North Iraq and North Syria, on the
other.[97]

Throughout this period the emperors had to deal with challenges to
their authority both at the level of imperial political theology as well
as in terms of attempted and successful coups orchestrated either within
the highest elite circles at Constantinople or by soldiers and their leaders.
This hardly contributed to their ability effectively to plan for the situation they faced, although it is clear that they were able to take advantage
of a favorable situation when it arose, as in the case of the two Arab-
Islamic civil wars. And, although I have already made the point, it is
worth repeating that the contraction of the empire's resource-base was
dramatic—had the empire failed to survive beyond the year 700 or the
siege of 717–718, we would probably have said that this was catastrophic
and substantially responsible for the demise of the east Roman state.

As I noted earlier, most accounts of the political history of the empire in the seventh century represent its survival largely as a reflection
of political events and actions and pay either little or no heed to issues
of resource and structure, or they offer merely a token nod in this direction. However important the actions of individual rulers and their
advisors may have been—and of course they did play just as crucial a
role as the other factors we will consider—it is nevertheless important
to remember that those actions and indeed the potential of those involved to act were entirely inscribed within the context of the struc-

tures, relationships, and resources—natural and social-cultural—of their world.

From whichever angle we examine the east Roman empire in the middle of the seventh century, it is quite clear that dramatic transformations were taking place, and in every aspect of social, political, and economic life. Yet, in spite of the total collapse of the old Justinianic state territorially, the empire not only survived but, by the middle of the eighth century, had also begun to stabilize the situation and recover. In the chapters that follow I will try to understand the mechanisms that lay behind this remarkable, indeed, paradoxical survival, and I will approach the issue by asking five linked questions:

1. Did the empire possess any ideological advantages that may have contributed to its survival, and if it did, how did they affect the situation?
2. What were the relative roles of the social elite of the empire; the people from among whom were recruited the financial, administrative, political, and military leaders; and the mass of the ordinary population, in these processes?
3. Did the empire, in the shape it took on from the middle of the seventh century in Anatolia, have any geographical and geopolitical advantages?
4. Were there any broader climatic or environmental factors that contributed to the survival of the empire?
5. Did the east Roman state have any organizational advantages?

Ideological Advantages?

The first question asks whether or not the empire possessed any ideological advantages that may have contributed to its survival, and if it did, how did they affect the situation? This is a complex enough question, but the complexity is greatly exacerbated by the dearth of sources, or rather, by the dearth of sources for what people below the secular and ecclesiastical elite thought. Since ordinary people did not write about contemporary events or their own experiences or views, we are entirely dependent upon a range of texts from which we must infer the views of the majority of the population as well as of the more educated and the elite in church and state. Yet it is not impossible to read between the lines in some types of text or document, nor is it impossible to use a range of proxies, such as patterns of behavior or indirect statements about certain events or ideas. Theological writings, hagiographies, and acts and canons of church councils as well as legal texts, quite apart from traditional chronicle or historiographical writings, all can reveal a good deal if used with care. Just as importantly, by examining carefully the actions of individuals and groups in terms of their behavior as described in our sources and in the ways through which such actions are embedded in a particular narrative, we can attribute with a reasonable degree of probability some aspects of the motives underlying the actions described, even if we can never know the intentions of the individual actors.

It hardly needs to be emphasized that we should distinguish between the attitudes and vested interests of members of local and Constantino-politan elites, on the one hand, and those of the vast mass of the "ordi-nary" population of the provinces, on the other, or that we ought to recognize that the actions and behaviors that we can ascribe to these varied groups depended both upon the immediate context in which they found themselves as well as upon the longer-term background situation that determined the way they led their lives on a day-to-day basis and the ways in which they amended or changed the key elements of the narratives that informed their lives and their understanding of the world.[98] Thus, the fact that the inhabitants of a particular region surrendered to an invading army does not necessarily mean either that they had given up all hope of their own cause or that they had abandoned former loyalties and political identities in favor of new ones. But it probably does mean that they were under enough pressure to need to compromise in order to survive the immediate situation, especially if there was some possibility of the situation being reversed in due course. In addition, the role of local elites, both in respect of their relationship to the government at Constantinople and the system of honors and social status that it embodied as well as with regard to their activities as representatives and enforcers of state policies in the provinces, was clearly of considerable significance in determining how local populations dealt with their own situations.

I will examine this question in greater detail in a subsequent chapter, but in the present state of our knowledge there is no evidence to suggest any overwhelming "national" sentiment or resistance on the part

of the indigenous populations of Asia Minor, so we cannot argue that
the response typical of the urban and rural populations in Syria and Palestine, for example (except where a particularly stubborn garrison
could offer resistance), was any different from that in Anatolia. Indeed,
the church appears to have been acutely conscious of the situation in
the provinces of Asia Minor, and it legislated through canon law to ensure that the populations were not permitted to drift out of its sights. Of
all the factors that contributed to Byzantine survival, we may wonder
whether the church and its activities were not one of the single most
neglected and underestimated elements in our discussions. One reason
for this might be that there is a scarcity of concrete evidence for the period
in question relating to ecclesiastical activity. But there are important
indications that can help throw a little more light on the situation;
indeed, when one looks for it, the evidence is there even if historians
have not, on the whole, taken it into account. The disciplinary arrangements of the church as reflected in the canons of the Quinisext Council
of 692, for example, suggest that the church maintained a relatively firm
grip over the provincial clergy and was able to ensure that there was
some continuity of the pastoral activities of the clergy. The same canons,
while showing up the nature of the problems faced by the ecclesiastical
establishment in Constantinople, also suggest, along with other evidence (some hagiographical and related material, for example) that few
areas escaped ecclesiastical control—even when in the 680s and 690s
provincial bishops from the areas most affected by warfare and disruption failed to show up for church councils in Constantinople, the
fact that they must still have been in their provinces is itself a strong
indication.[99]

In the context of a much-reduced imperial territory and the fact that
a single archdiocese was now the sole responsible ecclesiastical authority
throughout the eastern lands of the empire, it is also the case that
keeping an administrative, economic, and moral eye on the provincial
estates of the church as well as the population would have been much
simplified. And we should also bear in mind that the Byzantine church
had been, for over a century, a very clearly imperial church, and that
Christian orthodox faith and belief went hand in hand with acceptance
of—indeed, a need for—the empire, with its God-appointed and God-
loving emperor in Constantinople. Justinian's efforts to impose unity
on the church through imperial pressure and intervention were a failure.

Neither he nor his successors, up to and including Heraclius and Constans II, were able to resolve the fundamental divisions within the
church, both within and between different Christological parties. Yet
as the empire shrank in territorial extent, as it was reduced to what
would become its core, it was also reduced—more or less—to those
regions that accepted the imperially sponsored definition of orthodoxy.
Henceforth the identity of empire with orthodoxy and church, and orthodoxy and church with empire, was a crucial element and a key factor
in the story of east Roman survival. And there is little doubt that as
the Caliphate saw itself as a religious entity and justified its attack on the
eastern Roman empire ideologically on precisely those grounds, so the
religious identity of the empire became a key marker of distinction for
the emperor's subjects.[100] This is nevertheless by no means a simple or
monochrome picture, however, as I will show in Chapters 2 and 3.

  In the foregoing there has been reference to "the church" as well as
"the state" or "the empire." To avoid confusion, I want to comment very
briefly on these three terms here, since it must be clear that none of
these terms carried in the early medieval period the values and significance they do today. The standard term employed in medieval Greek
literature to describe what we would call the East Roman "state" is the
term *"politeia,"* the nearest equivalent to the Latin *res publica*. For most
inhabitants of the Eastern Roman Empire, this was hardly to be differentiated from the term "empire" itself, in its Latin form *imperium* or the
Greek *autokratoreia* (literally "autocracy"), and had an ideological and
symbolic as well as a practical, political meaning—the authority wielded
by the ruler, and the world he ruled over, along with the institutional
or administrative arrangements that accompanied them, as in the legislation of Justinian, for example, or the preface to the *Ecloga* of Leo III
and Constantine V. For a few—the educated and those who constituted
the service elite of the government, especially in Constantinople—the
term *"politeia"* also conjured up notions of an older Roman world,
whether that of Justinian a century or more earlier, or that of the empire of Constantine I, or perhaps also, for those familiar with the various
historical writings that were part of their educational background, the
world of ancient republican Rome. In contrast, "church" meant the
(orthodox) Christian community as a whole as well as its institutional
forms, just as *res publica* or *politeia* could refer to the totality of institutions that composed Roman rule, including the church. There was no

formal opposition between church and state as later evolved in the medieval west—to the contrary, from an eastern Roman perspective, while priesthood and empire were distinguished, they were also envisaged as different functions of a unity. Of course, in the practical, day-to-day realities of secular and ecclesiastical politics and theology, tensions as well as conflict arose over the interpretation of this relationship. In the course of this volume I will necessarily refer to "the state" and to "the church" in order to make some analytical distinctions and points. But this should not mislead us either into the anachronistic notion that medieval Byzantines differentiated in such distinct terms, or into the unhelpful idea that modern definitions and terms cannot be of value in attempting to understand pre-modern cultures.[101]

Elites

The second point relates to the social elite of the empire, the people from among whom were recruited the financial, administrative, political, and military leaders and their staffs. The dramatic changes of the seventh century, the loss of territory on a vast scale, the shifts and changes in civic culture and urban life, the narrowing of cultural and ideological horizons that the Persian and especially the Arab wars ushered in had many consequences. One is that late Roman culture, the culture of urbanized elites and the network of literary and political capital they maintained, disappeared. Only in Constantinople does there appear to have been much continuity, and even here it was attenuated. Many of the developments that led to this transformation were in train long before the seventh-century crisis, but that crisis brought things to a head and promoted the development of new structures and responses. Literary culture—the content, focus, and bearers of that culture—changed considerably as the relationships of power within the ruling elite to both land and office changed. The old "international" elite establishment, along with the cultural world and cultural media associated with it, fades away during the seventh century, to be replaced by a service elite, a pseudo-meritocratic elite, of more varied cultural background and social origins. True, the limited evidence suggests that the new elite incorporated many elements of the older establishment, but elite culture nevertheless underwent radical change. We shall have more to say on this in Chapters 4 and 5.[102]

The dramatic territorial shrinkage of the empire left it, as we have seen, with little more than Anatolia and the Aegean islands at its core, and important and wealthy provincials in these areas naturally turned to Constantinople, the seat of empire and source of wealth, status, and power, in which to invest their social capital in order to become part of that system. The Church provided an alternative and equivalent career structure, of course, but that also was centered in Constantinople. The emperor and the court became, more than ever before, the source of social advancement. And while there were many minor routes to power that were not directly pulled into that nexus, the imperial court nevertheless constituted the dominant mode of entry. Perhaps most significantly of all, these changes meant that the imperial government and the emperors themselves had a far greater and far more direct oversight of key officials and appointments. Of course, the ruler had always had a say in who received the most senior appointments, but with the territorial shrinkage came an increasing degree of centralization and, in many respects, an increase in "efficiency"—less institutional and spatial friction in the managing of the empire's remaining, reduced, territories. This contrasts somewhat with the situation of the empire across the later fourth, fifth, and into the sixth centuries, with increasing centralization of bureaucracy and administrative competences leading to less personal oversight by the emperor, even under Justinian. The contrast only goes to underline the shifts that a dramatic reduction in territory had brought.[103] Now "efficient" is, obviously, a relative adjective—what appears as "efficient" for one culture may not appear to be so for another. Indeed, this centralization appears to a degree paradoxical insofar as the administration responded to some of the problems it faced by devolving authority and power to provincial officials.

Individuals who had property or wealth in whatever form, and individuals who wanted to succeed and who had ambition, had little option but to invest fully in the survival of the system—or change sides. That being the case, it also meant that they collaborated 100 percent in the implementation of imperial policy, whether in respect of financial management, military commands, or religious politics. Probably not everyone responded in this way; indeed, there were particular individuals, about whom we shall have more to say, who were inflexible in their ideological hostility and opposition to imperial ecclesiastical policy. By the same token, there may well have been individuals or groups who

People renewed remarkably loyal

viewed constant enemy harassment and the threat of death and destruction as perfectly adequate reasons for fleeing, changing sides, or
whatever; and there is also good reason to think that under the right
circumstances people might well be inclined simply to give up. But
with certain notable exceptions, this does not appear to have been the
case in Anatolia, although the situation in other regions, such as North
Africa, was rather different and somewhat more complicated than this.
Yet under the conditions of the middle and later years of the seventh
century in Asia Minor, and facing the sort of prospect that the government in Constantinople had to confront, the survival of the territorial
integrity of the empire is, it seems to me, remarkable. We know of
only a very few cases of individuals hedging their bets—for example
Saborius, the general of the Armeniakon army in the 660s and his supporter Sergius—and often these are members of neighboring elites, such
as Armenians, whose loyalties depended very much on the immediate
context and the degree to which emperors in Constantinople paid
them appropriate attention and could afford to buy their continuing
support.[104] But while our sources are poor, it is unlikely, had this
been more common, that we would not have them reported to us—
indeed, had it been more usual, the empire would not have survived in
any case.

Geography

The answer to the third question is not difficult and is straightforwardly
positive. But it is important to put this into its wider context and especially to see how these advantages are just one key feature that, for their
effect, depended on combining with the other factors to be discussed.
The shrinkage of the empire that took place in the east in the course of
the few years following the Battle of the Yarmuk in 636 was, in hindsight, a distinct advantage. While the Taurus and Anti-Taurus Mountains marked a significant physical and political frontier only from the
early eighth century, they nevertheless represented a barrier behind
the Roman forward lines of defense in North Syria and Cilicia that offered considerable defensive possibilities and permitted Roman forces to
withdraw when necessary to regroup as well as providing a reservoir of
resources and manpower. Until the early years of the eighth century, in
fact, and in spite of the very dramatic reverses suffered by imperial forces

on several occasions, a hard-fought and bitter resistance meant that it was able to hold onto much of the rich Cilician plain and the open country in North Syria, south of the Taurus. By 710–715, however, these districts (Cilicia I and II, Armenia III)—subjected to almost half a century of constant to-and-fro warfare by that time—had to be relinquished, with the result that the Taurus/anti-Taurus line came into its own as a frontier barrier.[105]

As Map 1.2 shows, there are relatively few major routes through or across these ranges, and these can be defended or, alternatively, observed so that hostile activities can be monitored or ingress denied. Naturally there are a large number of smaller and less obvious routes, and while

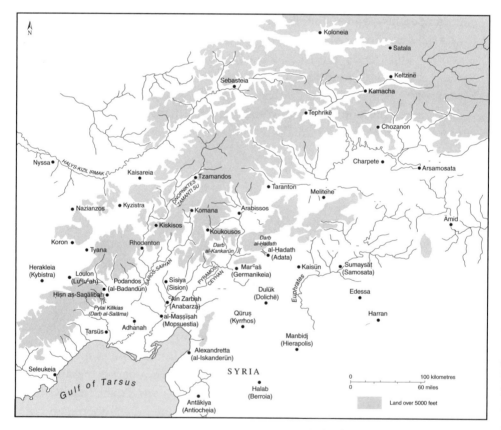

Map 1.2. The Taurus and Anti-Taurus region, ca. 740. (Reprinted from *The Palgrave Atlas of Byzantine History* by John Haldon, Map 8.8 with minor omissions. Basingstoke and New York: Palgrave Macmillan. © 2005 by John Haldon.)

The Challenge 65

these are more difficult to use or impose certain limitations on the size
of the forces that can pass along them, they are also more difficult to
control and observe. But the mountains themselves proved less of an ob-
stacle than the nature of the landscape behind them—together with the
nature of those attacking the Byzantine Empire; this was what proved so
effective a barrier to conquest. It is frequently assumed that the invading
Arab armies were fast, mobile, mounted Bedouin. In fact, while some
Arab forces consisted of horse- or camel-mounted warriors, and many
soldiers traveled on horseback or camel, the great majority of the early
Arab armies were made up of foot soldiers. While it is true that they were
certainly very mobile and that they exploited this mobility in their ability
to outmaneuver their slower Byzantine and Sasanian opponents, it is
also true that just as many, probably a majority, were men who would
ordinarily have been shepherds, farmers, or townspeople (traders, artisans, laborers). Very many, for example, were not from the Hejaz, the
central and northern desert regions of the Arabian peninsula, but rather
from the southern and eastern coastal zones. And while large numbers were relocated in the conquered lands, especially in Syria and
Iraq, they mostly continued to pursue the peacetime occupations
they had done formerly, except for those who permanently adopted a
military life, supported by the *dīwān* or military pensions of the new
regime.[106]

It is also the case that, while the climatic conditions in the Gulf and
the Hejaz and in central and northern Iraq and Syria were by no means
the same, they were not so very different in respect of the productive
activities they permitted. But they were very different indeed from those
of the Anatolian plateau. It is hardly a coincidence that, after an initial
period of conflict, followed by a short-term near abandonment, the landscape and urban centers of the Cilician plain (see Map 1.2), lying to the
south of the Taurus, were readily colonized by Islamic settlers and soon
became flourishing centers of economic activity. While the political context for this was the successful attempt of the first Abbasid caliphs to
reestablish their authority over the region, it nevertheless demonstrates
the real difference represented by the geography of the mountains and
plateau in contrast to that of the coastal regions and the flood plains of
the Sarus and Pyramus Rivers.[107] For no Arab settlements ever succeeded in establishing themselves permanently beyond the mountains,
on the plateau. The point of all this is that raiding expeditions across
the Taurus, lasting a few days or weeks, were one thing; settling there

and dealing with a very different climatic regime, which imposed a very different type of economy and agriculture, were something entirely different. The type of pastoral economy practiced by the Bedouin was impossible on the plateau; the type of farming typical of northern Syria or further south was just as different. Hot arid summers and harsh, bitterly cold winters demanded a very different type of economy, one that made permanent settlement by the Arab invaders (and, indeed, non-Arab converts from the Middle East who joined them) extremely difficult. The point is reinforced when we recall how easily the Turkmen nomads moved onto and occupied the plateau with their herds of sheep, goats, and horses in the eleventh century, for they came from lands and practiced a type of economy characterized by climate and geographical conditions exactly comparable to those they found on the central Anatolian plateau.

Byzantine views of the Arabs were, as we might expect, a caricature of the reality. Yet behind many caricatures lies an element of reality, and we should not dismiss entirely the somewhat simplistic, if not parodic representation of the Saracens presented by the early tenth-century *Taktika* of the emperor Leo VI, an account that may indeed be a caricature but was nevertheless based on east Roman experience of warfare on the eastern frontier:

> This people is hurt by cold, by winter, and by heavy rain. It is best, therefore, to launch attacks against them at such times rather than in good weather. Their bow strings become slack when it is wet and because of the cold their whole body will become sluggish. Often while making their incursions and plundering raids at such times, they have been overcome by the Romans and destroyed.
>
> They flourish, therefore, in good weather and in the warmer seasons, mustering their forces, especially in summer, when they join up with the inhabitants of Tarsus in Cilicia and set out on campaign. At other times of the year only the men from Tarsus, Adana, and other cities of Cilicia launch raids against the Romans.
>
> Therefore, it is necessary to attack them as they are marching out to pillage, especially in winter.[108]

This is not to propose a form of simplistic climatic and cultural determinism; of course the soldiers of the Greater Syrian region or the Arabian peninsula could deal with the cold, with snow, with harsh conditions. Indeed, they tried permanent occupation on a number of occasions and failed. In 666/667, for example, an Arab garrison was established in Amorium. It was quickly driven out when the Byzantines attacked in the middle of the following winter. Theophanes merely notes that the emperor sent a detachment to retake the city "when winter had fallen" and that the attack took place "at night when there was much snow." But the situation is indicative.[109] In 664 a major Arab raid affected the districts around Koloneia in Cappadocia, and the attackers overwintered in the area. In 665 another army wintered in Pisidia, not far from Pisidian Antioch, where it established a base of operations until it withdrew in 666, only to return again in 667.[110] Yet it is significant that during these attacks (and in others in the 660s and 670s) the invaders had little success in taking, occupying, and holding for more than short periods any fortified urban centers. It is true that they targeted a few major cities—Caesarea in Cappadocia, Trebizond, Ankara, Pergamum, and Amorium, for example, but—as with the example of Amorium noted already—they appear to have been quite unable to maintain themselves there. And without such bases, a permanent occupation was not possible. By the same token, they were able on occasion to seize and hold for a time some of the upland forts controlling access to or egress from the Taurus and Anti-Taurus from the south or southeast, such as Loulon, Podandos, Taranton, and others, but that entailed permanent garrisons and regular supplies from the lowlands in their rear.[111]

It seems that the opportunity costs of conquering and occupying Anatolia were thought to be just too high. The attacks on Constantinople were intended to avoid such expenses by short-circuiting imperial opposition and finishing the empire quickly. Settlement beyond the Taurus required both effective economic support and constant military backing. The former was only possible if local populations could be induced to provide it, by whatever means, but this would have required primarily the constant application of coercion and the absence of the constant harassment and pressure exerted by the Byzantine forces, a subject to be discussed in a later chapter.

It is hardly to be wondered at, therefore, that the only places the Arabs did hold onto were fortresses along the chain of the Taurus and Anti-Taurus Mountains themselves, usually in relatively inaccessible locations that could be supplied and reinforced from their Cilician or Syrian hinterlands. Permanent occupation beyond this was seen as impractical, and the climatic factor was such that even winter raids were to be undertaken only with great caution because of the lack of provisions, something clearly understood by Islamic commentators themselves: the early-tenth-century geographer Qudāma b. Jaʿfar, remarks that winter expeditions into Byzantine lands (in late February and early March) should not last longer than twenty days, the length of time for which the troops could carry their supplies with them.[112] And by the middle of the eighth century the caliphate had largely withdrawn into the Cilician and Syrian plains, where a little later under Harūn al-Rashīd a series of fortress-cities was constructed to maintain the frontier defenses and prevent Roman raiders from penetrating into the richer lands to the south. In effect the caliphate filled out the more hospitable and strategically more manageable plains, lapping around the mountains and the plateau to the north and west held by the Romans. Thereafter, and in spite of often very successful penetrative raids deep into Byzantine lands, no attempts were made to seize and hold on a permanent basis any major fortresses or towns, even though several were taken and their defenses destroyed.[113]

Time seems here to have played a role too. By the time the caliphate was moving into a mode that clearly involved trying to beat the Byzantine defenses down and destroy the Byzantine will to resist—that is to say, from the 660s on—the empire had had time both to restructure some of its military capability and to think about a different sort of strategic response to that employed up to then. Unlike in the provinces of Syria, Palestine, and Mesopotamia, the indigenous populations of Anatolia, particularly those of the frontier zones most regularly threatened by hostile action, seem to have been more closely supervised by the imperial authorities and were evacuated when attacks occurred or simply cleared out of areas that were constantly attacked. More importantly, imperial strategy moved very clearly from attempting to defeat the Arabs in the field to avoiding open battle; occupying and defending key forts, fortresses, and cities; and reoccupying and rebuilding them when driven out.[114]

Already under Muʿāwiya, the Islamic leadership appears to have recognized that an occupation of Anatolia was not practical and opted instead for the knock-out blow. Such an approach was always on the cards, and the major attack mounted against Constantinople in 667–669 exemplified the possibilities. Arab strategy appears to have shifted as

Byzantine strategic responses changed too, as can be demonstrated by a careful analysis of the pattern of raids. In the years up to ca. 679/680, the attacks were characterized by systematic attempts to penetrate deep into imperial territory, to seize key centers and to promote a collapse of Byzantine resistance and morale, to maintain troops through the winter on Byzantine territory, and to push the Byzantines out of what had become for a time the frontier regions in Isauria, Phrygia, Cappadocia, and Armenia IV. The failure of the siege of 668/669 does not seem to have affected this basic strategic plan in essentials, with frequent multiple annual raids to devastate the countryside behind the frontier and in the heartland of Asia Minor in order to destabilize the economy and force a collapse of the state through the consequent crisis of resources but with the same general aim of destroying resistance in preparation for a knock-out blow targeting Constantinople.

This policy seems to have been drawn to a close following upon the death of Muʿāwiya in 680. As we have just noted, the Arabs simply could not maintain a permanent presence behind the chain of the Taurus and Anti-Taurus Mountains, for every time they seized a Byzantine position and tried to hold it, they were quickly deprived of it—the main problem seems to have been the difficulty of maintaining communications and supply lines open across the mountains and through the winter period. It is clear that the frequent overwintering campaigns were deeply unpopular with the Arab soldiers: the caliph Yazīd is reported to have received requests from his troops that no more winter campaigns against Byzantine lands would take place; as has been pointed out, whereas there was an overwintering campaign virtually every year from 663 to 680, the sources mention only two or three thereafter. Between the early 680s and the year 715/716, the strategy shifted to one of wearing down Byzantine frontier defenses, paving the way for the great attack of 717–718 which, while it did not end this phase, was certainly its high point. Its failure brought with it a further shift in which the aim of actually knocking the empire out by one means or another appears to have been abandoned, an uneasy modus vivendi was achieved, and both sides focused on establishing what turned out to be a permanent frontier zone, although things were in fact a little more complex than this somewhat simplistic account suggests, inflected additionally, of course, by developments and internecine strife within the caliphate, a topic that will be addressed later.[115] Arab armies were neither able to gain a foothold behind the Taurus nor, apparently, to win over or subjugate any of the indigenous population—resistance was the norm rather than the exception, in striking contrast to the situation in Syria, Palestine, and Mesopotamia in the 630s, where urban centers had largely made peace with the invaders and reached an accommodation with them.

An Environmental Factor?

The fourth question concerned the issue of whether there were any broader climatic or environmental factors that contributed to the survival of the empire. This is a complex set of issues, and one into which we will go in greater detail in a later chapter. And we should begin by emphasizing that, as recent commentators have noted, there is no basis for the idea that any major civilizational development can be attributed to climatic changes *alone.* Climate is complex, and a great deal depends on whether we contrast longer-term trends with short-term data, the size of the area in question, the place of observation—different and apparently contradictory data need to be reconciled and fully contextualized before explanations can be offered.[116] Some climate scientists have talked in the past about systems collapse or societal catastrophe resulting from climatic changes, but when the phenomena in question are examined more closely from the perspective of a historian or archaeologist, they appear much more complex, particularly in light of the interaction between human societies and their ecology. Scale is often crucial, for any discussion of the relationship between climatic change and climate events and human history requires the incorporation of several additional layers of complexity, with outcomes varying according to environmental and geopolitical context as well as social, economic, and political structures.

A few salient features can be introduced at this point, however, simply to emphasize the potential that integrating historical with paleoenvironmental research has for interpreting the past and to sketch in some background. In general terms, it is broadly accepted that a phase of global warming dominated in Roman times and up to the later second century CE, and this favored both agrarian and pastoral expansion in the central and southern regions of Anatolia and in the Middle East more generally. Gradually, with different regional and microregional effects, a reversion to global cooling set in thereafter, until once again from ca. 900 onward what is referred to as the Medieval Climate Anomaly is documented to around 1200 CE. This means that in the period from the middle of the sixth century or a little earlier into the later seventh or early eighth century, some important environmental changes occurred that have important implications for the Middle and Near East as well as the regions around them. Recent interpretations of a range of proxy data for both land use as well as for climatic developments in the late antique period, combined with evidence for the activity of the sun and the impact of broader latitudinal climatic bands, suggest some interesting changes that seem to have affected the eastern Mediterranean and Near/Middle East during the period with which we are concerned. These developments form part of much broader climatic changes, and one of the problems is that general trends can have very different impacts on regions that are quite close to one another, depending on a range of local factors. Thus, on the one hand there is evidence to suggest a short-term slide in the east Mediterranean and Levant from the fifth into the middle of the sixth century toward a somewhat warmer, wetter regime than hitherto, which seems to have been beneficial to agriculture. This was followed by a generally drier and cooler period up to the ninth and tenth centuries. But there is also evidence to suggest that, as arid conditions once more imposed themselves on the Levant from the later sixth century, large parts of Asia Minor remained quite humid into the eighth century and in places into the ninth. The pattern in Europe north of the Alps is somewhat different from this again. And all regions were affected by a particularly cold period setting in from the late 530s, the result of a series of major volcanic eruptions, and lasting into the 660s, now referred to as the Late Antique Little Ice Age (LALIA).[117] These significant variations and their different impacts will be examined in more detail in Chapter 6, where we shall also see that reading off even generally applicable effects of such changes for individual regions is extraordinarily difficult. But for the moment we should note that climate may have had an impact on the political and economic situation that prevailed in the sixth to eighth centuries, and thus on the possibilities for survival of the eastern Roman state. Indeed, I suggest that, whereas the climate changes of the fifth and sixth centuries created conditions that adversely affected the later

Roman world, it was exactly these conditions that contributed—in the new international political and economic context that arose—to the survival of its successor in the east.

Organization and Management

The fifth question concerned the organizational advantages that the eastern Roman state may have enjoyed in its struggle to survive and to overcome the problems and challenges it faced during the seventh century. One does not need to examine the sources in great depth to see that, in spite of the disastrous loss of state income and the contraction of the empire to a rump of its former self, the military road system; the logistical arrangements for recruiting, supporting, and equipping armies; and, crucially, the tax system of the east Roman empire continued to function. While the exact mechanics of this remain to be clarified, it would appear that these conferred a distinct advantage, enabling the state to meet the economic and military threat to its existence, contain it, and, eventually, push it back. The government of an empire that had lost three-quarters of its revenues, that had retained effectively only its poorest set of provinces and yet still had to maintain, at least initially, armies of roughly the same size as before such losses, must surely have found itself in a major crisis. The point is generally admitted.[118] In looking for some of the reasons for the survival of the empire in a situation that would challenge any organized state system, our attention is inevitably drawn towards organizational factors. But while the empire entered the crisis period with a fully intact infrastructure, the question remains as to how and why exactly this infrastructure did not collapse but was able to respond to meet the challenges it faced.

Clearly, an infrastructure, a set of organizational and physical assets, consists not just of arrangements, or roads and bridges, or means of collecting revenues. Complex flowcharts may well indicate the complexity and relative sophistication of late Roman administrative concepts and structures, but they tell us nothing about how the system really worked.[119] For an infrastructure also consists—indeed, is crucially composed of—people. An appreciation of this is absolutely fundamental because it means that the institutions themselves are the effect of individuals acting according to a specific set of rules, within a particular social and institutional context, and with the aim, at least in principle, of achieving a certain set of results. These results are both personal and social, on the one hand, as well as institutional, on the other. For the former, the personal and social, this means in turn that the repetition of these particular forms of behavior and actions cements, or at least contributes to the maintenance of, a set of relationships that offers the actor a sense of self and identifies him or her with a particular social-cultural milieu. For the latter, the institutional, it means that certain organizational "needs" are met—the managing of resources, the keeping of records, and so forth. The two are, obviously, so intimately connected that they are hard to separate except somewhat artificially since the achievement of the organizational goals contributes toward and reinforces perceptions of personal competence, success, and identity (however, we may qualify these terms through the values of the culture in question).[120]

With these remarks in mind, therefore, we may ask, what is it that leads to the breakdown of a set of institutional arrangements and their failure to deliver the goods, so to speak? And by the same token, what sorts of arrangements, and under what conditions, manage to survive crises? To a degree, the answer lies in the ways in which social and ideological identities generate solidarities or not, and how people identify with particular sets of narratives about the way their world works, what is important to them, and how they can act to ensure stability and continuity. And the result of continuity and flexibility can be seen in what happens to the east Roman administrative and fiscal apparatus in the later seventh and eighth centuries (and to a degree beyond). Thus, in the course of the seventh century we find that the taxation of land in the established manner was able to carry on but that its administration was placed under a more direct palatine oversight; we find that the administrative pyramid typical of the empire hitherto, presumably because it no longer responded adequately to the exigencies of the times, was broken down into its constituent parts; and we see that the arrangements for producing weapons and supplying armies was radically restructured across several generations, and that a crisis-management system entailing, among other measures, the retasking of imperial customs depots and their officials to supply both the armies and Constantinople itself was set up, which better met the needs of the moment. We find that the court, the palace, and the patriarchate at Constantinople became the focus of virtually all elite social and cultural identity; and we find that the local elites of the surviving territories of the empire, such as Anatolia (previously largely invisible in the sources), rose to prominence, people whose investment in the imperial system helped to bind the provinces to the center in ways which facilitated imperial control on the one hand as well as resistance to invasion on the other. Finally, we find that these shifts and changes facilitated the capacity to maintain the physical infrastructure of imperial rule. Taxes continued to be collected; gold coins of a surprisingly high degree of purity continued to be minted, and in quantity; roads and bridges continued to be maintained; weapons and military equipment continued to be produced and soldiers continued to be recruited, trained, and equipped. But how was all this possible? Other state systems under comparable pressure have failed: the Western empire itself, indeed, is an obvious example (even if we concede that the difficulties it faced were somewhat different and that its cultural and political situation were also somewhat different). Our question is also, in fact, very much a question about the nature of a state and what makes it work—something to which we will return in later chapters.

The Challenger

The five key questions that we deal with in the following chapters represent factors and issues largely internal to the workings of the eastern Roman state and society, although it is certainly the case that no society is an island and that neither from the point of view of social and cultural life nor from that of economic and political activity was eastern Roman society independent from the world around it. The broader context is a major factor in the discussion, and in the foregoing I have offered a sketch of some important details that provide a framework for developments within the empire and a context that affected the ways in which those developments impacted on eastern Roman society and culture, economy and politics. The part played by the politics of the new Arab-Islamic empire is obviously a major consideration. For it is quite apparent that the internecine conflicts of the period 656–661, in the early 680s, and in the period ca. 689–691 undoubtedly played a role in Byzantine survival, giving emperors and policymakers, the army and provincial economies breathing spaces and allowing time to take stock and prepare for the next attacks. By the same token, we should remember that the Umayyad caliphs did not necessarily see the Byzantine Empire as their most important priority. They had to contend with enemies in the north and east as well as internal problems, and even when the east Roman enemy did take priority—Muʿāwiya was clearly particularly concerned with the taking of Constantinople—they were not able to muster all the resources necessary to its eradication. They faced problems of fiscal management and access to resources, and across a vastly larger territory than the Eastern Roman Empire—problems that remained intractable from the start and that were eventually to result by the later ninth century in the emasculation of caliphal power and the marginalization of the Abbasid caliphs themselves, except in ideological respects.[121]

The question of the distribution of resources and revenues and the degree to which the caliphs had access to the revenues from a given area was from the beginning a fundamental problem in the new polity. There is little doubt that already by the 670s, and certainly by the 690s, a tax system, fiscal apparatus, and centrally controlled army existed, administered (at least in theory) from Damascus—in other words, all the key elements for a state were present, apart from the dispensing of justice, which remained in the hands of local community religious authorities, although the caliphal court and the caliphs' representatives also wielded judicial authority. Yet the degree of control over resources exercised by the caliphs remains unclear—in the case of Egypt, where a considerable amount of detailed evidence for fiscal practices survives, it seems that the Islamic administration, based at al-Fustat, was more or less autonomous with respect to the financing and administration of its army and fiscal system.[122] Two institutions, and the practices and traditions that came to be associated with them, were central to the fiscal administration and the distribution of resources in the early Islamic state. The first was the *dīwān*, an institution with no real parallel in neighboring states (although there may be Sasanian precedents). Originally established by the caliph ʿUmar in response to the results of the first wave of conquests in the late 630s, the principle upon which the *dīwān* functioned was that Muslims would not settle on the land but remain rather as a separate caste of hereditary dependents upon the Ummah, the Islamic community (in effect, the state), established in garrison settlements or towns and drawing their incomes from the revenues of the conquered territories in their neighborhood. The term "*dīwān*" referred to the list of names along with the amount of the salary (*ʿatāʾ*) owed to each on a monthly basis (the rates were differential, according to seniority of association with the Prophet, acceptance of Islam, and the first conquests). The income to maintain the *dīwān* was raised in the province where the soldiers or their dependents dwelled, collected in the provincial capital, and both collection and distribution were administered by the provincial governor, appointed in theory by the caliph.

The second institution was that of *fay'*. This term meant the assets in respect of real estate and other immovables acquired through conquest. As a natural result of the conquests, the belief became widespread that all such booty could be divided up and distributed among the conquerors so that the revenues from such lands would thereafter simply be divided up, under local provincial supervision, without caliphal interference. The caliphs attempted from the beginning, however, to obtain control of some of these revenues for their own administrative purposes, without which they would neither be able to support a central governmental apparatus nor to expand or recruit to their military forces. From the beginning, this tension caused problems. The assassination of 'Uthmān has been associated at least in part with such a dispute, originating in al-Kūfa, although Byzantine victories at the same time may also have played a role in encouraging dissatisfaction with a leader associated with military failure.[123]

This conflict over resources and the functioning of the two institutions of *dīwān* and *fay'* constituted the single most important issue around which political struggle was focused in the early Islamic period.[124] By the time of Marwān I (AH 64/683–684 CE) the *dīwān* was in theory closed, although in a series of appeals for support, various contenders for caliphal power added the names of their supporters to the roll. This generally worked, so it is clear that the income derived for oneself and one's dependents through enrollment in the *dīwān* was regarded as significant. The income for the *dīwān* was collected at provincial level rather than organized from Damascus, again suggestive of the relative fiscal autonomy of the provinces, even those quite near the central lands of the state. The regional consumption of resources by the army is clearly reflected in the fact that military salaries were frequently paid in kind, as seems to have been the case in late seventh-century Egypt and, probably, in Palestine at the same period.[125] Efforts on the part of caliphal administrative officials to intervene directly in the col-

lection and distribution of resources for military pay were seen as det-
rimental to the local military.

Armies were supported by other means in addition to the salaries
derived to those listed on the *dīwān*. In some cases tribute from neighboring vassal peoples was paid directly to the army of a particular province or region; in others, resources from provinces where no soldiers
were based but that could produce an appropriate revenue were ascribed
to a specific army, as was certainly the case in parts of Iraq. Armies on
campaign were often raised on the basis of a promise of booty following
expected success, while provincial governors or caliphs could raise forces
on a temporary basis for specific campaigns, using revenue reserves or
income from other sources for the purpose. But as a general rule, all the
historical evidence points to the assumption on the part of those registered in the *dīwān* of each province that their pay—*'atā'*—was drawn
from the revenues of their own province, in turn extracted from the
conquered territories and other resources—*fay'*—and which belonged to
those so registered by right of conquest, not to the caliph or any other
central institution.

The costs of mounting the major expeditions against Constantinople
were enormous and required immense organizational effort as well as
the consumption of vast quantities of food and fodder; the preparation
of a huge number of ships; and a massive quantity of weapons and other
military gear.[126] That the caliphs were able to amass the resources and
assemble the armies for major attacks such as those in the 650s, 660s,
or in the period 716–718 against Constantinople shows that the problems were not insurmountable, but it also suggests that the shifts in
strategy reflect not just strategic but also social, fiscal, and political factional pressures on the regime in Damascus. In this context there is no
doubt that the civil wars in 656–661 and 682–692 helped the Romans
reestablish some equilibrium at moments when pressure had built up.
Yet it would be hard to argue that the empire survived only because of
these fortunate circumstances, and the extent to which this factor
should be seen as contributing toward the failure to eradicate the eastern
empire is a moot point. It seems to me that when we take into account
all the aspects with which I shall be concerned in the following chapters, the Eastern Roman Empire would have survived even had there
been no such "lucky breaks."

I began with the question of how the Eastern Roman Empire managed to survive the onslaught of the first Arab-Islamic empire, and I suggested a cluster of reasons for its success, so the issue becomes one of disentangling the relationship between the various different elements involved. Having sketched out the field for discussion, in the chapters that follow we will go into more detail about how these relationships in fact worked and how we can better understand the processes of historical causation and transformation that turned the recognizably still Roman empire of the late sixth century into the medieval Eastern Roman—the Byzantine—Empire of the eighth century and beyond.

2

Beliefs, Narratives, and the Moral Universe

Or what shall I name the holy chest of the martyr Artemios' precious relics? An abundant spring? Yes, it is a spring, a spring not simply nor in the ordinary sense but one which John the Baptizer of our Lord Jesus Christ cultivated . . . within His own church . . . It does not fail, it does not grow poor, it is not stopped by anyone, it is not held back by any force, it is not impeded by harsh tyrants . . . This spring serves the Christian people and as long as one draws from it, it is not exhausted but gushes up the more and furnishes water ten thousand fold.[1]

A Context for Change

There is no doubt that the social and political upheavals that affected the Byzantine world in the second half of the seventh and early eighth century generated a host of shifts, changes, and transformations in eastern Roman political, religious, and institutional culture.[2] But in order to understand the nature of the changes that affected eastern Roman society in the seventh and early eighth centuries more broadly, and indeed how those changes could come about, we need to sketch out some idea of how people might have perceived what was happening to the world they inhabited, and we need to find out how their perceptions and understanding might have affected their actions or affected how they thought about things. That is the primary purpose of this and the following chapter. The collapse of Roman power in the course of the seventh century threw the relatively stable symbolic universe of eastern Roman culture into confusion, challenging in a number of ways some of the fundamental narratives through which people

within the empire at all levels made sense of their universe. Secular
and religious texts of the period indicate that two major perspectives
evolved in this situation. Explanations for Roman military defeats were
founded upon a well-established biblical eschatology in which the sins
of the Chosen People (now the Romans) and in particular the sins of
their leaders—emperors and patriarchs—occupied a central position.[3]
As the patriarch of Jerusalem, Sophronius, put it in a letter to the patriarch Sergius in Constantinople: May God grant the emperors "great
victories and triumphs over the barbarians, . . . especially the Saracens who, because of our sins, presently rise up unexpectedly against
us."[4] There is nothing new in this logic,[5] yet in the difficult context of
the middle and later seventh century, such a rationale provided ammu-
nition for a sustained critique of individual emperors or their religious
and secular advisors, and the range of texts in which this motif appears increases dramatically. Emperors had to deal with the challenge of
maintaining their authority in the face of such criticism of both imperial religious policies and of political priorities, and with the problems
of keeping the fiscal and military apparatuses of the state in working
order. As the shape of the world changed around them, and as the narratives through which people made sense of the world and their place
in it began to break down, so individuals and groups took whatever
action seemed appropriate to them to attempt to make things better, to
redress the balance, to stabilize the situation.[6] This was not merely an
"ideological" problem—the usurpations and coups d'état that plagued
the empire in the period ca. 695–717, for example, show that soldiers,
members of the elite, churchmen, and courtiers all felt justified in
acting to adjust worldly affairs and "restore" the situation to one that
they could recognize, that is, to make "reality" fit once again the established narratives of how things should be. The deacon Agathon lived
through the events of the period and summarized his own feelings as
follows:

> For the frightful troubles which had come to pass one after another in
> the previous years as a result of our sins caused a weakening and a very
> great degree of destruction not only in the body of the God-guarded
> polity. They reached as far as the very head of the empire itself, so
> that at last, as a result of the frequent changes of ruler in the state
> brought about by tyrannous insurrections, its affairs were treated with
> contempt and valued at nought.[7]

Nor was this an issue for specific, limited groups. Ordinary people were just as interested in such matters, and discussion and concern were not confined to the level of sophisticated theological discourse, such as we find in theological treatises and discussions of dogma, or in the formal communications between popes, patriarchs, and emperors—the sort of discussion exemplified in the documents generated in the course of the controversy over imperial monotheletism between the 640s and 680–681, for example.[8] This is, after all, a society in which the political was understood and expressed through the prism and vocabulary of religion and faith. I do not mean to reduce either part of this equation to the other, but the discipline of political science was yet to be borne, while the world of Aristotle and of Plato, even if it influenced the theology of Christianity, did not impinge upon the thought-world of the day to day. At the core of those issues that attracted most intense discussion was the position held by the imperial authority in the chain of ideological connections between the divine authority of God and the Roman people. Associated with this issue were questions about divine causation, the extent and effectiveness of human free will, and the role of ordinary human beings in the whole equation—problems in the resolution of which emperors, soldiers, clerics, and laypersons all had a vested interest.

The evidence of historical accounts, contemporary letters and commentaries on the situation, and theological writings as well as the canons of church councils all reflect the ways in which eastern Roman understanding of their world evolved across the course of the later seventh century and how different aspects of this process played out in the direct action of groups and individuals. In the autumn of 681, for example, after the return to Constantinople from the Bulgar campaign of the emperor and (some of) the defeated troops and during the council at which monotheletism was in the process of being condemned, the soldiers and officers of the Anatolikon army gathered outside Constantinople and demanded that the emperor Constantine IV rule jointly with his two brothers (who were subordinate to Constantine himself as senior ruler); since they all accepted the Holy Trinity, then God's support would surely be guaranteed if they were ruled by a trinity of emperors: "We believe in the Trinity, let us crown all three," they are reported to have cried. The protests reflected both the troops' and their leaders' discontent with the shift away from monotheletism as well as dismay at the recent defeat at the hands of the Bulgars. As Theophanes put it,

"Both those who lived afar and those who lived near were astonished to hear that he who had subjugated everyone, those in the east and in the west, in the north and in the south, was vanquished by this foul and newly arisen tribe. But he believed that this had happened to the Christians by God's providence."[9] Constantine was thus faced with a military revolt hostile to the change in ecclesiastical policy, apparently focused around his two brothers Heraclius and Tiberius and at least originally with the support of senior members of the senate and government in Constantinople and perhaps also, according to the Syriac source tradition, the emperor's mother. He was able to win the elite to his side, however, with the exception of the *patrikios* Leo, possibly the commander of the Anatolikon forces that had campaigned in the Balkans, before having the latter along with eleven other leaders of the soldiers seized, mutilated, and executed. Heraclius and Tiberius were likewise mutilated and banished, probably to the Princes' Isles in the Sea of Marmara; their mother suffered a similar banishment.[10] In an edict issued in December 681 addressed to the Roman people in general, including the soldiers in the city, Constantine confirmed the results of the council, ordained unity, and condemned monothelete beliefs.[11]

The events illustrate the close association between notions of correct belief, military success, and the fate of the empire; they also underline the enormous coercive power and authority of the imperial government, since it is likely that much of the ordinary population of the empire, along with the clergy, had accepted and were indeed quite comfortable with the established monothelete doctrine. The collection of *Erōtapokriseis* (questions and answers) attributed to the monk Anastasius of Sinai in the later part of the seventh century is a treasure trove of contemporary popular concerns and worries of the period. One of the questions asks whether it is the case that every leader, king, or bishop is appointed by God. The answer was positive and was illustrated by an anecdote in which God is asked why he had sent the awful tyrant Phocas to rule the Romans.[12] The answer came: "because I could find no one worse"! The Romans had sinned, and this was their punishment. And although this logic already had a long history in the religious thinking of the times, it becomes especially pointed in texts by the later part of the seventh century, as indeed it had at other times of perceived crisis.[13] Many of the ills that afflicted the empire were thus understood as associated with the sins of its leaders or of heretics or non-Christians, such as Jews, within the empire. Anastasius of Sinai notes that "today, even if the race of the Saracens were to depart from us, straightway tomorrow the Blues and Greens would rise up again, and the East and Arabia and Palestine and many other lands would bring slaughter upon themselves"—a punishment meted out by God because of the sins of the Romans and their leaders (although reflecting in fact serious tensions within east Roman society, as we shall see in Chapters 3 and 4).[14] And in the answer to the same question, he notes: "Whenever you see an unworthy or base emperor or official or archpriest, do not wonder, but learn and truly believe that we have been delivered unto such tyrants on account of our lawless conduct." So it is quite clear that the evils perpetrated by the Saracens on the Romans were a result of God's will (although Anastasius points out that the pillaging of churches cannot have been God's intention, and that this and similar acts will in their turn receive their due punishment).[15]

By the same token, military success was seen as directly linked to God's support for an orthodox people, a motif that recurs in this and many other contemporary texts and is far older than Christianity. This was the more important because effective imperial leadership had always been one of the key attributes of a Roman emperor, and it remained so.[16] Apocalyptic literature and hagiological writings, such as collections of miracles that could be read out in church or in a monastic context, had a wide appeal and are similarly indicative of the matters that clearly concerned all levels of society. Two miracle collections, those of the healing saints Artemius (compiled probably in the 660s) and Therapon (probably of the first quarter of the eighth century), illustrate such issues, as does the so-called *Apocalypse of Ps.-Methodios*, which appears to have been especially popular and widely read by the year 700 in its Syriac, Greek, and Latin versions.[17] Andrew of Crete, the likely author of the collection of miracles of St. Therapon, compared the sins of the Chosen People to the Flood of the Old Testament and the invasions themselves as a "crawling embryo."[18] These assumptions are shared by some mid-seventh-century edifying stories ascribed to Anastasius.[19] And since internal purity was the hallmark of orthodoxy, it was thus also the guarantor of the imperial state, a notion applied to the political world as well as the spiritual.

Who to Blame?

Late Roman culture by the later seventh century had in some respects—
most especially, in those areas most associated with the government's
efforts to impose or drive a policy of doctrinal unity—become somewhat
more introverted than earlier, characteristics expressed in the ideologically antipluralist and antiheterodox tendencies of imperial rule, in
the apparent absence of external missionary activity, and in a focus on
internal order and correct belief.[20] At one level, this is revealed in increasing hostility toward Jews, for example, reportedly culminating
in imperial decrees imposing compulsory baptism as well as in the rise in
the quantity of anti-Jewish polemic at this time.[21] By the later seventh
century it is indicated in an increasing convergence of secular and ecclesiastical law and a very clear concern to ensure uniformity of belief
and enforce canon law, particularly marked in the canons of the Quinisext council of 692 and in the somewhat later summary codification
of secular law represented by the *Ecloga* of Leo III and Constantine V,
issued in 741, themes I will look at in more detail in Chapter 3. It was
underlined by the ecclesiastical establishment as well, which saw in the
activities of itinerant holy men, particularly in the more distant provinces, a serious challenge to its own authority and a threat to the stability of its moral universe. All these are indicative of a growing need
on the part of the establishment to reaffirm what was orthodox and to
exclude or suppress what was not.[22] Needless to say, the effect of ecclesiastical legislative activity was limited: many of the practices condemned
in the Quinisextum were still in existence several centuries later, as the
commentary of the twelfth-century canonist Balsamon shows.[23] Later
hagiographies, indeed, explicitly record their saints as involved in activities that the canons of 692 prohibited.[24]

There was a trajectory or evolution in the way in which these various
perspectives were expressed and in the issues upon which they focused.
Until the council of 680–681, for example, attention was concentrated
largely on the role of leaders—emperors, patriarchs, popes—key individuals whose policies and actions could be connected with the success
or failure of the empire against its foes. A close parallel was assumed
between orthodoxy (defined according to the perspective of the commentator, of course) and the fate of the empire, although it should be
stressed that wherever possible commentators and critics avoided attrib-

uting blame to an emperor directly, preferring instead to place responsibility at the door of the emperors' advisors or the patriarchs.[25] In the final decades of the century, Anastasius of Sinai himself clearly and explicitly relates Roman defeats to the adoption and enforcing of imperial monotheletism, and relates Roman success to its abandonment at the sixth ecumenical council:

> Then the emperor Heraclius died and Martin [pope, 649–653] was exiled by his grandson [Constans II]; but soon there arose the desert Amalek to punish us, the race of Christians. For that was when that first great, dreadful and irrecoverable fall of the Roman army took place, I mean the slaughter at Gabitha and Yarmouk and Dathimon, after which came the capture and conflagrations in Palestine and Caesarea and Jerusalem and then the destruction of Egypt, and after that the ravaging and devastation of the isles of the middle sea and of all the land of the Romans.[26]

This and other texts similarly allude to the fate of Constans II as a just punishment.[27] But note that such direct criticism of an emperor was largely written by those outside the empire, or written long after the events in question: it was held even by the fiercest critics of imperial policy as quite inappropriate to blame the emperor, a point that emerges from many texts but is especially clear in the account of the trial of Maximus:

> Lord Troilus, on hearing that the *Typos* was anathematized throughout the entire west, said to the servant of God (Maximus): "Is it a good thing that the reputation of our orthodox master (the emperor) suffer outrage?" The servant of God answered: "May God forgive those who caused the master to issue the *Typos* and those who allowed it." And he [Troilus] said: "Who are the ones who caused him to issue it and who are the ones who allowed it?" He [Maximus] answered: "The ecclesiastical officials caused him to do it and the state officials allowed it. Look at how the filth from those responsible has spread out over the one who is innocent and pure of any heresy." . . . "Let the one who now rules over us in an orthodox manner [repudiate the *Typos,* as Heraclius did the *Ekthesis*] too, and his reputation will remain completely undefiled by any censure.[28]

A letter of October 649 from Pope Martin and addressed to the young Constans on the issue of monothelete doctrine refers quite specifically to the association between the fate of empire and orthodoxy: "for the

preservation of the state is accustomed to go along with orthodox belief";[29] Sophronius of Jerusalem makes the same explicit connection.[30]
From a different point of view, George of Resh'aina, who was a contemporary of Maximus himself, penned in Syriac a hostile *Life* of the Confessor, and he saw divine retribution falling upon all those places and
individuals that had accepted Maximus's mistaken theology.[31] And if
explanations by theologians, hagiographers, and the writers of miracle
collections or apocalyptic texts were couched almost entirely in terms
of divine retribution,[32] those offered by the political authorities combined both secular and theological reasoning. Given the vociferous
opposition to the imperial position, Constans II's advisors sought to
explain the defeats of imperial armies by accusing both Maximus Confessor and Pope Martin of treachery. In the case of the latter, it was
because he purportedly supported the exarch Olympius's rebellion in
Italy and thus contributed to the loss of western territories as well as corresponding with the Saracen enemy.[33] Maximus is supposed to have
encouraged the general Peter to refuse to carry out imperial commands,
urged the exarch Gregory to rebel, insulted the emperor, and contributed
to the loss of Egypt, Alexandria, the Pentapolis, Tripolis, and Africa.
"And the *sakellarios* said to him: 'From what you have done it is clear
to everyone that you hate the emperor and his empire. I say this because
single-handedly you betrayed Egypt, Alexandria, Pentapolis, Tripolis
and Africa to the Saracens.'"[34] Martin was apparently refused permission during his initial interrogation to discuss issues of dogma on the
grounds that only political and secular matters were at issue, even
though it was Maximus's "heresy" that had provoked divine wrath.[35]

Constans II and his advisors naturally had a vested interest in locating an alternative reason for defeat; indeed, they may have promoted
apocalyptic writings in which the emperor was presented, in the context of the legend of the Last Emperor, as the savior of the Christians at
the end of days, picking up on aspects of the Alexander legend that had
been deployed in the time of Constans' grandfather, Heraclius.[36] In contrast, his son and successor, Constantine IV, while not admitting openly
that his father's policies were responsible, nevertheless tacitly conceded
as much when he convoked the sixth ecumenical council while at the
same time invoking secular troubles as a major reason for the delay in
reestablishing a dialogue between the imperial party and the opposition. But he too, of course, expressed the same fundamental assump-

tion that the health of the state is founded upon the rock of orthodoxy and the true faith.[37] Pope Agatho clearly relates the survival of the Christian community to the maintenance or not of orthodoxy.[38]

On the other hand, the logic of divine punishment was not limited in its applicability: the monothelete presbyter Constantine of Apamea argued at the sixth council that if only the synod had listened to him at the outset, when he wanted to propose a document of unity between the two camps, then the recent defeat at the hands of the Bulgars could have been avoided.[39] Indeed, it is probable that the threatened mutiny of soldiers in Thrace and the call for the emperor to rule jointly with his two brothers Heraclius and Tiberius is to be associated with this unexpected defeat, a defeat that clearly suggested to some, like Constantine of Apamea, that monothelete doctrine was indeed correct and had won divine support. Using the same logic, miaphysite texts relate the military disasters of the empire in the seventh century to the Chalcedonian position of the imperial government;[40] while the decision of the usurper Philippicus (711–713) to reimpose an official monotheletism as orthodoxy followed likewise a similar argument, attracting the support of churchmen such as Germanus, later patriarch, and Andrew of Crete.[41]

These developments need to be understood in the context of other shifts in perception, especially among some leading figures in the church; they were but one aspect of a larger picture. Churchmen and theologians, the writers of edifying tales and the authors of miracle stories and hagiographies, all placed a clear emphasis on the fundamental virtues of Christian belief and action, underlining for laypeople the importance of a strict adherence to ritual boundaries. The dialogues composed by Christian apologists during the seventh century, intended to show up the basic fallacies of Jewish thought in respect of Christology, representation, and the Cross, reflect these concerns in a particularly acute form, even if employing a much older rhetorical vehicle.[42] And they also broached issues that affected a whole range of Christian beliefs and practice. Across the course of the seventh century a focus on the eucharist and sacramental purity as the measure of right belief and therefore of divine support, a rigorous adherence to the established interpretations of the Fathers of the church, together with a strict demarcation between orthodox and heretic in respect of observance and practice, becomes increasingly evident and is especially notable in the writings of Anastasius of Sinai.[43] The practice of a straightforward,

day-to-day piety attainable by all (and not only by ascetics), and observance of the basic framework of ecclesial life and ritual through the
church and its hierarchy—these were the key precepts that were to
be defended in order to ensure salvation and that were preached in
churches throughout the Christian world. Such values are clearly
present in the canons of the Quinisext as well as in the range of texts
mentioned earlier.[44] They were the essential hallmarks that separated
the orthodox believer from the heretic or the nonbeliever and, in a
time of major and often dramatic political and ideological change, were
seen as the key to survival and to salvation. From the point of view of
the east Roman government at Constantinople, they were entirely consonant with imperial policy and thus with the future security of the
empire itself.

But such an approach created at the same time the grounds upon
which an unquestioned assumption of the identity of Christianity with
the Roman Empire could be challenged. Such an identity had already
become problematic as the senior representatives of the church—the
bishops who were intimately involved with local government as well as
with the spiritual welfare of their flocks—were seen to step in to fill the
breach left by the failures of the secular authority, either by taking the
lead in defending the interests of their communities following military
defeat or the hostile occupation of territory, or on occasion by encouraging military leaders to take the appropriate action to confront an
enemy. The church could continue to rule and guide without the Roman
state, as indeed occurred in greater Syria and Egypt from the mid-630s
and the 640s, so that to some extent it became possible to envisage
Christian Roman identity as separate from the imperial state. With such
an identity securely rooted in the presence of the church, it was the
bishop and the church that guaranteed the purity of soul and physical
survival of the Christian Roman people. Thus, while the empire depended on Christianity, the Christian church and people were not necessarily dependent on the empire.

For those who belonged to the Chalcedonian church, that could also
mean Roman.[45] If the anonymous author of the *Apocalypse of Ps.-Methodios*
was indeed a Chalcedonian (although this is not certain), writing in
northern Mesopotamia in the early 690s, it was certainly entirely possible to see the world as still basically Roman—those in the conquered
territories only had to wait for the redeemer-emperor to come on the

scene and save them.[46] But it is worth noting that the original Syriac version of this important text refers to "the Greek king" and "the Greek kingdom," whereas the Greek translation refers to the Romans and the Roman kingdom, illustrative perhaps of a perceived and significant difference between those who knew the text and lived under Arab as opposed to east Roman rule.[47] For those who belonged to the miaphysite congregations, a straightforward identity with the Roman Empire was not possible as long as its rulers were seen as heretical. But neither should this be seen as a clear rejection of the empire and an all-embracing Roman identity since the postconquest context in which the texts in question were compiled played a key role, and the term "Roman" was both highly evocative but also highly malleable. The late-seventh-century Egyptian bishop of Nikiû, John, expresses this sentiment thus:

> All these events and the separation of Egypt and Alexandria during the reign of Heraclius the emperor of the Chalcedonians fell out as they are recorded in the letters of the great Severus the patriarch of Antioch . . . wherein he prophesied against the Roman empire . . . "No son shall sit on his father's throne so long as the creed of the Chalcedonians prevails, who say that there are two natures in Christ after they became one, a creed which we cannot profess. Their doctrine that the manhood and the Godhead are two distinct natures after having become united, we believers cannot teach. It is not fitting that we should speak as the heretics."

And John continues: "When they (the Chalcedonians) rejected the orthodox faith, which is our faith, in like manner were they rejected from the imperial throne. And there has followed the undoing of all Christians that are in the world, and we have not experienced the mercy and compassion of our Lord Jesus Christ."[48] John bewails the fate of all Christians, not just miaphysites or Egyptians, and he is more concerned with the faults and sins of individual rulers such as Heraclius than with some generically heretical Roman world. But the *Chronicle* was written at a time when Islamic rule in Egypt was firmly established, a time in which Egyptian Christians could look back and reinterpret the past in the light of their present situation, and one in which the concept of "Rome" and "Roman" took on a specific significance. During the early years following the conquest, it had not yet become necessary to redefine oneself in terms of a distinction between being Roman or not-Roman. And similar considerations no doubt apply in the case of Syria and both the miaphysite and Chalcedonian communities.[49]

The idea that the church and the Christian community could be independent of the Roman state if the latter departed from the path of orthodox belief reflects ideas developed during the period of the Persian war in monastic circles in Palestine, particularly focused on the person of John Moschus, that were hostile to Heraclius's attempts at reconciliation with the non-Chalcedonian communities of the eastern provinces. It was reinforced in both theological discourse as well as at grassroots level, once the political disasters of the period ca. 634 onward could be ascribed to the failures of the secular state and its leaders to defend orthodox belief and practice. If salvation depended on strict and unwavering adherence to the established forms of orthodox belief and practice, then anything perceived as innovation had to be rejected outright.[50] Such was the rigorist position argued by churchmen such as Sophronius of Jerusalem already in the 630s, refined by Maximus Confessor and adopted by the papacy in the 640s in opposition to the compromise formulas (initially successful) developed under the patriarch Sergius aimed at bridging the divide between miaphysite and dyophysite doctrine. In itself, the question of the divine energy or operation *(energeia)* was not a new issue, having been an aspect of a long-standing discussion within both miaphysite and dyophysite Christology, as we saw in Chapter 1, whereas the issue of the divine will evolved out of the imperial effort in the 630s to find a form of language agreeable to all parties who had been involved in the discussion over the single operation.[51]

Thus, the emphasis on demarcation, on correct practice as a means of signifying and preserving orthodoxy that had been the hallmark of miaphysite opposition to the "imperial" church also encouraged an alternative strand of thinking within the Chalcedonian community about the relationship between Roman Empire and Christian faith. On this logic, if it was explicit and rigid adherence to the established forms of orthodox piety and practice that would bring salvation, then it was essential that the official church and the state also adhered to them. As the letter to the emperor Constans from Pope Martin puts it: "(the heretics condemned at the Lateran synod of 649 claimed that Constans had issued) the said impious *Typos,* enjoining as harmless a slight concession as regards excessive precision. This they have written, in no way heeding the conviction of the holy fathers that in the teaching about God and the divine that which falls slightly short is no slight matter."[52] A church or a government that compromised those forms could be justifiably and quite logically condemned as incurring God's wrath, while the unity and integrity of the church and the Christian faith could be understood as resting not upon the compromised and struggling secular empire, nor even on the vagaries of patriarchal politics, but upon correct observance of the established orthodox tradition, which should be pursued independently of, even in opposition to, the secular state and its interests. Those who most clearly and vociferously represented this perspective— Sophronius in opposing the doctrine of the single operation, Maximus and Martin in their opposition to the doctrine of the single will—thus came into direct confrontation with the government.[53]

Following the council of Constantinople in 680–681, the Christological issue seemed to have been resolved, at least as far as the government and the imperial church were concerned, although it is clear that monothelete sympathies lingered on within the empire for a generation afterward at least. Yet in spite of the fact that unity of the churches of east and west had been restored and the Roman state and its leaders were once more orthodox, the empire still faced enormous political and military problems; indeed, defeat remained a very real possibility. If the unorthodoxy of the emperors' advisors (or even the emperors themselves, if one was safely out of imperial reach) could no longer be blamed, then new reasons had to be found. In confirmation of this, it is interesting to note that the canons of the Quinisext council take imperial orthodoxy and the traditional parallelism of church and Christian *oikoumene* (the civilized world) with the Roman state for granted, which it reaffirms in the opening address to Justinian II. The council focused exclusively on day-to-day issues of Christian moral comportment, clerical and monastic discipline, and matters of appropriate Christian belief and practice. Unless one could correctly specify and identify the causes of the maladies affecting both individuals and the Christian community as a whole, it would not be possible to determine the form to be taken by the cure. But that church and empire were inextricably associated was taken for granted.[54]

Churchmen and the literate elements of east Roman society in the second half of the seventh century were especially concerned with the question: who had sinned in such a way as to bring down the wrath of God upon His people? What are the sins of omission or commission and

how can they be made good? What must be done to recover God's goodwill? One set of responses, as noted, was to be found in those advocates
of a doctrinal purity and rejection of compromise, such as Sophronius,
Maximus the Confessor, and others. They had come to look beyond any
direct association between secular empire and Christian salvation and
viewed the practical *oikonomia*—essentially, a willingness to compromise over details for the sake of what was seen as a greater good—of
those who worked toward a union of the miaphysite and dyophysite
communities as something to be rejected in favor of a rigorous adherence to doctrinal precision.[55] The impact of this thinking was not confined to the theoretical. On the contrary, it had—and was certainly seen
by the imperial camp as having had—dire material political consequences: political opposition in both North Africa in the mid-640s, culminating in the rebellion of the exarch, Gregory; and in Italy in the
early 650s, with the revolt of the exarch Olympius, clearly drew ideological succor from such an interpretation.[56]

For others, both before as well as after the council of 680–681—and
that included the imperial church and the patriarchal see—it was the
rejection of imperial authority and sinful and unorthodox behavior
among ordinary Christians that nevertheless remained the obvious
source of the evil, as implied by both the canons of the Quinisext and a
range of other hagiographical texts. Indeed, the Quinisext reaffirmed
a range of regulations intended to ensure conformity of appropriate
Christian behavior on holy days, in periods of fasting, and in relation to
what was considered seemly. Public theatrical events and festivities that
harked back to pre-Christian traditions were proscribed; the wearing
of theatrical masks and costumes—virtually anything that was part of
longstanding tradition and was thought to be tainted with pagan or
heretical customs or beliefs—was banned.[57]

How effective such regulations were away from the capital, Constantinople, is open to serious question. But they did mark the beginnings
of a longer process through which these ancient traditions were either
eradicated or transformed beyond recognition. The twelfth-century
canonist Zonaras often has to explain the festivities or celebrations of
which the canons of the Quinisext write since clearly few people in his
day understood what the *vota* or *broumalia* had been.[58] And following
the logic of divine retribution for sins, many texts continue to attribute
wars and invasions to God's wrath and justice. The late-seventh-century

writer of the collection of miracles ascribed to St. Theodore *tērōn* ("the recruit") states baldly: "In the fourteenth year of the reign of the God-protected and Christ-loving Constantine, when the peace between Romans and Saracens was over, and at the beginning of the seventh year of the indiction, the accursed Saracens went to war and devastated our whole country on account of our sins."[59] This was a view widely shared across different Christian communities. In Syria, for example, the devastation wrought by Arab raiders was likewise ascribed—with hindsight—to moral turpitude: "The Christians were reduced to despair, some of them saying: 'Why does God allow this to happen?' But the discerning will perceive that it is justice that allowed it to happen, because instead of fasting, keeping vigil and recitation, the Christians were practicing licentiousness, drunkenness, dance and other forms of debauchery at the martyrs' fairs and so angered God."[60]

Yet moral failure was still not the only concern. We have seen that before and up to 680, emperors and their religious advisors, the patriarchs, were made accountable by some for leading the Roman people into heresy. But now it seems that attention focused on the incompetence, ineffectiveness, or inability imputed to the ruler in dealing with the enemies threatening the empire's existence, and the military rebellions, mutinies, and coups d'état of the period from the 690s onward are part of the response to the situation. As the later chronicler Michael the Syrian (using a Syriac source that was almost contemporary with the events in question) reports, the usurper Tiberius Apsimar justified his coup with the words: "Just as Justinian [II] because of his mismanagement of the Roman empire, especially for pillaging Cyprus and breaking the peace with the Arabs, thus ruining many Roman lands, and other such things, was deprived of rule, so Leontius, though he had been enthroned for being one of the great men, has been cast out for lapsing into similar folly."[61] Things did not improve thereafter, so that the reimposition of monotheletism under Philippicus Bardanes in 711 was likely based on the assumption that perhaps it had after all been the correct and orthodox policy, a view that may have prevailed among the Anatolian military, in particular the Anatolikon soldiers who seem to have been hostile to the reestablishment of dyothelete doctrine at the council of 680–681. The effort was short-lived and died with the deposition of Philippicus in 713.[62] Such developments, while they generally had an immediate trigger or spark that set them in motion, reflected more broadly the efforts individuals and groups of people were making to take direct action to reestablish an order that was being lost. The extent to which some of the narratives through which individuals and groups understood that their place in the world had been shaken is reflected in the texts written and in the courses of action undertaken at the time. People in the east Roman world of the later seventh and eighth centuries could respond to the changes and challenges they faced only through the framework of belief they inhabited, which dictated the logic of their understanding and hence the courses of action open to them. It is those beliefs and the whole "thought-world" or "symbolic universe" that we need to take into account in our understanding of how Byzantine society dealt with the situation it confronted in the seventh and early eighth centuries.

Political Theology and the Framework of Belief

The political ideology of the east Roman world incorporated ancient traditions—Hellenistic, Roman, oriental, and early Christian. A formal and sophisticated set of ideas and concepts was embodied in what we might call the "political theology" of the empire. Christianity represented not simply the official political ideology and symbolic universe—the assemblage of beliefs, values, and assumptions of seventh-century people as well as the practices that went along with them—of the Byzantine world. It also represented a regional and individual system of moral values. It came to constitute—certainly by the seventh century for the majority—the metaphorical space within which society, politics, and the physical universe could be apprehended and through which it could be affected. And there were many day-to-day practices, such as the range of similar community burial traditions that had evolved from the fourth century that, while regionally nuanced, to be sure, may have underlined a shared identity and drawn a starker line under the differences between Christians and nonbelievers.[63] While overtly pagan beliefs and cults had largely disappeared by this time (which is not say that some remnants were not to be found in certain regions of the empire), many of the day-to-day beliefs and practices that had formed part of the cultural universe of rural populations in particular for centuries, if not millennia, remained and were given a Christian context and a Christian interpretational and explanatory gloss. The result was what Peter

Brown refers to as a sort of "modular" Christianity, a series of nested micro-Christendoms within a broader picture.[64] Indeed, it was in an effort to finally rid the Christian community of what contemporary churchmen viewed as such vestigial pagan practices that many of the canons of the Quinisext, as we have seen, were formulated. More on this later.

The Christianization of the older Roman imperial cult was another key element in this process, and the emperor was understood to represent orthodoxy and God's rule on earth. His rule was envisaged as striving for the maintenance and extension of the Christian *oikoumene*, the civilized—that is, orthodox—world, and thus the harmony and order of heaven in the earthly realm. This ideological system provided an explanatory model for contemporaries within which both the church and the state existed, it developed the framework and basis within and upon which imperial concepts of earthly political order were set. It provides one of the narrative possibilities through which Byzantines responded or reacted to the situations with which they were confronted—whether at the level of imperial politics or at that of individual beliefs and responses to personal issues. It also set the agenda for international as well as local politics.[65] And although there were other such threads within the east Roman symbolic universe running through local communities or the social elites of the empire, in Constantinople and elsewhere, the internal dimension of imperial authority is important both in its cultural and in its political forms, so it will be worth spending some time sketching in some of the key aspects of this dynamic.

A fundamental feature of the east Roman church by the mid-sixth century was the close political-ideological relationship it held with the secular power, embodied by the emperor. There evolved in the course of the fourth century an imperial Christian "political theology" rooted in both Romano-Hellenistic political concepts and Christian theology, which established an unbreakable association between emperor and church. In its most abstract form, it was understood as a relationship of mutual dependence, but the onus was on the secular ruler both to defend correct belief and to protect the interests of the church—in the form of the honor and respect accorded the priestly office—which catered for the spiritual needs of the Christian flock. As these ideas were expressed—at the council of Constantinople in 381, for example—it was the conviction that the health of the state was ensured only when the traditions of orthodox belief, as derived from the apostles and the Fathers of the church, were faithfully practiced and handed down.[66] This utopian expression of harmony and order was reflected in imperial religious and secular politics and in the ways in which the emperors understood their practical role in respect of the church, especially with regard to the convening of ecclesiastical councils and the incorporation of the principles embodied in these ideas in imperial legislation.[67] Needless to say, the actual process of Christianization of the imperial image, of the evolution of this political theology, has been shown to have been far more complex, contested, and multifaceted than the version encapsulated in the writings of the fourth-century propagandist and churchman Eusebius of Caesarea (and accepted by the majority of later commentators) would have us believe.[68]

But from the time of Constantine I in the period ca. 313–337, emperors had been involved in both church politics and theological matters, and imperial legislation and long-established tradition ensured that, by the time of Justinian in the sixth century, secular ruler, state, and church were inextricably joined in a complex whole. Justinian I's novel 6 issued in 535 summed up these developments, in which the two great blessings with which mankind has been endowed—priest and emperor—both deriving from the same divine source, were described. As God represented the ultimate source of law, so the emperor chosen by God was the ultimate source of earthly law, a formulation that, by defining the priestly authority strictly in terms of ministering to "matters divine," left some considerable scope for dissension thereafter. The imperial position itself became sacralized, a development that has been traced back to the early sixth or later fifth century as part of the response to the ideological as well as institutional challenges to the rulers of the second half of the fifth century.[69] The political theology of the east Roman state was not a static or closed system, however; to the contrary, it evolved and from the reign of Justinian in particular evolves an increasingly liturgical character. Indeed the liturgification of the imperial court and all that was associated with it that can be seen from this time on marks an important step-change in the process through which emperor-cult, church, and Christianity become elements of a single political theology of rule, in which the sacralized ruler appears—for a while—less subject to the contingencies that affected the lives of ordinary people in the empire and in which imperial authority becomes the mediating power between the earthly kingdom and heavenly authority. Even warfare and imperial expeditions take on a liturgical aspect.[70] This has been seen in part as a long-term and gradual response to the failure of both apocalyptic expectations and of traditional explanatory models for understanding natural calamities as well as human-induced disasters such as wars.[71] From the 550s and 560s on, imperial court ceremonial liturgy as well as the drama of the divine liturgy of the church reflected these ideas in a concrete and increasingly "ecclesial" form. None of this means that emperors were not equally aware of a range of secular concerns and interests, part of the traditional assemblage of the ruler's concerns for the welfare of all Romans, for the well-being of the state and for the preservation of the laws. But it does appear to be the case that, even when such issues came to the fore, whether in imperial action or in the accounts of imperial warfare and politics offered by contemporary or later Byzantine writers, it was more often than not this overarching political-theological identity that provided the context for the events described.[72]

By the seventh century—and even more obviously so after the Arab conquests—the church in the eastern Roman empire had become the East Roman Imperial Church, fully integrated into the apparatus of the state and its political ideology yet retaining at the same time a somewhat ambiguous position in respect of the emperors' rights to intervene in matters affecting dogma, however indirectly.[73] This is indeed one of the most important factors in the ability of the eastern empire to survive the challenges of the later seventh century. The Roman state in the east compromised with the church and the Christian community so that the two in effect blended. Unlike the Western Roman Empire in the fifth century, the east Roman state, its law, and its whole ideological apparatus became sacralized.[74] The relationship between emperor and patriarch may have been uneasy, and between emperor and pope even more problematic. But there could be no doubt that in the east, the Christian community and all that it represented and symbolized was headed by the Roman emperor, rather than by the patriarch; and that the Christian community was the Roman Empire, even if much of the former no longer lay within the territory controlled by the latter. Imperial law and canon law held equivalent status and value, as we shall see in Chapter 3.

In the east, church and state become in many ways different faces of a single institution. The views implicit in the theology of Sophronius of Jerusalem and of Maximus the Confessor, therefore, in which a successful and thriving Christian community could be envisaged independently of the Roman state, were highly damaging to the internal cohesion of the state and community. Such views were, in the end, marginalized by mainstream Christian Roman thinkers in the seventh and eighth century. That this was indeed the case is given clear expression in the address to Justinian II at the opening of the Quinisext council, where God's appointment of the emperors as guardians of the untarnished Christian faith is underlined.[75]

Non-Christian beliefs may have subsisted in many forms, and if the relevant canons of the Quinisext are a measure of the situation, the provincial clergy were aware of such cults and their associated practices, although they receive no mention in other sources.[76] Indeed, some caution is warranted, for as late as the last part of the sixth century it was observed during the trials of a number of so-called pagans in 579 that the province of Asia, in western Anatolia, had been noted for being a particular source of pagan beliefs.[77] On the whole, though, by the turn of the sixth and seventh centuries Christianity in one form or another was taken for granted by the inhabitants of the late Roman world; indeed, the notion of something different challenging the Christian church must have been virtually unimaginable for most, although awareness of the different religion of the Persians, for example, as well as of "heresy," depending on one's standpoint, can be clearly demonstrated. And while those large communities in the regions of Syria and Egypt in particular who had resisted the imposition by successive Roman emperors of the imperial orthodoxy—the neo-Chalcedonian dyophysitism established at the council of Constantinople in 551—may well have shared a common Christian faith, they accepted a somewhat different interpretation of the Trinity, to the extent that the disasters that befell the empire at the hands of Persians and Arabs were seen as God's punishment on heretical rulers and their followers.[78] As the Egyptian chronicler John of Nikiû later wrote, "This expulsion [of the Romans from Alexandria and Egypt] and victory of the Muslims is due to the wickedness of the emperor Heraclius and his persecution of the Orthodox [i.e., the miaphysites] . . . This was the cause of the ruin of the Romans and the subjugation of Egypt by the Muslims."[79] To what degree there continued to be appreciable numbers of miaphysites within the remaining lands of the empire after the loss of greater Syria and Egypt remains a moot point, but the limited evidence suggests that they were insignificant.[80]

In spite of these considerations, there is little to suggest that the blanket of Christian beliefs and devotional practices that covered the Roman Empire in the period up to the early Arab conquests was not relatively complete, even if there survived within its fabric a wide range of beliefs and practices, tolerated, or not, by the local church depending upon circumstances, and whether or not explicitly proscribed in the canons of the church. By the same token, the consonance of Christianity and the Roman Empire was also taken for granted. If opposition to imperial monotheletism had generated for a while a dissenting view, yet such a view was not adopted by the church within the empire, indeed it was limited largely to the few high-profile individuals who enunciated it most publicly, and to the papacy. Such ideas and arguments certainly inflicted some damage on the political fabric of the state in the west in the 640s and 650s, but the crushing of dissent by the imperial government and the confirmation of the imperial position at the council of 662 put an end to this particular problem.[81] And after 680–681 the unequivocal identification of the Christian Roman state and its emperor with Christianity and with God's kingdom on earth was once again unchallenged in the writings of churchmen and theologians in the West and within the empire. In the canons of the Quinisext, the Christian empire is contrasted with the heathen who assail it from without.[82] Andrew of Crete, writing in the early eighth century in an oration in praise of the birth of the Virgin, was absolutely clear that Christianity would triumph since for him the civilized world was already Christian, paying reverence to Christ and taking pride in their Christian name.[83] Even in the former eastern provinces, where miaphysite hostility to the imperial church remained, Christian thinkers could assume an eventual Roman victory. The *Apocalypse of Ps.-Methodius*, composed in the early 690s in Singara, certainly reflected this position and in doing so identified the Roman Empire as the only defense against the Antichrist and the Roman emperor as the leader of the Christian people: "For all rule and authority of this world are rendered null and void apart from her (i.e., the Roman empire). For war is also made upon her and she is not overcome, and all the nations which dash themselves against her

will be destroyed by her. . . . For where is, or where will there be, a
kingdom or another power that excels her?"[84] A slightly later apocalyptic
text, that of *Ps.-Daniel*, presents a similar view.[85] All these writers assumed the parallel between imperial orthodoxy and imperial success.
The opening address of the assembled clergy to the emperor Justinian II
at the council of 691/692 in Constantinople (the "Quinisext") notes
that the divine grace of Christ has covered the earth, that ignorance and
error have been exchanged for knowledge and that "Christ our God,
who steers this greatest of ships, the entire world, has now set you over
us, the wise governor, the pious emperor, our protector indeed: you who
dispense your words in discernment, safeguard truth always, render
judgment and justice upon earth and walk in the blameless path."[86]

Shared Narratives, Common Loyalties?

Such ideas expressed a longer-term process through which eastern
Roman—imperial—Christianity became interwoven with the biblical
past. This was encouraged through ever-increasing parallels between the
religious practice of the everyday and biblical antecedent. The extent to
which such ideas reached beyond the literate elite of the empire or the
clergy remains open to question, although as we will see much of this
way of understanding the world reached a much wider audience through
the medium of the clergy and regular contact with the local church and
its preaching. But the attitudes and beliefs these ideas embodied were
also promoted through the integration of the celebrants themselves into
liturgical practice and into the liturgical drama through the introduction of appropriate texts, especially from the New Testament. As one
commentator has pointed out, the performance and ritual activities
associated with liturgical celebration across the year draw those involved, clergy and congregation, into the roles of those represented in
the sacred narratives, forging an identity with the events and the times
they depict, promoting a common shared narrative among all partici-
pants, and reinforcing a common set of assumptions across social and
geographical space.[87] The growing emphasis that we have noted already on the eucharist as the key marker of Christian observance was
one aspect of this process, of course. Importantly, it seems to have been
during the second half of the seventh and early eighth centuries that
the east Roman liturgical calendar was standardized, reflecting the

increasing pace of these processes.[88] Through both liturgical performance and the presence and preaching of the clergy, the inhabitants of
the empire, as well as of all those regions no longer under imperial rule,
knew that they were members of a common moral universe.

How effective was the preaching of the church in the provinces and
away from the larger urban centers? This is a difficult question—sermons
(homilies, i.e., "conversations") were intended for a congregation, and
although often very long, dealt with theological and moral values relevant to the "ordinary" Christian. That the texts themselves were
usually understood, except for some particularly high-language compositions, is more than likely—formulaic constructions, repetition,
well-known motifs, and stories as well as straightforward language
all contributed. Their purchase on people's minds and attitudes, however, depended on context and frequency, and while the populous cities
of the late Roman world provided an ideal forum for such forms of
preaching—and the evidence suggests that they were often effective[89]—
churchmen had to confront a very different, deurbanizing world from
the 640s and 650s. In Constantinople, or perhaps Thessaloniki, the urban
environment meant that the established patterns of preaching could
continue.

The same was no doubt true of many other urban contexts, but there
are interesting indications in both the structure and the themes of later
seventh- and eighth-century homiletic compositions by preachers
such as Andrew of Crete or Germanus that some important changes
had taken place. First, sermons were increasingly delivered outside
the standard liturgies, during the offices and vigils. Second, their subjects tended to concentrate more than in the preceding centuries on
scriptural comment and exegesis or on specific feasts, explaining to the
laity the significance of specific passages from the Old and New Testament. The Quinisext insists that homilies should be preached on a daily
basis, most particularly on Sundays, and is most particular that clergy
should not indulge in their own interpretations but follow those of the
Fathers of the church: "If a Scriptural passage should come up for discussion, they shall in no wise interpret it differently than the luminaries
and doctors of the church have set down in their writings. In this way
shall they distinguish themselves, rather than by composing their own
works, being at times incapable of this and thereby falling short of what
is proper."[90]

Whether this reflected a perception that people were failing to pay attention to the basic message of the church is unclear, but the passage continues: "For through the teaching of the aforementioned Fathers the people are given knowledge of important things and virtues, and of unprofitable things and those to be rejected: thus they reform their lives . . . and escape being taken captive by the emotions of ignorance; giving heed to this teaching they . . . work out their salvation in fear of the punishments hanging over them." And on the topic of preaching in church and the behavior of the congregations, Anastasius of Sinai notes in one of his own sermons that pious behavior was not always what we may imagine it to have been: people yawn and doze off if the preacher is too long-winded; some leave before he has finished, others show up only just before communion before rushing off as soon as they are finished; disruptive chattering and gossip about matters of day-to-day business, money, or similar secular topics is common; men even stand around ogling the women who might be present.[91]

It is not clear whether Anastasius's comments refer to urban or rural society—perhaps both. And of course he is talking about people in Palestine and Syria rather than in the provinces of the empire, although, as we have seen, the newly imposed political limits on imperial Roman authority still barely impacted on the ecumenical Christian world. Preaching in the countryside was likely a very different affair from in towns, chiefly because of the relative isolation of rural settlements, the much lower levels of basic literacy, and the limited number of appropriately qualified clergy. Those provinces that had been heavily urbanized before the 640s were in the second half of the seventh century increasingly less so. Furthermore, the high level of insecurity in those regions exposed to hostile raids seems often to have meant a flight of even senior clergy, thus depriving the populace of regular contact with ecclesiastical authority. Canon 18 orders the return of clergy to their flocks, while canon 37 deals with bishops who live away from their sees for the same reason. The insistence in canon 19 of the Quinisext that clergy rely only on the written word of the Fathers hints at the nature of the problem the church faced here. Several other canons, mostly repeated from councils of the fourth and fifth centuries, refer to a range of disorders within the church, such as conflicts of authority between provincial bishops or unwarranted absences from their sees or parishes (canons 17, 20, 25, and 80, for example). These indicate the difficulties of maintaining both clerical discipline and the regular activities of the church in the provinces. Such a situation also meant increased possibilities for fraudsters, for misunderstanding, for heterodoxy, for laxness of observance. Canon 60, for example, condemns those who feign possession by demons and ordains that they should be subject to the painful rites of exorcism applied to those who were genuinely so afflicted; canon 63 ordains the destruction of false martyrologies while canon 68 prohibits the destruction of volumes of either Old or New Testaments or their dismemberment for the use of perfumers.[92]

This shared moral universe was thus somewhat patchy in its coverage, variable in the way it reached its members. But it was reinforced nevertheless by practices and beliefs associated with the devotion accorded to saints and martyrs, whose churches and cult centers were spread throughout all the provinces of the empire, and devotion to whom established a bond across the whole of society, among ordinary provincials of all social strata as well as members of the social elite, the church, and the imperial household. Importantly, these were both local and empire-wide at the same time. All the saints, martyrs, and apostles were part of the heavenly host that interceded with God on behalf of humankind but who also protected, so it was believed, the earthly kingdom from its enemies. And they were represented in turn by an empire-wide patron, the Mother of God, the Theotokos, who from the second half of the sixth century had been promoted by the imperial court in particular as a patron saint of Constantinople and hence of imperial fortunes more broadly.[93] Constantinople itself also housed the saints of the provinces. Justinian I had endowed some thirty churches in Constantinople, for example, many for saints popular in distant parts of the empire: St. Theodore, whose cult was already widespread although centered at Euchaïta in the Pontus; St Sergius, for whom many churches in the provinces were built but who was at home on the Syrian frontier; St. Thecla from Isauria; St. Stephen; St. Nicholas; St. George; and many more, some of them far less well-known.[94] The point is that through the widespread and shared cults of saints, people in the provinces received both a sense of local and a regional identity, a provincial "patriotism," but were at the same time linked one to another and to the seat of empire, Constantinople, the home of many of the same saints and martyrs and a city that stood under the direct protection of the Virgin Mary.

Saints' cults generated a range of devotional and related practices in
common, even if regionally divergent, connected with healing, with the
driving out of evil spirits, with protection against the vast range of haz-
ards outside human control. The wearing of amulets aimed at warding
off evil spirits was common and widespread, for example. The practical
nature of the cult of relics integrated a belief in the intercessory powers
of a saint with a conviction that a physical presence, through the saint's
relics, was an essential facilitating medium.[95] Physical remains, such
as bodies, objects that had had touched bodies,[96] or oil sanctified by the
saint's presence in the form of physical remains of one sort or another,
had certainly by the seventh century become vital aspects of the intercessory process.[97] The cult of martyrs, with almost daily commemora-
tions, came to equal the great liturgical occasions celebrating aspects of
the life and passion of Christ in time and devotional energy.[98] The *laudatio* for Therapon and the collection of miracles of Artemius show how
important physical contact was believed to be for the process of intercession and the associated healing for which prayers were offered. When
these saints healed, touch and physical contact were an essential element. Mistreating or abusing saintly relics or the saint's sanctuary could
also have unpleasant consequences, as one of the provincial miracle accounts of St Theodore relates:

> At that time, when that hateful race of enemies filled our city and were
> spending the winter there, their leader happened to be moved by some
> demonic malice, and he ordered a number of picks and levers to be used
> against the most beautiful and pleasing shrine of the saint, with the in-
> tention of destroying it utterly as far as its foundations. So he sum-
> moned all his men into the said honoured shrine and explained to them
> his evil plan concerning it. But while the words were still in his mouth,
> God's anger rose up against him and he fell headlong to the ground,
> rolling about, foaming at the mouth and chewing his tongue. The
> barbarians, snatching him up, laid him to rest in his own lodging; and
> while in this way he was cut short in his satanic undertaking, yet he
> was not released from the hostile spirit that opposed him.[99]

Many of the practices associated with the cult of saints were not officially sanctioned, however, unlike the focus on relics and the shrines
of the saints. Entrenched beliefs and anxieties about evil spirits, the
causes and cures for disease and various forms of physical or spiritual
affliction, meant that "superstitious" practices abounded, albeit in a

Christian guise. The miracle stories associated with cult centers reflect tales and wonders typical of this mix, and while much of this was not far from or tantamount to magic, holy men and monks were often involved in exactly the same sorts of activities—the miracles of the sixth-century saint Nicholas of Sion, in Lycia, have him involved in driving out evil spirits from a tree as well as sacrificing animals to various saints, for example; St. Theodore of Sykeon in early seventh century Galatia is likewise credited with driving evil spirits back into a hole in the hill from which they had accidentally been released, while the holy monk Ioannicius in the early ninth century demonstrates his divinely granted powers to a group of villagers in Bithynia through making a bear do his will.[100] Again, the stories can be multiplied and represent a well-established stock. Many other stories are equally fantastic, entailing the slaying of dragons, the feeding of other wild beasts, the calling forth of springs of fresh water, and so forth, quite apart from the more usual cures affected through incubation (sleeping in the saint's chapel or crypt overnight and dreaming that the saint comes to cure the patient). Devotees of individual saints disagreed about the relative efficacy of their patron; for example, cursing or exclaiming by the name of one's favorite or patron saint was part of everyday speech. And several canons of the Quinisext council address questions and practices suggestive of some of the issues the church faced in dealing with popular and often superstitious beliefs.

Still, all this is to be understood within what was, by the middle of the seventh century, a solidly Christian world. It was a world in which certain groups played an important connective role. Monks, for example, were throughout the lands of the empire, in both town and country, in direct contact with the people of the provinces, in towns and villages, and undoubtedly acted as a mode of transmitting commonly held beliefs and ways of thinking about the world as well as acting upon it in respect of day-to-day piety and practice. They might also, of course, act as a disruptive or even dangerous element at times, threatening the established order—hence the regulatory canons of the Quinisext. Collections of tales about the deeds of monks and holy men, such as are found in the writings ascribed to John Moschus or John Climacus in the first half of the seventh century, as well as the references to the role of such men in the Questions and Answers of Anastasius of Sinai suggest their importance in this respect.[101] The material point is that they acted to transmit notions of shared Christian identity across the Roman world, an identity that was clearly expressed as much in terms of Christian as in that of Roman—the two were effectively equivalent in their symbolic and political-cultural value and implications.[102] Yet there is also evidence suggesting that, within the empire at least, monks may have lost some of their status and played a lesser role than hitherto in the period from the middle of the seventh century into the later eighth century. Of course there were exceptions—the Palestinian monks who moved westward in the face of the Persian and then the Arab invasions, Sophronius and Maximus among them, while Anastasius of Sinai is a similarly outstanding figure. But of major monastic centers and monastic activities in Anatolia, for example, other than the issues of monastic discipline and public comportment that came to the attention of the Quinisext, very little is heard. One reason for this may have been the physical disruption to the rural landscape as well as to many urban contexts following from the Arab invasions and raids, a change in context that must have impacted on both numbers as well as on the possibilities for a reasonably secure monastic existence in many provinces.[103]

A second clearly identifiable body was constituted by the regular clergy, for it was they who were responsible for ensuring that orthodox observance was respected, that the eucharist was celebrated properly and at the assigned intervals, and that the message of scripture was faithfully transmitted and explicated to the vast majority of the population. It was they who were the focus for many of the canons of the Quinisext as the church attempted to maintain the uniformity of practice across the provinces.[104] In the rural hinterland, they were the main, if not the only, contact between the senior clergy and the ordinary populace and the only regular source of teaching about the faith. But we know very little of their activities, their level of education and literacy, or, indeed, their numbers. Not every community had a church or a priest; the organization of the church was largely focused on the city and its bishop, who appointed so-called *chōrepiskopoi* (country bishops) to care for the rural communities around the towns, although these clergy had very limited authority and powers; by the time of the council of Nicaea in 787, they had been reduced effectively to the status of regular priests.[105]

In the early seventh century it seems that it was not unusual for some villages to have no church or chapel and no regular clergy attached to them for their spiritual care and education. The *Life* of Theodore of Sykeon mentions village presbyters, but they are clearly not a universal feature of rural society. According to the Justinianic legislation, local chapels and churches were largely the responsibility of local landowners or village communities and seem to have been poorly integrated into the church administration, a fact reflected to some degree in the canons of the Quinisext, some of which are concerned with the clergy who attended them—who were paid, when at all, by the landowner or the community who had endowed the chapel or church in the first place. Some clergy were supported from episcopal funds, although the proportion of those remunerated in this way is unknown, and many were supported either from donations made by the parishioners themselves in return for the services or from their own landholdings, as tenants of the person who had endowed the church.[106] The situation is unlikely to have improved much in the conditions that prevailed across many provinces from the middle of the seventh century, and this raises the question of just how much influence the church really had in such areas—indeed, the evidence suggests that it was only by the later eighth and ninth centuries that an effective ecclesiastical establishment had been evolved in much of the countryside.[107] It also suggests that the shrunken urban centers of the period continued to be a vital link between the bishops and their flocks, a role that has received surprisingly little attention in research on the period.

Eastern Roman society, and society in the eastern Mediterranean world more broadly, was heavily stratified. While vertical associations and loyalties existed that cut across the barriers generated by wealth and poverty, by access or lack of access to justice, power, and the ability to defend one's interests against the more powerful, the horizontal divisions produced by social inequality were systemic.[108] It is hardly surprising in such a context—as we would take for granted in most such social formations—that dissatisfaction with economic and social conditions might at times have manifested itself in terms of beliefs and related social practice. This is occasionally apparent, for example, when the texts suggest that a degree of skepticism affected what people thought about the efficacy of the saints to intercede or to affect divinely inspired cures or other wonders as well as their attitudes and at times reactions to the social order, although it is true that we have very little direct evidence for this during the seventh century. I will return to this theme later.

Christian Roman culture and the range of beliefs it encapsulated was, therefore, by no means an undifferentiated, unquestioning monolith, no more than is any belief system. To the contrary, lively, vituperative debate was a feature of the period, particularly in regard to the issues just mentioned. In the sixth and seventh centuries in particular, the tension between a "rationalist" and "populist" perspective was very clear, in respect of intercession as well as of other issues, even if this had been a feature of Christian theological reflection from the beginning. For example, in the later seventh century Anastasius of Sinai argued that, since neither saints nor ordinary mortals have a physical presence after death, the soul of the ordinary human loses all its powers of memory, self-identity, and recognition and must await the Last Judgement in this state of limbo.[109] But while those of the saints do retain a degree of consciousness, it is the heavenly angels who represent them on earth, taking on their customary apparel and appearance in order to demonstrate the power of the Holy Spirit to those who inhabit the world of mortals. In partial proof of his argument, Anastasius notes that the same saint has often been observed in different places at the same time.[110] Such a view was debated already in the later sixth century, when Eustratius, author of the *Life* of the patriarch Eutychius, penned a treatise on the nature of the soul and the relationship it bears to the body after death, in which he set out to refute such "rationalist" arguments in an explicit attempt to provide a theologically grounded explanation for such miracles in which divine intervention and the direct mediation of God through the saints were fundamental elements.[111]

The texts that assume a real physical presence for the saints who appear and intercede on behalf of those who have prayed for their assistance outnumber those in which a more careful somatological or "rationalist" approach is evident. The former is the norm in collections such as the *Miracles* of Cyrus and John (in Alexandria),[112] of Cosmas and Damian (set in Constantinople),[113] of Demetrius (at Thessaloniki);[114] of Theodore Tiro (Euchaïta),[115] of Artemius (Constantinople),[116] of Therapon in Constantinople,[117] and a number of others. Anastasius seems, in fact, and by the time of his writing, to reflect a minority opinion (although the debate simmered on into later centuries).[118]

It is important to bear in mind that this debate about intercession was not confined narrowly to the Roman world—similar debates were taking place in Armenian and Iranian Christian communities at the same time.[119] And this was just one aspect of a broader discussion concerning the degree of human freedom of choice and of divine intervention in human affairs, in which hagiography played a central role in reaffirming the centrality of the divine in human affairs—as in the first collection of the miracles of St. Demetrius at Thessaloniki, for example, where only the wrath of God and divine intervention are admitted as real causal factors; physiological or natural explanations are dismissed. Some collections included a variety of arguments "proving" the rationalist position wrong by repeating the fact that the miracles and acts of the saints in question had occurred in the form described in the miracle stories—a good example is found in the *Life* of Isaac of Nicomedia, for example, dating to the later eighth or ninth century.[120] That the issue was a constant is reflected in the canons of the Quinisext: "We command that martyrologies which have been faked by enemies of truth, in order that they may dishonor Christ's martyrs and cause their listeners to lose faith, should not be read publicly in churches, but should be consigned to the flames. As for those who receive them or accept them as true, we anathematize them."[121]

Whatever the vagaries of this ongoing discussion, there can be little doubt that there was room for skepticism and doubt, as in the case of the cathedral deacon Dometianus in the late sixth century, who refused to believe in the miracles of Theodore of Sykeon, for example.[122] Sometimes this skepticism or annoyance took the form of direct action.[123] Long before the promotion of an official position on sacred imagery under Leo III, images had been on occasion a point of contention. Thus in 588, for example, in an incident reflecting the frustration of the soldiers on the eastern frontier with the imperial authorities' attempts to reduce their pay, the general Priscus displayed the sacred *mandylion* (towel) from Edessa bearing the image of Christ (called by the Romans *acheiropoiēton,* "not made by human hand") in an attempt to quell the rioting troops. But the soldiers are reported by the near-contemporary historian Theophylact Simocatta to have hurled stones at the image, seeing through the attempt to overawe them, before later attacking the images of the emperor Maurice himself.[124] Neither did the angry soldiers show any respect to the bishops of Constantina and Edessa who were sent to calm them.[125] Over a century later, during the siege of Nicaea by the Arabs in 727, a soldier hurled a stone at an image of the Virgin and damaged it. The motives for his attack are ascribed by the chronicler

Theophanes (who reported the incident in his *Chronographia* just under a century afterward) to the soldier's impiety and iconoclastic sentiment; yet, assuming the event happened at all, it is far more likely that it was a symptom of frustration—whether at the naivety of the population or of soldiers who believed the image would help them or a reflection of the soldier's own anger will never be known.[126]

Whether or not such incidents took place more frequently than the sources record, they demonstrate that piety and respect for the church, for religious symbols, and for authority always depended upon context, and that observance of a faith and how individuals or groups practiced their beliefs could vary, often considerably, within a single system. We should not be overly hasty in assuming a uniform and passive acceptance of the established structures or political-ideological order.[127] While the overarching belief system represented by the Christian Roman Empire served as a powerful unifying force, reflected in both official political and theological as well as a whole range of less formal forms of discourse, there was space for other ways of thinking within and between these modes of believing and doing—for modes of behavior in church, for example, not entirely consistent with the forms of piety we may imagine to have been desired by the clergy. These were challenges not to the edifice of Christian belief and the imperial state as such, but they nevertheless permitted the coexistence of perceptions and beliefs that were not always entirely consonant with officially sanctioned views.

Conformity, "Orthodoxy," and Heterodoxy

How uniform, how "orthodox," was Byzantine society and Christian orthodox culture in these core territories by the later seventh century? A specifically "east Roman" identity certainly existed, within which the population of the early medieval eastern Roman empire could be represented as an "orthodox" and Roman community. But "identity" is above all functional and performative, a set of operational strategies in which situation and context determine which elements are invoked in which combinations: many subsets of identity exist, some reflecting regional cultural, linguistic, or ethnic traditions and lifeways; some heterodox beliefs; some social status and situations; some a mix of all of these. The crucial point about any identity is that it differentiates those who self-describe in a particular way from those who do not so describe or who can be described as "other," as different in some fundamental way. Some identities embrace a whole cultural system and serve as a backdrop against and within which other more localized and personalized identities operate, identities that dominate the day-to-day lives and activities of most people.[128] Thus, while the notion of "Christian/Roman" itself was to a degree a universalizing discourse, it served different sociocultural groups in different ways and came to prominence or was invoked only under certain very specific circumstances and at particular moments. On the one hand, it represented above all the self-identity and vested interests of the social elite whose continued loyalty to the status quo was essential to the survival of the state and the whole imperial edifice. On the other, it represented the difference between all those who understood themselves as members of the Christian Roman world and those outside it—pagans, barbarians, whatever. And it could also represent the identity of all subjects of the Roman emperor and all inhabitants of the Roman Empire, humble or elite, when contrasted with those perceived to stand outside of the boundaries of this world. In other words, while elements of this particular notion clearly penetrated to the roots of society, both in the metropolitan regions as well as in the more distant provinces (even if only in the form of coins bearing the emperor's image),[129] the notion of a Roman identity needs to be deployed with care, since it had different valences according to social and cultural circumstances and according to the demands of the moment.[130] And unfortunately, we cannot really say with any confidence whether or not it was invoked in ordinary communities and among ordinary people—farmers, peasants, herdsmen, artisans, and craftsmen in the provinces—at those crucial moments when they had to face the invader. It probably was, since it demarcated the enemy from those they attacked, and this is fairly clearly expressed in some of the hagiographical literature, including the seventh-century miracle collections of St. Demetrius and those of St. Theodore.[131]

The Church represented one of the most powerful ideological and economic institutions of the late Roman and Byzantine world. It represented at every level of society the single correct form of belief, through its formal teaching and liturgical calendar, embodied in the clergy and the ecclesiastical hierarchy. But we have already seen that there existed significant variations within the fabric of eastern Roman Christian belief: in respect of the cult of saints, for example, as well as in respect of

attitudes to symbols of imperial and religious authority. The lack of uniformity behind the veil of the imperial church and its official ideology
is revealed in the canons of the Quinisext council, which make clear
that there were ongoing challenges to the formal definitions of "orthodoxy" and to the formally "correct" modes of orthodox behavior that
the church promoted through official acts and conciliar decisions.[132]

The frequent repetitions and elaborations on lists of various heretical beliefs that were produced by leading churchmen and theologians
throughout the Byzantine period testify to the crucial importance both
of combating heterodox and heretical beliefs as well as of defining and
refining the way in which "orthodoxy" and its attendant practice were
to be understood, applied, and taught.[133] The patriarch Sophronius of
Jerusalem in the 630s, Maximus the Confessor in the 630s–640s, and
Anastasius of Sinai as well as John of Damascus in the first half of the
eighth century, all produced heresiological works, works that by definition worked with an assumption about what constituted orthodoxy.[134]
Germanus of Constantinople is likewise attributed with a heresiological
tract (although this has been shown to be by another hand and the
main body of the tract was probably compiled before the Quinisext
council of 692).[135] The acts of church councils, on the one hand, and
sophisticated theological texts, on the other, served to define key tenets; and alongside the conciliar texts a wide range of homiletic and
liturgical literature helped clarify and explain for believers how theology was to be translated into the daily practice and understanding
of the world around them. The church specified in great detail how
heterodox believers were to be readmitted or admitted for the first
time to the church—social inclusion through baptism was an important element of belonging both to the Christian as well as to the
Roman community.[136] But in practical terms, the day-to-day practice
of Byzantine Christianity incorporated, under the unifying system
presented in theological discourse, a plurality of ways of interpreting
basic tenets, influenced by the inherited patterns of belief from the
various cultural traditions in which it developed and upon which it
had been imposed. How this plurality was reflected in terms of social
differentiation can only be described in very broad terms, through the
differences in the degree and choice of investment of wealth, time,
and energy made by individuals of different socioeconomic and cultural status, for example—in the endowment of church decoration or

building, in membership of a religious organization focused on a saint or martyr, and so forth.[137]

The geographical and cultural variety of the east Roman world thus meant that in many regions traditional, pre- or non-Christian practices could linger on unobserved for centuries, albeit in isolated and relatively limited groups. Heresy and heterodoxy were two of the constant issues that the Church, and the emperors, had to confront. The church tried to deal with a whole range of beliefs and practices with which it did not approve, some seemingly trivial—canon 96 of the Quinisext forbids men to "arrange their hair in elaborate plaits, offering allurements to unstable minds," for example. By the same token, heterodox beliefs could evolve that might, and did in some cases, develop into major challenges to the imperial authority. Heresy, at least when it made its presence obvious, was equated with political treason, conflating the religious-spiritual with the secular ideological spheres, and directly involving the imperial government in the issues thus raised. Local synods and ecumenical councils tried to grapple with some of the causes of heresy, such as the lack of clerical discipline or supervision in far-flung regions, the ignorance of some of the lower clergy as well as of the ordinary populace, or the arrival of immigrant population groups with different views or different understanding of the basic elements of Christianity. The church was constantly active in this respect, often on a very low-key basis.[138] The Quinisext legislates on the admission of heretics to the church, an issue that had become acute as a result of considerable demographic disturbances in the later seventh century. Canon 95 notes: "In the case of Eunomians, however, who are baptized by immersion, and Montanists, referred to here as Phrygians, and Sabellians . . . as well as all the other heretics—there are many here, especially those from the land of Galatia—."[139]

The loss of the eastern provinces to the Arabs in the seventh century offered a partial practical solution to one of the most difficult theological-political issues faced by the emperors of the period: how to overcome the hostility and suspicion that had evolved between the Chalcedonian, or dyophisite, Christians and the miaphysites of Syria and Egypt. But since Constantinople did not give up on the idea that the lost territories would at some point be recovered, the problem did not go away. More importantly, the Constantinopolitan patriarchate still had to deal with its sister churches in the east as well as ecclesiastical provinces under its

own authority, which now lay outside of imperial control. While monotheletism ultimately failed, this was not because it had no support or
purchase among the population—quite the contrary. Rather, there took
place a radical shift in imperial policy, a shift that was rigorously and to
a degree brutally enforced. The whole story offers a good example of
how the state was central to matters of dogma, and how it was embroiled
in the imposition of an official position. But after the council of 680–681,
Christological issues no longer rocked the imperial church. Only the
iconoclastic policies of the eighth and ninth centuries—which also
had, eventually, a Christological element—stimulated further major
internal rifts, and it is by no means clear that these commanded the interest or commitment of more than a handful on either side, at least
until the iconophiles rewrote the history of the period during the ninth
and tenth centuries.[140]

An insight into the degree of local variation and the different levels
of engagement with basic Christian teaching that the church had to contend with is afforded by some writings of the second half of the seventh
and early eighth centuries. We have already seen some examples of dissident belief or behavior. The fascinating collection of "questions and answers" attributed to the wandering monk Anastasius of Sinai provides
invaluable information about the worries and concerns of ordinary
Christians at this time. Anastasius seems never to have visited the provinces of Asia Minor, but the sorts of issues put to him can be taken to
reflect many of the concerns of people across the eastern provinces,
including Anatolia. People were concerned about rules of purity, about
how to worship under a non-Christian ruler, about how often they
should take communion, about the state of the world more broadly,
about the reasons for Arab victory and Christian defeat, about such
things as why the poor have many children and the wealthy few, about
the connections between diet and health, or between correct belief and
success or sinful behavior and divine punishment. Indeed, the motif of
sin and punishment was an extremely common theme among ordinary
believers, appearing in popular hagiographical writing, in sermons, and,
as we have seen, in apocalyptic writing as well as in the explanations
offered by theologians and others.

We should not lose sight of the fact that the east Roman government
seems to have been remarkably successful, given the constraints on its
political authority imposed by circumstances, in policing or managing

dissent and in controlling the sources of dissent. After the council of 680–681 in Constantinople, for example, it seems that nearly all traces of promonothelete literature and writing was destroyed or suppressed, including the records from an important synod of the church held in Constantinople in 662.[141] We know of their existence only through occasional oblique references in texts from both within as well as outside the empire, including the Syriac versions of some of this material that survived in the monothelete regions of northwest Syria. What potential opposition there was toward the end of the council—voiced in the activities of some military units and their leaders, in particular the commander of the Anatolikon forces, Leo—was ruthlessly crushed and the troops sent back to their provincial bases.[142] And before the council of 680–681, when official imperial policy was itself monothelete, the writings of Maximus the Confessor himself, among other opponents of imperial policy, were sought out and destroyed, just as those who circulated or kept them were suspects in the eyes of the imperial authorities.[143] A similar situation prevailed after the first and second periods of iconoclasm (730–787 and 815–841), when it seems that the imperial church and the government were very successful in hunting out iconoclastic material and destroying it, just as the governments of the iconoclast emperors in the period 815–830s, when we have somewhat better evidence than from the first period of iconoclasm, appear to have been equally successful in locating and controlling dissidents.[144] By the same token, imperial officials were frequently able to intercept both people and documents, for example, in the 640s and 650s or in the 720s, when papal emissaries as well as private persons carrying letters were held up, searched, and on occasion arrested. The brothers Theodore and Euprepius, opponents of imperial monotheletism, were arrested at Abydos in 648, trying to leave for Rome, for example.[145] To avoid such problems in the 640s, Stephen of Dor, a key figure in the opposition to imperial monotheletism, had to travel from Rome to Palestine via North Africa, for example: "They sent out orders concerning me by place and province, that I should be arrested and delivered up to them in chains."[146]

It might be thought that it would be difficult for a premodern state to control its borders as carefully and as efficiently as a modern state, with all the advantages of industrial surveillance technology at its disposal. But it was made much easier by virtue of the fact that most people who wished to travel across substantial distances preferred to do so in a group simply for reasons of safety, if not for companionship. Such groups of travelers were dependent on hiring guides or various modes of transport for themselves and their baggage and accompanying servants and were relatively easy to manage and to monitor.

Of course individuals could, and no doubt did, manage to slip across frontiers or avoid points of egress and access, but this was always extremely risky and could end in disaster—robbery, enslavement, or capture—at worst, death. There were certainly in the period up to the 690s, a number of regions where this would have been possible, especially as the Anatolian and Balkan "frontier" or border regions were undoubtedly highly permeable, while along the Levantine coast, where Byzantine naval activity and raiding was a significant factor in the 640s and early 650s and again in the later 670s, a number of districts and towns probably existed in a partial political vacuum, acknowledging whichever military power was currently present and permitting the movement of individuals with very little control. The numismatic evidence may support this, given the continuing presence of imperially minted copper coinage in northern Syria in quantities that would undoubtedly have facilitated ongoing relations between imperial and former imperial districts.[147]

Nevertheless, groups of travelers were more readily monitored, when necessary, and individuals who wished to escape the notice of the imperial officials traveling in such parties were easier to detect. The late Roman government controlled key points of entry or exit from the empire efficiently,[148] and the arrangements that had evolved appear to have been maintained without a break well into the later Byzantine period. Each traveler generally required formal letters authorizing their departure. For churchmen even within the empire, official letters *(grammata)* from their superiors were required. Such documents—referred to as *formatae* or *epistulae formatae* in Latin—were necessary when moving from one episcopal province to another, for example, or when visiting the capital, as canon law stresses repeatedly—although the limited evidence indicates that such regulations were frequently ignored or abused.[149] For laypersons, these papers were known as *sigillia* or *sigillia kai sphragides*— "sealed/validated documents," and without them the traveler could encounter serious problems, as a number of cases attest. The seventh-century Armenian chronicler Sebeos does not find it implausible that imperial authorities could surveille roads and forts to effect the arrest of a fleeing senior commander.[150] St. Gregory the Decapolite suffered arrest on suspicion of spying for the Arabs when he arrived without papers at a port in the early ninth century, for example.[151] And internal movement, particularly when making use of the *dromos* or *cursus publicus,* the public post, was subject to the issue of the appropriate paperwork and warrants (although, again, as the legislation makes eminently clear, subject to very considerable abuse).[152] The close cooperation between provincial clergy and state officials, particularly fiscal officials, even made it possible for the government to legislate to compel widows to marry foreign captives (presumably of an appropriate age) in order to support continued payment of taxes.[153] Imperial officials were efficient in gathering information as well as in keeping watch on individuals, and control over information that was taken into Arab territory could lead to accusations of spying or instigating opposition to the imperial government—as we have already seen, this was the case, albeit in a very different geographical context, with Maximus the Confessor in the 650s.[154]

There is a further complicating factor in respect of distinguishing levels of uniformity or conformity of belief and practice across the provinces of the empire. In the period from the middle of the seventh through into the ninth century the imperial government followed a policy of moving populations—sometimes in huge numbers—from parts of Asia Minor to the Balkans and vice versa in order to repopulate devastated regions. While it no doubt had economic benefits, it also proved an effective means by which heterodox views were transferred from one region of the empire to another, so the church had to be constantly vigilant in its managing of local populations.[155] And quite apart from the more important heretical movements, the church had to combat many less significant heterodox beliefs. We know next to nothing about how it tackled such issues, apart from the reflection of reality in the canons of the Quinisext. But the fact that groups such as the Athingani (in Lycaonia and Phrygia), who may not even have been Christian, were still apparently flourishing in the early ninth century, or that the Paulicians in eastern Anatolia appear to have continued to exist in spite of reported interventions from both church and state from the seventh and throughout the eighth into the ninth century (there were attempts to convert or rebaptize them as well as to persecute and destroy their leadership in the seventh century and in the following centuries) shows that Anatolia contained a variety of creeds not necessarily (as with the Paulicians) reconcilable with the basic tenets of dyophysite Christianity.[156] The dangers of heterodoxy in the context of near-constant conflict with the caliphate and a rival religion were clearly recognized, although whether these dangers carried with them all the implications that have been ascribed to them is yet another question that remains at issue.[157]

Finally, the church also had to contend with Judaism, a religion with which Christianity had from its very beginnings an ambiguous relationship, the more so since the Jews, by failing to acknowledge the Messiah, had lost their status as the Chosen People, which had now been transferred to the Romans. Anti-Jewish polemic becomes especially prominent from the middle of the seventh century; indeed, Christian texts defending a range of key practices—devotion to the Cross, to relics, the cult of saints, for example—appear to have been composed to answer accusations that Christians were idolaters.[158] Some of this has been assumed to respond also to early Islamic criticism of Christian belief and practice, and although this remains debated, it seems clear that the Christian polemic becomes especially strident in the course of the seventh century, reflecting the increasingly difficult circumstances in which Christians in the conquered provinces as well as in the empire found themselves.[159] It has also been suggested that the Athingani represent a Judaizing sect.[160] In general, until the sixth century, Jews were officially tolerated, although often treated with considerable prejudice. From the reign of Justinian, however, they became increasingly isolated within the Roman world, a process greatly exacerbated by the results of the Persian and then the Arab conquests, for which the Jews were partially held to be responsible, and a development that reflects the introversion and defensiveness with which east Roman culture seems to have responded to the catastrophic losses and defeats of the seventh century. Compulsory baptisms of Jews were carried out under Heraclius and later (probably) under Leo III. Jews were prohibited from a wide range of public activities as well as participation in the state in any form and were frequently blamed for whatever ills befell the empire. While they were not alone in this, since various heretical groups were usually listed alongside them, they were regularly singled out for ill-treatment.[161]

The number of repetitions dealing with heterodox belief and practice that occur among the 102 canons of the Quinisext is a sufficient demonstration of the fact that, even if most communities identified with or claimed to be "orthodox" in their own view, there remained substantial variations in Christian liturgical practice and worship across Anatolia, and that such differences were looked upon with some concern by both church and state. But what is important is not the fact that Jews, rather than any other identifiable group, continued to be singled out: rather, by failing to accept the dominant religious ideological system, the "Roman" identity of such groups—Jews, Montanists, or others—was placed in doubt. Whereas under Justinian they had still held a particular place in Christian Roman theory—as a living proof of the Christian interpretation of the Old and New Testaments—this position was rapidly eroded from the time of his successors onward. Their implicit or tacit hostility and opposition jeopardized their belonging to the East Roman Empire at all and made them potential enemies, a fifth column within the empire. The continuing ability of the imperial government and the church to police people's beliefs and what they could read, however imperfect this oversight actually was, must have seemed particularly important in this respect. In the following chapter we will look at the ways in which secular and canon law affected how people saw their world, and how the redrawing of political and cultural boundaries affected them.

3

Identities, Divisions, and Solidarities

*And God waits patiently over the tribulations of the just and faithful . . .
And after the tribulation under the Ishmaelites has come about . . . these
barbarians will be eating and drinking and joking, boasting of their victories and of the desolations to which they have reduced Persia and Ro-
mania, Cilicia and Syria, Cappadocia and Isauria and Africa and Sicily
and those who live near Rome and the islands . . . they say "the Christians have no rescue from our hands."*

*Then a voice will come out of the heavens, saying, "This same pun-
ishment suffices for me." And the Lord God will then snatch the cowardice
of the Romans and thrust it into the hearts of the Ishmaelites and take
the manliness of the Ishmaelites and cast it into the hearts of the Romans;
they will turn and drive them from their homes and crush them without
mercy.*[1]

Confidence versus Reality

With all the caveats about regional, local, and cultural variation that we
have discussed in the preceding chapter, it is nevertheless very clear that
the church, supported by the state, represented a symbolic universe
within which a Christian Roman political theology legitimated and promoted the projection and maintenance of east Roman power, both internally and externally. In formal and official texts, the Romans remained the Chosen People and the Roman Empire was God's kingdom
on earth. As the prefatory address of the Quinisext to Justinian II puts
it, the Roman state under its God-appointed ruler is the Holy Nation, the
Special People; and in the canons of the Quinisext and their insistence

on conformity with the Constantinopolitan church we can detect a self-awareness in this respect.[2] Here we see a presentation of the order and discipline of the Byzantine imperial church as the standard for the whole Christian community, Eastern and Western, in which the Byzantine church reflected the political *oikoumene* represented by the orthodox emperor. Of course, military coercive power, the ability to tax and extract resources in manpower and agricultural, pastoral or mineral produce (with the underlying threat of coercion to reinforce it), and the ability to defend and maintain its frontiers played an equally fundamental role. But in terms of beliefs, motives, and the rationale of empire, imperial orthodoxy—however contested within the bounds of empire and however defined and refined in theological discourse and conflict across the years—was a *sine qua non* for Roman identity and presentation of self to the outside world, evident in such official proclamations of imperial orthodoxy as Justinian II's *iussio* of 687, or the imperial letters to the papacy included in the acts of the sixth ecumenical council at Constantinople in 680–681.[3]

Many in the conquered lands continued to believe, at least so it would seem from some of the surviving literature of the period, that Roman recovery was something to be taken seriously and to be hoped for. An anti-Jewish text ascribed to Anastasius of Sinai and composed apparently in the last decade or so of the century sees the Christian community as a whole—both outside and within the empire—as unbowed, in spite of defeats and disasters, enslavements and calamities.[4] Contemporary apocalyptic texts such as *Ps.-Methodius* and *Ps.-Daniel* look forward to a future great victory of the Roman emperor, in spite of the chastisements and catastrophes that have befallen the Romans (i.e., the Christians) so far.[5] To what extent such views prevailed broadly within the empire is not clear, except to note that the Greek versions of these texts and others like them were certainly widely known within a very short time of their composition. Another late-seventh-century, highly tendentious anti-Jewish polemic known as "the Trophies of Damascus" and written probably about the time of the sixth ecumenical council in 680 makes the point: "This is the most remarkable, that the church, having fought, remained invincible and indestructible, and while all struck it, the foundation remained unmoved. While the head and the empire stood firm, the whole body could be renewed." Empire and Christian community went hand-in-hand.[6]

A Moral Framework of Shared Values:
Secular Law and Canon Law

This broader pattern of beliefs provided the ideational framework within which the political theology of the eastern Roman state is to be understood, and the latter was itself underpinned by two sets of regulatory precepts, sets of values inscribed in certain institutional arrangements that promoted a distinctly Roman imperial community of interest, if not a conscious identity across regional and social divisions, within the remaining territories of the eastern Roman state. These are the continuing application of Roman law, on the one hand, and the canon law of the church. Perhaps more significantly, there also took place an ever-greater convergence of the secular and ecclesiastical realms in law and regulation, a phenomenon that has recently and rightly been highlighted and underlined.[7] Roman law was a crucial element in the way the state functioned, and it represented, along with the church, the fiscal system and the military, one of the instruments through which the state as the dominant political structure could operate. Law-making was the prerogative of the emperor, and the law and all that was associated with it thus also symbolized the imperial Roman state. Indeed, just as correct belief—orthodoxy—was a fundamental element in maintaining divine support, so was a proper regard for the law and for justice as defined by the divinely elected Roman emperors:

> Since God has put in our hands the imperial authority, and given us thereby an acknowledgement of the love which we reverently hold for Him . . . we believe that there is nothing higher or greater that we can do in return than to govern in judgement and justice those who are given over by Him to our care, to the end that the bonds of all manner of injustice may be broken, the oppression of agreements imposed by force may be relieved, and the assaults of wrongdoers may be repelled, and that thus we may be crowned by His almighty hand with victory over our enemies (which is a thing more precious than the diadem we wear) and thus there may be peace in our palace and stability in the state of our realm.[8]

It is true that the pattern of imperial legislative activity changes radically from the early decades of the seventh century. No longer do emperors legislate through edicts and *novellae constitutiones* as had emperors before Heraclius. Instead the business of the state is regulated through

imperial orders or commands—*iussiones* or *keleuseis*—that dealt with immediate issues, while the legal and moral framework established by
Justinian's codification in the sixth century was taken as the norm to
which government, church, and people should conform. Indeed, the
sort of legal activity pursued by the emperors of the sixth century became both impractical, in light of the difficult conditions of the times,
and ideologically redundant. Imperial commands and orders—legislation
in the broadest sense—were aimed at rectifying a situation and restoring
the norms of the (lost) Justinianic moral and administrative universe.
The *Ecloga*, the slimmed down codification of Justinianic law issued by
the emperors Leo III and Constantine V in 741, aimed specifically to
make the Justinianic code more accessible and usable, and the changes
it introduced were not understood as novelties but rather as reaffirming
and reinforcing the moral universe of the older laws.[9] Interpreted through
a Christian lens, applied casuistically, regionally very variable in its application and diluted in some cases by the persistence of local custom
and tradition, especially where issues of kinship, inheritance, or the punishment of various criminal offenses was concerned, it nevertheless penetrated to the roots of Byzantine society.[10] The preface of the *Ecloga* sets
out the aims very clearly:

> . . . recognizing that the laws issued by our imperial predecessors are
> written down in many volumes, and knowing that for some the meaning
> contained within them is difficult while for others it is completely inac-
> cessible, indeed especially for those who dwell outside this, our God-
> protected imperial city, we have, therefore, with the collaboration of our
> most glorious *patrikioi,* of the most glorious *quaestor,* and of the most glo-
> rious consuls and secretaries and other God-fearing persons, ordained
> that all those books should be assembled in our presence. And after a
> thoroughgoing examination of all these tomes, and making use both
> of what is well-expressed in the aforementioned volumes as well as of
> that which we have ourselves decreed in new laws, we have held it ap-
> propriate to set out more clearly and more concisely in the present book
> those decisions and contractual matters that arise frequently, as well as
> the punishments for offences, with the aim of offering a more manage-
> able understanding of the sense of these pious laws, easier decisions for
> legal cases, the just punishment of evildoers and the discouragement
> and correction of those who tend to sin.[11]

Legislation and managing the state remained crucial interests of the
ruler;[12] indeed, without the maintenance of the established framework

of the law, neither government nor elite would have been able to maintain their control of the provincial populations. While its application was patchy in the provinces, it was the instrument through which the imperial administration dealt out justice and it served both as a means of reinforcing Christian (Roman) identity as well as of imposing a common set of socially effective norms in respect of property and inheritance.[13] Its existence reflected and symbolized the remarkable infrastructural reach of the eastern Roman state into the lowest levels of society, affecting the family; the rights of the head of a household; the ways in which property, both movable and immovable, was to be disposed; the rights of children, male and female; and the rights and duties of husbands and wives, in-laws and parents.[14]

When the reach of the law was challenged, then the government was worried. As we have just seen, the preface to the *Ecloga* noted as one major reason for its promulgation the shocking state of jurisprudence in the provinces, the ignorance of legal literature, the corruption of those entrusted with judicial office, and the influence of the powerful and wealthy.[15] Yet provincial courts and judges are mentioned in the body of the text, and a little incidental evidence suggests that justice and the judicial framework, however attenuated by circumstances, continued to maintain a provincial existence, even though the emperors go on to hope that their code would facilitate a general rehabilitation of imperial legislation in the provinces, suggestive of the erosion of much of the traditional fabric of civil administration.[16]

Importantly in this regard, a legal text known as the Farmers Law *(Nomos geōrgikos)*, closely associated with the *Ecloga*, deals with a specific and very limited field of interest, namely property relations within a rural community. While the precise date of its compilation remains debated, it is generally agreed that it was produced at some point between the middle of the seventh and the early ninth century, and more likely was associated from the start with texts such as the *Ecloga*.[17] Given its structure and content, which are neither antiquarian nor reflective of a classicizing compilation for the purposes of jurisprudential study, its very existence demonstrates a perceived need for a formal regulatory procedure that would deal with issues of property law, land-use, tenurial rights and obligations, trespass, livestock, theft, and a host of related issues. This in turn implies very strongly the direct intervention of the state in the form of local magistrates, and since some of the provisions of the *Nomos geōorgikos* are related quite clearly to fiscal matters, it may be that the magistrates in question were in fact fiscal officials.[18] Roman law continued to embody the empire and imperial rule in the provinces; it was as much an aspect of imperial administration and surveillance as it was a legal system in any modern sense. And while it is likely that the numbers of individuals who actually came into formal contact with it was very limited, we should also bear in mind that, as the legislation of the emperor Justinian in the sixth century makes quite clear, the presence in Constantinople of ordinary subjects, such as peasant farmers, among many others who had come to seek justice in imperial courts, was entirely usual—indeed, was a problem in terms of increasing the city's population, even if temporarily.[19] Such a tradition was not readily forgotten; appeal to imperial justice in the capital, however difficult of access for most, would certainly have reinforced ties between metropolis and provinces; and the existence of the Farmers Law at the very least indicates that for most an awareness of "the law" at some level or other was entirely standard.[20]

Roman law in the eastern empire after the sixth century was increasingly affected, both in terms of practice and interpretation, by the growing moral authority of the church. Indeed, in the context I have described, the church and its clergy were likely at least as important, and probably more important, in daily life than the civil law or the judicial apparatus, along with the fiscal officers and the local military who must have represented for a substantial part of the provincial population their major contact with the state and the representatives of the established order. This brings us to the second key element, canon law, the law of the church.[21] In the *Ecloga* in particular, the close association between justice and Christian philanthropy has long been recognized, along with what has been termed a "scriptural turn" in both the language of the law as well as in respect of some of the sanctions outlined.[22] While it is the case that there had always been an association between the secular and the sacred in the Roman world, even before Christianity (indeed, in all ancient cultures), the affinity between the canons of the Quinisext council in 691/692 and the language and moral universe of the *Ecloga* is clear, and indicates the increasing formal convergence we have noted already between these two spheres—a convergence that meant for contemporaries the effective blending of church with state, conceptually if not necessarily in daily practical respects.

The close relationship between secular and spiritual authority was of particular importance for it was, of course, only through the armed might of the state that the orthodoxy of the day could be properly and effectively enforced or defended, at least within the empire's borders.[23] So it was in those areas of social and moral life where state and church met that the effectiveness of a Christian and Roman identity was determined and reinforced.[24] From the time of the emperor Justinian in the sixth century, canon law—the moral and disciplinary code of the church—had been endowed with the force of the law of the state. The evolving relationship between church and state is summed up in the introduction to Justinian's sixth *novella constitutio,* issued in the year 535:

> The greatest blessings of mankind are the gifts of God which have been granted us by the mercy on high—the priesthood and the imperial authority. The priesthood ministers to things divine; the imperial authority is set over, and shows diligence in, things human; but both proceed from one and the same source . . . Nothing, therefore, will be a greater matter of concern to the emperor than the dignity and honor of the clergy . . . For if the priesthood be in all respects without blame . . . and if the imperial authority rightly and duly adorn the commonwealth committed to its charge, there will ensue a happy concord which will bring forth all good things for mankind.[25]

In the 620s a particularly important codification, the so-called *Nomokanon in fourteen titles,* assembled in a single work under a series of thematic titles all the key legislation concerning both secular civil law and canon law, reinforcing this relationship.[26] One of the effects of this was to permit secular authorities to invoke a Christian moral universe in arriving at legal decisions;[27] another was to introduce a particularly Christian approach to the family and personal social relationships, entailing a reduction in the power of the *paterfamilias,* increasing the range of options open to women in respect of inheritance and control over their own property, limiting the possibilities for divorce, determining degrees of consanguinity in marital relationships (and thus directly impacting on patterns of inheritance and the disposition of property), and, perhaps most significantly, making it clear that while the duties of the ruler included the protection of the church and the implementation of its laws, emperors were subject to exactly the same moral code as their subjects.[28] These developments were intensified and can be said to have culminated in the canons of the Quinisext council held in Constantinople in 691/692,[29] a council that Justinian II attended and where he presented himself as the mediating authority between God and human-kind, as the shepherd who guides the Christian flock, and in which canon law was effectively deployed as an aspect of the legislation of the state.[30] Justinian II's letter to the pope in 687 confirming the decisions of the council of 680–681, the opening address of the council of 691/692, and the preface to the *Ecloga* all imply an emperor who was both the divinely appointed and divinely guided ruler as well as the shepherd and defender of the Christian flock under God's divine protection. The opening address to Justinian II put it thus:

> Christ our God, who steers this greatest of ships, the entire world, has now set you over us, the wise governor, the pious emperor, our protector indeed: you who dispense your words in discernment safeguard truth always, render judgement and justice upon earth and walk in the blame-less path. Wisdom bore you in her womb and nurtured you well with virtues; she brought you up and educated you and filled you with the Spirit of God; she has made you the eye of the universe, you who brightly illumine your subjects with the pureness and splendor of your mind. To you she has entrusted her Church and has taught you to meditate on her law day and night, for the correction and edification of the peoples subject to you.

And again: "For this reason, then, we have assembled at your command in this God-guarded imperial city, and have drawn up these sacred canons. Wherefore . . . even as you have honored the Church with your letters of convocation, so may you finally confirm our resolutions through your pious signature."[31] In some respect the canons of the council of 691/692 represent the bridge between the Justinianic corpus and the *Ecloga*, in which the Christian Roman emperors themselves were incorporated into the soteriological teleology of Christian history as heirs of the Old Testament prophets. While these developments were not uninterrupted, and while the *Ecloga* reflects a somewhat different reaction to the situation with which Leo III had to contend during his reign, their overall direction cannot be mistaken.[32]

The close association between secular and religious law thus in-tensified the penetrative authority of the state while at the same time strengthening the role of the imperial church as a key reinforcing and structuring element in Byzantine notions of empire and imperial rule at the humblest level of village society. The direction these developments took was to become clearer over the following centuries. Not only did there never develop a specialist class of canon lawyers in the eastern Roman context, unlike in the medieval West, but ecclesiastical office-holders functioned also in secular justice. Churchmen acquired proficiency in civil as well as canon law, with the ultimate result that the canon law of the Byzantine church entirely subsumed the civil law tradition, rather than evolving along its own separate course.[33] While the ways in which this Christian symbolic universe inflected different levels of society and social praxis certainly varied, underlying such variations was a single message: the Eastern Roman Empire was God's empire on earth, its ruler appointed by God, and its destiny—as reflected in the apocalyptic and eschatological literature of the times (as well as in later tradition)[34]—was both to recover "lost" Roman territory and to extend orthodoxy, and to overcome the faithless and those who challenged the rule of the emperor. That it reached deep into society is not in doubt, in light of these considerations. But the extent to which such beliefs generated a shared identity, to what extent they promoted a unity of ideological purpose in terms of social action beyond the level of the literate and the privileged—whether in respect of day-to-day life or in respect of the ways in which the state could mobilize resources in manpower and materials—still remains unclear.

The canons of the Quinisext are an important source in this context and are especially revealing. Dealing with a wide range of topics connected with clerical discipline and the day-to-day presence of the church in the community, they range widely in their subject matter. Wandering hermits and monks are condemned and should be either driven out or taken into the disciplined environment of a monastery. Condemnations of fortune-telling and prophecy and the use of sympathetic magic, amulets, and charms were likewise repeated, such behavior and practices being seen by the church as a challenge to its established spiritual authority, offering as they did an alternative means of access to divine guidance and succor: "Regarding the so-called *eremitai* who go about the cities clad in black and with long hair, associating with men and women and making a mockery of their calling, we decree that, if they choose to have their hair cut and to assume the habit of the other monks, they should be placed in a monastery; but if they choose not to do this, they should be driven from the cities altogether and dwell in the wilderness, from whence they fabricated their appellation."[35]

As I have already pointed out, similar concerns are expressed in ha-giographies, miracle collections, and the *Questions and Answers* litera-ture. And one question in a seventh-century collection notes that it is not just "true" holy men who can work miracles: sorcerers and magi-cians are also at work—indeed, the ability to work miracles is no guar-antee of sanctity, even if a divine purpose is somehow at work.[36] While often repeated from earlier conciliar collections, new canons were from time to time added to address new problems, even if the flight of many of the clergy from areas threatened by "barbarian" raids—mentioned in another repeated canon—leaves us unsure as to the extent to which their prescriptions could be implemented.[37] The established church was concerned about channels of access to divine authority, and it redirected its anxiety about divine causation into legislating how that access worked and who controlled it.[38] The canon on wandering hermits is a case in point. People needed local and more tangible forms of spiritual guidance than those offered by the relatively distant institutions of formal reli-gious or secular authorities, and the authorities were always worried about this.[39] But the peculiar context of the later seventh century lends to both well-established practices and beliefs and to those that were in process of evolving, a very different force and effect from that which they had possessed in less troubled times.[40]

The canons of the Quinisext are dominated by issues connected with the question of ecclesiastical authority and correct Christian obser-vance among both clergy and laity. But the key point remains that in the form and context in which they are framed here, they are in effect to be understood also as imperial law. As we have just seen, in the introductory address to the emperor, as well as in the very first canon of the council, they decisively reject the challenge to imperial au-thority in the church presented by the views of Maximus and his fol-lowers, while in a later canon they equally decisively reaffirm the especially privileged place reserved to the emperor in the liturgy. They mark in many respects the final stage in the conceptual merging of secular and ecclesiastical authority under the God-appointed and Christ-loving emperor, itself a long, drawn-out process that had begun in the fourth century with a Christian "resacralization" of the emperor.[41] But the later seventh century saw a further stage in this process: a progressive assimilation of the institutions associated with the secular authority into a God-protected and divinely ordained structure headed by the ruler chosen by God.

Of fundamental importance in this development was the often overlooked or taken for granted fact that, in Constantinople, both emperor and patriarch shared the same conceptual as well as physical space, whereas in the city of Rome itself from the later fifth century the popes had no secular counterpart of equivalent status.[42] In Constantinople this led to tension as well as to occasional disagreement between these two powers. But it also meant more significantly that imperial authority tended, with only occasional exceptions in this period (and into the later eighth century), to far outweigh patriarchal authority—emperors continued to crown both themselves and their successors well into the middle Byzantine period, for example, with the patriarch in attendance as a witness and guarantor of imperial orthodoxy.[43]

In the west after the fifth century, in contrast, and in the absence of both an imperial court and a strong imperial presence,[44] the papacy alone represented the church, and in an international context of competing "successor" polities rather than within a single political formation. While the pace and nature of papal autonomy at Rome has often been exaggerated, the political realities of the later seventh century did endow the popes, in comparison with the patriarchs at Constantinople, with a greater degree of leeway and autonomy.[45] Imperial authority was, of course, present in the form of the exarchate and the various military commands that survived into the later seventh and early eighth century. Its symbolic presence was a constant, reflected through ceremonial, through the assumption that the emperor continued to wield authority over Rome and its territory as well as over the popes themselves (in terms of ratifying papal appointments, for example, either directly or, after 685, through the exarchs in Ravenna), and through the forwarding of taxes raised on papal properties in Italy to Constantinople (until the reign of Constantine IV). Occasionally it was physically present, as with the arrival of Constans II in 663. But in terms of practical, day-to-day realities, the popes had to fend for themselves, regardless of this imperial backdrop and the occasional infusions of imperial military and financial support.[46] And we should also recall that in the west, in strong contrast with the east, there was no other apostolic see. From the early days of the foundation of Constantine's new capital, there had always been competition between a city like Antioch, which was apostolic, and

Constantinople, which was not. The greater weight of imperial influence on the see of Constantinople as an ecclesiastical authority was yet another factor in the emergence of Rome and of papal primacy.

We should not exaggerate these developments. We should remember, for example, that not even Maximus the Confessor was prepared to claim absolute primacy for the Roman see, conditioned as it was—like Constantinople—by historical circumstances in which popes were just as fallible. Nor were disagreements framed or conceptualized in terms of "west" and "east," even if, according to the pro-Maximus account of his interrogation at the hands of high-ranking imperial officials in 655, a distinction between "Romans" and "Greeks" was employed as a shorthand for the papal and imperial positions. As the text has it, the *sakellarios* (chief treasurer) asks, "Why do you love the Romans and hate the Greeks?"[47] Final authority derived, in Maximus's view, through the Fathers of the church and the councils rather than through an individual, and he does not separate out the Roman church as such (or the papacy) from the church of the Romans in general. Had the papacy accepted the imperial position—which under Pope Honorius and later, if tacitly and briefly under Pope Vitalian, it did—then Maximus and his allies would have condemned it just as roundly.[48] Yet there is little doubt that the political and cultural situation of the 640s and after, and in particular the antimonothelete challenge mounted by Maximus the Confessor and his allies, gave further emphasis to the very different situations of patriarch and pope as well as to the growing political and ideological distance between Rome and Constantinople (regardless of the compromises made by both parties across the remaining decades of the century).[49] It promoted in Rome the space for pragmatic and independent action in respect of papal handling of regional political and religious matters as well as an increasingly vocal assertion of Roman theological primacy and ecclesiastical independence. It also strengthened the already close ties between Rome, North Africa, and Sicily, given the inability of the eastern patriarchates of Alexandria, Jerusalem, or Antioch to do more than observe from the sidelines: Alexandria remained loyal to the imperial position; Jerusalem was likewise under the authority of the monothelete Sergius of Joppa; and the see of Antioch was vacant at the time.[50]

The government response to the antimonothelete challenge was, once compromise had failed, to isolate oppositional voices through banishment and imprisonment, with the result that imperial oversight of ecclesiastical and theological matters within the see of Constantinople was intensified. When formal reconciliation with the papacy became necessary, first under Constantine IV and his advisors and later under Justinian II, spiritual and secular authority were presented in effect as a single, unified institution under the banner of imperial orthodoxy, as we can see in the *prosphōnētikos logos* addressed by the council of 680–681 to Constantine IV as well as in Justinian's *iussio* of 687, in the canons of the Quinisext, and in the *Ecloga*. Indeed, while the political situation certainly warranted the move, it is perhaps significant that it was the emperor, not the pope or the patriarch, who took the initiative in this respect.[51]

The full implications and impact of the Christianization of the imperial cult—completed in the course of the fifth century—had taken many decades to become apparent.[52] From the beginning it was widely accepted that the emperor was representative of both the secular as well as the spiritual authority. A law of Valentinian II of the year 384 illustrates the tendency: "There must be no dispute concerning an imperial judgement, for it is a kind of sacrilege to doubt whether the person whom the Emperor has selected is worthy." The harmonization of the two forms of authority was at the heart of the imperial position as summed up in Justinian's novel 6, issued in 535, even if there remained a tension and debate around this theme and in particular around the role of the emperor in formulating dogma.[53] Focused primarily on the imperial court and the position of the ruler, the process was marked at progressive stages by the legislation and ecclesiastical politics of Justinian and his successors as well as by the liturgification of court and palatine ceremonial already noted and now reasonably well understood.[54] From the fourth to the seventh century and beyond, the acclamation of emperors as "new Constantine" and "new Justinian" recalled this, and "new Solomon" or "new David" evoked the biblical heritage of the Christian Roman emperor, just as in the preface to the *Ecloga* Leo III could attribute the authority of a bishop to the emperors.[55] In the context of the seventh century, from Heraclius onward, these epithets received a new valency. And the language and tone of the canons of the Quinisext council, on the one hand, and of the *Ecloga*, on the other, suggest that, in more than one sense, the late seventh century saw, beyond the already well-advanced liturgification of the court and imperial ceremonial, a sacralization of the Roman *politeia* (state) itself.[56]

New Boundaries, New Divisions

After the initial phase of Arab conquests, the Christian community was divided by more than just matters of Christology and the nature of the Trinity, for there now evolved a political and geographical divide between those areas still under Roman imperial governance and those outside. The emperors continued to claim universal sovereignty, regardless of the political situation and, as just noted, many assumed that the empire would eventually recover its lost territories. But the Roman state was very clearly no longer coterminous with the Christian community. And so the question arises, to what extent did a specifically Roman, imperial, Christian identity evolve in the course of this separation and within the territories remaining to the empire, an identity that differentiated "Romans," the subjects of the one God-protected and Christ-loving emperor, from the rest of the Christian population of formerly imperial lands—particularly in light of the fact that the latter continued to consider themselves "Roman" for a period thereafter? To what extent was such an identity shared across socioeconomic boundaries? And to what extent did it contribute to what appears, at least on the face of things, to have been the peculiarly stubborn resistance to conquest and occupation on the part of the populations of Asia Minor?

Both the patriarch Nicephorus and the chronographer and monk Theophanes, writing in the late eighth and early ninth centuries, respectively, took it for granted that Romans were Christians and that Christians were Romans. Indeed, in the *Ecloga* the subjects of the emperor are described throughout as Christians rather than Romans—the formal identity of the two is complete.[57] This does not seem ever to have been an issue, except for those who, briefly in the middle decades of the seventh century and under very particular circumstances, had challenged the notion. But additional factors played a role that contributed to this parallelism. First, it is worth pointing to the increasing degree of estrangement, geographically as well as ideologically, between the surviving imperial territories and their populations and the conquered provinces. Movement across the frontier between the empire and the caliphate appears to have become ever more limited and, as we have seen in Chapter 2, was subject to many constraints. While the movement of both pilgrims and, more importantly, clergy and monks between the two realms appears to have been possible (but with some limitations, as we shall see in a moment) during periods of peace, the ongoing warfare and the lawless conditions of much of the frontier zone during the decades from the 650s meant that regular traffic was exceedingly difficult and hazardous.[58]

There are indications of travel between Constantinople and Jerusalem or Alexandria in the period 657 to 662, for example, or between 678 and 691, both periods during which the empire had concluded a formal peace or truce with the caliphate.[59] Contacts between the empire and monastic communities or the church in Palestine and Syria or in Egypt are attested in the first period, which followed the assassination of the caliph 'Uthmān; the second period following the peace concluded in 678 after a series of Arab defeats. Eastern clergy were present at the council of 680–681 as well as at the Quinisext in 691–692, although in both cases the numbers were small.[60] By the same token, it seems clear that information about affairs in the empire filtered only very slowly to Syria, so that Anastasius of Sinai, for example, had only the most garbled information about political events there.[61] In general, it seems that from the 650s onward, contacts between the Byzantine world and Syria and the former eastern provinces became fewer and fewer. No doubt some travelers—merchants and the occasional pilgrim, along with those who knew the least dangerous tracks across the frontier region—continued to journey in one direction or the other. But the evidence suggests that a real estrangement was growing up between the two worlds of east Rome and the caliphate.[62] As I noted in the Introduction, within sixty years of the first Islamic conquests in Syria, the east Roman hagiographer who wrote the *Life* of Andrew of Crete could refer to Palestine and Greater Syria as "the land of our enemies."[63]

Such an estrangement was undoubtedly reinforced by the deliberate actions of the Byzantine government, and possibly that of the caliphate as well. It is highly likely that imperial control over several key routes into Syria was in part responsible for the slowing down of communications between Anatolia and North Syria, and it had long been the practice for imperial officials to be posted to control access to and egress from the empire.[64] As we have already seen, careful watch was kept on key points of transit, and the consolidation of a frontier or border that stretched across lands that were occupied by Christian communities on both sides cannot have done much to promote a shared political identity. There is reasonably good evidence that from the early

640s the imperial government began a policy of fortifying and controlling access to the passes from North Syria and Mesopotamia into Anatolia. It is a long and difficult frontier, especially in its less readily defended eastern section, but there are enough indications in the problematic Arabic historiographical tradition and in the Syriac tradition to suggest that Heraclius, in his final years, had inaugurated a policy of devastating some border regions and of defending key routes through the Taurus Mountains into Asia Minor. From then through the remaining years of the seventh and into the first decade of the eighth century the Romans were able to hold onto outposts along the southern and southeastern flanks of the Taurus-Anti-Taurus range as well as in the Cilician plain. How effective these measures were we shall see in a subsequent chapter, but it is the case that the pace of Arab-Islamic conquest in North Syria and southern Anatolia slows down dramatically from this point, developing from conquest and absorption to raiding and economic-political disruption.[65] Whatever the details, it is clear that for the first time in many centuries a "frontier" was evolving between North Syria and Anatolia where there had been no frontier before. Yet there is little doubt that it remained for many years a highly permeable borderland; especially along the coastal regions in both North Syria and southwest Anatolia, it is likely that many communities frequently found themselves on different sides of a notional "frontier" from time to time as the fortunes of warfare and politics fluctuated to and fro.[66]

A second important feature lies in attitudes to the invaders, as reflected in a range of texts, both theological and popular. As I noted in the Introduction, eastern Roman/Byzantine and Christian awareness of Islam as something substantially theologically different from Christianity had barely begun to evolve by the later seventh century. Islam was generally viewed as a deviant heresy, when it was mentioned at all.[67] Anastasius of Sinai is the first writer who, in his *Hodēgos* or *Viae dux*, makes an explicit reference to Islamic teaching in this respect. Written before 680 and revised in about 686–689, the ideas he expresses in this text, as those of John of Damascus in the 730s to 750s, are often relatively crude characterizations of Islamic teaching and practice.[68] Indeed, the dominant perception of the Saracens from the very beginning of their conquests, across the whole of the eastern empire, had less to do with their beliefs than with the fact that they were a barbarous people of the desert, either godless and impious or God-hating and hostile to

Christianity, its churches, and its practices, destroying what they hated or did not understand, contemptuous of Christian values and thus of all forms of civilized culture. Yet awareness of the ideological-religious hostility of their enemy certainly helped to consolidate the notion that the Roman Empire was distinguished in particular by its Christian faith, a message that, as we have seen, permeated well beyond the metropolitan and provincial elites.[69]

Such views were slowly modified by experience over the course of the eighth and into the ninth century, especially among diplomats and those who traveled in Islamic lands. But it is a constant of all Byzantine texts that deal with the Arabs and the invasions across this period and well beyond, and it served both to caricature the "Saracens" and to turn them into the ultimate "Other" that threatened both Christian society and *mores* as well as God's chosen empire, that of the Romans.[70]

While this hardly needs to be demonstrated in detail, it is worth mentioning here because it is often forgotten as a factor in determining how we might imagine people of the time responding to the Saracen challenge. The reverse of the medal lies in the attitude of the Islamic authorities to the different Christian communities with which they had to deal, and who until at least the early ninth century constituted by far the majority population of the greater Syrian region. Christians, and more importantly Melkite Christians—those who adhered to their Chalcedonian faith and could thus be seen as loyal to the eastern Roman emperor, the "king" *(malik)* of the Romans—were clearly suspect on occasion and thus liable to persecution, harassment, or surveillance. In the context of the relatively fragile nature of Islamic rule in the conquered lands during the first Islamic century, of the obvious threat posed by imperial naval as well as land forces, and of the occasional desertion to the Romans of individuals as well as groups, a good number of Christians were killed on suspicion of being spies at various times. Some of the most important Christian neomartyrs of the period appear to belong to this category, as has been pointed out: the sixty martyrs of Jerusalem (in 725), for example, and many others. By the same token, Islamic suspicion about Christians in respect of the ongoing conflict with the Roman Empire has also been suggested as one reason underlying the promulgation of anti-Christian discriminatory laws.[71] The contrast between those lands under the emperor's rule and those under that of the caliph must have been very clear and can hardly have done other than to reinforce a growing perception of political and cultural difference.

A Common Cause?

To what extent, therefore, did this Christian Roman identity generate or support an awareness of common interests across the whole population of the Eastern Roman Empire, and did this help in the defense against hostile attacks and the invasions of the Arab-Islamic armies in the second half of the seventh and the first part of the eighth century? The archaeological and historical evidence coincides in showing that, in spite of frequent attacks and sometimes the sack of a city, the population generally resisted or took refuge somewhere until the enemy had gone before reoccupying their settlement. The best textual account comes from a collection of miracles ascribed to St. Theodore "the recruit" and associated with the town of Euchaïta in Helenopontus (north central Asia Minor). Here the author describes in detail how the population took to their fortified acropolis behind the town during "the yearly raid" of the enemy before returning when the enemy had departed with its booty.[72] But although we have no specific texts for them, the same was clearly the case for many other settlements. And sometimes, especially in those areas most exposed to constant raiding and attack, the settlements were ultimately abandoned. In 711 the inhabitants of the town of Sision, in the Cilician plain and the subject of continuing attacks, finally decided to abandon their city and relocate northward, into the Taurus region and away from the exposed lowlands.[73] The question as to the nature of resistance to invaders (if that is what it was) as well as when and why it took place or did not take place, however, remains as yet unanswered.

To understand the context within which we can address this issue, it is worth briefly reviewing the course of the Arab attacks across this period in order to highlight some important features, bearing in mind the general political historical background as outlined in the introductory chapter.[74] First, there is general agreement that, commencing in the 640s and gathering in both pace and intensity under Mu'āwiya (first as governor of Syria, then as caliph from 660), the attack on the Eastern Roman Empire was explicitly aimed at its conquest and eradication. The Byzantines became—and remained for more than two centuries thereafter—the main opponent of Islam, posing both a military as well as a fundamental ideological challenge.[75] But it seems that there were significant shifts in emphases, first in the early 660s and again after the year 680, the year in which Mu'āwiya died and his son Yazīd I succeeded to the caliphate. Across the later 640s and 650s substantial raids were mounted into Anatolia, but from the early 660s until 679 they became yearly, sometimes two or even three times in a single year. Fortresses and settlements in the zones immediately adjacent to territories firmly under Islamic rule were raided, other columns pushed deep into the provinces of Anatolia, and virtually every year between 663 and 679 one or more Arab armies also wintered on Byzantine territory. These armies lived off the land and raided for captives, livestock, and other forms of booty. Thousands of prisoners were taken and carried off to Syria to be enslaved. The infrastructural damage to the hardest hit areas must have been substantial, and I will give a specific example in a later chapter. The targets of these attacks ranged across the whole of the Anatolian hinterland, aimed apparently at a "softening up" of resistance as part of a plan to wear the empire down, disrupt communications and organizational cohesion, and, as in Syria and Egypt, encourage a political and military collapse. They reached cities as far afield as Trebizond (in 654), Ankara (also in 654), and Euchaïta (possibly in 641, certainly in the 660s on more than one occasion). More regularly, fortress towns such as Koloneia, Amorium, Antioch in Pisidia, Tarsus, and Mopsuestia in Cilicia, and other fortresses and settlements in the provinces of Lycia, Isauria, Phrygia, Cappadocia, and Armenia IV were targeted. Although many of these cities or towns were taken and sacked, they were almost immediately retaken and reoccupied so that Arab forces rarely succeeded in maintaining a hold over a key fortified center for more than one winter season, never for more than a few months at any time. And Constantinople itself was the target of a major assault in 654–655, although the assault was defeated before it began when the main fleet was destroyed in a storm, and the accompanying land forces were defeated as they marched through Anatolia shortly thereafter.

The first Arab civil war that broke out in 656 and lasted until 661 meant a pause in the continuous nature of the assault and permitted Constans to rethink imperial strategy and in particular permitted his march through the Balkans to Italy in order to reinforce imperial interests in the west. But from 663 a more deliberate strategy was begun by Mu'āwiya aimed not only at wearing down opposition and morale and

disrupting administrative continuity but also at destroying local economies throughout Anatolia, crushing the will to resist. The siege of
668–669 marks a high point in terms of Arab ambitions, but the yearly
attacks continued uninterrupted. Only with Muʿāwiya's death in 680
did the strategy change and the overwintering raids ceased almost
completely (only two are recorded between the accession of Yazīid I in
680 and the year 717, for example).[76]

A crucial factor for Byzantium were the internecine conflicts within
the caliphate, known collectively as the first and second *fitna*, or civil
wars, conflicts that saw the assassination of the caliph ʿUthmān in 656
and the final victory of Muʿāwiya in 661; and the accession and demise
of Yazīd I (680–683), Muʿāwiya II (683–684) and Marwān I (684–685)
before the accession of ʿAbd al-Malik (685–705), whose caliphate saw, if
not an end, then a dampening down of the strife and witnessed the rise
of a stronger and administratively innovative regime.[77] Two elements
were important here. First, the emperors of east Rome were able to take
advantage of these problems to achieve truces highly advantageous to
the empire. During the first civil war Constans II had been able to campaign in the Caucasus and reinforce imperial authority there before
turning his attention westward. In 678–679 negotiations had already
begun, promoted by Muʿāwiya (as he attempted to deal with opposition
to his wish to secure the succession to the caliphate for his son Yazīd)
and by the emperor Constantine IV (as he prepared to deal with the
newly arrived Bulgars on the Danube, the preparations for the sixth
ecumenical council, and negotiations with the papacy). A peace was
of course highly desirable on the Byzantine side in any case, simply to
permit the consolidation of frontier defenses and to free the provinces
from the constant raiding. While the initial truce seems to have been
slow in starting (Arab raids are reported after it had supposedly begun),[78]
the internal troubles of the caliphate continued for some time, permitting
a second peace treaty to be agreed on even more favorable terms for the
imperial side in 685 and confirmed in 688–689 as ʿAbd al-Malik struggled to impose his authority over oppositional forces in Iraq and the Hejaz,
and as the east Roman ruler went onto the offensive in Cilicia.[79]

Second, with the final defeat of his "internal" enemies in 692, ʿAbd
al-Malik could turn his attention to matters of administration and finance
and to the ongoing struggle against the major enemy of Islam in the west,
the eastern Roman state. While the Byzantine presence in Armenia and

Iberia was probably not the immediate cause of hostilities, following on as it did from the treaty of 688–689, tensions over the form in which ʿAbd al-Malik's payment of the tribute in gold coin and a possible Byzantine claim to all the revenues of Cyprus (divided between the two parties according to the treaty of 685) led to a renewed outbreak of hostilities.[80] Following the defeat of imperial forces near Sebastopolis in 693 the Arab offensive was renewed, yet the strategy was markedly different from the one Muʿāwiya had promoted. From this point and into the 720s, the focus is on the "frontier" regions ringing the imperial heartland in Anatolia, from Armenia IV and the regions to south and east around into the Cilician plain and into Isauria, although on occasion raids penetrated more deeply, as far as Amaseia in the north and Dorylaion in the center. Hitherto the Byzantines had been able to hold onto several key fortresses in these regions—Kamacha, Theodosiopolis, Taranton west of Melitene, and Tyana north of the Cilician Gates as well as a string of much smaller fortified strongholds whose names are only rarely noted in the sources. Indeed, the peace of the years after 688–689 had almost certainly permitted the imperial forces to reform and strengthen the frontier defenses.

But from the late 690s, this began to change as the Arab strategy concentrated on the destruction of these installations and the eradication of any organized frontier. The Cilician plain, abandoned by the Byzantines but regularly attacked when Arab forces were there, was now for the first time occupied—in 703 Mopsuestia was rebuilt, fortified, and garrisoned in large part because it served as an advanced defense for the more important city of Antioch;[81] Sision, to the northeast of Mopsuestia, was finally abandoned by its population and garrison in 711;[82] by the time the series of campaigns that culminated in the second siege of Constantinople in 717–718 was under way (715–716), Cilicia was entirely in Arab hands and the Byzantines were forced back on the Taurus-Anti-Taurus line, losing Kamachon, Theodosiopolis, and Armenia on the eastern front and defending the Cilician Gates and other passes into Cappadocia and Isauria with the greatest difficulty. Surveys of the pattern of Arab attacks clearly bears out the fact that strategy had shifted, with the main aim now being to grind down Byzantine defenses— whether preparatory to the great campaigns of 715–717 from the beginning or, as seems more likely, initially as a reflection of the failure of Muʿāwiya's strategy to achieve its end of forcing the empire and more especially its provincial populations simply to give in. The attack on Constantinople was intended again, of course, as a final knock-out blow, this time prepared by the destruction of the imperial capacity for defending the capital. While its ultimate failure did not stop the raiding or mounting of large-scale expeditions through the 720s, 730s, and into the 740s, Byzantine resistance and willingness to confront and defeat the invaders in battle increased. Arab-Islamic strategic objectives changed—while the long-term intention remained the destruction or subjection of the Roman state, expansionist conquest was replaced by a longer-term war of attrition. Raids deep into Asia Minor continued but less regularly, the capture and sack of major Byzantine centers occurred less often (Ikonion in 723, Caesarea in Cappadocia in 726, for example),[83] the border zones remained the chief target, and the warfare settled down into a routine with which imperial forces were able to deal fairly effectively, permitting the slow recovery of the inland regions. As has been pointed out, the warfare now largely takes the form of small-scale raiding, focusing especially on the *sa'ifa,* or summer raid.[84]

Yet it is clear from an examination of the chronology of Arab attacks and of the abandonment or sack of Byzantine towns and fortresses that, even if on occasion the population despaired of their situation, whole districts that submitted to the enemy rarely stayed under their control for long. The seventh-century Armenian chronicle of *Ps. Sebeos* states that the population of those areas of Anatolia through which Arab forces marched during the invasion of 654 submitted wholesale: "When he [Mu'āwiya] penetrated the whole land, all the inhabitants of the country submitted to him, those on the coast and in the mountains and on the plains." Theophanes likewise records that the garrisons and population of Cappadocia submitted to Maslama in 715–716 when that commander appeared at the head of a major expeditionary force: "When Masalma had come to Cappadocia, the Cappadocians despaired of their own safety and went out towards him begging him to take them."[85] Such capitulations are hardly to be wondered at, given the circumstances. But unlike in the provinces of Syria, these never seem to have become permanent and indeed reflected the exceptionally high numbers of the hostile forces. Of the hundreds of Anatolian settlements, large and small, that lay behind the Taurus-Anti-Taurus line and that were attacked on one or on many occasions in the course of the period ca. 640–740, the number that can be shown to have been abandoned as a result is not as great as one would expect from the frequency and ferocity of the attacks and warfare. As we have just seen, the towns that were given up and whose populations were driven off entirely, either as refugees or taken prisoner, were for the most part in the regions immediately adjacent to the frontier zone behind the Taurus and Anti-Taurus.[86] Most other settlements shrank, certainly. Many populations simply moved to a safer nearby site. But absolute abandonment was not the rule. At first sight it might appear that the populations of these settlements did not—would not—give up but returned, often time after time to rebuild and reoccupy their towns or cities. A clear illustration of the refusal to abandon territory can be found in the lists of signatories to the church councils, for at the Quinisext in 691–692 there is evidence of the transfer of a number of episcopal sees, displaced from their original locations due to the pressure and impact of hostile activity and established at less exposed settlements, creating in the process entirely new sees—three in Galatia II, one in Lycia, five in Phrygia Pakatiane, four in Pisidia, and one in Armenia I.[87] It would be difficult to find a clearer indication of the determination with which the church and the government at Constantinople held onto their lands and the inhabitants of the provinces. But was it the ordinary inhabitants who led this resistance and reoccupation? This was undoubtedly one part of the equation.[88] But a careful consideration of the evidence suggests that things were a little more complex, as we shall see in the following.

Retrenchment and Resistance

One important reason for the ability of the Romans to hold onto territory in this way was that the defended cities and towns of Anatolia were more easily relieved by imperial forces, more easily defended against hostile incursions, and, perhaps crucially, more easily within the reach of imperial wrath than were those of the Syrian provinces after the great defeat at Yarmuk in 636. Provincial elites, bound to Constantinople through a range of measures and relationships, also played a key role, which is examined in the next two chapters. The proximity or possibility, or not, of imperial help seems to have been a key factor in determining the levels of resistance. While there was certainly a long-standing tradition of Roman cities resisting hostile attack where they had adequate defenses, their prospects for success depended on a wide range of factors, whether or not the ordinary citizens of the town were involved,[89] and it is clear that the large number of smaller and medium urban centers that fell to the invader in the course of the extensive raiding does not speak for much stiff local opposition or commitment to defend to the last.[90] In Syria after 636, with few exceptions, towns and cities surrendered because there was little or no hope of imperial relief. According to a story transmitted by al-Ṭabarī, the inhabitants of Emesa were keen to resist precisely because they thought the emperor would come to help them. This is an old history—even in the sixth century and at the height of Justinian's empire, Syrian cities tended to concede fairly easily to invading Persian armies, less a reflection of their pusillanimous nature than of a sharp awareness of the remoteness and unlikelihood of imperial succor. Only where a substantial Roman force could be expected was resistance stiffer.[91] After the Battle of Yarmuk, no help was forthcoming, and cities quickly realized that it was better to preserve what they had than to lose everything in what would probably be a futile resistance. Only strongholds that could be supplied and supported from the sea held out—places such as Caesarea in Palestine or Aradus, off the Syrian coast, for example.[92] A similar phenomenon can be observed in Anatolia in the seventh century—the fortresses and cities that surrendered usually did so when there was no hope of relief, as with Tyana in 707–708 for example, which resisted an initial Arab attack, observed the crushing defeat of the relieving army, and then surrendered to a renewed siege.[93]

By the same token, it is also the case that the proximity or not of Islamic occupying forces must also have made a difference—whereas substantial Arab forces were within easy reach of and often encamped close to the major cities of Syria, there was no occupation of the Anatolian provinces, and it was the imperial armies that exercised both the threat of reprisal and punishment as much as the promise of relief. This is an important point, and one to which I will return in due course.

A second key factor in this context is the Byzantine strategy of refusing battle that, according to a later report, although following a near-contemporary tradition, appears to have dominated policy in the years after 637–638: "Heraclius wrote to all the Romans in Mesopotamia, Egypt and Armenia, saying that no-one should engage with the Arabs in battle, but whoever could hold on to his post should do so."[94] In Syria and Mesopotamia the imperial forces had been trounced in a series of full-scale battles, the result of which was both to deplete the garrisons and defensive capacity of the cities of the area and at the same time to deprive them of any hope of relief if they were attacked. It can hardly be accident or coincidence that in the years following the Byzantine withdrawal from Syria there are so few full-scale battles between imperial and Arab armies recorded by the sources in the main theater of conflict in Anatolia, apart from those associated with the attack on Constantinople in 654–55, imperial expeditions to the Caucasus (a challenging situation involving both imperial and Armenian troops and the complex princely politics of the region), and in the late 660s and 670s—situations, then, where the imperial forces were able to assemble and prepare an attack on enemy troops occupying defensive positions or demoralized by news of the defeat of the main assault on the imperial capital.[95] This cannot be an oversight since the Byzantine, Arab, and Syriac sources present the same picture and it seems likely; in contrast, Byzantine attacks and open battles do take place in the period after the renewal of hostilities in 693. Just as significant is the fact that there is no question but that Byzantine field armies were active throughout the period in question, with campaigns in the 640s and in 653 in Armenia, 658 and 680 in the Balkans, and 663–668 in Italy. So there were substantial numbers of men under arms in Anatolia across these years,[96] and yet these troops appear deliberately to have avoided contact with enemy forces, except to harry or harass them. To what extent this reflects any orders issued by Heraclius remains unknown, of course. But it is credible that such a policy appears to have been practiced, the more so in light of the relatively unsuccessful performance of the imperial armies in Armenia and Anatolia as well as the failures in the 630s in Syria and the early 640s in Egypt.[97]

By avoiding battle, possible (or even probable) defeat, and the consequent loss of military potential, the empire achieved three crucial results. First, and regardless of whether active local resistance on the part of the provincial population was effective (and it seems as often as not to have been readily brushed aside by the invader), it retained the wherewithal quickly to reestablish its control over areas raided or devastated by Arab forces, once they had retired, and where necessary to reoccupy and refortify key positions. Second, it retained the potential and the organized manpower to garrison, strengthen, or reconstruct major fortified centers or bases when they were attacked, thus negating very quickly any gains the Arabs were able to make in the course of a campaign. This explains why the Arabs were rarely able to establish a permanent presence north of the Taurus and Anti-Taurus, even though the period from ca. 660 to 680 was one in which overwintering campaigns were the norm. On the one hand, smaller forts and fortresses changed hands as they were seized by Arab forces only to be recovered, refortified, and regarrisoned by imperial troops (a process paralleled in sixth- and seventh-century Italy, for example, which successfully held up or prevented Lombard expansion on several occasion);[98] on the other, while a good number of smaller, mostly unfortified urban settlements in the regions of Cilicia, Cappadocia, and Isauria were abandoned by their populations, important urban centers further inside imperial territory might be taken and sacked but were also for the most quickly reoccupied and refortified—a few exceptions underline the general rule, such as Tyana.[99] And third, it meant that the government, through its local military and other officials, never relaxed its control over the provincial population—it could continue to tax and appropriate resources, where conditions allowed, and it could thus continue to raise armies, however straitened its fiscal circumstances, a theme that will be taken up in a later chapter. The last point is especially important, as we shall see. The armies that were, from the 640s, now garrisoned across Anatolia were based largely in and around defensible urban centers, further adding to the resistance potential of the cities.[100] The continued presence of the military in the provinces was itself only possible because of certain other key factors, notably the adherence of local elites to the imperial cause (see Chapter 4). These two elements combined gave the empire a considerable advantage when it came to holding on to and rapidly reoccupying or reestablishing control over provincial centers of resistance.

And finally, it may be that the very nature of the Arab raiding attacks discouraged local populations from giving up. As it became evident to the Arab military commanders and soldiers, notably after the mid-690s, that they could not maintain a permanent foothold in Anatolia, their warfare became increasingly destructive and punishing, and one consequence may have been that surrender to the raiders became far less appealing than continued resistance. But this is hypothesis, and, without evidence to support or challenge the contention, it must remain so.

While by no means the only factors in the survival of the state, these must be seen as some of the most significant in terms of grand strategic concerns, along with the failure of the Arab attacks on Constantinople. The capital city of the empire was, of course, the major target of the first seventy-five years of warfare. Its loss would probably have led to the collapse of east Roman resistance in Anatolia, since the elites who were the backbone of state resistance in the provinces depended directly on the imperial court and government at Constantinople for income, social status, and power. Without an imperial government at Constantinople— even if the seat of empire had been transferred to Sicily with Constans II in the early 660s—it is unlikely that the empire could have survived. Of course we cannot know, but this seems the most likely outcome. But it did not fall, partly because of its defenses, partly because of the enormous cost to the caliphate of mounting a single, knock-out blow along with all the strategic and logistical difficulties associated with such an effort (as in 654, 668–669 or 717–718, for example), but also because of the flexibility of the imperial resistance in the provinces of Anatolia. The vital importance of the capital was well understood by both sides, and the Theotokos, as the protector of the capital, could in consequence be portrayed as the protector and patron of the empire as a whole. The patriarch Germanus expressed this in a sermon on the dormition, for example, and the message was given voice even more explicitly when he noted, in his sermon on the Akathistos hymn, composed at some point after the defeat of the attack of 717–718:

> Our city had never before experienced threats such as these, indeed not even the most distant regions of the whole civilized world, where the name and polity of the Christians exists. For the whole body of Christ's flock would doubtless confess that it would have been at risk along with us if the Saracens who range themselves against the confession of his glory had attained the aim of their campaign against us.[101]

The apocalyptic tradition associated with the city is considerable, as one might expect, but there was a parallel early Islamic apocalyptic tradition devoted to the theme of the conquest of Constantinople underlining just how important this was for the invaders, both ideologically and in practical terms. As one such text has it: "You will invade Constantinople three times. In the first one you will face affliction and hardship. In the second there will be a peace treaty between you and them, so that the Muslims will build mosques in it, join them in a raid beyond Constantinople and return to it. And in the third invasion God will open it for you." The tradition had a long history well into the early Ottoman period. But it took until May 29, 1453, for the prophecies finally to be realized.[102]

Provincial Society

The ways in which the developments we have now outlined affected the populations of the provinces, both in the countryside as well as in towns, is a topic about which we have only limited evidence. Towns and cities had been foci for markets and meetings, and even if the views of the local rural and urban populace rarely reached Constantinople, they could not be ignored by local representatives of the empire. But we now know that, however varied the fate of individual urban centers after the middle of the seventh century may have been, there had taken place a drastic change in the nature of traditional civic culture. Those major centers that survived without a significant reduction in their occupied surface were relatively few and tended to be foci for fiscal, military, and church activities. Even so, many larger cities contracted to a smaller fortified area, sometimes with the continued occupation of substantial suburbs outside the new defensible center, sometimes not—the microregional variations have been shown to be substantial.[103]

Yet the character and content of urban culture was certainly transformed. Civic life in its late Antique form virtually vanishes; secular education contracts and almost disappears from the provinces, along with the study of the law; literary output, before the seventh century firmly anchored in an urban context, highly diverse, and reflective of a lively urban culture, likewise shrinks, with many genres more or less invisible in the surviving manuscript tradition but with a much more obvious emphasis on the various forms of literature associated with the church, popular piety, and monasteries. This was a reflection of two developments—the physical and institutional disruption just noted and the changing character, priorities, and concerns of the social elite in both provinces and capital.[104] In the absence of populous towns and the civic culture and institutions typical of the period up to the 640s and perhaps the 650s, along with the possibilities they offered for the expression of the views of ordinary people, we may ask how the urban populace of the empire, and how provincial populations more generally, were able to voice their opinions and communicate their views. Other

than in Constantinople or perhaps the few other remaining major provincial towns, such as Thessaloniki or Trebizond, for example, civil opposition or simply representation through the traditional means (including rioting) had little point.

It is perhaps indicative of the complex changes that were taking place
that the decline in the independent political activities of Blue and Green
factions (the popular chariot-racing fan clubs) in the cities of the east
more or less coincides with the changes in function and form of cities
in east Roman culture and government. Indirect confirmation of this
comes in the form of the surprising absence from the canons of the
Quinisext of references to the involvement of members of urban monastic communities in political disturbances of all kinds, from riots and
street protests and related activities to factional strife, topics that occupy
an important place in the canons of earlier councils such as Chalcedon.
Apart from canon 34, prohibiting clergy and monks from "conspiracy
or forming secret leagues," there is no hint that monks might be involved in urban politics as they had been in an earlier age. At the same
time these developments are paralleled by the increasingly vocal appearance of soldiers in politics.[105] And so it would appear that, throughout
the greater part of the later seventh and eighth centuries and beyond,
the ordinary rural population was represented, implicitly and infor-
mally, through one particular institution, and in a form—the only form—
through which they could make their opinions at least partially known
to those in power. For it was from the peasantry of the empire that the
vast majority of soldiers were recruited, and it was through the army, in
its various provincial divisions, that popular opinion could on occasion
be given expression.[106]

Following from the changes in the way the field armies were garrisoned or billeted across the Anatolian provinces from the 640s, it is
likely that soldiers gradually—over a generation or so—became much
more integrated into provincial society and the many urban and rural
communities into which they had been introduced, probably largely
through a process of intermarriage and through replacement and recruitment as units came to be recruited from the districts where they
were based—a situation that can be paralleled in Egypt in the sixth
century, for example, or more immediately comparable with Italy in the
later sixth and seventh century.[107] It should be recalled that soldiers enjoyed a higher than average social standing, especially cavalry soldiers,

bringing with them a range of legal privileges for themselves and their immediate dependents. These included advantages in respect of inheritance and the transmission of property as well as exemption from extraordinary fiscal levies. This gave them significant social advantages both in respect of status and in terms of income.[108] And these established privileges were confirmed and to a degree expanded in the provisions of the *Ecloga*.

The Italian situation, while certainly differing in several important respects from that in Anatolia, offers a number of very useful parallels. Already by the last decade of the sixth century in the exarchate, soldiers were purchasing property, both urban and rural, from which they drew rental income. During the seventh century this was in Italy apparently sufficient to permit them to remain active and to maintain their equipment, with only very minimal cash remuneration from the government. Rations and supplies were provided by the local military administration through the fiscal system. Military recruitment was a mix of conscription (based on land-tax assessment on estates) and volunteers, and together these tendencies certainly reinforced the localization of service and the ever-closer incorporation of soldiers into local society.[109]

And so a similar situation appears to have developed in Anatolia half a century later, with local variations, as the field armies of the east were withdrawn and dispersed in garrison towns and across the countryside. A process comparable to that which took place in Italy is nicely illustrated for other parts of the empire by an important and suggestive legal text from the 740s, which shows that provincial soldiers could support their military service from the revenues derived from their properties, a development that must certainly have reinforced the highly local ties of such men.[110] And just as in Italy, soldiers recruited from particular localities served in the units based in that area and thus tended to share loyalties and political and other views; the sections in the *Ecloga* relevant to soldiers' testamentary rights give the impression of a highly localized provincial military.[111] Likewise, just as in Italy, their cash *rhogai*, or salaries, were rationalized but paid at much greater intervals—on a three- or even four-yearly basis, rolled into the payment of donatives from the emperor.[112] The important role attributed to soldiers receives especial emphasis in the *Ecloga*, which repeats and reinforces earlier legislation, especially with regard to soldiers' privileges of inheritance and testamentary rights as well as of prohibitions on soldiers' leasing land or serving in the households or on the estates of others: as the text states explicitly, their only concern is to fight for the *politeia* against its enemies. To what extent the repetition of such regulations should be taken to mean that they were in fact (still) being ignored, or alternatively that these paragraphs were incorporated because the compilers of the law code felt they should be included, remains unknown. Later evidence (from the tenth century) would certainly suggest that there was a genuine and continuing need to enforce rules that were being slighted.[113]

An indication of such changes is that soldiers and the provincial units they made up became political in a way that they had not been during the sixth century, in spite of the fact that there had, in constitutional terms, always been a military element in, for example, the acclamation or choice of a new emperor. Politics in the very broadest sense was not new for soldiers—one has only to consider the developments of the third century to appreciate this. But the political context in the later seventh and early eighth centuries in the east is quite different from that of the preceding century, and in terms of imperial administration and structure, governance and international context, is utterly different from that of the third century—and it is, in the end, context that matters here. The absence of any other focus *except* the armies for nonmetropolitan or provincial opinion and the central position of provincial commanders in imperial politics—these were important aspects in this development.[114] Such tendencies were by no means unique—as demonstrated by the behavior and responses of soldiers of the Roman forces in Gaul during the later fourth century, for example.[115] The process may have been reinforced by the fact that the east Roman armies of the later seventh and eighth centuries were, as far as the evidence allows us to say, mostly indigenous and relatively homogeneous, from the cultural as well as the economic perspective. Within a couple of generations of their relocation to new bases in Anatolia—let us say, by the 670s at the latest—they had come to be rooted in local society and recruited regionally from peasant communities. They were officered at the lower levels, again as far as the evidence permits any conclusion, by local men, and even if the senior commander of each army was not local—indeed, the evidence suggests that the government made efforts to ensure that this was not the case—the unit and brigade commanders were for the most part members of local elites.[116] We can naturally see these developments from a longer-term structural perspective: the increasing prominence of the military during a period of political crisis and transformation and the systemic responses to the various pressures and stresses to which the eastern Roman state was subject, as in the third and early fourth centuries, for example. From the point of view of the comparative study of political systems and empires, this is quite legitimate. But as I noted in the Introduction, my aim in this discussion is to get beneath the surface of such descriptive models to locate the mechanisms of change and transformation at a particular time and in a specific region.

The interest of soldiers and their leaders in imperial affairs and in the way the empire was being governed—or misgoverned—during the later seventh and eighth centuries is indicated by their involvement in the series of rebellions and coups between the years 695 and 726 in particular;[117] although it had become evident in a number of interesting cases before then, and it supports the suggestion that provincial soldiers were conscious enough of matters that seemed to them to be relevant to their own situation and to that of the empire as a whole, to make their views known. I have already mentioned the ostensibly promonothelete demands of soldiers toward the end of the council of 680–681 and the events of 654, when soldiers in Thrace were concerned about supposed slanders against the Virgin. One of the soldiers at the fortress where Maximus had arrived went off to the nearby camp and proclaimed, "The monk who blasphemes against the Mother of God is on his way here!," causing an immediate uproar. The soldiers expressed no interest in the whole matter of monotheletism and Maximus's opposition—the crucial issue to them was a reported insult to the Theotokos, an issue that affected ordinary pious Christians and indicates the nature of their concerns. A similar accusation was made against Martin, an accusation claimed by Anastasius of Sinai to be typical of monothelete slurs on the orthodox.[118]

Such views cannot have been too different from those prevailing among the provincial population, given the origins of the majority of soldiers. And that the potential for the armies to function as a possible alternative power base was understood is reflected in the recognition accorded them in official pronouncements: Constantine IV acknowledged their role in his opening statement to the Sixth Ecumenical Council in Constantinople in 680.[119] Even more obviously, Justinian II attempted to integrate the imperial armies into his scheme of authority when he listed them in his *iussio* of 687 as being present at his ratification of the Sixth Council, possibly bearing in mind the military opposition to his father's shift in religious policy in 680–681. This is hardly surprising when we also recall that, while soldiers had always seen themselves as "Roman" and were thus addressed in rhetorical exercises in both historical texts as well as in other documents (such as Vegetius' *Epitoma de re militari*), it was loyalty to a specific emperor, affirmed in the "military oath," rather than to an abstraction such as the state or even the Roman Empire, that was crucial.[120] For an emperor to jeopardize or lose the support of the troops was a serious and very dangerous problem, as the usually very harsh response to military opposition illustrates. Emperors traditionally took care in this respect, of course—the payment of donatives and of occasional largesse is adequate testimony to that and hardly requires documenting here.[121] Indeed, and clearly a reflection of the centrality of soldiers to both society at large and to the emperors, the *Ecloga* introduces an entirely new regulation on the division of booty in which the soldiers are specifically singled out for rewards as opposed to their officers. The paragraph is worth citing in full:

> Those who march off to war against the enemy must desist from every wicked word and deed and should direct their thoughts and prayers to God and wage war with prudence; for help will be vouchsafed from God through a prudent heart since *the victory of battle standeth not in the multitude of an host; but strength cometh from heaven* [1 Maccabees 3. 19]. Thus when God grants victory, then a sixth of the booty should fall to the fisc, all the remainder should be distributed equally among the whole army, both high and low. For their additional salaries are sufficient for the officers. But should some officers have excelled through their bravery, then their commander-in-chief [*strategos*] should award them something from the fisc's sixth portion and permit them to receive the appropriate reward. Proportional to the share of those who take place in the battle, let the portion of those who serve in the baggage-train be assigned according to regulations.[122]

Especially where noncampaigning emperors were concerned, and in particular across the period from Gratian to Tiberius Constantine, regimes and their apologists took great care to cultivate images of Christian victory and to emphasize that the success of generals was ultimately derived from imperial piety and devotion.[123] When emperors were effective campaign leaders—as with Heraclius and his successors—then the rhetoric focused on their deeds while the propaganda of imperial victory reinforced the message. It is no coincidence that the military opposition faced by Constantine IV followed immediately after a major and humiliating defeat at the hands of the Bulgars; and Justinian II's actions point to a sharpened awareness of this relationship as well as to a shift in the place of the military in the rulers' consciousness. It is notable that in this list the provinces are in fact represented by two key groups: on the one hand, the soldiers' and some of their officers; on the other, the metropolitan and suffragan bishops of the church.[124]

This is a striking indication of the central role attributed to soldiers by the emperor at this time and of the lack of any other significant provincial representatives other than the clergy: the latter and the soldiers *were* the provinces and represented provincial opinion. They themselves cannot have remained unaware of this. Not only were soldiers picked out by their special legal status and other privileges; they and their leaders and officers were involved in facing and repelling the incessant raids and attacks of the Arabs. They were the front line of the empire and the Christian world, and some of them knew it: the popular *Apocalypse of Ps.-Methodius* is quite clear that the Romans, with God on their side, will eventually triumph over their enemies—specifically, the Saracens in the east—under the leadership of a new Constantine or Heraclius: "And the king of the Romans will set upon them his yoke which is sevenfold what their yoke was upon the earth . . . And they themselves will be slaves . . . and they will serve those who used to serve them, and their servitude will be a hundred times more bitter and hard."[125] It is no accident that Justinian II's reformed coinage of the early 690s bears an image of Christ on the obverse, with the emperor now on the reverse. Whether or not this emission follows on from the Quinisext and canon 82 (ordaining that Christ should no longer be represented symbolically by a lamb but shown in his incarnate form), and whether or not it was part of a "war of images" between the caliph ʿAbd al-Malik and the emperor Justinian, are debated issues, although as we have seen, the more likely explanation resides in the internal theological politics of the imperial decision to abandon monotheletism and reaffirm a traditional dyothelete creed, and the use of imperial iconography as one element in this message. Coins could certainly have a considerable impact, or at least they were thought by some contemporaries to be so.[126] John of Nikiû noted the rumor that circulated to the effect that "the death of Heraclius is due to his stamping the gold coinage with the figures of the three emperors—that is, his own and of his two sons on the right hand and on the left—and so no room was found for inscribing the name of the Roman empire." Underlining the importance of producing an acceptable coinage and the fact that people who used it noticed what it represented, a near contemporary Syriac chronicle notes that after his election as caliph, Muʿāwiya minted gold and silver coinage, but "it was not accepted, because it had no cross on it."[127] The new issue of Justinian certainly emphasized the close association between emperor, Roman state, and Christ. Coins, even gold coins, were regularly seen by both rural populations and soldiers and represented once again a form of imperial and Roman propaganda and persuasion that penetrated to the heart of society. Indeed, the soldiers continued to receive some payments in gold, and at regular intervals, payments which no doubt served to reinforce their Roman and imperial identity.

The other clearly demarcated groups that deserve mention in this context are monks and the clergy, both in the metropolis as well as in the provinces. We have already had reason to mention the latter in the previous chapter as intermediaries between state, elite, and church, on the one hand, and the mass of the ordinary population, on the other. Along with soldiers, many rural clergy and monks came from relatively humble backgrounds and, to a degree at least and as reflected in canon law legislation and in hagiography, they represented an aspect of ordinary day-to-day culture and social life and offer us a window into the values and mores of ordinary society. As noted in Chapter 2, their presence in the provinces reinforced the idea of a common Christian symbolic universe of ideas and social practice—including the elements of skepticism and doubt already discussed—that was shared across all levels of society.

Monastic communities suffered in the provinces much as did the ordinary population, and there is good evidence for the migration of monks from threatened areas, both those that remained within the empire as well as those that were conquered; the number of monastic houses in Constantinople seems to have declined, although exact figures are difficult to come by; the church clearly saw a problem of monastic discipline in the provinces as well as the capital, as some of the canons of the Quinisext suggest.[128] Yet while members of monastic communities maintained contact with both urban and rural communities and were aware of their concerns, they are more or less absent from the political scene in the period after the 650s and on into the early eighth century. The evidence of hagiography and miracle collections, our main source for these sorts of activities, rarely shows them as representing matters other than the highly local, dealing with illness, offering advice, banishing evil spirits, and praying for souls.[129] The exceptions are those individuals whose particular activities and public statements attracted the attention of the government or the church, such as Maximus the Confessor and his immediate associates, or the monothelete monk Polychronius at the council of 680; or those who through one means or another became associated with the court, such as the monk Menas, involved in the interrogation of Maximus, or the Theodotus who served as general logothete under Justinian II.[130] Nevertheless, it is likely that in the later seventh- and eighth-century context (a rapidly shrinking urban culture and the transformation from a late Roman *polis*-based society to one organized around Old Testament and Christian perceptions of rich and poor, powerful and powerless), monks and monastic communities in fact took on a greater significance as mediators between the secular and spiritual worlds.[131]

The Power of Ideology

Like any other hegemonic ideological system, any other "ruling ideology," the east Roman political order could only function effectively and over the long term if coercive power was embedded in a broader set of relationships, including the law, custom, and religion: it had to function and be seen to function within the framework of what people understood to be the natural order of things, it had to be able to offer plausible explanations of how the world worked. Indeed, belief systems generally serve to legitimate the world as it is perceived and as it functions so that the coercive potential of the state—for example—is in many contexts either invisible or understood only as a potential rather than a real aspect of social and political relationships while social and economic relationships are presented as part of the natural order. Such legitimating systems are not free-floating, of course; they are grounded in the structure of society itself.[132] As far as the evidence permits us to say, the imperial system, represented through what I have termed its political theology, was indeed morally and intellectually hegemonic. The Christian, Roman symbolic universe within which it was itself embedded was both a powerful focus for community- and self-identity across all social divides as well as for representing the empire under the ruler chosen by God as the only imaginable form of polity. Belonging to it and supporting it, actively or not, was the only option. The inhabitants of the Eastern Roman Empire bought into the imperial ideology for two reasons: first, it was the only world and the only polity they could envisage; second, there was, save for those few theologians who could envisage it, no alternative that made sense. And the constant presence of the imperial administration throughout the provinces, embodied in local secular and religious elites and in the imperial armies, permitted both central government and the church to reinforce imperial authority and, where necessary, maintain their control over the provincial populations.

None of this is to suggest that undercurrents and occasionally much more open forms of hostility and opposition to the established social and political order did not exist, as we will see in the next chapter. Nor is it to argue that the vast mass of the rural population of peasants and farmers of one sort or another, quite apart from the poor and those with few means of support in the towns and cities of the empire, enthusiastically embraced the official ideology and leaped to its defense and the defense of the empire. But the empire did represent the world they understood—the world with which they were familiar, within which they had a place and a sense of self, and which embodied their own identity. Like people in all socially stratified societies at all times, therefore, and especially in an age long before nationalism had become part of everyday thinking, it was possible to express dissatisfaction, hostility, and opposition to the established order while also being able to identify with it.[133] However oppressive it might on occasion have appeared to some or possibly all, and particularly under the sort of conditions that prevailed throughout the course of the seventh and early eighth centuries, tacit support or active defense of the empire and all that it stood for was something the imperial government probably took for granted, even if it could not always rely upon it.

The unintentional and unplanned combination of the pervasive presence of the church with the equally pervasive activities of the secular authority (military and fiscal arrangements) reinforced and underlined the consolidation of an identity of Roman and imperial, Christian and orthodox, different from and thus inimical to "barbarian" ways and beliefs. Already from the sixth century the official recognition accorded bishops—generally members of the social elite in any case—in the running of their cities, in which they cooperated or collaborated with the local gentry, had secured them a position in society at large that tended toward the blending of secular and ecclesiastical authority.[134] The increasing overlaps and intersecting of secular with canon law promoted what was in effect an identity of state with church and church with state. The east Roman state became a sacred state, ruled by a God-appointed emperor under divine protection. The sacralization of the empire had been effected by the year 700 and was confirmed in the *Ecloga* of Leo and Constantine. The evidence reviewed in this and the previous chapter leaves no doubt. It can be inferred from the ways in which ordinary people were concerned about the interpretation of biblical texts, along with the influence the church wielded at all social levels; or the ways in which soldiers, among others, reacted to questions of belief: we have already seen some examples. It can be observed reflected in the ways the government and court expressed their concerns regarding the opposition led by Martin and Maximus, as we have seen. It was reflected in the blending of secular and ecclesiastical law—indeed, as we have seen, in the *Ecloga* the empire is a Christian empire rather than a Roman one.[135] And it was reflected in the symbolism of the Cross and the close association between emperor, orthodoxy, the leadership of the church, and popular conceptions of divinely approved imperial victory. Perhaps most of these features were already present in various forms before this. But the conditions and developments of the second half of the seventh century brought them together and articulated them in a particular configuration and with the specific results that we see.

The impact of the clergy, at least the senior clergy, in the provincial cities of the empire is reflected in letters written in the later 720s and 730s to two provincial bishops on the issue of the devotion shown to sacred images in churches, with the patriarch's urgent request to them not to say or do anything that might cause confusion among the lay populace. In the later letter, written in the 730s to the bishop Thomas of Klaudioupolis, the patriarch Germanus is anxious that Christians should not become confused by theological sophistry and insists that unbelievers should not be given the opportunity to slander the church. In a clearly marked emphasis on the differences between Roman

Christians and others, he lists the ignorance of both Jews and Muslims in this respect and asserts that there can be no community of interest between Christians and such idol worshippers. And whatever Germanus's reservations in the 720s or the opposition and criticism voiced by Maximus the Confessor and Pope Martin in the 640s and 650s, the church as a whole accepted imperial policy with little dissent and no effective opposition within the bounds of the Roman state itself.[136]

Where the church preached, so the community generally followed, whatever dissenting undercurrents may also have subsisted. It is not without significance that John of Damascus notes in his "second sermon against the iconoclasts," written probably shortly before 754, that already the church—and thus the population of the empire—had more or less entirely followed the imperial line.[137] The position of churchmen may have been that the ordinary population of the empire was often naive in matters of theology. This is implied by Germanus in his letter to Constantine of Nakoleia. It is made equally clear by Anastasius of Sinai in his answers to questions about theological debate and devotional practice, where he is careful to emphasize the importance for the ordinary Christian of leading a godly and pious life to the best of their ability according to their circumstances and to avoid becoming enmeshed in theological debate beyond their abilities. But this did not stop people being concerned with matters of dogma, because their own health and happiness as well as that of the empire depended upon matters of correct belief. There was probably a substantial difference between the reception and awareness of official doctrine in towns and cities and other larger settlements, on the one hand, and in the rural hinterlands, on the other, where the bulk of the population were to be found. But we have virtually no evidence as to how such differences presented themselves and, if the suggestion is correct that soldiers now reflected some at least of the attitudes and beliefs of a good part of the provincial populations, the difference may not have been as great as might otherwise be assumed.[138]

4

Elites and Interests

Philippikos . . . decided to make on the Saturday of Pentecost an entry on horseback, to bathe in the public baths of Zeuxippos and to lunch with citizens of ancient lineage.[1]

Elite Interests

As I noted in the Introduction, a key role in the process of transformation and survival of the east Roman state must be ascribed to the social and political elite in all its various shades and manifestations—provincial local gentry, both secular and ecclesiastical; senatorial elite; the powerful "establishment" clans; and individuals who dominated central government and the imperial court. In this chapter I will look more closely at how this aspect of east Roman state and society worked. These people constituted the administrative and military apparatus that served the interests of the state. But they also needed to be paid or rewarded in such a way and by such means as would secure their loyalty as well as the effectiveness and cohesion of the institutions and bureaucracy they represented. State salaries and privileges, which increased in quantity, scope, and esteem with rank, title, and proximity to court and emperor, were a key ingredient in securing such loyalty. They were seen as desirable objectives of social and political competition in themselves. So long as the state was present, actually or potentially, to defend elite interests—land, property, office, and status—its survival was perceived as an essential prerequisite for the survival of the members of its apparatus and of the elite more widely. But while the east Roman state was undoubtedly understood as essential to the fortune of individual members of the elite, it was largely and understandably taken for granted, so what we might perceive as short-sighted internecine conflict was not obviously understood as a threat to the empire's continued existence. Political and military opposition in the regions distant from the capital, as expressed in the rebellions of the exarch Gregory in North Africa in 647, or of Olympius in Italy in 651, should be seen not as deliberately tending toward political and military autonomy but much more as reflecting both local disquiet about lack of imperial military support (or about imperial fiscal oppression) as well as a desire to respect and respond to local religious ideological sentiment and politics. In this case, the belief that the key to salvation lay in adherence to the established Chalcedonian orthodoxy promoted by men such as Maximus and Pope Martin was a clear reflection of the strength of such sentiment.

Somewhat simplistically stated, members of the late Roman elite tended to belong, according to our sources, to one or another of two categories.[2] First, there are those who had an international, multiprovincial aspect to their property or who filled the highest civil and military offices, who dominated in the imperial court and administration at Constantinople, most of whom were regularly transferred from post to post and region to region according to imperial requirements. From their ranks was drawn the "power elite." This was a select, oligarchic group, constantly shifting in its composition, that dominated at court and filled or controlled admission to the key palatine posts—the senior military commanders; praetorian prefects; and chief judicial, fiscal, and administrative officers: the men (for they were all men) who ran the empire from the top and worked directly in association with the ruler.[3] Many were insiders, benefiting from their parents' privilege and situation, inherited wealth and education; but just as many were outsiders—military commanders and soldiers whose talent and skill won them recognition, high-ranking foreigners who entered the imperial system at a senior level, reflecting their background; while others came from the provinces and had been able, through patronage and networking, to improve their lot.[4]

This last group represented one element of a second, much larger body of individuals and families that constituted the late Roman elite in the provinces, internally more diverse both in respect of wealth and property as well as in respect of status, people who represented the "gentry" in each province, in provincial administration at all levels, and on the councils of their cities. The elite as a whole thus had a cellular aspect—individuals belonged to overlapping or intersecting interest-groups at city, local territory, regional, and provincial levels. For the great majority of those in this second stratum, their influence and their standing were confined largely to their own regions, and it was this lo-calized middle stratum of landowners in the provinces of the empire that comprised the leading members of society in their cities or regions, and supplied the personnel from whom provincial governors and impe-rial *curatores* appointed fiscal and managerial officials. In Italy and North Africa from the later sixth century, this body also provided many—perhaps the majority—of local subaltern military officers and officials.[5] But as we have also noted, members of this broader provincial elite could also rise to join the first group and achieve the highest imperial posi-tions and offices. They thus joined a broader circle of connections and associations and extended their interests and connections across to the capital and the imperial court. The two groups were not exclusive, and while they were no doubt aware of their social status and identity vis-à-vis those above or below them, this did not translate into any sort of "class" awareness, except perhaps at a highly local and personalized level and in respect of their immediate circle—the other members of the *curia*, or governing council, of a city, for example, with whom they might be connected through networks of patronage and friendship also. Family and kinship connections far outweighed most other associations, with the exception of ties to the imperial court and household.[6]

The role of members of the old senatorial establishment in the provinces—most of whom held high imperial office or titles of one sort or another—was one important facet of the glue that held the empire together, for it was in the interests of the government to support the eco-nomic structures from which the elite benefited and thus through which their loyalty as well as their fiscal contributions to the maintenance of the state were secured, while it was in the interests of the members of the elite to participate in and contribute to the system that ensured their status and privilege. Many exploited their lands through bailiffs and managers as absentee landlords, in which their most important pur-pose was to optimize the income from rents. Just as important were those individuals—sometimes the same people—who were able to obtain appointments as *curatores* or senior managers of imperial estates, positions they could use to expand their own wealth and to swallow up neighboring properties through intimidation as well as more legal methods. The imperial household possessed vast estates—in southern Thrace, Egypt, Syria, Phoenice, Mesopotamia, Anatolia, and Greece as well as in North Africa, Italy, and Dalmatia[7]—the rents from which contributed to the upkeep of the imperial household as well as the fisc. The middle-ranking managers of imperial estates were, like their superiors, able to exploit their position to their own advantage, and many similarly maintained private estate militias.[8] Estate lands were leased out to tenants of varying means and status, ranging from smaller local and provincial, non-Constantinopolitan landowners to farmers of yet humbler status.[9]

A novel of the emperor Justin II in 569 makes it clear that many officials of the provincial administration as well as those of the central fisc were members of the local landed elite; indeed, provincial governors were thenceforth to be appointed by the choice of the landowners and bishops of the provinces.[10] A combination of the impact of the plague of the 540s on the availability of labor power, consequent shortages of labor on private and ecclesiastical estates, and the fiscal needs of the state in turn meant that the identity of the interests of the state with those of provincial elites and the church as landlord was further reinforced.[11] It was the fact of state service, in whatever form, that facilitated an improvement in, or a confirmation of, status and position. This was true throughout the empire, whether in Egypt, Syria, Anatolia, North Africa, or Italy. It remained the case thereafter, as can very clearly be seen in the exarchate of Ravenna. In the cases of both North Africa and Italy, however, only recently reincorporated into the empire, a combination of strong local identities and cultural traditions with an equally powerful concern in Constantinople for the security of imperial interests meant that senior officials were largely appointed from outside (in light of their record as loyal servants of the emperors), while very few locals extended their ambitions to achieve posts in the imperial court or elsewhere in the empire.[12]

This meant that the vested interests of this middling stratum of the provincial elite, while focused on the imperial system and the court on the one hand, were also focused on their home territories and their local power, for it was imperial service in the provinces that gave them admittance to the imperial court and the system it embodied. With the vast losses of territory incurred by the state and the accompanying damage inflicted on the property and sources of wealth of the highest level of the senatorial establishment in the course of the seventh century, the remaining provinces and their local elites—the strata from which both the older curial elite had been drawn as well as the most prominent provincial magnates—became far more important than hitherto to the survival of the empire, and hence even more closely bound to the capital and the imperial system. It remains unfortunately the case, nevertheless, that we do not have the sort of textual or literary evidence for the attitudes and values of this Anatolian elite that we have for the Gallic elite in the fifth century, in the letters of Sidonius Apollinaris, for example. The situation, both politically and culturally, was very different, so it is difficult even to employ this earlier resource comparatively for the seventh-century Antolian world.[13] Yet certain elements were to be found in common—epigraphic and other evidence for pious donations to churches and for the support of the clergy from local elites (as well as humbler persons), for example, indicate the common Christian inheritance shared across the centuries and indicate one form of cultural investment found throughout the empire and beyond.[14]

The advantages an individual had over both local landlords and peasantry if he occupied a position of military or civil authority in the provinces were considerable—a monopoly of armed force, for example, the power to seize or confiscate food or other produce for the army, and so on. Persons appointed to such posts had every opportunity to further their own interests if they desired. While we can only guess at the process for Anatolia, once again the better-documented situation in Italy offers useful comparisons for the later sixth and seventh centuries, where the senatorial elite was whittled down through losses in land, personnel (through death or migration to Constantinople, for example), and low birth rate as well as loss of authority and prestige in competition with officials and more powerful or influential nonsenatorial neighbors. As we have said, of course, Italy was not Anatolia, and there must have been significant variations that we can no longer identify. Yet the effects of a combination of warfare, economic dislocation, disease, and competition from office holders and the patronage they were able to exercise on behalf of their own clients, all of which were present in Anatolia, can hardly have been very different.[15] The *Ecloga*, for example, repeats and summarizes the Justinianic legislation about the activities of the managers and bailiffs of ecclesiastical, monastic, and imperial estates in the provinces or their subordinate administrators (*chartoularioi* and *dioikētai*).[16]

A major outcome of such developments was a partial militarization of provincial society and the evolution of a very different ruling elite. In the context of imperial efforts to maintain an effective defense and mobilize the necessary resources, this process had already contributed to a further diminution of the social and economic importance of the Italian senatorial elite.[17] There is no doubt that a similar process took place throughout the surviving territories of the empire.

Toward a New Elite: Continuities and Contingency

The evidence for these changes can be perceived in several developments. While service in the bureaucracy of the eastern part of the Roman Empire undoubtedly served to assimilate disparate provincial elites into the imperial system, there remained cultural and factional divisions, and there had since the fifth century at least existed a tension between the interests and concerns of the senatorial as opposed to the palatine elements of the elite at Constantinople.[18] Until the period of Justinian's reforms in the 530s, the bureaucracy in the east, with its distinctive mode of administrative practice and "professional" culture, had possessed a degree of relative autonomy from the court. But Justinian challenged this tradition, reinforcing the emperor's control of the central bureaucracy both practically and symbolically.[19] Administrative departments were largely enclosed within the imperial palace and were thus subject to direct oversight, while palatine ceremony and ritual drew the members of the various bureaus directly into the symbolic world of the court. At the same time this provided the emperor with a means of managing both potential opposition and factionalism within the system.[20] The developments of the later seventh century furthered this tendency toward imperial oversight and control, and under the pressures of the political as well as social demands of the times, the palatine establishment became increasingly dominant. The established hierarchy of senatorial dignities and titles (the *clarissimi*, the *spectabiles*, and the *illustres*) gradually dropped out of use, and only the leading category of the *illustres* group, referred to as *gloriosi* (*endoxos*, or *endoxotatos* in Greek) retained any significance after the later seventh century.[21] Titles that no longer corresponded to power-political realities became irrelevant, disappearing entirely or being fossilized at a lower level of the system of ranks and status.

By the end of the seventh century a restructuring of the whole system of titles and precedence was in train, in which the importance of titles and posts dependent directly upon imperial service in the palace and at court increased, to the disadvantage of older titles associated in one way or another with the senatorial order. There was a series of overlaps across the seventh and eighth centuries, but the general pattern is very apparent. Power was concentrated and focused more than ever before on the figure of the emperor and in the palace, radiating into the provinces in the form of imperial officials of all kinds and ranks. The older, more pluralistic system of rank, privilege, wealth, and power was transformed.[22] In short, the reconfiguration of the system of precedence indicates that the conditions of the times were having a solvent effect on the established hierarchy of privilege and rank. Even before the major changes of the later sixth and seventh centuries, service in the military had been a major—the major—channel of social advancement. The conditions of the middle and later years of the seventh century can only have enhanced and facilitated this tendency.[23]

The political and military challenges faced by the emperors and their advisors encouraged the need both to appoint competent and able persons to positions of military and political authority as well as to move such persons around to carry out functions the emperors deemed necessary. Prosopographical analysis of senior military officials in the seventh and eighth centuries shows that the government was able to rotate many individuals from post to post and from region to region after fairly short periods in each position.[24] In a highly patrimonial context, where personal connections and associations with those in positions of power were especially vital, this promoted a shifting and fluid bureaucratic-military establishment. Individual insecurity in such contexts is often high, promoting both maximum exploitation of the possibilities open to the officeholder during their period of tenure, and inhibiting the tendency toward the building of factions and cliques intended to secure the fortunes of particular—constantly fluctuating—groups of individuals at court and in the provinces. Ever greater competition between post-holders and an intensification of the exploitation of offices promoted increasing dependence on the personal favor of the ruler.[25] The

more insecure the members of the state establishment, the more secure
the ruler, who thus maximized the dependency of office holders and
senior personnel upon his goodwill, at least potentially. Naturally, this
could also work to his disadvantage—a fine balance was necessary,
between pushing too many of the leading elements of the elite too far
into insecurity and causing anxiety for their positions and physical
safety. The reign of Justinian II provides some useful illustrations.[26]

The imperial court was the focus of the state's administrative apparatus and consisted of several associated elements. Justinian I had
introduced a major reform of the senate, reaffirming its role as the
curia or *boulē* (city council) of the capital. From that time, the senate had
consisted chiefly of the leading officials of state, retired as well as active, and all persons of *illustris* rank (the highest grade of senator) in the
territory of the city of Constantinople itself. The senior officials who
managed the daily business of government comprised a select group
of civil and military administrators. Most of these also belonged to the
so-called consistory (which might also include individuals with no
official position but whom the emperor chose to include), from among
whom an even more select group might meet more frequently with the
emperor to make policy or deal with a specific problem. From the early
seventh century the highest-ranking members of the senatorial order
were those with the title of *patricius,* including the urban prefect of Constantinople, followed by consuls *(hypatoi),* proconsuls *(anthypatoi)* and ex-
consuls *(apo hypatōn),* praetorian prefects, *magistri militum,* and other *illustres.*[27] The *sacellarius* (manager of the imperial privy purse, or *sacella,*
with oversight of the central fiscal departments)[28] also figured among
the leading senators: at the trials and interrogations of Pope Martin in
Constantinople in 653, for example, he is mentioned as the highest-
ranking of the senators along with the urban prefect.[29] We no longer
hear of the consistory by this time, but it is clear that a select group of
senior officials of senatorial status made up the chief governing body
with the emperor at Constantinople. This group included also all those
senior officials with major imperial appointments in the provinces,
including both military commanders and officials such as the *curatores* of
the imperial estates already mentioned—the "power elite" to which I
referred earlier in this chapter.

Many members of the establishment survived and prospered because
their property had been based largely in the metropolitan area, in and

around the capital, or because such properties in the provinces had been preserved.[30] Many were members of the senate, a body that seems during the seventh century in particular to have taken an increasingly active role in government affairs and policymaking decisions. The high profile of the senate, in particular during the reign of Constans II, who acceded to the throne at the age of eleven years, was surely a reflection of the increased dependency of the young emperor on the ruling elite in the capital, and we have some indication in this case of who some of his leading advisors and policymakers are likely to have been: in his first year or so, the *sakellarios* Philagrius and the general Valentinus; later the *koubikoularios* Andreas and the general Theodore of Koloneia.[31] Yet, paradoxically, across the second half of the seventh and into the eighth century the status of all but the highest grades (*hypatos, anthypatos, apo hypatōn*) associated with the senate was reduced. The gradual loss of status of many senatorial grades clearly indicates the declining importance of the order as such and hence of the social elite that it had represented.[32]

True, not all these metropolitan families will have escaped entirely from either enemy depredations or internecine strife—as when, for example, troops under the Armenian general Valentinus attacked the gardens and vineyards of Constantinopolitans located around Chalcedon on the Asian side of the Bosphorus in 642.[33] And the process was not overnight. The wars of the first half of the seventh century and the persecution of certain members of the Constantinopolitan elite under Phocas must have had some impact, although exactly what this meant in terms of numbers is not clear. Yet they were relatively untouched when compared with the loss of lands and property of those who hailed from the conquered provinces on the one hand or those whose estates had been subjected to the raids and attacks inflicted on provinces such as Cappadocia or Isauria, Pamphylia or Pisidia. The warfare of the second half of the seventh century must have done a great deal of damage to elite interests in the provinces, especially in the years 662–678 and then again in the 690s and afterward, when Anatolia was raided annually, and usually by several different armies. It is unfortunate that for the provincial elite there is no evidence relating to the fortunes of named individuals in this respect. But we may usefully compare their fate with that of members of the Roman elite in the fifth-century west, such as Paulinus of Pella, for example, whose property in southern Gaul was destroyed by Visigothic federates in factional conflict with the Roman authorities and who was reduced to poverty thereafter.[34]

The evidence is, yet again, sparse but indicative of some considerable continuity at Constantinople. In 676/677 a certain John Pitzigaudes was sent by Constantine IV to conduct delicate negotiations with the caliph Muʿāwiya. John is described by the source used by the chronographer Theophanes as "the *patrikios* John, surnamed Pitzigaudes, a man of ancient lineage in the state and possessed of much experience and excellent judgement." It may not be clear what "ancient lineage" really means, but it certainly implies an old and established family with roots perhaps going back at least into the sixth century. It is a term that recurs: Philippicus Bardanes is reported to have dined with "citizens of ancient lineage," suggesting at the least that there was some awareness of who the older families in Constantinople might have been.[35] Theophanes also remarks on the oppressive fiscal demands made during the reign of Justinian II of highly placed persons and of confiscations of land and property.[36] Occasional glimpses of individual members of the older elite are afforded by our limited sources. Thus, Nicephorus, the father of the usurper Philippicus Bardanes, was a *patrikios* and may possibly be identified with the *patrikios* and general of the same name who commanded an army under Constans II in 667;[37] the *patrikios* Justinian, father of the patriarch Germanus, was involved in the rebellion of Mizizius in Sicily in 668 and appears to have been a member of the established senatorial elite and very possibly related to the family of the emperor Justinian I;[38] the *patrikios* and prefect of the city Troilus appears to have been a member of this same established elite group, as do the brothers Theodore and Euprepius, sons of a wealthy patrician Plutinus and supporters of the antimonothelete position in the late 640s.[39]

The senate, or its leading members (all men of high rank and office), came into its own when it intervened in order to maintain political stability at Constantinople and to uphold imperial policy when no effective emperor occupied the throne. This was particularly the case at times during the later sixth and especially during the seventh century when the sources record a direct involvement of the senate in the appointment or deposition of a ruler, all during moments of political uncertainty: at the accession of Phocas in 602, that of Heraclius in 610, during the tensions surrounding the succession to Heraclius in 641–642, in the revolt against Justinian II in 695, at the deposition of Philippicus Bardanes in

713 and the accession of Anastasius II, and again in 717 at the abdication of Theodosius III and accession of Leo III. The senate was prominent in supporting or leading government at times during the reigns of Heraclius, Constans II, Constantine IV, and Philippicus Bardanes.

These aspects of elite continuity can also be traced through the higher echelons of the church, for example, although it is impossible to follow the appearance of "new men" on account of the adoption of an appropriate Christian name by most of those who had progressed to senior ecclesiastical rank—bishop or beyond. Thus, of 135 signatories from the patriarchate of Constantinople at the final session of the council of 680, and 183 at that of 691/692, only one is "foreign"—the (probably) Frankish Segermas, bishop of Horkistos in Galatia II, at the council of 691/692.[40] Yet this would certainly accord with the fact that the decline in provincial municipal culture and the concentration of resources (including educational resources) in Constantinople meant that the church henceforth provided one of the most stable environments for the continued influence of the cultural inheritance of the traditional social elite. The structures of provincial urban culture that had supported secular literary activity were, with a very few exceptions, no longer there; and it is worth noting that in terms of literary production, it is precisely in the realms of the church and theology, which encompassed an enormous variety of genres and subtypes of literature (ranging from popular apocalypses to theological commentaries on causation, and from miracle collections and hagiography to Christology), that the emphasis is found after the middle of the seventh century and until well into the eighth.[41] In the context of the later seventh and early eighth centuries, it seems to have been the educated members of the old establishment who provided the church with the literacy, learning, and cultural capital it needed to maintain this tradition, and provided the central administration in the palace with the bureaucratic know-how and literacy to manage the state. But while its survival in and around Constantinople seems clear, it was an element in society more broadly that seems no longer to have dominated in the way it had previously.[42]

So who were the people who made up the new elite, and just how new was it? Although the evidence for its changing composition and character is fragmentary, its members seem by the end of the century to have been drawn from four intersecting pools. First, we have that group of individuals and families who belonged to the "old" establishment, as we have just seen. They will have overlapped to a degree with the second group, those men who came from among the provincial elites in the lost eastern provinces. As we saw, the property and estates from which derived the wealth of a large proportion of the highest-ranking and wealthiest members of the established elite were no longer within the empire. If they had not accepted the new regimes in the conquered territories of the East or in the Balkans, such men seem largely to have fled, many of them probably losing much of their former wealth as a consequence.[43] We cannot know for lack of evidence how many wealthy or influential persons from Syria left for imperial territory, for example, but the evidence does suggest that quite a few important persons from the Syrian provinces ended up at court or on imperial territory and survived by virtue of service within the imperial system. This was but one aspect of a wider movement—the flight of people from Greater Syria to Anatolia, Constantinople, or beyond, to Africa, Italy and to Rome, is a recognized feature of the period. They included, for example, nuns from Palestine and Egypt who removed to North Africa during the 640s.[44] Better known are the popes or senior clergy who stand out in the second half of the seventh century: Theodore of Tarsus (archbishop of Canterbury 668–690),[45] for example; Sergius (687–701), born in Sicily, but whose Syrian father, Tiberios, hailed from Antioch;[46] John V (685–686), also from the region of Antioch;[47] Sisinnius (708);[48] Constantine (708–715);[49] and Gregory III (731–741).[50] Sergius and John V also had connections with the Syrian monastery of St Saba at Rome.[51] In the period 685 to 688 Antioch in Syria was again in imperial hands as the emperor Constantine IV exploited the situation within the caliphate to push against Mopsuestia and beyond, and its loss thereafter may well have set off a further wave of refugees, especially among those members of the regional elite who had welcomed the return of imperial authority.[52]

A few other individuals who clearly hailed from a Syrian background can be singled out in the imperial administration or in the eastern church: the patriarch Anastasius, appointed by Leo III after the abdication of Germanus in 730, was apparently of Syrian origin, had no obvious association with Rome, and may represent those who had arrived originally as refugees.[53] In the secular and administrative establishment of the empire, one or two figures are known. Thus, George "the Syrian," *patrikios* and general logothete in 711, held high office and in a post that required literacy and a good education.[54] Similarly Isoes, *patrikios* and *komēs tou Opsikiou* (commander of the field army stationed near Constantinople) in the year 718, bears a Syrian name (Ishō) and was probably the son of refugees of some status and influence.[55] He is likely the same man as the owner of a seal of Isoes, *patrikios* and *kuaistōr* (quaestor), on a seal of the same period, that may represent an earlier stage of his career (given the relative scarcity of this name in the Byzantine sources). The position of quaestor was one of the most important palatine offices and required a familiarity with the law and a high degree of literacy, so Isoes must have been a man of some education.[56] Both men reached the highest levels of the palatine system and their example suggests the ways in which elements of provincial elites could penetrate to the heart of the empire.

Other groups were also present. Already in the late sixth century members of the Armenian nobility had become prominent in the eastern Roman world, most especially in the military. Many leading commanders were drawn from their ranks, and they were frequently accompanied by their own personal armed retinues.[57] This increased their value to Constantinople because of their practical experience as well as their local contacts. Their numbers increased in the course of the second half of the seventh century, as has been widely recognized—an illustration of the tendency for the imperial government to rely on skilled senior men of "provincial" origin. And while Armenians are especially prominent in our sources, other non-Romans also played a role—Turkic, Slavic, Iranian, and Semitic names begin to appear in greater numbers than hitherto in chronicles, histories, and on lead seals.[58] The *patrikios* Sisinnius Rhendaci(u)s, a senior confidant of the emperor Artemius, bore a Slavic name and is representative of these high-ranking newcomers to the establishment.[59] Similarly, there were senior military commanders who had been transferred from duties (and homeland) in the West to serve in the East. Such were surely at least two generals with obviously Western names—Florus and Cyprianus—who, along with a third commander, Petronas, appeared in command of a victorious Roman force in Anatolia in 673. Their case illustrates also the point made earlier about the transferability of senior personnel across the breadth of the empire to meet imperial needs.[60]

The third group that we can identify consists of persons of higher status in provincial society, landowners with possessions in both town and country in Anatolia as well as elsewhere. Whether or not they had obtained senatorial rank, families from a curial background—those whose official status classed them as eligible for the *curia* or governing council of their city—made up the majority of landowners in their urban territories. They represented for the most part a well-established local elite, even if the financial independence of some could be threatened with absorption (for example, through indebtedness) into the estates of bigger landowners in their locality (including imperial estates), especially where a more powerful neighbor might have been able to acquire fiscal exemptions.[61] Hardly anything is known of the provincial elite outside areas that are relatively well documented, such as Egypt or Italy, and we have even fewer sources to tell us about this group after the sixth century. Only in the case of the clergy, especially the episcopate, do we have some indication of their local importance and role in society. But it is very probable that many of the important "new" families or individuals of uncertain background who come to dominate the army and civil administration of the empire from the later seventh century came from this context, relatively well-off families rooted in provincial administrative traditions, who had remained invisible in the sources of the preceding centuries.[62]

In the peculiar conditions of the middle years of the seventh century, in particular, as armies began to be permanently settled across the provinces of Anatolia, it would undoubtedly have been sensible for members of those local elites whose provinces were most affected to associate themselves closely with the military. No doubt the militarization of elites was greatest in those regions most affected by warfare and the presence of soldiers, and there must likewise have been regions where the process was much less developed. A similar process has been remarked for the provinces of the western empire during the fifth century, as well as in later sixth and seventh-century Italy although, while there are important similarities, we should not draw too close a comparison, given the different conditions of, say, late Roman Gaul, largely occupied either under treaty or by conquest by "barbarian" groups, and Anatolia, subjected to economic dislocation and warfare but never occupied.[63]

Nevertheless, association with the military was both a source of power, authority, and access to the government at Constantinople as well as a means of protecting local interests and promoting those of family, kin, and clients. The family of the later eighth-century patriarch Tarasius, born ca. 730–740 in Constantinople, may be indicative. Tarasius's paternal grandfather, Sisinnius, had been a *komēs* of the *Exkoubita* (commander of an imperial guards unit),[64] his maternal grandfather was a *patrikios* also, and both sides of the family are reported to have come from a line of *patrikioi* largely associated with military positions. His father, George, became a quaestor, one of the leading judicial officials in Constantinople, and his brother, also named Sisinnius, was a high-ranking military officer. The limited evidence indicates with little doubt that the family was originally from Isauria or the immediately neighboring provinces (Tarasius is a name closely associated with Isauria), clearly of provincial origin, and clearly associated closely with the military, through which they were probably able to improve their fortunes.[65]

In the mid-seventh century Theodore of Koloneia appears as a high-ranking military commander in the 650s, and later an important senior and influential figure at court. His epithet, "of Koloneia," indicates a provincial origin, possibly Armenian, although this is again by no means certain.[66] Daniel of Sinope, *patrikios* and prefect of Constantinople, dispatched by the emperor Anastasius II on a diplomatic mission to Damascus in 714, may be of similar background.[67] Similarly representative may have been the future emperor Leo III, whose family was transferred from Syria (although probably of Isaurian origin) during the first reign of Justinian II (685–695) to Mesembria in Thrace. Leo seems to have prospered sufficiently to donate a flock of five hundred sheep to the emperor, in return for which he was given the rank (and possibly also the function) of *spatharios,* from which position he was then able to advance his career at court and through active military and diplomatic service. The reliability of all the details of this tale, including his mission to the Caucasus region (and there are variations) is questionable, but the outline of the story likely reflects one plausible and recognized means of advancing a career and the fortunes of a provincial family that had hitherto no direct association with the court and was of modest means.[68] By the same token, the *Life* of St. Philaretos, a Paphlagonian landowner born at the beginning of the eighth century whose estates are described in the hagiography as being very extensive, may also be representative of such middling elite provincials. The *Life* itself, written in the 820s, is to a degree invention and follows classical models. Yet the details of Philaretos's property and flocks may again be taken to reflect a recognizable reality for the times, and again reveals a little about the provincials at whose existence our other sources only hint.[69]

The lack of precision and the absence of specifics about most of the people mentioned in the sources makes it in most cases impossible to be certain. Yet there is the faint outline of a trend. And it is entirely possible that the distinction between these groups was far less clear and that there were far more overlaps between them than we can say. This is the best we can do with the limited evidence at our disposal, and the general picture fits the overall framework. But there is a vast mass of sigillographic evidence for provincial military careers, for example, with men rising through a series of steps, from relatively humble positions such as *komes* to more elevated ranks such as those of *drouggarios* or *tourmarchēs*. Some of these can be shown to have continued to advance to even higher rank and status; a greater number probably moved only a relatively short distance in status over their lifetimes, although the lack of specificity makes it very difficult in most cases, although not all, to trace continuity across an individual's career. Nevertheless, the existence of the considerable body of sigillographic material from the seventh into the later eighth century illustrates the fact that there was a substantial number of these middle-ranking provincial officers and officials who most probably came from the middling to lower levels of the provincial elite.[70]

The broad direction of the tendencies outlined so far is illustrated by a number of indications. The shifting pattern of personal names of those at the top as well as those occupying key positions in the provinces suggests that the composition of both the senate in Constantinople and of the power elite, the people who actually ran the empire at Constantinople, began to change, especially from the middle decades of the seventh century. There had always been a place for "newcomers" under imperial patronage in the state establishment during the later Roman period, and it is likely that it was now primarily people from the Anatolian territories of the empire, of whatever social background, who came to dominate the imperial bureaucracy at court, and certainly in the provinces. While caution is necessary in evaluating the evidence of names and naming patterns, the number of non-Greek names of officials who appear in the sources is very striking from the 660s and after, suggesting that there took place a significant shift in the cultural and social origins of key personnel in the imperial establishment at all levels, many of whom may well have belonged to refugee groups who had resettled within the empire north of the Taurus mountains.[71]

A final group, although only very dimly discernible in the sources, is represented by individuals who had risen from much humbler social origins, often through becoming members of the retinue of an important person. One or two are mentioned in the narrative sources from time to time, although we have no clear examples from this period, and it may be that some of the hundreds of seals of imperial officials were issued by people such as this. Theophanes implies, very indirectly, that the logothete of the general treasury, Theodotus, during the first reign of Justinian II, formerly a monk and hermit, was of humble origins, although this is not certain.[72] Vertical mobility was not an unusual feature of eastern Roman society, even if constrained structurally by the strong socioeconomic divisions that existed, and as we have seen the potential for upward mobility was increased in a context where warfare and the military came to dominate.

The possibilities were further enhanced because the absolute authority of the emperor at court made palatine service at once both highly desirable and remunerative as well as insecure and potentially dangerous, while at the same time the consequences of the universal patron–client relationships that permeated society always left upward channels of access open. Personal service on an individual powerful person and proximity to him or to her on a day-to-day basis—whether this was a member of the provincial elite, of the imperial court, or the rulers themselves—could mean promotion and upward mobility.[73] Thus the imperial *chartoularios* Paul, for example, Leo III's senior chancery official, was sent to Sicily in the year 717/718 to deal with the usurpation of Basil Onomagoulus (Tiberius III) and promoted directly to *patrikios* and *stratēgos*, or military commander, of Sicily.[74] Whether Paul came from this social background is not known, of course. And there is really no evidence to identify such people from the humblest levels of society, although neither can there be much doubt that it was possible to rise from relatively lowly status to high rank.[75] It is likely as well that some of the lead seals of military and possibly also fiscal officials from the provinces belonged to people from this sort of background. As we have seen, there is a great deal of evidence from lead seals for movement from lower to more senior military ranks in the provinces. While a number of such individuals did go on to achieve even higher rank and status, the evidence nevertheless reflects the fact that most middle-ranking provincial officers likely came from these lower-elite strata.

The nature of the changing elite in the core regions of the empire, dimly discernible though it is, does seem to differ in some respects from those in more distant regions, especially Italy and Africa. In Anatolia, the admittedly very slender evidence suggests some degree of access to the higher positions for those from the middling levels of provincial society, for example. The higher stratum of imperial officials and military commanders is the most prominent, mentioned individually by name in the sources and sometimes traceable also in the sigillographic record. And while the vast mass of imperial provincial officials, known almost entirely through their lead seals, remains otherwise silent, there does seem to have been some interpenetration of the two groups.

In contrast, in both Italy and North Africa there appears to have been a relatively clear distinction between the "imperial" elite of high-ranking officers appointed largely from outside their province or region and the remaining members of the military, predominantly local men commanding local units. The conditions that led to this development were by no means the same in both regions, but in both cases there was little crossover between the two, with individuals within the former group more frequently moved or transferred, to be found in the course of their careers in several very different commands or geographical situations. So in these more distant regions we are faced with a two-level system, with the troops and the lower and middle-ranking officers or officials drawn almost entirely from local society, while the higher-ranking individuals came from the cosmopolitan, "imperial" class of functionaries. For North Africa, for example, it seems clear that while the reconquest meant the arrival of a considerable number of eastern officials, very few Africans were employed in the east or at court. Movement from the level of provincial magnate or official into the senior ranks of the imperial service elite was limited, and even more so in respect of access to the imperial court itself.[76] This contrast between the core regions and the periphery—North Africa and Sicily—may well have been another factor influencing the loyalties and political choices of elites in different areas of the empire to Constantinople.

To summarize, the shrinkage of the empire territorially, the centralization of fiscal administration, and the effective disappearance of cities as social and economic intermediaries between the provinces and Constantinople all played a role in the shift in emphasis in elite culture and in the composition of those who ran the east Roman state. Imperial focus from the middle years of the seventh century on the immediate hinterland of the capital, Anatolia, may have encouraged a further re- gionalization or localization of society and administration in the more distant regions. New networks of power and patronage between capital and provinces and within the provinces evolved. Yet all this can also be seen as another key factor that in fact contributed toward the resilience that permitted the Byzantine world to confront the problems it faced and to survive.

Social Conflict: Resistance, Coercion, Collaboration

So far, then, we have reviewed a good deal of evidence for the various ways in which the populations of the empire—provincials, members of elites, the church, and monks—shared or did not share their views of the world and the particular developments that marked the seventh century, and for how they responded to the challenges they perceived. We can now return to the questions posed in Chapters 2 and 3, about the extent to which the vast mass of the "ordinary" population of the empire—in particular the farmers, peasants, pastoralists, and towns- people in the provinces—shared in the Roman imperial world repre- sented by the government at Constantinople and its administration, by the law, and by the church. To what extent did they identify themselves and their interests and concerns with those of the state? And to what extent were their actions a reflection of such a common or shared iden- tity of interests?

The first thing to be said is that, when faced with the overwhelming presence of non-Roman forces, the provincial population generally submitted—this applies as much to the population of Syria during the early conquests as it does to the population of provincial Anatolia in 654 or 715–716, for example, or to the rural inhabitants of southern Italy when faced with the constant harassment of Lombard raids and devastation. As noted in Chapter 3, the numbers and the pace at which Anatolian cities and towns fell to the invader in the years from ca. 660–720 does not speak well of the strength or commitment of local re- sistance. The only occasion on which we read in the sources of a military force recruited from the rural population is in Theophanes, for the year 706/707. Described as "a peasant auxiliary force" (λαὸς χωρικοβοηθείας), it was raised in order to relieve Tyana in Cappadocia but was resoundingly defeated and the city fell.[77] This single reference may not represent the only such incidence, but they seem to have been rare: it is possible that the citizens of Thessaloniki, or at least a select group of them, fought alongside regular soldiers.[78] But we read of no other similar attempts to muster the active military support of ordinary provincial populations. For the cities themselves, this may not say very much—faced with such odds, submission or flight were likely expedients and in very many cases clearly did not preclude a return to the imperial fold as soon as the enemy had departed, and perhaps more importantly, when the imperial state reappeared in the form of the local elite, fiscal, and military officials and the church.

Second, we should probably draw a difference between the rural hinterland of Constantinople, directly under the influence of the court and its palatine elite, and the more distant provinces. People were certainly concerned about the fate of the Roman Empire as such, representing a world order that few could imagine vanishing. But it is likely that the fate of their own city or town or district took priority in the face of an imminent threat. It is difficult to see this in the sources, representing as they do the bias of their genre or particular perspective, and there is not necessarily any contradiction or paradox here. As we have already said, local and personal identities and interests were embraced within the broader framework of being Christian and Roman. In the miracle collection of St. Theodore Tiro, for example, where the key motifs are the fate of the city and its populace under the protection of their martyr and miracle-working saint—"our city," "our land" are the phrases used—the emperor is a distant figure (mentioned respectfully, of course, but only once as part of a dating formula), the enemy are the "accursed Hagarenes" or, in the earlier miracles, the Persians, who are simply *"barbaroi"*(barbarians). When help arrives (during a siege by the Persians), it is in the form of a *"rhōmaikon ekstrateuma"* (Roman army) but no details are given, and the Roman force in question has no further association with the city of Euchaïta. Otherwise it is the saint, his city, and its surrounding country that preoccupy the writer, and this is no more than we should expect from such a text. The inhabitants of the city flee to their defenses when they are attacked, and they defend their town because it is their home rather than because of some grander, imperial motive. There is no explicit mention of any "imperial" sentiment here, any special concern for the fate of the Roman state, except insofar as it was, as we have seen, assumed to be coexistent with Christianity itself.[79] Given the nature of these texts, this should not surprise, and there is a well-established tradition of ordinary people as well as various forms of "urban militia" in both the provinces as well as the capitals defending the walls of their cities reaching back through the late Roman period into Antiquity. This may reflect loyalty to a higher authority, but it certainly has everything to do with the immediate interests of survival and the protection of property and kin.[80]

Third, we need to bear in mind that eastern Roman social-economic relations were highly stratified and exploitative: this was a society marked by extremes of wealth and poverty, in which the members of local elites, landlords, and the state's representatives overlapped substantially; in which the vested interests of these groups in respect of land, property, and the extraction of resources were supported and bolstered both by the secular law of the Roman Empire and longstanding custom; and in which the vast majority of country people had few opportunities and little power to resist the demands made either by private landlords or by state officials. We have remarked on the potential dangers to the government offered by religious dissidence or dissent, whether regional or focused within the leading elements of the church and among religious intellectuals. Accounts in later sixth- and early seventh-century sources suggest that social tensions within the empire were high as well, a consequence in part of an increasing rate of exploitation of the agrarian and rural populations by state, church, and private landlords and the fisc and of parsimonious treatment of military units by a cash-strapped government.[81] Factional strife within cities at moments of crisis (such as while under siege or when threatened by the action of an enemy such as the Persians), military mutinies, attacks on the wealthy, all suggest that social relations were stretched to breaking point. At the same time regional discontent focused on local issues, whether religious, fiscal, or political, had been endemic in the later Roman state. Leaving to one side regions notorious for disorder and "banditry" (i.e., rejection of imperial authority at various levels), such as Isauria, Justinian's legislation for provinces such as Pisidia, Lycaonia, Phrygia, and Lycia as well as for the Pontic provinces suggests a fairly constant low-level disorder in which only military policing was effective.[82] This was a systemic issue and reflected the three-way conflict between the needs of the state for manpower and support for its armies, the vested interests of the social and political elites and private landowners, and the willingness or ability of the producing population to pay, to offer resistance to such demands, or to passively accept them.

The issues that led to the problems faced by central government in the provinces in the sixth century are unlikely to have disappeared in the conditions of the second half of the seventh century, although there may well have been shifts in the ways in which they were expressed. Internal conflict of this sort is rarely mentioned in discussions of the east Roman world in the seventh and eighth century unless it is to do with religious disputes. Yet we have already noted the remark of Anastasius of Sinai in the later seventh century to the effect that, even if the Saracens were to disappear as a threat, social unrest and particularly the factional strife between the Blue and Green chariot-racing fan clubs would still tear the empire apart. The bishop John, author of the first collection of miracles of St. Demetrius in Thessaloniki, remarks likewise that during the reign of Phocas (602–610), the provinces of the eastern empire were racked by violence and civic disorder, a situation that should not be seen as simply a reflection of the policies of that emperor. In the *Vita* of Philaret the Merciful, compiled in the early 820s but concerning events in the middle years of the eighth century, the fear of (and latent hostility toward) the military officials of the region and their treatment of those obliged to serve in the local army is clear, even in a text that, while also heavily dependent on ancient fable and *topoi,* is nevertheless intended for a Constantinopolitan audience or readership sympathetic to the Roman imperial state.[83] A similar situation, albeit a century and a half or so later, is evident in the account in the *Life* of St. Anthony the Younger concerning a Saracen attack on the saint's city of Attaleia in the 820s. Here Anthony, who commands the city, points out to the enemy leader that the people of the town were not to be treated as one with the Roman army and should not suffer for the actions of that army, which is under the direct command of the emperor and obliged to fulfill his commands. As far as the author of the *Vita* is concerned, the people of Attaleia, while they may be Romans, have nothing to do with imperial politics and wish to be left alone.[84] Roman and Christian identity is clearly a given, but uppermost in the minds of the townsfolk and the hagiographer in these cases is the fate of the local people and their city—there is no suggestion that they will sacrifice themselves for some higher political symbolism. Again, we should allow for the effect of genre and context, but we may at least draw the conclusion that there was an audience for which the automatic identity of local populations with imperial interests was not at the forefront of their concerns. Similar sentiments can be found in texts of the fourth to sixth centuries.[85]

What is very obvious in the written sources, of course, are the various military rebellions that took place in the later seventh and eighth centuries. These were, so far as the sources inform us about them, never to do with pay or conditions of service, unlike the great majority of mutinies and soldiers' riots that took place in the sixth century. On the contrary, they were concerned either with explicit political-ideological issues or with questions of status and rewards.[86] The role of the leaders in these affairs remains obscure, but in light of the observations made regarding the localization of military forces, their gradual integration with the provincial populations among whom they were distributed and where they were based, and the role of local elites in constituting their officers and commanders, we may surmise a considerable element of local, provincial sentiment underlying many of the disturbances that the sources record. In the case of the mutinous Anatolikon soldiers in the fall of 681 toward the end of the sixth ecumenical council, their feelings about both recent military defeat and the change in imperial religious policy certainly seem to have figured as key grounds. Regional and provincial hostility to Constantinople or to the established orthodoxy may well have constituted one of the elements that at times underlay some of the actions described in the sources, rearticulated by the eighth century through the provincial military commands. The evolution of such local identities no doubt took some time, and we should assume a long-term process, culminating in the much clearer provincial identities that had become apparent by the ninth century. Nevertheless, it seems likely that by the later decades of the seventh century the soldiers could give voice to the concerns of the provinces. Again, the example of the impact of the process of localization of the military forces in the exarchate in Italy offers useful parallels.[87]

It is unlikely that the wide range of such social and cultural tensions that we have described were without consequences for the willingness to resist among the population of many areas attacked by the Arabs in the 630s and afterward, although it is impossible to say how exactly its impact was manifested. The legislation concerning slaves and freedmen and regarding military booty in the *Ecloga* shows that the government was aware of the need to maintain provincial loyalties among the ordinary population.[88] And although there are only the vaguest of references in the written sources to internal social conflict, by drawing on parallel situations in the provinces for an earlier period where the evidence is much better, we may get some idea of the sort of problems the government must have faced in the later seventh century, and the sort of responses to invasion, fiscal demands, and the presence of the military that were manifested on the part of provincial populations, whether urban or rural. Demands for tax in cash or for a range of equivalent prestations could generate substantial discontent, opposition, and sometimes armed rebellion.[89] Late Roman governments were concerned to maximize fiscal revenues but were not oblivious of the fact that overly heavy fiscal pressure could ruin the tax base upon which it depended and on occasion legislated accordingly.

In the years after Justinian I the government had to deal with a range of problems that were in many respects the forerunners of those that challenged it in the decades from the 650s, even if we would not characterize the sixth-century situation in terms of crisis. The conflict with Persia, the threats from the Lombards, Avars, and Slavs from the 560s and 570s, combined with the financial difficulties that had followed Justinian's expansionist military policies and the longer-term demographic impact of the plague of the 540s, generated a number of serious difficulties for the fisc. In spite of an ever-worsening fiscal situation, by the mid-570s the government had to recognize that the rural population of many provinces, notably those most directly affected by warfare, was simply unable to bear the enormous burden of tax placed upon it and was forced to concede reductions in tax or outright remissions. Yet at the same time the production and delivery of grain was a constant requirement that could not be relaxed. In novels of 566 and 575 the rural populations are named as the beneficiaries of substantial tax remissions, on the grounds that they are simply unable to pay the demands made of them without ruination. In the novel of 575, the basic taxes are reduced by a quarter each year for a four-year period, but that part of the land-tax normally required in the form of grain or other produce was exempted from this since the army still needed to be provisioned, and tax-payers could obtain a rebate for this portion in gold. A papyrus of the same period confirms that the reductions were actually carried out in this way.[90]

Concern over the situation of the rural producers, or rather their tax-paying potential, is expressed also in respect of legislation over marriage and inheritance. In a novel of 572 intended to deal with the recalcitrant population of Samaria, only the peasant producers of the region are permitted to transmit their property to their heirs, "not on their account, but with regard to the situation of the lands they till and the taxes and obligations due from them." Similar concerns are expressed in the novel of 566 already mentioned, which includes stipulations relating to inheritance rights of the children of mixed Roman-barbarian unions in the frontier provinces of the east, and in novels of 570 and 582 dealing with, among other things, rights of inheritance of the children of tied tenant farmers in Africa.[91] The chief concern was twofold: that the producers should not simply abandon their farms and fields as a result of excessive fiscal pressure and that exploitation and oppression from state officials should be stopped. Prescriptions in novels issued in 566, 569, 574, and 579 thus forbid the latter, and especially the managers of imperial estates, from making overly burdensome fiscal demands for their own profit, and were held accountable even after they had relinquished their post. One of the major complaints of the government was that poor peasant farmers were driven to abandon their lands entirely, being reckoned thus as a net loss to the state in fiscal terms, or to give them into the hands of wealthy landlords, usually state officials themselves, who could also buy up or seize lands that had been abandoned and were in a position to minimize or even write off their own fiscal contributions.[92] Such legislation seems to have been relatively ineffective, however; its application depended, after all, precisely on those people who were its prime target.

The oppression of rural producers of all kinds by their wealthier neighbors; by imperial officials, military, and civilian; and by the fisc led to different forms of opposition. In some areas, banditry and armed resistance were particularly noticeable and, indeed, had been common for centuries beforehand, as in the mountain and hill country of Pisidia and Lycaonia or Isauria in Anatolia. Legislation from the time of Justinian makes mention of populous villages in these regions, whose inhabitants lived outside the law of the state and paid no taxes, where clan and kin relations determined status and power, and where internecine conflict was endemic, accompanied by regular attacks on representatives of the state. A similar situation prevailed in parts of the Pontus and

Cappadocia, and the empire attempted to address the problem by appointing military commands specifically to deal with it.[93] Such hostility to the state and its officials in the more intractable regions of the empire will hardly have improved during times of stress and increased fiscal pressure. Religious differences must also have contributed, as the concern of both state and church with heresy and heterodoxy clearly indicates.[94] In Egypt peasant resistance to the demands of both government and landlords can be detected in the papyrus documentation concerning the large estates in the later sixth and early seventh centuries as well as in armed revolts that took place in the last years of the sixth century;[95] in the Balkans a situation comparable to that in Asia Minor can be seen far earlier, from the later fifth century through into the early seventh, reflected first of all in references to various "outlaw" gangs known locally (in Noricum, Pannonia, and Thrace) as *scamares* and later simply as bandits and robbers, and secondly by imperial legislation, which again underlines the role of the army in limiting their depredations and attempting to control the situation. Since many of the robbers or bandits were armed deserters from military units, this was all the more difficult.[96] When the government was unable to help them, some communities took matters into their own hands and were quite hostile to the authorities, as the story of the town of Asemos in Thrace and its imperially approved but locally raised and funded militia suggests.[97]

That the government continued to face such difficulties and occasional armed opposition during the seventh century is indicated by the more limited evidence at our disposal. The situation in parts of Phrygia, for example, appears to have been similar throughout the seventh and into the eighth century, although concealed to a degree behind the fact that local rural opposition is ascribed to heretical "Montanist" beliefs. Punitive expeditions were mounted against the Montanists under Justinian and Leo III, in whose time they were still seen as a source of opposition to the central government, even if there is some debate about their religious identity in the eighth century. It is not insignificant that the heartland of the "heresy" of the Athinganoi, first mentioned in the early eighth century, was also in Phrygia and Lycaonia.[98] And it is certainly likely that the identification of these communities with heretical beliefs reflected at the same time traditional opposition to the central government and its demands as much as it reflected an ideological difference. It is entirely possible that the Paulicians who, according to Theophanes, first appear in eastern Anatolia during the seventh century, are also representative of local hostility and opposition to the state and its fiscal apparatus as much as of their particular religious beliefs. For other parts of the empire, we simply have no evidence other than the references to representatives of various heresies in canon 95 of the Quinisext.[99] But it would be reasonable to assume that the situation did not improve as the seventh century progressed, given the devastation of the landscape in many areas and the continuing oppression of the government's fiscal administration.

In the Balkans during the sixth century, it appears that the situation for much of the rural population was such that on occasion it became simpler to accept paying tribute to enemy invaders. Even imperial legislation recognized this problem, along with the reality that the peasant farmers of the region suffered more from local state officials and the army than from the enemy.[100] John Lydus, an imperial official in Justinian's reign, describes the oppressively burdensome demands of a passing imperial military force for food, provisions, and money, remarking: "they find the raids of the barbarians easier to bear than the oppression of the officials and the army."[101] For the seventh century, we really have very little direct evidence for the situation in the countryside in the remaining Balkan lands of the empire, although it is unlikely to have improved.

For Anatolia, the evidence is no better. What it suggests is a highly inflected response determined by the immediate circumstances in which a community found itself. As we saw in Chapter 3, from the 650s and 660s at least the army came to be recruited largely from among the communities it defended. It thus also mirrored to some degree provincial and local concerns, but at the same time under its locally recruited subaltern officers and its imperially appointed commanders, it also represented the imperial ideology and the Roman Empire as a political idea and an administrative, cultural, and institutional reality, and civilian fear of soldiers was a well-recognized and generally well-grounded phenomenon.[102] The troops under the command of the usurper Tiberius Apsimar did not hold back from plundering and robbing the citizens of Constantinople when they entered the city in 698, for example, no more than did soldiers of the Opsikion in 715 during the usurpation of Theodosius III—although this likely reflects urban–rural hostility as much as the general behavior of soldiers.[103]

Still, on the basis of the very slender evidence we have, such as the accounts in the miracles of St. Theodore and St. Demetrius, there seems little doubt that provincial populations had no obvious ideological alternative than to identify with their empire. For much of the time when not under threat, of course, local loyalties and identities probably loomed larger than a distant imperial ruler and a relatively oppressive state apparatus that explicitly supported the interests of local elites, whether secular or ecclesiastical. When threatened, they no doubt looked to the army to protect them. But where the state was absent, it is likely that local interests and loyalties prevailed, especially if a community was threatened by an enemy and no help was forthcoming. Where the army was nearby morale and resistance were probably stiffer; where the local elite was present (along with the military, fiscal, and church officials with whom it probably to a large extent overlapped), with the coercive authority it wielded on its own behalf and on behalf of the government, imperial Roman identity likely trumped local concerns. Distance from the army and the long arm of the state was a crucial element in the success or failure of the empire in maintaining its hold. For provincial populations, this distance was in turn inflected by a range of local factors about which we can say very little: the degree of presence of the church and other ideologically reinforcing elements, the strength of local networks of patronage, and conjunctural factors such as the frequency or intensity of enemy attacks or raiding—these all played a role and no doubt influenced people's willingness to support and identify with the empire and a Roman identity.

Imperial legislation from the sixth century regarding the situation in those provinces most affected by warfare—in the Balkans and on the eastern front—provides, therefore, a valuable source of comparison for the sort of situation that would have prevailed throughout much of the empire in the years after 640. It indicates both the gravity of the problem that the government faced as well as awareness of the need to negotiate a careful path between the interests of the state and those of the provincial populations at all levels—both farmers as well as landowners. This is made clear, for example, in the late sixth-century *Strategikon*, which repeats warnings in imperial legislation as well as older treatises to military commanders to respect the property and interests of the provincials.[104] But such concerns hardly addressed the issues of social-economic polarization and elite exploitation, especially by managers of imperial or ecclesiastical estates noted earlier, even if they suggest some awareness of associated problems. That the imperial government was itself aware of the issues is clear, however; indeed, the *Ecloga* specifically introduces new regulations concerning slaves and freed persons that seem to reflect a desire to stiffen popular morale and to encourage resistance to enemy attack or occupation.[105]

The very real cultural and political distance that existed between the imperial capital and the provincial elites that were bound to it, on the one hand, and the ordinary people of the provinces, on the other, a distance that existed regardless of any shared Christian and Roman identity, is a motif from all periods, evident in particular in hagiographical writing but occasionally in the sort of action already noted, where provincial soldiers were able to plunder the inhabitants of Constantinople. It meant that the relationship between state and elite, on one side, and provinces and more distant populations, on the other, was always double-edged. In Constantinople especially, this relationship could be problematic for the ruler. But it is also the case that while we have references to the hostility or hatred of the urban populace for a particular emperor— Constans II after the murder of his brother Theodosius, for example, or that directed against Justinian II and some of his ministers[106]—there is no evidence for any massive popular rebellion or opposition to imperial authority, other than that which we could read into the references to persecutions of groups such as the Montanists. It is true that Justinian II fell victim to a coup and that this certainly had popular support, but the events affected the city only, and briefly, whereas the eventual assassination of Constans II in Sicily had nothing to do with his popularity as an emperor or not. Opposition or dissatisfaction with imperial policy or with a particular emperor or commander is most often expressed through the activities of the soldiers. But in spite of the tensions within eastern Roman society, the basic fabric of social relations in town and country seems to have been maintained with little disruption to the running of the state.

Yet, having underlined and drawn attention to the horizontal divisions and tensions within east Roman society, we need also to bear in mind that even in the most stratified social contexts there exists a wide range of vertical solidarities too, solidarities that may bridge or overcome the social and economic divisions of wealth, status, family, and occupation. These may take the form of loyalties across social strata to a particular creed, for example, as in membership of a monastic community or of a confraternity or ceremonial/community organization (such as a devotional society associated with a church or a saint's cult, for example, or with a particular annual commemorative liturgy)[107] or more commonly and far more widespread between tenants and clients and their landlords and patrons; and of course networks of friendship can regularly transcend social divides, as with the circle surrounding Maximus the Confessor.[108] There is virtually nothing from the core lands of the empire at this period to provide details of such associations apart from the relationships of patronage we might assume between provincial and metropolitan officers and their soldiers. Some of the "political" activities of soldiers may well have been spontaneous responses to specific events or information. But underlying more explicit oppositional acts there appear to have been ties of loyalty between officers and men, likely reflecting patron–client relationships of one sort or another, even if we have no details. There is very clear evidence both from fifth- and sixth-century legislation and from tenth-century imperial legislation that military officers and commanders employed soldiers in nonmilitary capacities and in their personal retinues or service, often apparently to the advantage of the latter, suggestive of the forms of patronage and the loyalties or obligations that such ties generated. Such relationships certainly existed during the seventh and eighth centuries, even if we have few indications of them.[109] Vertical associations and loyalties, whether coerced or voluntary, have always served to mitigate, undermine, or subvert the effects of horizontal stratification and in most societies have often been perceived as more important to the individuals in question, particularly where the relationship is confirmed through oaths or rituals that are considered binding on the parties in question. Such ties can be public or private—the oaths of loyalty sworn by troops to the emperor in the Roman army, for example, offer a particularly clear case. Their existence means that, however hierarchical or exploitative the social relations of a society may have been, social and economic relationships were never straightforward.[110] In the last analysis, and as we have now seen in this and the preceding chapters, the concordance of empire with salvific, Christian polity reinforced through church and imperial military and administrative presence certainly reached down to and influenced all levels of provincial society.

The evidence presented or summarized thus far suggests a number of conclusions. First, the developments of the second half of the seventh century need to be understood in the context of the social and economic changes that affected the empire as a whole, including an increasingly close relationship between Constantinople and the provincial elites upon whom it had to depend. Second, people throughout Byzantine society were aware of different challenges and threats according to their social and economic position or their geographical location. Thus, while they may have shared similar concerns regarding some of the affairs and changes of their times, they expressed these concerns in different ways and through different means according to these other factors and the ways in which they impinged upon their "identity," as determined again by context. So much is apparent from the evidence about the way in which soldiers responded in different places and times to some of the political developments they experienced or had heard about, about what issues and worries concerned "ordinary" people, and about how the rural populace responded to fiscal pressures and hostile attack. Third, the effects of the distribution of the armies across Asia Minor and the high levels of localized recruitment and garrisoning or quartering of soldiers have to be seen within the framework of an increasingly de-urbanized, more militarized, and less civic cultural environment. Soldiers were, or at least came to be, recruited largely from the rural populace of the empire in Anatolia, and soldiers thus reflected, in however refracted and distorted a way, the views of provincial populations.

But at the same time soldiers were led and officered by provincials who, along with the fiscal and judicial administrators of the provinces in which they were based, were drawn at least to some extent from the middling and upper echelons of local society. Churchmen were likewise part of the picture, contributing to local governance and forming an element in the local elite. Each set had its own particular vested interests and concerns, and at times these coincided. Both soldiers and their leaders, on the one hand, and provincial churchmen, on the other hand, had in common a commitment to the imperial idea, to emperor and government, and to church at Constantinople. How this commitment was given expression varied, of course, compromised by local loyalties and concerns, interests that appear only rarely and indirectly in the sources describing their actions.

Thus, the ways in which totalizing or universal concepts, such as "Christian," "Roman," or that of the orthodox Roman Empire, impacted on different sectors of society and motivated a response must have varied considerably. Reinforced through the various mechanisms we have described, such concepts meant that those who did not share that idea or buy into that identity could be presented as Other, as alien, and thus as a real or potential threat to the very existence of that Roman world within which people understood themselves and made sense of their lives. This was the reaction of the east Roman state to perceived challenges to authority such as the supposed Montanists of Phrygia and other such groups, whatever they may have thought of themselves. It is true that much of the urban population of greater Syria or Palestine or the Roman province of Mesopotamia remained loyal to the empire in the initial wave of Arab attacks,[111] and that the notion of Roman Empire served to bind the provinces and especially their elites to the capital. And it is also true that into the very last decade of the seventh century and perhaps a little beyond many in the conquered provinces still hoped for a Roman victory and the destruction of the caliphate. This was a hope reflected in the apocalyptic literature and in anti-Jewish polemic of the period as well as in the fact that, in spite of the damage inflicted by the constant warfare on the economy of the areas most affected, the empire was at times able to take the offensive both on land and by sea and to threaten Arab control of substantial regions of northern Syria, most spectacularly in the first years of the reign of ʿAbd al-Malik.[112]

Our evidence is so slight, unfortunately, that such pro-imperial sentiments only occasionally appear in the form of armed resistance to the invaders or, after the conquest, to rebellion, as with the sailors from Syria in the year 653/654 and again in the period 717–718. Abandoned by many members of their own elites during the first phase of the conquest and without any hope of real imperial counterattack, resistance in these areas thus tended to be fragmented and ultimately ineffective. In Anatolia, in strong contrast to what had happened in Syria or somewhat later in Africa, the imperial government seems to have been able to evolve a series of strategies that helped it cling onto its core territory. Even near-contemporary Arab sources noted the stubbornness of

Roman resistance in Anatolia. As an early Islamic apocalyptic text puts it, "The Romans are severest of all peoples on you."[113]

Three key points can be underlined. First, as this and the previous chapters have now demonstrated, the political theology of the eastern Roman state, embedded within the broader Christian and Roman symbolic universe of late Roman culture, offered the only framework through which people could understand their world and through which political, social, and other forms of social discourse could be comprehended.

Second, a policy of largely avoiding open battle in the period up to ca. 680, except in the most favorable circumstances, permitted the government to consolidate its fiscal and military presence under the new conditions and to cling onto all its major fortresses and strongpoints along the Taurus/Anti-Taurus line (in spite of the frequent changes in control over many of them). The premise for all this was, of course, the survival of Constantinople through the attacks of the 650s, 660s, and the great siege of 717–718, but it was at the same time precisely these policies in the provinces that permitted this and that bound provincial elites and their interests to the capital and the imperial system.

Third, while resistance was certainly given direction through the coercive authority granted to provincial elites by the imperial court and household at Constantinople, it cannot have been coercion alone that facilitated imperial resistance in the provinces. True, provincial elites wedded to the Constantinopolitan establishment were the instrument through which the imperial government could coerce the rural population into maintaining production, paying taxes, supplying manpower to the armies, and reoccupying their land and settlements where they had abandoned them in times of danger. Similar considerations applied to more distant regions such as the Ravenna exarchate or Sicily. The umbilical ties between provincial elites and the imperial court, with its power to reward and to punish, to honor and to shame, bound fiscal managers, military commanders, and the local powerful, including members of the ecclesiastical establishment, directly to the interests of the imperial government. But the eastern Roman elite was not just a dominant elite: it held in the thought-world of east Romans a legitimate position of authority. While its coercive power undoubtedly came to the fore at times—consider the role it must have played in dealing with the provincial unrest or rebellions mentioned earlier—it was also directly invested by the emperors with symbolic and practical power and legitimacy. Nested within the framework of the eastern Roman symbolic universe, these various factors made for a powerful alliance between the widely held beliefs of people throughout eastern Roman society, on the one hand, and the state system that both depended upon them and could be seen to be acting in their interests as members of the same community, on the other.

5

Regional Variation and Resistance

In this year Gregory, the patrician of Africa, raised a rebellion together with the Africans.

The Saracens invaded Africa and, after joining battle with the rebel Gregory, routed him, slew his followers, and drove him out of Africa. Having laid a tribute on the Africans they returned home.[1]

Dissent, Disaffection, or Loyalty: Elite Choices

The issues reviewed in the previous chapters all had important implications for the relationship between the government and the elite, both the established elements and those elements that evolved during the seventh and eighth centuries, and this brings me to one of the most important issues that this book will touch upon. As we have now seen, the late Roman elite, internally diverse and highly regionalized though it was, was the bearer of late Roman literary culture and the guardian of the urban-centered cultural traditions of the earlier Roman and Hellenistic worlds.[2] The changes of the seventh century—changes in the role of cities, the huge losses of imperial territory that the Persian and especially the Arab wars ushered in—affected this in many ways.[3] As we noted in Chapter 1, a number of key identifying aspects of late Roman literary culture vanish almost completely, along with much of the cultural capital it carried with it. Cultural and ideological horizons become narrower, and the older senatorial establishment, with much of the literary cultural baggage associated with it, faded away during the seventh century. Instead there develops a new elite, a service elite of heterogeneous ethnic, social, and cultural origins, certainly incorporating many elements of the older establishment, especially in the metropolitan region and in the senior church hierarchy,[4] but nevertheless representing something rather different from what had gone before. Imperial political life, career, and status had always revolved around Constantinople, but as the eastern provinces were lopped off, the Constantinopolitan focus became even more pronounced. The transformations in settlement patterns and urban life in Anatolia and the southern Balkans along with the territorial reduction of the eastern Roman state and the loss of the great international urban centers such as Alexandria and Antioch on the Orontes meant that now only Constantinople could serve as a focus for acquiring wealth, status, and power. As the seat of empire, home of the imperial court, and the largest city remaining to the empire, it was now the only focus for the investment of social capital. Whether seeking a post in the metropolis or in the provinces, Constantinople was the only option. The church provided an alternative and equivalent career structure, but even the church, in the form of the bishop of Constantinople, the patriarch, had its focus there. The emperor, the court, and the church became, more than ever before, the sources par excellence of social advancement. And while there were many minor routes to power that were not directly pulled into that nexus, it was these, and the imperial court in particular, that nevertheless constituted the dominant mode of entry.

The hallmarks of belonging to this elite Roman world were a degree of literacy (no doubt very variable according to origins, background, and educational opportunity) and participation in the established literary culture in some way; an absolute acceptance of the Roman imperial system with the God-appointed emperor at the apex; and membership of the state or church establishment at whatever level an individual's social, economic, and cultural capital permitted. The chronicler Theophanes, writing in the early ninth century, defines "becoming Roman" quite simply as knowing the letters and language of the Greeks and accepting the ways and traditions of the Roman polity.[5] Christianity, and more particularly orthodox Christianity, was taken for granted. Being a member of the sociocultural and political elite, whether in the provinces or the capital and at court, meant also being a Roman in this sense.

It is clear that the government could not hope to maintain its authority in the provinces, and thus extract the fiscal resources it needed, without the collaboration and active support of provincial elites. And that implied both ideological consensus as well as pragmatic politics. Many studies have shown that states, whether far-flung imperial systems or geographically compact polities, must before all else secure the loyalty of their various local elites if they are to retain control over the conquered lands—short of eradicating the former elite and replacing them (as the Normans did more or less effectively after the defeat of Harold in 1066), there are few alternatives, although there have been many means of achieving this end. Coercion can work for a time, but in the end some degree of reciprocity between center and province, between ruling elite and provincial elites, is essential if the system is to survive over any length of time. This holds not only in the case of newly conquered or absorbed territories and their formerly dominant elites but also where old established aristocracies or dominant social groups are concerned.[6] In the case of the Roman Empire in particular, it has been shown very clearly that it was not some supposed eventual identification of the populations in the conquered territories with the Roman state and its values that explained the absence of rebellion and opposition on a systemic basis to Roman rule—the vast mass of the population had little say in the matter. Rather, Roman hegemony was secured by coopting local elites and by assimilating them both culturally (primarily linguistically) and politically into the Roman governing establishment, with its ability to impose authority through direct physical coercion. This is not to suggest that no assimilation or identification of the broader masses of the conquered populations might not or did not eventually take place because at certain levels and in certain areas it clearly did—linguistically, for example, in the evolution and spread of various dialects of Latin in the west, or in the case of the eastern parts of the empire from the later sixth and seventh centuries on, through a common adherence to the imperial church and the Roman state (even with all the local variations we have discussed). This was never a straightforward process, but it is clear that it was above all the ideological and political incorporation of provincial elites into a Roman establishment that contributed toward the stabilization and indeed the longevity of Roman rule.[7]

But provincial elites were loyal to a distant government—indeed to any government—only so long as their own interests were protected by the state, and insofar as the state was able effectively to impose sanctions in some form on those who challenged its authority or failed to support it. Disaffection from or hostility to the imperial center was about a slippage in the correspondence between the perceived vested interests of a local elite and those of the state. And elites have been historically remarkably consistent in preserving their interests, whatever the compromises they may have had to make in order to do so. The North African elite, for example, did little to defend the interests of the church and its clergy against the Vandals in the 430s and thereafter, preferring to preserve their own interests. The somewhat precarious ideological loyalty such a response indicates underlines the self-interested nature of elite society, examples of which can be multiplied and from widely different periods and societies.[8] While this was certainly an indication, by the middle decades of the fifth century, for example, if not already some decades before then, it is clear that local loyalties among the Gallic senatorial elite and their interests were more powerful than loyalty to the imperial government in Rome, and that willingness to tolerate the demands of the fisc in the context of a decreasingly effective military defense of their lands and property was rapidly dissipating.[9] The case of the praetorian prefect of the Gauls, Arvandus, accused in the 470s of writing to the king of the Visigoths to suggest the partition of Gaul among Goths, Romans and Burgundians, may not be typical, but it is certainly an indication, and he was not alone in his sentiments.[10] The difficulties faced by the state in financing and maintaining its armies in the west, the challenges to the ideological hegemony of Roman imperial authority, and the inability of the state to defend elite vested interests in the provinces meant that, by the third quarter of the century, compromising with the new powers in the western provinces—the Visigoths and the Franks in particular—seemed preferable to many, in order to maintain social status, wealth, and influence.[11] For the eastern empire in the seventh century, the demands of the situation were not so very different in several respects.

The eastern Roman state had several means of consolidating its hold over a local elite. Coercion and sanctions represented one approach. In seventh-century Anatolia, in contrast to more distant regions of the empire, the government at Constantinople was in effective striking distance of those who challenged its authority, even if applying sanctions was not always a straightforward matter. This is perhaps most apparent in Constantinopolitan dealings with Armenia and the various local rulers whose policy with regard to the empire was often ambivalent, especially with the constant threat of reprisals or attacks from the caliphate. Imperial titles and offices were often efficacious in winning members of the Armenian elite over to the imperial cause, although in the conditions of the time this was often for the short term only. Yet even this far from the capital it was generally the case that the fear of imperial military reprisals or loss of prestige with the Roman court could secure loyalty to the Roman cause.[12] Admittedly, imperial policy in this region was not especially successful, but the point is that if the imperial arm could reach as far as the Armenian highlands, both militarily as well as in respect of ecclesiastical politics, even under such very straitened circumstances as prevailed across much of the period from the 640s onward, then how much more effective was it nearer to home? Even with substantial interference from the caliphate, Roman political control over central and eastern Anatolia was rarely in doubt. As the example of the attempted rebellion by the general Saborius, commander of the Armeniakon division, in 667/668 indicates, the government of Constans II was very quickly able to dispatch a substantial punitive force to deal with this while also pursuing a diplomatic offensive to dissuade Muʿawiya from lending his support to the rebels.[13] In spite of the continuous Arab raiding and occasional major offensive operations, Roman forces were ubiquitous, whether dispersed in their local provincial bases or in more concentrated numbers for particular campaigns. In consequence, it is a reasonable assumption that no member of the provincial elite could afford to abandon the imperial cause without fear of relatively swift reprisals and punishment. Without wishing to introduce a circular argument, the results speak for themselves: again as we have seen in Chapter 3, once behind the Taurus/Anti-Taurus line, virtually no territory and hardly any significant forts or fortresses were abandoned by the state. If the empire was able so effectively to hold onto its territory in this respect, there is little reason to doubt it was able to reach out to the provincial elites to ensure their loyalty.

Different Region, Different Outcome: African Problems

But coercion alone was not enough, at least not over the longer term, and without some degree of reciprocity on the part of the government, provincial loyalty to the center was ambivalent. By way of contrast and comparison, the examples of Syria, North Africa, and Italy with Sicily offer good illustrations of these points. In Syria, as we have now seen, the failure of the empire to protect its territories and to relieve the cities besieged or threatened by the Arabs led either to the flight or to the surrender of members of the elite, and it seems largely to have been the upper levels of the urban-centered Greek-speaking elites who left—many stayed and threw in their lot with the conquerors as the best way to preserve their property and position. The family of John of Damascus may be a good example.[14] Here the problem for the both the government at Constantinople and for the indigenous populations was relatively clear—the empire was basically unable to help, and the only recourse was flight or compromise.

The situation was complicated by other factors than the purely military or logistical. Issues of doctrine and dogma were intimately bound up with issues of political identity and beliefs about the relationship between the divinity and humankind, about the relationship between the heavenly and earthly kingdoms; as we have seen already, the politics of belief had a direct impact on the politics of the period.[15] The theological position represented by Maximus clearly had implications for the way in which members of the church and the secular elite understood and acted within their world.[16] The issue was about both the preservation of unity within the dyophysite—the Chalcedonian—church as well as about the definition of operations/energies and wills. But there were two diametrically opposed standpoints. The government saw challenges to its own position as challenges to the unity of the secular empire, to the authority of the emperor, the empire and the imperial church, and thus to their survival in the face of external threats and challenges—in this case, the challenge from the caliphate. But where a ruler, his advisors, and the "official" church deviated from what others saw as correct understanding, then not only was the life of the polity threatened, but the unity of Christianity as such was broken since there could be no communion with innovators.

The two positions are made very clear, both in the trial of Maximus in the 650s and in the earlier disputation between Maximus and the former patriarch of Constantinople Pyrrhus in 641/642, to be discussed shortly. As we saw in Chapter 2, recent scholarship has emphasized the fact that in the development of the theology of John Moschus, Sophronius of Jerusalem and Maximus the Confessor in particular, the Eucharist had become the defining sacrament, the one key symbol through which the difference between correct and incorrect belief and practice was demarcated, and it is certainly the case that during his trial and interrogations Maximus based his resistance to monotheletism on an absolute refusal to enter communion with Constantinople.[17] How far these ideas penetrated below the level of the theologians and statesmen who were involved in the debates and in the trials of Martin and Maximus is not known. But the imperial government had to take the public challenge seriously or lose both face and credibility, and as we have noted, the centrality of the Eucharist was certainly an important element in the work of Anastasius of Sinai, for example, and in the advice contained in his questions and answers.[18]

The personal associations that Maximus had developed were crucial to the impact his theology had on contemporary political developments, and in the context of his own theological position it has been suggested that his move westward in the early 640s was associated with the fact that leading elements of the African provincial government were already at odds with the imperial government at Constantinople. It was in fact at just this time that a disagreement arose between the (praetorian) prefect of Africa, George, and the empress Martina, over an order to release some nuns from Egypt accused of heretical beliefs. Martina's fall from power in 641 seems to have temporarily resolved the situation, but it did not improve.[19] Maximus became the focus of opposition to imperial monotheletism. The position from which he argued, and which forms the basis and clarifies the nature of his evolving hostility, is made quite clear in a public disputation with the former Constantinopolitan patriarch Pyrrhus, held in the presence of the military governor of North Africa, the *patrikios* and exarch Gregory, in 645. In the course of this debate, Maximus defended the principle of *akribeia*, exactitude, in matters of dogma, contrary to the position adopted by his opponent, who made the case for a pragmatic approach, for *oikonomia*, or accommodation.[20]

Imperial prestige had already suffered as a result of the disasters that beset the empire in the 630s and early 640s with the loss of the eastern provinces and Egypt.[21] Military victory was a key element in the legitimation of Roman rulers and political regimes, and while the problems that arose in its absence were not new to this century,[22] the very particular challenges faced by the empire from the 640s and 650s onward rendered them especially acute at a time when success against an external threat and political and religious legitimacy were, as we have seen in

Chapter 2, so closely bound together. The exarch Gregory's own position in consequence becomes a little clearer at this point. First, he permitted a debate, contrary to the prohibition enunciated in the *Ekthesis*
(the fact that a former patriarch was his co-disputant, cannot have altered this). In 646 he permitted the holding of two local provincial councils (in Africa Proconsularis and Byzacena), following which a number of
bishops from these and other provinces, including the bishop of Carthage,
appear to have made their support of the traditional Chalcedonian
position public. Maximus's influence and Gregory's failure to stifle
opposition to the imperial cause clearly had dramatic and very unwel-
come results from the point of view of the empire. There is no evidence
for antimonothelete sentiment before Maximus's arrival, although the
dispute between the praetorian prefect of Africa, George, and Constantinople suggests a degree of tension between the region and Constantinople; within a year North Africa had become the focus of anti-imperial
propaganda and ecclesiastical opposition.[23] And finally, probably in 646,
Gregory was proclaimed emperor in a direct challenge to the government at Constantinople that acted for the still young Constans II.[24] His
motives remain debated. He may have intended seriously to replace the
rule of Constans II and his advisors, reflecting or stimulated by disap-
pointment or disillusion at the failed imperial attack against Egypt in
645,[25] and would perhaps have made an attempt on Constantinople itself,
as Heraclius had done. He may have intended to establish an autonomous
subimperial state in order the better to resist Arab incursions.[26]

It is impossible to say. And in the end, he died in battle while confronting an Arab raid at Sufetula (Sbeitla) in 647.[27] But there is little
doubt that this was a genuine challenge to the existing regime and that
it was very likely morally supported by Maximus, who, during his later
trial in Constantinople, did not deny reports that he had had a dream
in which the eventual victory of the usurper Gregory was symbolically
represented by the victory of one angelic choir over another. While this
may at first sight seem trivial, we should not underestimate the considerable authority or significance ascribed to such dreams, as has been
pointed out: they were taken very seriously indeed, as indications both
of divine support or opposition as well as pointers to potential popular
and elite opinion, whether positive or negative. From the later sixth to
early eighth centuries Maurice, Justinian II, Leontius, and Philippicus
Bardanes were all associated directly or indirectly with dreams or proph-

ecies purporting to indicate the success or failure of their rule, and so it is not surprising to find that the government of Constans II regarded the report of Maximus's dream with some concern.[28]

Just as during the Persian wars, North Africa (along with Sicily) had had to shoulder the burden of supplying Constantinople with resources. The importance of Africa to the fisc as well as to the grain supply of Constantinople had already become very clear in the period immediately after the loss of Egypt in 618, when the civic *annona* for the capital was cancelled.[29] From this time a number of seals of *kommerkiarioi* associated with Carthage and North Africa testify to the activities of officials who, it has been plausibly argued, were associated with the measures taken to supply Constantinople with grain during the years after the Persian occupation of Egypt and lasting up to the usurpation and defeat of the exarch Gregory in 647.[30] In the early 640s the *sakellarios,* Philagrius, who had been exiled briefly in 641 to North Africa (the province of Septem, focused around mod. Ceuta in Morocco, opposite Gibraltar) had begun implementing a new empire-wide tax assessment, and it is likely that North Africa figured in his calculations as a major source of revenue, especially in light of the loss of Egypt.[31] And North African wares were still being exported to southern Italy and to Constantinople in the period ca. 640–680 and a little beyond, for example, probably reflecting both private commercial transactions as well as state-sponsored movement of goods.[32] African landowners, already facing economic and political disruption from Arab raids and with little military assistance from Constantinople, were left in a difficult situation. The expedition of 645 may have been seen as a real opportunity for an improvement in the situation.

But the hope was dashed, and it may well have been this that lent support to Gregory's actions, further bolstered by the ideological support given by Maximus and many bishops of the North African church. As we have seen in the preceding chapter, the leading members of the imperial civil and military administration were largely, although not entirely, non-African in origin, and this remained the case into the seventh century. In contrast, although many subordinate officers were easterners or at least not of African background, the process of assimilation with the indigenous Romano-African population meant that by the middle of the seventh century the majority were locals while the secular elite and ecclesiastical elites remained largely Romano-African.

There was thus a clear division between eastern appointees and the indigenous Romano-African elite, but the *patrikios* and exarch Gregory, possibly related to the family of the emperor Heraclius, had strong African connections.[33] The distinction between Romano-Africans and "Romans"—that is to say, eastern Romans/Byzantines—was noted by Procopius; and as has also been pointed out, a later Arab chronicler similarly distinguishes between Romano-Africans, Romans, and Moors.[34] Such clear demarcation between groups can have contributed little to the solidarity of any resistance to an invader or, under stressful conditions, to loyalty to a distant emperor. It remains unknown whether the rigorist theological arguments defended by Maximus first promoted unquiet and then outright opposition to Constantinople, or whether his arguments fell on fertile ground because of a North African clergy and elite already partially disaffected from the government because of harsh fiscal demands. There is no doubt that his views, like those of other important theologians, could exert a good deal of influence, especially among the literate social-cultural elite who were in receipt of his letters.[35] But it appears clear that Gregory enjoyed the support of the provincial elite as well as the North African church hierarchy.[36] It was members of the African elite who negotiated with the Arabs thereafter over the subsidies intended to buy the Arabs off. As in the Ravenna exarchate, it is likely that a significant element of the North African elite was by this time made up of members of provincial origin, Romano-Africans who held imperial military commands and offices, a possibility perhaps reinforced by somewhat later reports that at the battle near Sufetula in 647, many of the "notables" of the province were killed along with Gregory himself.[37]

Following more than a year of pillaging and raiding deep into the provinces of Roman Africa, and with no imperial assistance in sight, the African elite were certainly willing to pay very substantial sums to buy off the invaders: the fantastic sums mentioned by Baladhuri and al-Waqidi are probably not to be taken at face value, but they clearly indicate a massive tribute, possibly partly made up from the revenues that had been held back.[38] The Arab withdrawal was followed—according to al-Waqidi—by an imperial demand that the African provinces pay a similar sum to the treasury, at which the notables of the region claimed they could not, since their tribute to the Arabs had exhausted their resources. That such a demand alienated the elite even further seems highly likely (a later somewhat embellished Arab account reports that one notable went to Damascus to persuade Muʿāwiya to pursue the conquest of North Africa in order to relieve the nobility of such fiscal afflictions).[39] The continuing tensions between Constantinople and the North African church can be clearly seen in the Acts of the Lateran council convened in Rome in 649. Somewhat later the oppressive tax demands imposed upon both the Italian and North African provinces after 663 (the year that Constans II established his headquarters in Sicily, surely with the aim of being the better able to defend these fiscally important western provinces) are mentioned in the *Liber pontificalis* and were no doubt typical of the central government's attitude to the western provinces, especially Africa and Sicily.[40] The presence of an imperial commander in charge of parts of Tripolitania in the 650s indicates continuing imperial government, but the resources to resist a determined Arab campaign and raiding were clearly inadequate, and Roman control over much of Byzacena was lost in the years 665–668 in spite of the reported dispatch of substantial forces in the year 665/666.[41]

In any case, local dissent, rejection of imperial authority, and tendencies toward provincial autonomy were all a serious challenge to the government's ability to maintain its authority and to extract fiscal resources. But such challenges appear not to have been systemic; that is to say, they were responses to specific imperial policies—imperial monotheletism, for example, or fiscal demands seen as especially harsh or unfair—rather than to the Roman Empire and its rulers as such, as a recent study has persuasively demonstrated.[42] Constantinople recognized the crucial importance of local elites but also took their loyalty under extreme pressure for granted. Even where the government was unable to provide military assistance or relief it strongly resented local efforts at defending provincial interests and making peace with the invader. Such initiatives, as seem to have occurred in Mesopotamia in the late 630s, in Egypt or in North Africa after Gregory's defeat, were perceived as threats to central authority and frowned upon.[43] But in the light of all this, and of the evidence presented at the trial of Maximus in 655, it is hardly surprising that high treason—his reported encouraging of the imperial commander in Numidia, Peter, to disobey a direct order to attack the enemy, for example—was the charge, and indeed the available evidence does strongly suggest that Maximus had deliberately aimed at undermining imperial authority and thus destabilizing the empire.[44]

Although the North African situation is difficult to follow because of the near total absence of written sources after the 650s, it does seem that, apart from Carthage and its immediate hinterland, in particular the grain-producing districts with easiest access to the port, the wider region slowly slipped out of imperial control across the following half century, in spite of occasional government efforts to reverse the process and the continuing identity of the Romano-African populace with the empire.[45] Imperial forces were based in and around Carthage until the end and were clearly both active and remained loyal to the government: North African units were involved in suppressing the rebellion of Mizizius on Sicily in the wake of the assassination of Constans II in 669. The mint at Carthage continued to operate.[46] And while the strategic situation needs also to be taken into account in this long, drawn-out process—the geography of the territory to be defended along with the defensive capacity or potential of the major towns and fortresses[47]—the role of local elites would have been crucial to any resistance. Whether the North African elite was really as drastically affected by the defeat at Sufetula as to be almost annihilated or not,[48] their role in (or absence from) this process must have been significant, and the relatively oppressive fiscal demands of the government can have done little to help their situation. Coastal towns and cities remained under imperial authority until the 690s. In the end, however, and in spite of the continued presence of some imperial troops, the occasional much larger expeditionary forces dispatched from the east, and a clear desire to hold onto North Africa, the government was simply unable to devote the resources necessary for an effective long-term defense and, more importantly, to inhibit local tendencies to compromise with the invader.[49]

Italian Questions

The situation in Italy was complicated, as in North Africa, by the conflict between the papacy and Constantinople over imperial religious policy and in the later seventh and first half of the eighth century by the fiscal demands of Constantinople. Already by the 640s local feeling and local identities could overcome loyalty to the emperor in Constantinople, and central control was a precarious matter of compromise, diplomacy, the occasional use of force and coercion, which was not always successful. The situation for the government was only worsened by the arrival in Rome of Maximus the Confessor in 645/646, who came in order to win papal support for his position.[50] Here further connections and associations served him well since the pope, Theodore (642–649), was himself the son of a Palestinian bishop. Theodore had been elected without imperial sanction and, like his predecessor, John IV (640–642), officially rejected the *Ekthesis*.[51] The gulf that was already opening between Rome and Constantinople was dramatically widened as a result of the influence exercised by Maximus and his monastic supporters, which appears to have been both substantial and effective. In a public break with Constantinople, perhaps encouraged by the fact that the former patriarch, Pyrrhus, had meanwhile come to Rome and renounced his support for the imperial position, Theodore deposed the current patriarch of Constantinople, Paul, having first dispatched a letter to Constans II (or his councilors) denouncing monotheletism.[52] The pope summoned a general council—the so-called Lateran Synod—although he died and this meeting was held under his successor, Martin (649–653). Again, monotheletism was condemned, and although the suggestion that the acts of the council had been scripted by Maximus and his followers in advance is probably to be rejected, he certainly had a decisive influence over the council's proceedings and its outcome.[53]

Our knowledge of events in Italy during these years is hazy, to say the least, in part because the *Liber pontificalis*, a key source, omits or appears to have tendentiously modified some events in order to preserve papal reputations.[54] The imperial response to these developments was nevertheless slow, no doubt because of a rebellion or mutiny of soldiers led by a *cartularius*, a certain Maurice, in 643, and at the same time new encroachments on imperial territory by the Lombards, who inflicted a series of defeats on the forces of the exarch. Interestingly, Maurice claimed that the exarch was plotting his own rebellion against the empire, but it is impossible to know whether this was actually the case, and both Maurice and the exarch, Isaac, died in 643.[55] The new exarch, Plato (ca. 643–649), took no immediate action, and it was only in 649 that the government was able to make a move.[56] This time the exarch, Olympius, was ordered to Italy to snuff out the papal opposition, but by now it seems that increasingly strong local sentiment and inadequate investment diplomatically and militarily on the part of Constantinople had made the situation very difficult for the government of Constans II. The *Liber pontificalis* claims that Olympius was first to have sounded out the

Italian forces and only act against the pope (by arresting him) if he could count on their support. If he could not, he was ordered to wait until such time as he had won them over. If they would support him, then he was to compel the bishops and clergy to sign up to the *Typos* issued by Constans II in 648, prohibiting further debate on the issue of divine wills.[57]

As it turned out, it would appear that Pope Martin was protected by both the army of Italy and his clergy, and although we cannot know how he and Olympius were reconciled, it was later believed that Martin supported Olympius's subsequent usurpation—something he claimed during his trial in Constantinople that he simply could not have prevented.[58] Having declared himself emperor, Olympius set off to deal with an Arab attack on Sicily, very possibly at papal instigation, given the importance of the island to papal income.[59] When shortly thereafter the usurper died, probably in an outbreak of disease that had affected the Roman forces, the new exarch, Calliopas, was able in 653 to arrest both Martin and Maximus without opposition and have them taken for trial to the capital, where they were charged with treason.[60] Opposition to Constantinople suffered a serious blow as a result, but hostility and discontent smoldered on, with further disorders during the pontificate of Martin's successor, Eugenius (653–657), ending only when the pope undertook to reject the synodical letters of Peter, the new patriarch of Constantinople.[61]

The ecclesiastical estrangement that ensued lasted until reconciliation at the council of Constantinople in 680, although in the period 663–668, while the emperor was in Italy and Sicily with significant forces, an informal modus vivendi prevailed. The acuteness of the disagreement seems to have been dulled by a period of relative quiet following some imperial political and military successes, in particular after the failure of an Arab naval attack on Constantinople in the mid-650s. The emperor was now able to conclude a treaty securing a few years of peace with the caliphate, and he could in consequence reestablish a degree of Roman control over the Armenian principalities before campaigning through the Balkans, restoring a short-lived degree of Roman authority there, and then into Italy and to Rome.[62] Although it cannot be shown beyond doubt, this campaign, followed by his prolonged stay in Sicily, was aimed at reestablishing imperial control over the western regions still in imperial hands. It is true that his campaign against the

Lombards of Benevento was not crowned with complete success, although his forces certainly recovered several towns and fortress, began the fortification of a large number of mountain refuges, and created a defensive infrastructure that had been lacking hitherto. He also constructed a fleet to safeguard the coastal waters of the region. This did little to halt Arab attacks in North Africa, of course, which continued in spite of the dispatch (and subsequent defeat) of a substantial force under the *patrikios* Nicephorus at some point between 663 and 668. On the other hand, thanks to a conciliatory position adopted by Pope Vitalian (657–672), some harmony was reestablished between Rome and Constantinople, while Constans also succeeded in protecting and securing the wealth of Sicily as well as politically reconciling with the papacy (even if imperial monotheletism was still a bone of contention).[63] The fact that emperor and pope celebrated the Eucharist together, thus at least on the face of things overcoming the breach in communion that had been so clearly highlighted by Maximus and Martin, must have been especially significant for contemporaries, especially in light of the apparent silence (according to the report in the *Liber pontificalis*) of the Palestinian monastic community in the city that had so fervently supported Maximus.[64] From his new capital at Syracuse, Constans then issued legislation on fiscal matters regarding the western provinces—Calabria, Sicily, Africa, and Sardinia—imposing taxes that, while resented by the church, appear to have aroused little or no resistance or opposition.[65]

But in 668 the emperor was assassinated in his residence in Syracuse in what was clearly a palace coup (and in the course of a major Arab assault on Constantinople), and there is no evidence to suggest that local forces, or western units more widely, were supportive of the plot. The exact course of events remains obscure, and scholars have proposed a variety of theories about the background, none provable, ranging from a plot engineered from Constantinople to an assassination planned by the caliph Muʿāwiya.[66] The immediate outcome of the emperor's death was the usurpation of the throne by an Armenian general, the *komes* of the Opsikion, Mzez (Mizizius) Gnouni. Exactly how long this lasted remains unknown because of the contradictory sources, but the imperial forces sent from Constantinople cannot have arrived before the end of the siege of the capital in 669, and in fact it was probably not ended until

672.[67] It was followed very soon by an Arab naval raid that was able to take and sack Syracuse and return to Egypt loaded with booty. Yet Italian and African troops responded to suppress the rebellion, a clear indication of their loyalty to the established order; while Pope Vitalian, perhaps conscious of the empire's importance in protecting papal estates on Sicily, similarly supported the legitimate regime in Constantinople, as indicated by a letter from the emperor Constantine IV to the pope, preserved in the acts of the council of 680, in which the emperor thanked him for his support against usurpers.[68]

One likely consequence of this rapprochement was Constantine IV's decision to reverse imperial policy with regard to the doctrine of the single will. In the period prior to the convening of the council of 680, Roman ecclesiastical privileges were confirmed, fiscal exemptions were granted, and the church of Ravenna—granted autocephaly by Constans II—was returned to Roman authority. The council of Constantinople, held in 680–681, saw the abandonment by Constantinople of imperial monotheletism, reestablishing formally once again communion between the two patriarchates.[69] The rapprochement was continued under Justinian II, although Roman rejection of a number of the canons of the so-called Quinisext Council, held in Constantinople in 691–692, caused some difficulties in Constantinople. This eventually resulted in an implicit recognition of papal authority with a compromise on the part of the emperor when, during the pontificate of John VII (705–710), Justinian invited the pope to convene a synod in Rome formally to accept those canons of the Quinisext that it could and to reject the others. The clear shift in imperial approaches to the papacy and to Rome is evident in Justinian's reign in particular. No longer could an emperor intervene in the direct way that Constans II had been able to do. To the contrary, Justinian's desire to maintain Roman support becomes especially obvious in the marked display of imperial humility and goodwill during the visit of Pope Constantine (708–715) to Constantinople.[70]

All this certainly exacerbated the strained relations that had been developing between Constantinople and Ravenna and may have further promoted sentiments in favor of regional autonomy and even alienation from the capital of the empire. And while papal support was certainly regained, caution still had to be exercised. When Philippicus Bardanes (711–713) formally reestablished a monothelete policy, the news was met with armed resistance to the new emperor's appointment of the *dux,* or military commander, of Rome, while the papacy and Roman elite rejected the policy out of hand, the *Liber pontificalis* even taking the unprecedented step of denouncing the emperor as a heretic.[71]

Thus, from the middle of the seventh century, the Italian territories in the north and center, in particular those within the exarchate of Ravenna, seem slowly to have slipped away from direct imperial control in spite of efforts by Constantinople to pay attention to their affairs. Eastern officials certainly came and went regularly, although members of the local establishment had only limited access to Constantinople and the titles and status it could bestow.[72] Nevertheless, the elite remained, with few exceptions, more or less loyal to the imperial capital and the emperor, even if independent-minded on key issues. The imperial position could be reinforced from time to time by the arrival of new officials and senior officers or the imposition by an emperor through the exarchs of imperial political decisions. But the situation was inevitably complicated by the fact that, as in North Africa, while the leading elements of the administration—the exarch and his immediate entourage—tended to be appointed from Constantinople, it was locals and members of the provincial elite who filled many senior posts and dominated at all lower levels.[73] Nominal loyalty went hand-in-hand with a largely provincial political perspective and orientation. Again, while the response of western units and the occasional appearance of eastern forces might be sufficient—as in the period 663–668—to impose a stricter imperial authority and stifle any potential disloyalty, Italy was simply too far from the center of imperial attention to be seriously threatened by costly centrally directed military intervention. The income that could be drawn from imperial lands in Italy was not great, with the exception of Sicily and, possibly, the grain-producing areas of the south, as we shall see.[74]

Unlike in much of Anatolia, an effective and constant Constantinopolitan oversight over local elites was not possible to the same degree, no more than were injections of cash or of troops. But perhaps more importantly, in Italy there was no potentially overwhelming challenge from a united enemy. Instead, the remaining imperial territories, under their various increasingly autonomous local elites and with the church, faced a generally disunited, even if at times quite powerful, enemy in the form of the Lombard kingdom in the north and the duchies of Spoleto and Benevento in the center, with frequent shifts in the relationship between the imperial administration and local Lombard notables.[75] Local and regional identities flourished in the conditions of the period, but loyalty to the empire and to the government at Constantinople was not something that needed to be surrendered in order to survive. Indeed, even in Rome it was possible to retain a nominal loyalty to the empire in a period of increasing local autonomy and growth of an independent elite while at the same time opposing imperial religious policy;[76] at the same time imperial naval forces were able to maintain relatively unbroken communications with the capital as well as a flow of imperial officials, at least until the military and economic strength of the exarchate had been whittled away to almost nothing in the 740s and early 750s.

Although information is sparse, imperial interests in the far south were also maintained and were possibly more securely represented than in the north. This was partly because of the immigration of populations from the Peloponnese, a process beginning already in the sixth century,[77] and partly also because the region was, with Sicily, an important source of both grain and wine, and not just for Rome. This importance is reflected in the fact that Sicilian officials seem to have had greater access to the imperial court and to positions in the east than those from the exarchate.[78] We noted earlier that Constans II ordered a reassessment of fiscal burdens in the western regions of the empire, including Calabria (along with Sicily, Sardinia, and Africa), in the early 660s;[79] and in 681 Constantine IV issued orders reducing the rate of assessment of the *coemptum frumenti*, the annual tax in grain, for Sicily and Calabria, implying that Constans had increased it in order to support his court and military during his presence there. Indeed, the proxy climate data for the region show that it enjoyed an especially mild, humid climate regime from the later fourth into the middle of the eighth century, thus rendering it a reliable source of grain so long as the government could draw upon it securely.[80]

From the fourth and especially the fifth centuries, Apulia (later part of the east Roman military command or *thema* of Langobardia) had already become a major producer of grain but apart from its southernmost districts around Gallipoli and Otranto was effectively lost to imperial authority after the death of Constans II in 668, to be recovered only in the ninth century.[81] Calabria (Bruttium and Lucania) had likewise become a major producer of cereals from the first half of the sixth century as well as a source of horses and produce, and, while often threatened, a substantial part of it remained in imperial hands.[82] The fortification of the region as a consequence of the ongoing warfare with the Lombards and especially the military activities of Constans II also contributed to the transformation of the demography and settlement pattern of the region, but state and church operated closely together in reinforcing imperial as well as ecclesiastical moral authority and Roman identity. Just as in the exarchate in the north, many urban residents became part of a local militia while the traditional class of landowners merged with the imperial bureaucracy to generate a new social elite of office and birth.[83]

Although considerably reduced in extent by Lombard encroachment and with a population in serious decline from the later sixth century, the continued strategic importance and relative agricultural wealth of the region meant a continued, if small-scale, imperial investment and concern. In 686/687 Justinian II reduced the fiscal burden on some papal estates in the region, for example.[84] Calabria was a source of grain, wine, wood and manpower as well as, significantly, of minerals, in particular copper and silver, but also of gold. And it also seems clear that it continued to export produce beyond its immediate hinterland, at least so far as the ceramic evidence suggests.[85] The relatively gradual processes of change that accompanied warfare with the Lombards meant once again that the region was never faced with the sort of overwhelming conquest that took place in Syria, even if warfare caused substantial devastation at times, especially with the renewed attacks on Roman territory after the death of Constans II.[86] Imperial fiscal oppression nevertheless drove many among the ordinary rural and urban populations to accept Lombard control, as the limited evidence shows.[87] But even under such pressure, the continued imperial presence and interest in its resources, close association with Sicily (with which it formed economically part of the same subregion, the coinage from the mint of which dominated in the area), contact with the exarchate at Ravenna, and the identity of the interests of the elite with those of the empire ensured a continuing loyalty—again in spite of the evolution of a semi-autonomous local elite—in contrast to the North African situation.[88]

The importance of the resources of Sicily meant that the government paid a great deal more attention to the island. It remained under the more direct imperial management that had prevailed since the time of

Justinian in the sixth century. It was a smaller and relatively easily controlled region compared with North Africa, for example—or, indeed,
with the Italian peninsula itself—and relative to its size was extremely
wealthy in terms of grain production. The fact that it was an island and
that imperial naval forces could protect it from Lombard attacks, if not
from the Arabs, protected it from economic disruption. In Sicily, indeed,
the government took particular pains to ensure the continued support
and loyalty of the local elite, issuing especially countermarked coins
when, in the period ca. 620–641, it required additional supplies of grain,
for example; while Constans II's presence on the island, whatever the
burdens the arrival of the imperial court and army brought with them,
would certainly have enhanced the possibilities for social and political
advancement open to the local elite. In this respect it is not hard to see
why Sicily, in contrast to most of the other western provinces, remained
firmly under imperial control until the second decade of the ninth
century. The church of Ravenna had estates there as well as the papacy,
and their interests combined with those of Constantinople certainly made
the island of continuing and central importance to all three parties.[89]
The *strategos,* or military commander, of Sicily makes a fairly early appearance, ca. 700, and its economic as well as strategic value is indicated
by the fact that there are more seals and references in texts for military
commanders of Sicily for the eighth and ninth centuries than for any
other single military province of the empire.[90]

The very different histories of the ways in which the empire was or was
not able to hold onto its provinces in Syria, Anatolia, North Africa, and
Italy illustrate the difficulties the government at Constantinople faced
in dealing with the elites of the different regions; in extracting fiscal
revenues, whether in cash or in kind; and in mobilizing the resources
in manpower and matériel with which to secure them against internal
dissent and opposition as well as against external threats. There were
clearly some developments that affected all areas, in particular the militarization of the Anatolian elite. Yet it seems that in the east there
also remained a powerful civic elite in and around the capital. The two
were by no means rigidly distinct, but the tension between their different perspectives and ambitions may well have contributed once
again to an internal social balance of power and to the ability of the emperors to maintain a fairly firm hand on all aspects of imperial admin-

istration in the capital. In any case it is quite clear that it was the continued adherence of provincial elites to Constantinople that constituted the central element in the ability of the empire effectively to resist attack. Coercion worked, when circumstances and geography favored it. The maintenance of longer-term loyalty depended upon an identity and overlap of interests—social, political, economic, and ideological—between these elites and the metropolitan and imperial center. In contrast to its relationship with the indigenous elite of North Africa, the government was indeed able to maintain the loyalty and adherence to the imperial cause of the Anatolian elites; in contrast to the elites in Italy, those in Anatolia were never distant enough to inhibit direct government intervention to stem opposition or regional resistance to imperial policy. And in contrast to elites in more distant regions, the Anatolians could not but see Constantinople as the direct source of status, privilege, and wealth.

Their identity as Roman undoubtedly entailed a desire on the part of individuals to see the continued existence of the status quo in which they lived (the social, cultural, and political structures of their world, in our terms). But they also saw service for the state as a means to an end—for their own personal and family interests—at least as much as, if not more than, a form of public service to "the state" as an abstract entity or notion. Such a concept was certainly part of the symbolic universe of the elite and brought with it a sense of certain duties and responsibilities as well as rights. Office and title were aspired to as part of the process of realizing vested interests, even if being in the service of the emperor, at court or in the provinces, was in itself an esteemed and praiseworthy attainment.[91]

So while we have no information about the response to imperial monotheletism of the church or the elite in Anatolia, we may assume that the majority conformed because it remained in their interests to do so, because they still identified with the interests of the east Roman state and the political-ideological world it represented. This is certainly what the absence of references to secular opposition suggests, and it is what the evidence for the response of the clergy suggests. At the council of 680–681, for example, the lists of signatories to each of the sessions clearly show a reluctance on the part of the majority to attend until the direction of imperial policy had become clear, at which point—from the eleventh session until the end (session eighteen)—all those who had reached Constantinople were in attendance, and by which time the whole episcopate had clearly pledged themselves to the imperial position.

The key determinant was the emperor and court. It is also what later examples of the response to imperial religious policies suggest, as with monotheletism under Philippicus Bardanes (however briefly) or with iconoclasm, for example.[92] In contrast to North Africa, and to a lesser degree Italy and the islands of the western Mediterranean, virtually all the remaining territories of the east Roman state were, after the 650s, within relatively direct striking distance of Constantinople. The government was therefore also in a position to deliver—quickly and effectively—in terms of a military presence and an organized and coherent defense. Reciprocity was possible, and it was the combination of defense of vested interests, incorporation into a system of social and cultural status and esteem, and injections of substantial cash payments to the provincial elites, in their role as officials of the government and leaders of the army, through which it was achieved.

6

Some Environmental Factors

When winter had fallen, the emperor sent the same koubikoularios, *Andreas, and he reached Amorion at night when there was much snow. He and his men climbed on the wall with the help of planks and entered Amorion. They killed all the Arabs, all 5,000 of them, and not one of them was left.*

In this year there was a severe cold, and many men as well as beasts suffered hardship.[1]

Agriculture and Rural Production

So far I have looked in some detail at the ways in which people in the East Roman Empire viewed their world, as reflected in texts about Christian dogma and faith, polemical writings, hagiography and miracle stories, legal texts—both church law and secular law—and historiography. I have also looked at how people at different social levels and in different social and cultural contexts responded, insofar as our texts and other monuments shed light on this, to the world around them. It is now time to take a look at the physical world of seventh- and eighth-century Byzantium because all these activities are inscribed within a physical, spatial context, which itself both constrains or sets limits to beliefs and actions as well as being in turn subject to those beliefs and activities. In particular, and in light of the situation of the eastern Roman state and its inhabitants in the seventh century, we need to account for the products and the wealth from which the government ultimately drew its taxes to see if there were any significant changes that took place that may help to explain the empire's survival. And in order to do that, we need to understand what the rural producers of the empire were growing and harvesting, and under what conditions and circumstances. Since we now know that there were some important changes in both the broader climate of the late Roman world as well as in patterns of agriculture and rural production, we should inquire what impact, if any, these may have had and what brought them about. In the preceding chapters I showed how the transformed political and economic situation that arose in the middle of the seventh century generated changes in the composition, cultural identity, and values of the various elements that made up what we may refer to broadly as the dominant or ruling elite. In the next chapter I will show how these same circumstances compelled the government to revise the ways through which it managed its resources. This was not a set of specific actions or reforms (although there probably were some of these too) but rather a series of reactions at different levels to different stimuli resulting in a very different administrative apparatus from that which went before. What we have not yet done is to locate all these social and political arrangements in their environmental context.

As noted in Chapter 1, by the middle of the seventh century the empire consisted of some two-thirds of the Anatolian subcontinent, together with the Aegean Islands and long coastal stretches around the southern Balkan littoral, with some of the plains lying behind them. In addition, it held Sicily, a rich source of grain, with a hazy presence in Sardinia and in the Balearics as well as in parts of southern Italy and, of course, the circumscribed territory of the so-called exarchate of Ravenna in the northeast. Until the 690s it controlled much of North Africa—a control, however, that was increasingly challenged from the 660s by Arab raids and attacks. As far as we can tell from the extant textual and related evidence, especially the testimony of the lead seals of imperial fiscal officials, the main sources of imperial income were Asia Minor and Sicily, with North Africa playing a secondary but still important role into the 680s, as we have now seen. Here I want to look at climate, landscape, and products.

What sort of agrarian economy had generated the revenues of the late Roman state in the east before the changes of the seventh century? The Anatolian plateau, with its steppic climatic environment, is dominated by a largely pastoral and cereal-growing economy and, in spite of the relatively harsh winters and long arid summers, is not unfavorable to cereal production, which depends as much on the seasonal pattern

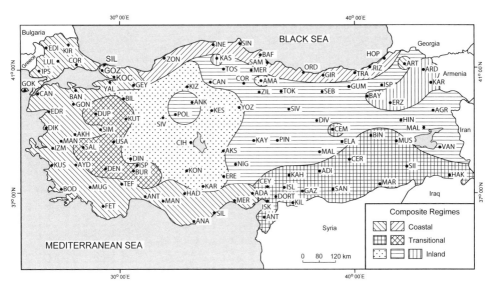

Map 6.1. Anatolia: Seasonal rainfall régime zones. (Reprinted from F. Sariş, D. M. Hannah, and W. J. Eastwood, "Spatial Variability of Precipitation Regimes over Turkey," *Hydrological Sciences Journal* 55, no. 2: 234–249, Fig. 8. © 2010 IAHS Press. Reprinted by permission of Taylor & Francis Ltd., on behalf of IAHS Press.)

of rainfall (in this case with a marked spring maximum) as it does on the volume of precipitation.[2] (See Map 6.1.) In contrast, the coastal plains reflect a Mediterranean or transitional Mediterranean environment where cereals, fruits, and nuts as well as vegetables, olives, and vines flourished. The coastal regions and islands, whether mountainous or consisting of plains and river valleys, all share certain key features that permit them to support a very wide range of agricultural and pastoral activities. All around the Mediterranean as well as inland in the river valleys and less exposed plains, vines, olives, fruits, and cereals were grown while fowl, goats, pigs, cattle, and sheep were raised. The proportions of each of these to one another depended on local terrain and established patterns of land tenure as well as market demand, on the one hand, and the need to sell produce to pay taxes, on the other (Map 6.2).[3] This agrarian culture involved a mixed regime of cereals, fruit, vegetables, olives and vines, and livestock in different proportions according to local conditions. It is characteristic of the large-scale human environmental impact found across a wide territory stretching from the southern Balkans, through Anatolia, and into the Caucasus and

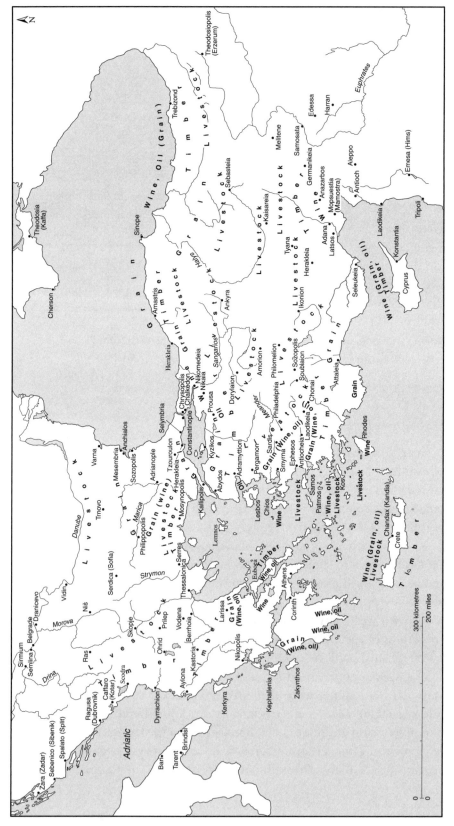

Map 6.2. Agricultural production and land use, ca. 500–1000 CE. (Reprinted from *The Palgrave Atlas of Byzantine History* by John Haldon, Map 10.4. Basingstoke and New York: Palgrave Macmillan. © 2005 by John Haldon.)

southwestern Caspian area. Known to historians of the environment as the Beyşehir Occupation Phase (BOP), it reflects a period of anthropogenic activity stretching approximately from 1500 BCE until 800 CE.[4] From the point of view of archaeologically identifiable cultures it covers the centuries from the Hellenistic through into the early Byzantine period (ca. 300 BCE to ca. 700 CE). It can be shown from the evidence of pollen (found at archaeological sites or in a variety of natural deposits such as lake beds) that the BOP begins and ends in different places at slightly different times. Its final phase stretches from the fifth into the later seventh or early eighth century, depending on site location. At some sites with well-defined timescales, the end of the phase is dated to the middle or later seventh century CE, while at other sites its termination is set somewhat earlier.[5] While most clearly evidenced in the upland valleys of southwest Anatolia, where it is characterized by the cultivation of nut trees, cereal growing, and pastoralism,[6] it is also recorded in pollen diagrams from sites in northwestern Turkey, parts of Greece, and other sites in the eastern Mediterranean.[7]

The reason for the uncertainty and debate about the end date for the BOP lies partly in the imprecision of the chronologies derived from the various datasets. This raises the questions of whether major landscape change occurred at the same or at different times across different regions and what the causes of such changes may have been. But all the records show a sharp decline in anthropogenic indicators and a rise in pine pollen at some point during the middle of the first millennium AD. These different landscape types, the range of crops they supported, and the general patterns of seasonal temperature and rainfall produced across the areas in question have all been well studied and the broad regional variations are well understood.[8]

Climatic Fluctuations

That human activity has always been one of the most significant features impacting on the landscape in historical times is a point that is apparent as soon as we consider issues such as deforestation, erosion, alluviation, the impact of overexploitation, overgrazing, soil-exhaustion, and abandonment. But the way people affect the land is itself influenced by certain factors outside human control, particularly climatic factors.[9] Quite minor shifts can have significant effects at a local level, so before looking at their possible significance for the Byzantine state in the period with which we are concerned, we will review very briefly what is known about the climate history of the region across the later Roman and into the medieval period.

It is generally agreed that records for ancient climate indicate that the regime prevailing across western Eurasia from the later third century BCE into the late second century CE was relatively stable, warm, and moist—in general, conducive to intensive agriculture. This is frequently referred to as the Roman Warm Period (RWP) and was characterized by relatively low-risk conditions with limited decadal variability, associated by many historians with the growth and consolidation of Roman military and political power and economic expansion. Such a situation was also favorable to the expansion of agriculture and population in central and northern Europe.[10] Records of solar activity reinforce this picture: there is general agreement that a correlation exists between observed paleoclimate records and changing solar activity. Low solar activity—solar minima—is reflected in low temperatures and high solar activity in higher temperatures.[11] Some scholars have associated climate and solar activity with historical events or developments, although of course this is never a one-to-one relationship and in many cases remains hotly debated—a point to which we will return à propos of our period below.[12] The solar evidence derives chiefly from certain isotopes, notably C14 (radiocarbon) and 10Be (Beryllium 10). Thus, known-age tree rings offer an absolutely dated and highly resolved record of changing atmospheric C14 levels through the Holocene for the northern hemisphere,[13] while 10Be records, extracted chiefly from polar ice cores, have annual resolution and have been shown to correspond exactly with sunspot activity, matching also the absolute chronology offered by the C14 data.[14] The point is that climate historians can be fairly certain about the major climate changes that have affected the earth over many millennia. What is usually much less clear are the minor fluctuations within these major phases because they are inflected by a range of factors that remain in many cases to be fully investigated.[15]

A great deal of highly technical literature has been published in recent years, and historians together with climate historians have recently begun to pull this material together and try to synthesize some of it.[16] This is not a completely new development, of course, since prehistorians, for example, have for many decades been thinking about the relationship between climate, environment, and the evolution of early human society and economy.[17] But it is really only in the last twenty or so years that attention has turned to more recent history.[18] Nor is this the place to enter the technically dense forest of paleo-environmental studies, depending as they do on a range of highly specialized disciplines—the study of solar activity, tree rings, glaciers, C14 and other isotopes, speleothems (stalactites), pollen, ice cores, and sea-level changes. But there is enough data now available, and more being collected and published, to enable us to fill in some significant details about the ways in which climate changed across several millennia, particularly over the last two millennia.[19]

The longer-term framework is set by the positive climatic conditions that lasted from ca. 250 BCE to ca. 200 CE but that then gave way to a less stable climate, with a considerable degree of fluctuation between cold and dry, and warm and wet periods. Thus, whereas in the southern Levant the climate became somewhat more humid after about 400 until the middle decades of the seventh century, when a more arid phase began, regional variation in Anatolia across these years appears to have been fairly marked, with wetter conditions in the center and west beginning in the early sixth century and lasting into the middle of the eighth century.[20] A wetter regime for the period ca. 500–900 in the northern Aegean and southern Balkan region is also indicated by an analysis of the evidence for ancient sea-surface temperatures.[21] The story is complicated by the impact of volcanic eruptions and a so-called dust-veil event, which meant that the years from ca. 536 to ca. 545 saw a particularly sharp drop in temperature with corresponding impacts on agriculture and human health more broadly.[22] While there seems to have been some stability in the years 480–520 and 545–560, there were also several short dry spells. In 541 the great Justinianic plague broke out, but the exact relationship between this, human health, and a changing climate context remains unclear.[23] In the Levant the short-term shift to a wetter regime that can be documented from the later fourth century into the seventh century and in parts beyond has been associated by some historians with the revival and consolidation of the Eastern Roman Empire at this time. While this association remains debated, it is certainly the case that ceramic and other data is suggestive of an intensification of economic activity during the same period.[24]

In general terms, the instability and the deterioration in climate after the second century CE indicated by the data marked the end of the relative stability that had been characteristic of the previous four hundred years. It also marked a clear increase in regional variation as the changes impacted with different results in different regions. While some fairly clear causal connections have been posited between the different historical trajectories of east and west and these climatic trends, it is still difficult to demonstrate how these actually worked, and in view of both the absence of data from many areas as well as inadequate chronological control over some datasets, we should proceed carefully before making overly hasty causal associations. The many parallels between climatic history and the evolution of states and societies on the larger scale suggest at the very least that such associations should exist and do need to be teased out. Climate and the ancient environment must play a more important role in understanding the political, social, and economic history of past societies and state formations than they have done in our interpretation in the past.[25]

So a brief word is in order about the problems that come with trying to relate climate and environment to the changes in social, political, and cultural life that our other evidence indicates. First, it needs to be made clear that shifts in climatic conditions, unless they are unusually severe and dramatic, rarely have the sort of direct impact in terms of changing patterns of social organization and behavior that more simplistic presentations of their effects would have us believe. Climate scientists are generally aware of this, so the real issue is how to relate the differential effects of climate and related environmental change to social and political change.[26] Some fairly dramatic claims can be made, of course: for example, it has been argued that the collapse of the eastern Turk khanate in the period ca. 630 was the direct result of a volcanic eruption in 626, an eruption that generated a substantial stratospheric dust cloud. This in turn had the effect of forcing a period of sudden cooling that impacted catastrophically on nomadic herds and pasturage and led to mass starvation and internal societal collapse. Chinese sources report in detail on the unusual snows and frosts for the period ca. 626–630 since China was similarly affected. Ash was apparently also observed in Constantinople. Of course, political and other structural factors must be taken into account as well, but this is an example of a situation in which a relatively fragile and inflexible social ecology would have been damaged beyond redemption very rapidly. Given that this must be set within the broader context of the "Late Antique Little Ice Age," itself probably stimulated by volcanic activity in the southern hemisphere and now thought to have prevailed from the later 530s into the 660s, it seems all the more likely.[27] The relationship between climate and culture is generally synergistic and usually asymmetrical, although such cases as this express an unusually intense socioeconomic and cultural impact.[28]

Most social-cultural systems can absorb a certain degree of change in their environment and make the appropriate adjustments without breaking down. And the degree of change evident in their response can vary enormously and depends in turn on the internal structure and articulation of the societal systems in question. In other words, their ability to adapt at different levels of social praxis will determine the success or failure of the system as a whole to respond effectively to change. Resilience, adaptability, and flexibility are thus crucial aspects, and these are the sorts of quality about which the historical and archaeological record can often tell us a great deal. Climate generally acts to amplify preexisting tendencies without being the direct cause of anything, and the intensity, length, and spatial extent of the climatic changes that can be observed in the proxy data will be key determining elements. But because it can have this amplifying effect, it is important to build it into our understanding of social, political, and economic evolution. This will become obvious in this chapter and in Chapter 7. Forcing by climatic factors—that is to say, the impact of, say, increasingly cool or humid periods on agricultural practices or on water-management systems and the social praxis and attitudes that accompany them—can be very important. But by the same token we should also bear in mind that cultural or sociocultural forcing can also occur—human activities that impact on the environment in such a way as indirectly to bring about shifts in societal behaviors and even of patterns of belief are just as important.

Another important point to bear in mind is the different levels at which climatic impacts can have an effect. Larger regional shifts can have very different impacts at subregional and microregional levels, determined by local features such as proximity to the sea, the presence of absence of mountainous terrain, and so forth. The differences in the consequences of changing climatic conditions on Anatolia and its subregions, on the Balkans, and on the Levant in the fourth through eighth centuries CE, for example, make for very significant variations in their economic histories and to some extent their political histories.[29]

As I suggest in this and the next chapter, there are some interesting possibilities arising from the evidence that is available.[30] In the case of Anatolia, the major single landmass remaining to the eastern Roman state by the late seventh century, it is becoming possible to detect some interesting and significant developments. Set in the context of other parts of the empire and their climate history, such as Sicily and southern Italy, for example, these developments can help us to understand how the Byzantine state responded to the dramatic events and transformations of the seventh and eighth centuries.

Anatolia: Climate and Land Use

The southern Balkans and especially the Anatolian peninsula are influenced by three global weather systems that affect the Mediterranean zone: the Atlantic, the south Asian monsoonal system, and the continental climate system anchored over Russia and Siberia.[31] In light of the particular geography of Anatolia, this makes for a particularly complex and nuanced regional subsystem,[32] although interpreting the complexities of environmental change in central-interior and eastern regions of Turkey is particularly problematic because of very poor records from before the twentieth century. But recent work has shown up some interesting developments, and we can exploit these to help us to understand the Byzantine response to the crisis of the later seventh and early eighth centuries. Firstly, the broad context is framed by the onset in the 530s of the so-called Late Antique Little Ice Age, a period of unusually cooler seasonal temperatures following a series of major volcanic eruptions in the 530s and 540s. The extent to which this was causally related to the Justinianic plague and to the movement of nomadic peoples on the steppe westward remains unresolved and indeed has barely begun to be discussed seriously and in detail. Secondly, it is now broadly agreed that much of Anatolia experienced a somewhat wetter climate during the sixth and up to the later seventh century, possibly stretching in some areas into the early eighth century. The end of this phase varies depending on the site from which the evidence is drawn—at Nar Gölü in central Cappadocia and at Çöl Gölü near Çankırı (Gangra) to the east of Ankara, regions typical of the central sections of the plateau, it ends ca.

750; at Tecer Gölü in northwest Cappadocia it becomes more arid from the later eighth century, whereas evidence from Gravgaz marsh in southwest Anatolia suggests an earlier onset of aridity, from the middle of the seventh century.[33] (See Table 6.1.) While it is important to be aware of the limited nature of the data, this pattern seems to be repeated with minor chronological variations across Anatolia. Indeed, the available textual evidence from the wider eastern Mediterranean and Levantine context certainly hints at the instability that these conditions promoted, with a comparatively greater number of very severe winters and apparently unusually severe frosts and snows across the later sixth and into the eighth century in Anatolia, but with relatively few droughts and aridity-related events.[34]

Whether this picture of the climate coincides with changes in land use is another question. Pollen from a range of flora reflect human activities—the pollen from cereals, olive, and nut trees, for example, or the types of grasses favored for grazing livestock. They also reflect the natural vegetation that grows to replace anthropogenic crops or expands to occupy formerly tilled arable land. Pollen can thus indicate particular patterns suggesting both what was grown and when it was grown or ceased to be grown. Pollen data taken from sites across Anatolia show that the exploitable arable and pastoral land across the region was relatively intensively exploited into the sixth and seventh centuries, with subregional variations according to local conditions. Both the palynological record as well as the archaeological evidence suggest that an often densely inhabited landscape characterized by mixed farming was typical of much of the region and included often quite marginal land. But beginning in the middle of the sixth century this intensive and relatively homogenous exploitation of land in Anatolia receded, along with the bundle of crops and activities associated across the southern Balkans and much of Anatolia with the established BOP agricultural regime. At different rates according to area, the established pattern is gradually replaced either by natural vegetation or by a more limited range of crops. There appears to have been a simplification of the preexisting agrarian regimes.[35]

Even though all the indications point to an overall decline in human activity,[36] cereal production and stock-raising appear to increase in significance proportionate to this reduced level of production. The cultivation of vines and olives recedes dramatically from many areas, and there

Table 6.1.   Varying estimated end dates for the BOP in Anatolia

Site name	Est. end date	Radiocarbon dates (no.)	Publication
SOUTHWESTERN ASIA MINOR			
Ova	2nd c. BCE?	Radiocarbon-based (2)	Bottema et al. 1984
Köyceğiz	2nd–3rd c. CE	Radiocarbon-based (2)	van Zeist et al. 1975
Söğüt	4th–5th c. CE	Radiocarbon-based (2)	van Zeist et al. 1975
Gölhisar	Mid-7th–mid-8th c. CE	Radiocarbon-based (11 for 3 cores)	Eastwood et al. 1999
Pinarbaşı	9th–10th c. CE	Radiocarbon-based (2)	Bottema et al. 1984
Ağlasun	7th–8th, or early 11th c. CE	Radiocarbon-based (5)	Vermoere 2004 / Bakker et al. 2012
Bereket	Early 4th c. CE	Radiocarbon-based (11)	Kaniewski et al. 2007
Gravgaz	Mid-7th c. CE	Radiocarbon-based (7)	Bakker et al. 2011
Beyşehir Gölü I	4th–6th c. CE	Radiocarbon-based (2)	van Zeist et al. 1975
Hoyran	4th–6th c. CE	Radiocarbon-based (1)	van Zeist et al. 1975
BITHYNIA			
Adliye (n/Iznik)	6th–7th c. CE	Radiocarbon-based (2)	Argant 2003
Göksü (Iznik)	6th–7th c. CE	Radiocarbon-based (2)	Argant 2003
Manyas	8th c. CE	Radiocarbon-based (2)	Leroy et al. 2002
Küçük Akgöl	5th–6th, then 11th c. CE	Radiocarbon-based (2)	Bottema et al. 1993/ 1994
Melen	10th–11th CE.	Radiocarbon-based (1)	Bottema et al. 1993/ 1994
Abant	11th c. CE	Radiocarbon-based (5)	Bottema et al. 1993/ 1994
PONTUS			
Ladik	8th–9th c. CE?	Radiocarbon-based (4)	Bottema et al. 1993/ 1994
Kaz	5th–6th c. CE	Radiocarbon-based (2)	Bottema et al. 1993/ 1994
Demiryurt	6th–7th c. CE	Radiocarbon-based (1)	Bottema et al. 1993/ 1994
CAPPADOCIA			
Nar	670s (first changes in 590s) CE	Varve years	England et al. 2008

Source: Reprinted from J. F. Haldon et al., *Journal of Interdisciplinary History* 45, no. 2: 113–161, Table 2 with minor omissions. © 2014 by the Massachusetts Institute of Technology and The Journal of Interdisciplinary History, Inc. (Based on Izdebski 2013b, 145–201.)

Note: Only those pollen sites in which the BOP can be clearly identified and which are provided with radiocarbon dates or varve chronology are listed.

is also a marked reduction in the presence of pollen from nut trees of all types. There are, nevertheless, clear exceptions. In the Miletus region, for example, the pollen data show uninterrupted continuity in the agricultural pattern from the fifth to the fourteenth century (while at the same time indicating a marked reduction in production levels).[37] Likewise, in parts of Bithynia in northwest Anatolia, close to Constantinople, the traditional BOP suite of cultivars seems to continue. In the coastal regions of Bithynia, in contrast, the evidence suggests an increased reliance on pastoral farming and a reduction in cereal and fruit production. While this has been seen by one scholar as a reflection of the less secure situation of the second half of the seventh and early eighth centuries, when Arab seaborne attacks on the northwest Asia Minor coastal regions were frequent, we should not lose sight of the possibility that changing market demand in the metropolitan hinterland might also have played a role.[38] In the inner Pontic region the limited pollen data suggest, in apparent contrast to the coastal zones, a decline in general cultivation after the seventh century (evidence from Ladik, Demiryurt, and Kaz). While the chronology from this material remains problematic, it nevertheless seems to indicate a trend, with no obvious signs of increasing agricultural activity that far inland after ca. 700.[39]

A simplified and more regionally diverse agropastoral regime and a reduced level of activity across the region as a whole were therefore common features across much of Anatolia from the later sixth or seventh century. A retreat from many marginal areas that had been farmed formerly and in some cases a dramatic reduction in the intensity of farming are suggestive also of a reduced rural population in many, if not most, areas. This seems to be the case in Cappadocia, in parts of southwestern Asia Minor, to a degree in Bithynia and the northwest, and in eastern Paphlagonia in the Sinope region.[40] Apart from one or two cases, the chronology of these changes remains very broad, stretching from the sixth into the eighth century. But while we should recall that the evidence is patchy and that many more sample sites are needed to offer a fuller coverage, the overall picture does seem to fit well with what is known from the textual and the archaeological evidence about conditions at this period, conditions described briefly already and discussed in detail elsewhere.[41] Another feature common to a number of sites is that, after a period of some 100–150 years, a further shift becomes evident in the pollen, namely an intensification of this simplified regime, an expansion of large-scale pastoral farming but with the reappearance in some contexts of vines, olives, and fruit. These developments coincide both with the political and economic recovery of the empire in the course of the later ninth and tenth centuries as well as with the end of the arid period that lasts from the seventh to eighth century into the tenth to eleventh century.[42]

It should by now be clear that the onset of this simplification cannot be made to coincide neatly either with known political events, such as the Arab invasions, nor can it be made to fit neatly with a single "climate change" event. The high degree of regional variation across Anatolia indicated by the paleoclimatic data does suggest that climatic instability was a significant factor in the variable rates of change evident in the pollen, and indicates different rates of change across the sixth and seventh centuries. In some areas, such as around Lake Beyşehir on the western edge of the plateau or around Sagalassos in Pisidia, the change sets in across the period from the first half of the sixth into the mid-seventh century but with a high level of local variation across quite a small area; at the coastal sites in Lycia and on the southern Aegean littoral it appears even earlier; in Bithynia the seventh century marks the key shift, in parts of Paphlagonia and Pontus likewise, although the traditional suite of cultivars may have survived into the eighth century in certain localities, while in much of Cappadocia the 670s appear to denote the end of the BOP.[43] The results of intensive archaeological survey in the southeast part of the Sinope region indicate a very clear rise in settlement density from the fourth century associated with an intensive market-orientated olive oil production. But the environmental record and the archaeology also suggest that at some point in the seventh century there was a dramatic decline in settlement density and numbers. This has in turn been linked to a collapse of olive production in the region, indicated in the pollen record.

This may have been associated with the onset of cooler temperatures, to which the olive is especially sensitive, and which are certainly suggested anecdotally by the documentary record for the period, as already noted. But the proxy climate data do not suggest any significant shifts at this point for Anatolia, and the paleoclimatic evidence for temperature for this microregion is still inadequate to determine whether the wetter conditions of the period were also part of a generally cooler climate.[44] For the present, therefore, we might hypothesize that, while cooler average temperatures may have played a role, it may just as likely have been changing market conditions, both in the Sinope hinterland as well as further afield, that were primarily responsible, with the longer-term impact of the endemic plague that sets in from the 540s across the whole eastern Mediterranean and Anatolian region (the archaeologically attested extremely dense settlement-pattern of the Sinope peninsula region could certainly have been negatively affected by plague). Such changing market conditions combined with a demographic downturn would certainly fit the broader pattern of change in the east Mediterranean and Aegean regions detectable in the archaeological record. Interestingly, the pollen indicators for the region around the site of Küçük Akgöl in Bithynia, a site much closer to Constantinople, show the introduction of oleoculture around the last quarter of the seventh century. It is tempting to link the two, even if no direct relationship can be clearly demonstrated.[45]

In all of these cases a fairly clear degree of subregional variation can be read off from the data to suggest that, within the big picture, the shift depended on a number of highly localized factors. Thus, the generally drier conditions were interspersed with a few short, wetter, periods, as illustrated by the proxy climate data from the Küçükçekmece lagoon near Istanbul.[46]

Yet, while the first half of the eighth century marks a change from humid to more arid, even where we are fairly sure that the climate really was changing, there is no change at all in the agriculture of many regions until much later. In areas of Paphlagonia other than around Sinope, or in the Pontus, for example, as well as on the central plateau and at certain sites in the western coastal regions of Anatolia, old and new regimes existed for a while side by side. In much of Cappadocia the 670s appear to denote the end of the established pattern of agriculture.[47] As I have already noted, in the coastal regions of Bithynia the evidence indicates an increased reliance on pastoral farming and a reduction in cereal and fruit production, whereas inland the agriculture typical of the previous late Roman regime appears to continue without a break.[48] So while in some areas changes in what farmers grew may be paralleled by climatic shifts, in others there is no such parallel. It seems clear that climate cannot alone have accounted for the changes. (See Table 6.2.)

Last, but by no means least, there are some interesting climatic phenomena associated in the Mediterranean region with inverse patterns

Table 6.2.   Patterns of agrarian production from the seventh century CE
            in Anatolia

Site name	Production
SOUTHWEST ANATOLIA	
Beyşehir Gölü	Slight indication of stock-raising
Hoyran Gölü	Some stock-raising; + cereals from later 8th c.
Karamık Bataklığı	Stock-raising
Bereket	Stock-raising and cereals
Gravgaz	Stock-raising and cereals
Ağlasun	Stock-raising and cereals
Pinarbaşı	**Cereals, later stock-raising**
Gölhisar	None indicated
Söğüt Gölü	**Stock-raising 6th c.–8th c., grain c. 815 +**
Ova Gölü	**Stock-raising, small-scale cereal production**
WEST ANATOLIA	
Köyceğiz Gölü	**Cereals**
Bafa Gölü	**Cereals and olives**
Gölçuk	Cereals, olives, stock-raising
Alakilise	Cereals, fruit, livestock, olives, vines
NORTHWEST ANATOLIA	
Adliye valley	**Stock-raising, small-scale arable farming**
Iznik Gölü	Stock-raising
Manyas Gölü	Fruticulture until ca. 9th c.
Göksu river delta	Stock-raising
Küçük Akgöl	Cereals, vines, fruit; olives from late 7th c.
Abant Gölü	**Stock-raising, cereals, vines**
Melen Gölü	**Stock-raising, cereals; vines from later 7th c.**
NORTH-CENTRAL AND CENTRAL ANATOLIA	
Ladik Gölü	Cereals and stock-raising
Demiyurt Gölü	Cereals and stock-raising
Çöl Gölü	Cereals and stock-raising
Nar Gölü	None until 10th c.
Tuzla Gölü	None
Çadır Höyük	Livestock and some cereals
Pessinus	Livestock and some cereals

Note: **Bold** typeface denotes continuity of agriculture from fifth to sixth centuries
into ninth to tenth centuries.

of precipitation and temperature on either side of a line at around 40 degrees latitude north. This is an effect of the contraction or expansion of horizontal climatic bands (the movement toward or away from the equator of the so-called Intertropical Convergence Zone). In periods of global cooling, Europe north of central Italy becomes cooler and drier— again with some regional variation—while proxy data and climatic modeling suggest that under such conditions the Mediterranean south of approximately 40 degrees becomes warmer and wetter. In contrast, during periods of global warming this pattern is reversed: the region south of 40 degrees becomes drier and that to the north, wetter. It is not yet clear what the implications of this are for the period with which we are concerned, and until more proxy climate data are available, it will not be possible to integrate this information into the regional picture.[49]

In summary, the palynological evidence is very suggestive of a re- treat of the traditional patterns of land use from several areas, its con- tinuation in others, and the increasing importance of stock-raising and cereal farming in other regions, all accompanied by a probably declining population. The archaeological evidence for the nature and extent of urban settlement corroborates this, even though there continues a ro- bust debate on exactly how to interpret some of this data. But relating these changes in the agrarian regime to the shifts in climate that can be documented remains problematic.[50] Whichever perspective is adopted, it seems clear that the less stable, mostly wetter conditions in much of Anatolia across the period from the later fifth through into the first half of the eighth century and the ensuing greater aridity of the following years rendered some agricultural activities more marginal than before and might suggest one reason for the forcing, microregion by microregion, of a less vulnerable, simpler, and thus, from the human perspective, safer mode of agrarian economy.[51]

Complexity and Causes

Other key factors that affected demography, agricultural production, and farming strategies included epidemic disease and warfare—very often linked in one way or another. The Justinianic plague is one impor- tant factor that needs to be taken into account and placed in the longer- term context of the eastern Mediterranean basin and the Levant and their history. Beginning in the early 540s, it rapidly engulfed the western Eurasian world, with estimates of the overall mortality ranging between 25–50 percent of the population in some areas. But it is difficult to find any quantitative evidence in order to gage its precise impact in demographic terms. Its effects certainly varied according to population and settlement density or natural environmental factors, such as the dust-veil event of the late 530s. That it did have an impact, and in some regions a very dramatic one, is not at issue, and scholars who have attempted to estimate the size of the population of the Eastern Roman Empire at this period are all in agreement that the population shrank dramatically between the mid-sixth century and the later seventh. Thus, estimates of the population of the eastern part of the Roman Empire ca. 400 vary from 24–26 million, declining to a low of anything between 10 or 12 to 19 million ca. 600, and to a mere 7 to 10 million by the early ninth century.[52] Such calculations or estimates do not take the loss of territory explicitly into account, so the degree of decline within a particular region such as Anatolia remains unknown (and probably unknowable). And, of course, all such estimates remain extremely hypothetical.[53] The shifts in patterns of urban settlement, again heavily nuanced by subregion within Anatolia, must also reflect shifts in the availability of human resources, the demands of local and interregional markets, and, thus, levels of production.

Additionally, the invasions and warfare of the second half of the seventh century had a noticeable effect, and, although there is to date only one site where paleo-environmental data can be tied in exactly to the historical evidence, it is starkly suggestive of the impact the constant raiding and hostile activity of the second half of the seventh century could have. The evidence from Lake Nar, some twenty kilometers southeast of Nazianzos and thirty kilometers southwest of Malakopea (Derinküyü), is located in the center of areas that were the subject of repeated Arab attacks in the seventh century (Map 6.3). The analysis of the pollen sequence provides a very high-resolution record of vegetation patterns in the surrounding district for some 1,700 years, back to about 300 CE, information that tells us about the changes in vegetation that took place over this period. It shows that during the period ca. 300–ca. 670 CE the pollen signature reflects a mixed and fairly intensive agrarian regime dominated alongside areas of deciduous oak, woodland, and grass-dominated steppe, a regime reflected also in the pollen from

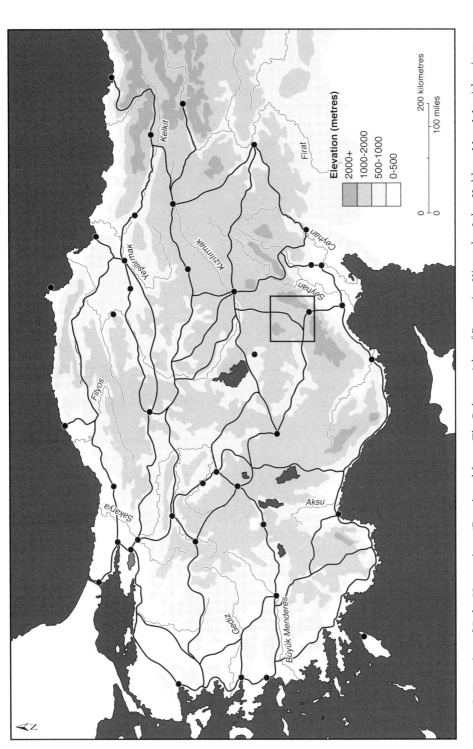

Map 6.3. Location of Lake Nar region. (Reprinted from *The Palgrave Atlas of Byzantine History* by John Haldon, Map 1.1 with minor additions. Basingstoke and New York: Palgrave Macmillan. © 2005 by John Haldon.)

other sites in southwestern and western Turkey and associated with the BOP.[54] This agrarian regime comes to an end during the seventh century, and the near disappearance of anthropogenic indicators implies a period of marked decline in agricultural activity and an expansion of woodland, while the sustained increase in pine pollen percentages, typical of many other western Anatolian pollen diagrams for this period, thus seems to reflect a fairly dramatic expansion of pine forests across the Taurus and Pontic mountain chains, albeit probably at some distance from Nar.[55] Pollen percentages for grasses associated with steppe vegetation also decline in this period, possibly implying that some areas previously dedicated to livestock grazing were also recolonized by scrub.

Unlike other sites, however, the annual sedimentation from the lake bed at Nar permits exact dates to be achieved for the major changes in representative pollen types, so the end of the BOP can be fixed within a fairly tight timeframe and placed with great precision in the period from 664 to 678 CE.[56] During this short time most of the evidence of human agricultural and pastoral activity decreases markedly, to be replaced by an increase in the percentage values of pollen from arboreal species associated with secondary scrub and woodland development generally related to encroachment onto recently abandoned agricultural land.[57] This is significant because specialist pollen distribution analyses suggest that most pollen deposited in Nar Gölü was regional rather than local in origin—although local land-use changes in the immediate vicinity of the lake (an area of some five square kilometers) probably affected the composition of the pollen, the record also reflects landscape and vegetation changes across much of Cappadocia (thus, from an area of some five thousand square kilometers or more).[58] The Nar record reflects a regional pattern in which the evidence for extensive human agricultural activities appears to cease or be reduced to a statistical minimum in the period ca. 664–678, to resume again, albeit with different emphases, only in the middle of the tenth century. (See Figure 6.1 and Table 6.3.)

In the year 664 a substantial raiding force struck Koloneia in Cappadocia (Aksaray)[59] and the region around it, a focus for attacks into imperial territory for invaders from this time onward. Frequently devastated by passing armies, its smaller towns were destroyed or abandoned and its more significant centers transformed into fortresses.[60] In the following years many other hostile forces moved through or occu-

land use and vegetation   **climate**

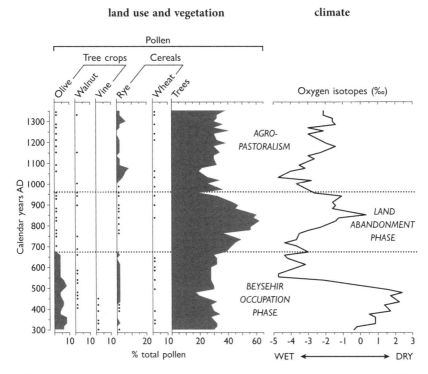

Figure 6.1. Summary of vegetation, land use, and climate change, Nar Gölü, Cappadocia, 300–1400 CE. Reprinted from J. F. Haldon et al., *Journal of Interdisciplinary History* 45, no. 2: 113–161, Fig. 4. © 2014 by the Massachusetts Institute of Technology and The Journal of Interdisciplinary History, Inc. (Modified from Anne England et al., *Holocene* 18, no. 8, December 2008: 1229–1245.)

pied the countryside; in 665 another army wintered in Pisidia, not far from Pisidian Antioch, where it established a base of operations until it withdrew in 666, only to return again in 667. Further expeditions passed through both Pisidia and Cappadocia in the next five or six years, both preparatory to the attacks that coordinated with the blockade of Constantinople in 667–669 as well as part of other thrusts into the empire's heartland.[61] A near-contemporary source describes in dramatic terms the effect of such warfare on the landscape through which they marched or where they were based:

> Armenia and its inhabitants will fall into captivity and to the sword; Cappadocia to ruin and become a desert, and those who dwell in it will be consumed by captivity and slaughter . . . Cilicia will become a desert and its inhabitants will perish by the sword and be led into captivity . . .

Table 6.3.   Summary interpretation of high-resolution pollen and stable
             isotope data, Lake Nar, 270–1400 CE

Climate		Rural land use and population	
270–540 CE	Dry	pre-680 CE	Dense settlement; cereals and tree crops
540–750 CE	Very wet	pre-680 CE	Dense settlement; cereals and tree crops
750–950 CE	Moderately dry	680–950 CE	Greatly reduced agrarian activity, forest recovery, rural abandonment
950–1400 CE	Moderately wet	950–1400 CE	Agro-pastoral economy, demographic growth

Source: Reprinted from J. F. Haldon et al., *Journal of Interdisciplinary History* 45, no. 2: 113–161, Table 3 with minor modifications. © 2014 by the Massachusetts Institute of Technology and The Journal of Interdisciplinary History, Inc.

> The land of the Romans will be given over to ruin and slaughter and its inhabitants will be turned to flight, and the islands of the sea will become a desolation and their inhabitants will be destroyed by the sword and by captivity.[62]

This is a dramatic record, no doubt exaggerated for rhetorical effect, of the perceived impact of such warfare on the land and its inhabitants. It is corroborated by the evidence of the chronicles.[63] Apart from the archaeological and survey evidence, there are also the references in the sources to the compulsory transplanting of captive populations from the Balkans into devastated regions of Asia Minor, noted in an earlier chapter, in order to make good the loss of manpower through captivity and death.[64] There is also written and archaeological evidence for the flight of populations as well as the movement of settlements to more defensible locations. Hagiographies of a slightly later period all make reference to the devastation caused by such warfare; indeed, in some cases it seems that areas in Asia Minor first attacked in the seventh century, and regularly thereafter, were still only at the beginning of recovery in the later tenth century—another point nicely confirmed by the Nar Gölü data. And this is, of course, apart from the narrative evidence of the chronicles and histories of the period.[65] In the seventh-century account of the miracles of St. Theodore "the recruit," the population of the beleaguered fortress town of Euchaïta, much further north than the area discussed here, consider abandoning their homes in an effort to locate a less hazardous environment (as did indeed happen in one or two doc-umented cases), and the text speaks almost mechanically in terms of "when the yearly raid of the Saracens came."[66]

Allowing for all the biases in the written sources, this material nev-ertheless offers a context for the interpretation of the Lake Nar pollen data. They suggest beyond any reasonable doubt that at some point be-tween 664 and 678 the region around the lake, an area certainly encom-passing Koloneia (Aksaray), suffered a massive retrenchment in terms of traditionally cultivated crops. Oleoculture and viticulture cease or were seriously curtailed, while cereal production disappears from the record almost entirely. There is no climatological explanation for this phenom-enon; indeed, such a dramatic change can only be explained in terms of the devastating warfare of the period that affected this area. Human occupation did not cease: the continued existence of a number of small settlements and fortresses, located archaeologically or referred to in the written sources, makes this clear. But the data do indicate a complete change in the economy of the region accompanied, it may safely be assumed, by a considerable reduction in population. And in view of the geographical coincidence of the warfare of the period with other sites as-sociated with this change, it would seem clear that the traditional agri-cultural regime—characterized by the BOP discussed earlier—was ended in these regions entirely as a result of anthropogenic factors and associ-ated phenomena: warfare and its accompaniments, pestilence and famine.

As significant as the pollen data for the radical and dramatic re-trenchment of human agrarian activities in the period 664–678 may be, the later recovery indicated by the pollen data that took place some 280 years later is equally impressive. This evidence presents a somewhat different configuration of the human economy of the region, with a more obvious emphasis on cereal production and pastoral farming or ranching—in contrast to the greater extent of orchard and garden crops of the BOP before its abrupt termination. Here there is a coincidence of the pollen evidence for a reviving agrarian economy and the broader economic and political recovery of the empire in this region in the later tenth century, as well as a further downturn ca. 1100 CE and a subse-quent recovery about a century later. This can most likely be associated with the occupation of this area by the Seljuks, the abandonment of cereal production on a substantial scale, and its gradual reinstatement as the area became politically and economically stable again at the be-ginning of the thirteenth century.[67]

But the main point of this is that the effects of warfare should be neither overestimated nor underestimated. Many of the economic changes that affected the patterns of urban and rural settlement, production, and population of Anatolia in the seventh century were of a longer-term character. Warfare was just one of several factors to be taken into account, and in some areas may have played no or only a very limited role. In others, though, such as this region of Cappadocia, its impact seems to have been much more severe than elsewhere. In the region of Gangra (Çankırı), for example, pollen from Lake Çöl show a sudden decrease in the evidence for anthropogenic activities ca. 750 (±twenty-five years). It has been suggested that this may reflect Arab raiding in the first half of the eighth century (specific attacks are mentioned in the sources for 712 and 727), among other potential causes.[68] The demographic impact of the warfare is difficult to judge exactly for want of evidence, but it is worth pointing out that movements of refugees and of groups transferred by the government from without the empire are prominent in our sources. Refugees of all social categories fled their homes in the conquered territories or abandoned lands that had been subject to enemy ravages. Already by the 650s communities of monks from Armenia and Cilicia had established themselves as far afield as Rome and Sardinia, for example, suggestive of a wider tendency, while other monks, some of them originally from Palestine, fled to Italy from Saracen attacks on the North African provinces after 647.[69] It is likely that other elements of the population fled to Anatolia, notably many from northern Syria from the late 630s onward.[70] Some Byzantine settlements along the Syrian and Cilician frontiers, such as Sision, were abandoned by their populations; the inhabitants of the city of Euchaïta, as we have just noted, considered abandoning their town; and the canons of the Quinisext themselves make reference to the abandonment of settlements and of the land as a result of hostile attacks, as well as to the flight of clergy from such areas.[71]

An analysis of the regions represented by the bishops who were present at the late seventh-century church councils of 680–681 and 691–692 shows that the western and southern regions of Anatolia were far less well represented than those from the north and east, and it has been argued that this reflects the impact of the warfare on these areas, districts that formed the main corridor of attacks into Asia Minor and toward Constantinople in the 650s to 670s.[72] The movement and resettling of refugees cannot have been unusual: canon 38 of the Quinisext deals with the conditions under which new or refounded cities were to be established, and as an example canon 39 deals with the case of the transplanting of the Cypriots of Constantia under their bishop, John, who were established by Justinian II at Nea Ioustinianoupolis in the Hellespont. Canon 95 is concerned with heresy, and it names various heretics as being among the refugees.[73] At different times according to the exigencies of the moment, many of these may have been Armenians who came in both larger and smaller numbers, usually under their own leaders, and as a result of Arab pressure, although in many cases returned quite soon to their homeland. Some certainly stayed: in 661 a number of "heretical" Armenian Paulicians settled in the Pontic region between Neokaisareia and Nikopolis; some of the later military magnate families of Cappadocia could trace their origins to such migrations and settlements in that area.[74] Where exactly the refugees went is generally not known, apart from these few cases, but in the case of the Cypriots, northwest Anatolia was clearly the destination. In addition to refugees, the government also transplanted captive populations en masse to Asia Minor during the reigns of Constans II (in 658) and Justinian II (in 688/689), mostly to Bithynia or to Cappadocia, a clear indication of the damage inflicted by almost constant warfare on the indigenous populations. The lead seals of some of the high-ranking officials who dealt with these settlers survive to illustrate just how important such transfers were for the government.[75] Yet even such moves could not always undo the damage. An eighth-century Syriac chronicle notes of the transit of the invading armies in 716: "the regions of Asia and Cappadocia . . . as far as Melitene and by the river Arsanias as far as Inner Armenia . . . had been graced by the habitations of a numerous population and thickly planted with vineyards and grain and every kind of fruitful tree; but since that time (they have) been deserted and . . . have not been resettled."[76]

Grain and a New Agrarian Regime?

As the political situation in the empire in the years around 700 worsened, so did the chances of its surviving for much longer seem ever more slender. As well as a demographic decline, a regional retreat of agriculture, and a simplification of agricultural production, it also had to deal with the impact of warfare and insecurity across many areas, a retrenchment of urban life, and a reduction in the agricultural products upon which the state based its taxation and supported its armies. This makes the issue of supplies, of grain in particular, for the capital, Constantinople, and for the armies in the provinces of especial importance. The loss of Egypt in 618 to the Persians, and then for good to the Arabs from 641, was a serious blow to the government because Egypt had been the bread-basket of the empire. The great grain fleets carrying the annual harvest from the Nile delta to the Aegean and on to Constantinople no longer operated; indeed, the Arabs waged economic warfare as much as they waged a war of attrition against Constantinople. The government at Constantinople, having discontinued the public bread dole in the cap-ital, a deeply unpopular move, needed to find new sources of grain for the capital.[77] Not only that, but with the withdrawal of the field armies into Anatolia from the 640s and 650s onward, the provinces now had to supply substantial numbers of additional mouths, both human and animal. This consideration is rarely if ever discussed, important though it is, and it is the issue of the empire's grain supply and of supplying the armies to which I now want to turn.

The possible sources of grain are not many. Studies have shown that there were, in effect, only four realistic options. At first North Africa, and then Sicily, may have served this purpose—the evidence of both the seals of imperial fiscal officials, *kommerkiarioi,* associated with both re-gions is suggestive, as is the ceramic data for the movement of goods between both provinces and the capital in the period from the 650s to 670s.[78] Indeed, the numismatic and sigillographic evidence from Sicily shows that it was an important and valuable source of grain for the Con-stantinople government during the reign of Heraclius, when the Per-sians were in occupation of Egypt, and again for a time during the reign of Constans II (so, from the 650s) as well as those of his successors. But as Lilie also noted, Sicily was a long way from Constantinople and could hardly guarantee a secure and regular annual delivery after the 660s. Indeed, from the 650s, with Arab sea power henceforth a serious chal-lenge to Roman control of the sea-lanes, such a source of supply became doubly problematic, and Constans II's move to Sicily in 662 was almost certainly connected with the grain supplies of Sicily and North Africa. Just as importantly, the appearance of a *strategos,* or generalissimo, for the island at a comparatively early date, ca. 700, suggests that Sicily figured fairly prominently in imperial priorities.[79] More military commanders are known from seals and texts for Sicily for the eighth and ninth centuries, for example, than for any other single military province of the empire, suggestive of the economic as much as of the military strategic value of the island.[80] Africa was endangered by Arab raids by land from the 650s, and with the defeat and death of the exarch Gregory in 647, the North African provinces appear to have lain under tribute to the Arab authorities to the east for over a decade. It is worth noting that the seals of imperial officials who have been associated with the management of North African grain disappear at about the time of Gregory's usurpation and defeat in 647 and reappear only in 673–674, shortly after the government at Constantinople tried to reimpose fiscal control over the region.[81] In any case, its last outpost at Carthage was finally lost in 692. A second option lay in Thrace and the southern Balkan regions, but for much of the later seventh and eighth century they were in no position to provide a regular and reliable supply; production was easily disrupted by raids and attacks from Slavic invaders throughout the first three-quarters of the seventh century, and thereafter from the Bulgars, although at a later date—in a more stable political and economic situation—these regions provided a good part of the city's supply in grains, vegetables, and meat.[82] A third possibility lay in Bithynia and the northwestern regions of Asia Minor. They certainly produced grain, and there is evidence to suggest that enough could be produced to supply the garrison and residual population of Constantinople after the siege of 717–718 was over. In the later eighth and ninth centuries grain from Bithynia was certainly a significant product.[83] (See Map 6.4.)

This leaves the Pontic regions, Paphlagonia and Pontus, with the important ports of Trebizond, Amastris, Heraklea, and Sinope. Textual as well as limited archaeological evidence shows that these were comparatively flourishing across the seventh and eighth centuries.[84] We know that grain ships traveled from the southern Black Sea coast to Cherson in the middle years of the seventh century.[85] Throughout the eighth century and well into the ninth century there is clear evidence for Amastris as an important focus of Black Sea trade, especially to Cherson.[86] The evidence of lead seals of imperial officials in charge of storehouses and granaries for several regions and major ports along the southern Black Sea coast, dating to the later seventh or early eighth century, illustrate the relationship.[87] And there was certainly a regular

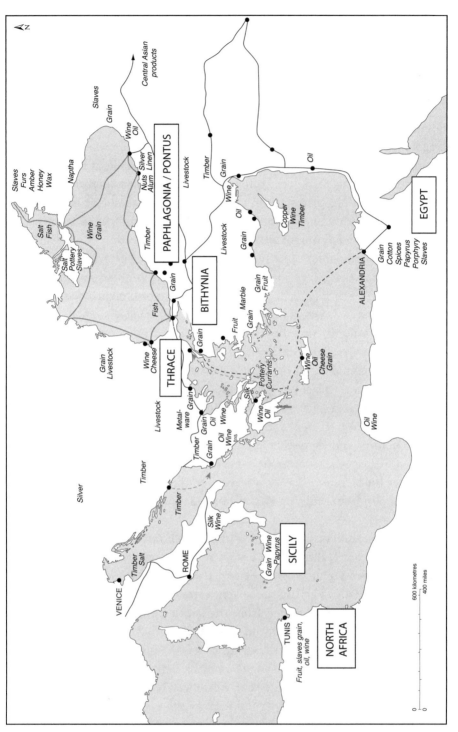

Map 6.4. Sources of grain in the seventh century CE. (Reprinted from *The Palgrave Atlas of Byzantine History* by John Haldon, Map 1.4 with minor modifications. Basingstoke and New York: Palgrave Macmillan. © 2005 by John Haldon.)

annual grain traffic to Constantinople in the first half of the ninth century, conducted by contracted ship owners or *nauklēroi*, from particular regions such as the Aegean and Paphlagonia to Constantinople, and managed through the general *logothesion*. The emperor Nicephorus I introduced a series of measures intended to indemnify or insure the government in respect of the activities of such ship owners. Ships' masters from the island of Androte, located off the Paphlagonian coast, who had defrauded the government of some of the grain they were to transport are mentioned in a letter written in the 820s.[88] According to the tenth-century *De administrando imperio* ("On governing the empire"), Cherson was supplied with grain by sea from the southern Black Sea coastal ports, just as it had been in the second half of the seventh century: "If grain does not pass across from Aminsos and from Paphlagonia and the Boukellarioi and the flanks of the Armeniakoi, the Chersonites cannot live." Aminsos (Samsun), Paphlagonia, and the Boukellarion region as well as the Armeniakon are named, and there is no reason to doubt that such grain could also be shipped to the capital.[89]

While the limited palynological data suggest a reduction in agricultural activity in general after ca. 700 in some parts of inland Paphlagonia-Pontus, it is clear that these regions in their widest sense could supply both themselves and more distant parts of the empire in the period from the seventh to the ninth century and beyond. Consider, for example, the case of the region around Euchaïta, on the whole not a particularly favored agrarian environment. In ancient times this was the southerly portion of the district of Phazemonitis, running alongside the region of Diakopene. It was described by Strabo as "in general bare of trees and productive of grain." In one of his letters the eleventh-century bishop John Mauropous also describes the region as "very desolate, uninhabited, unpleasant and without trees, vegetation, woods or shade, a total wilderness full of neglect . . . It abounds, however, in the production of grain."[90] The wetter conditions of the seventh to eighth centuries would certainly not have impacted negatively on this regime.

It should also be remarked that while a decline in agrarian activity probably indicates also a demographic decline, it may at the same time disguise an increase in production relative to total population. In the conditions of the period in question, such a potential increase may well have had significant consequences in respect of the carrying capacity of the landscape. In addition, the presence of *nauklēroi* contracted by the government shows quite clearly that the state continued to have a direct interest in the sources and delivery destinations for grain. The letter in question was written on behalf of the ships' captains to Democharis, the general logothete, to beg for leniency. Particularly important is the fact that this concerns the annual shipment for the public treasury (*dēmosios logos*), the department under whose remit the earlier general *kommerkiarioi* had fallen, and which in the early ninth century administered the imperial *kommerkia*, the warehouses or granaries.[91]

It might be appropriate at this point to consider briefly production techniques and matters relating to the yield on seed sown for cereals, among other crops. This is a subject about which we do not have a great deal of specific information from the early Byzantine period, but evidence from somewhat earlier as well as from the tenth century and later, and evidence from comparable situations in other parts of the Roman world does permit some general conclusions. Byzantine agriculture was organized throughout on the basis of the peasant family household, normally forming one element in a village community that served as the basis for both fiscal assessments as well as social life. The amount of land farmed and the types of crops produced varied by region, terrain, size of family, relative degrees of wealth and poverty, and similar factors. Most peasant households possessed a garden that produced essential vegetables for the family, although the semi-free waged workers on large estates were more dependent on their landlords for their sustenance (and the evidence is too slender to hazard even the most general estimates of the proportion of different types of tenant one to another). With few exceptions it would appear that most farming was mixed, even where cereals dominated, with some legumes being an important element of the productive cycle and the system of crop and field rotation; and, again with the exception of those of the lowest social and economic status, most households had some livestock, although again numbers varied considerably.[92]

Production levels—the size of harvests—are, of course, very difficult to assess, and on the basis of the limited evidence, some interpretations and proposals about returns on seed for wheat in both the ancient and the later Byzantine periods have been made. Thus, at one extreme the rate fluctuates between 1:3 on the poorest land or in a bad season to an average of perhaps 1:4 or 1:5 and, occasionally, in especially favorable circumstances, to as much as 1:8 or 1:9. At the other end of the scale, outputs between 1:9 or even 1:15 have been suggested, depending on area, the textual source in question, and the willingness or not of historians to generalize from sparse data. Byzantine farming in the Balkans in the eleventh and twelfth centuries was fairly intensive, with a sowing of some three hundred grains per square meter (following the *Geoponika*, which were certainly read by landlords at that period); whether such conditions applied in Anatolia in the seventh and eighth centuries is impossible to say, but it is certainly the case that a return of less than 1:4 would barely generate a marketable surplus.[93] A papyrus document from the Nessana archive in the Negev, dating to the middle of the seventh century and relating to irrigated fields in the area, records returns of 1:7 for wheat and an even higher rate of 1:8 or 1:9 for barley, showing what sort of return could be managed from a less favorable agrarian environment.[94] Since it is evident that cereal harvests from Paphlagonia and Pontus did indeed generate such a surplus, the conclusion is unavoidable that returns on seed sown were at least as high as this and in most years may have been considerably higher.

We do have some figures from tax documents and from handbooks for fiscal officials from the tenth and eleventh centuries that tell us a little about relative levels of production in different parts of the empire. Thus, arable land in western and southwestern Asia Minor was considered more productive by an order of some 19 percent than equivalent land in Thrace and Macedonia, and by an order of some 30 percent than land in the central and eastern regions.[95] Interestingly, the Pontic region and Paphlagonia are not mentioned specifically, but since they were certainly at all times somewhat more fertile and suited to intensive farming than the inland regions, we might assume that they had at least the same productive capacity as the European provinces mentioned. While again we have no comparable information for the seventh and eighth centuries, such differences are unlikely to have changed a great deal in the intervening period and thus give some idea of the relative and potential wealth of Byzantine agriculture even in difficult times.

In the middle of the tenth century, even the military district or *thema* of Anatolikon, much of which lay on the plateau or in the Taurus mountains and foothills, could generate enough surplus in cereals to supply some 20,000 *modioi* of barley and as much as 30,000 of wheat for a military expedition. Assuming the standard value for the so-called *annonikos modios* of 18.6 pounds or 8.5 kilograms, this approximates to about 170 metric tons, or 187.4 US tons of barley and proportionately more in wheat.[96] If we risk a somewhat hypothetical exercise, and following the advice of the *Geoponika,* according to which the traditional sowing of wheat was one *modios* of seed per *modios* of land,[97] and if we assume an average rate of return on sowing of 1:5,[98] then the wheat represents the produce of some 6,000 *modioi* of land, or 1,500 acres (approximately 608 hectares), the barley (assuming a similar return on seed sown) 4,000 *modioi* of land, or 1,000 acres (approximately 405 hectares). Given that this must be a surplus extracted as levies from the rural populations of the regions in question, it is suggestive of the productive potential of the land. We should recall, of course, that considerable areas of this district were particularly insecure in the later seventh and much of the eighth century, so it was probably not such a ready source of grain at that time. Yet the region still had a substantial military force to maintain.

There are some significant indications that the empire had been able to reorient its management of both the Constantinopolitan supply as well as the centers of grain production for some of its provincial armies. We have already noted briefly that the palynological data for parts of Paphlagonia and Pontus suggest not only that the suite of crops associated with traditional late Roman agriculture continued to be cultivated in some limited areas into the eighth century but also that production after the middle of the seventh century placed increased emphasis on cereals and the herding of livestock. While the evidence is ambiguous, it is possible to see a proportional increase of cereal production in these areas compared with more exposed regions to the south.[99]

Such a simplification of agrarian output across Anatolia, and more especially the greater emphasis on cereal production suggested by the palynological data, would in fact have been very opportune for the east Roman state under the sort of intense pressure that it experienced at this time. The fact that northern, northwestern, and central Anatolia experienced a period of greater humidity from the sixth into the eighth century—lasting at least into the 730s—than had hitherto been the case may well have acted to encourage cereal production also. The importance for cereal farming of the regular winter and spring rainfall (November to April) was emphasized by medieval writers such as Michael Psellus (in the eleventh century) as well as in the Roman agronomical literature that learned Byzantines read.[100] Although it is clear that the change from the established pattern to the simpler grain and livestock regime was under way in a few places from the fifth century onward, the proxy data suggest that in most cases the shift took place in the seventh to eighth centuries. Whether or not this process was the result of local conditions and evolved at different rates in different regions, the desperate straits in which the government found itself from the 650s on must certainly have constituted a further pressure on the fisc to generate the supplies needed by its armies—livestock and grain, precisely the products that the pollen record suggests came to dominate.

Market-orientated produce such as vines and olives, still "essentials" in an eastern Mediterranean cultural context, continued to be produced but on a much-reduced scale, as the pollen evidence appears to indicate. And as I noted earlier, the introduction of oleoculture close to Constantinople during the later seventh century may well reflect the apparent collapse of the Sinope region industry at roughly the same time. The evidence from the Miletus region would support such an argument.[101] Whether this reflects a shrunken market demand, a breakdown in production due to economic or climatic factors, or a combination of all of these still remains obscure.[102]

A final indication of the centrality for the government of issues of military supply and the production of key provisions—grain and meat in particular—is the way in which the armies were accommodated in Anatolia after their withdrawal from the regions in which they had originally been based. It is a significant feature of this process that the different divisions appear to have been billeted or based across provinces according to the ability of the districts to support them. This ought to be obvious, yet for many years it simply was not noticed. Of course, the exact rationale underlying the withdrawal remains obscure, but the outcome is clear enough.[103] Thus, a force of some 12,000–15,000 from the field army of Armenia was garrisoned across a vast swathe of territory but in a landscape that was both less strategically vulnerable, consisting largely of mountain and inhospitable terrain relatively difficult of access from the major Arab forward bases and with only limited agricultural potential; whereas a nominally larger force withdrawn from the eastern frontier in Syria and Mesopotamia was located in a smaller but more productive and certainly strategically more vulnerable landscape. I will deal with this in the next chapter. Suffice to say that the government clearly had a plan, and a sophisticated one, for the garrisoning, supplying, and maintaining of its armies, and it also had a plan for the continuation of grain supplies for the capital as well as, we may assume, for the soldiers. I will deal with these aspects also in the following chapter.

These were hard times for the east Roman state. Yet in spite of the sparseness of the sources and the ambiguity of many of them, we can glimpse the basis for its survival. Shifting and unstable climatic conditions in this period seem to have had a significant—indeed, transformative—impact on agricultural production and farming across Asia Minor and beyond. Population declined, the amount of land productively exploited receded, the agrarian regime was in many places considerably simplified, and all this in the context of a reshaping of urban life and a refashioning of urban–rural relations. In the context of the wars with the Persians but much more dramatically with the Arabs after the 640s, the government had also to completely rethink the ways in which it supported its armies, supplied Constantinople, and defended its core territories, issues that I will address later. Imports to the capital from North Africa or Sicily remained important at times, as we have noted and as we will see in the next chapter—and the proxy climate data from Sicily and southern Italy show that the humid climate that this region experienced in the period 450–750 CE was highly favorable for the intensive production of cereals.[104] Nevertheless, Anatolia continued to produce the essentials for survival. In fact, if the palynological data reflect the situation accurately, the production of grain in Anatolia appears to make up an increasing proportion of a declining total agricultural output, a proportional increase that could be seen to compensate for the decline or disappearance both of sources of grain no longer available and of other activities (fruticulture, oleoculture, and viticulture), while stockbreeding appears likewise to become a more prominent aspect of the agrarian economy. In the context of a marked demographic decline and a dramatic shrinkage of territory, this might have been enough to provide for the needs of the government and the provincial producing populations. When we combine this information with organizational aspects of east Roman government to be discussed in the next chapter, we can begin to see through the haze surrounding these developments to generate a more rounded and, I hope, plausible account of the way in which the medieval Eastern Roman Empire emerged from the crisis conditions into which it was plunged in the middle of the seventh century.

7

Organization, Cohesion, and Survival

As long as the armed forces of the Romans were in good order, the state enjoyed divine assistance . . . and the toil of the most valorous was mingled with discipline and, for the most part, was crowned with the splendor of victory.[1]

Money and Resources

In the first chapter of this book I noted the importance of organizational advantages that may have contributed to the ability of the east Roman state to survive the challenges of the seventh and early eighth centuries. It is easy to overestimate or exaggerate these advantages, and we should not forget that, in the early years after the Arab conquests, at least, much of the state infrastructure that was in place at the time of the conquests remained functional thereafter. Not only were many of the officials who had been responsible for the state's fiscal operations in the eastern provinces still there, but the conquerors were themselves fairly familiar with late Roman logistical and fiscal arrangements, for many of them had served as federates of the Romans or Sasanians; indeed, some groups had worked alongside Roman soldiers and administrative officials for generations.[2] In this chapter I explain how the east Roman government's arrangements contributed to its survival and how a set of well-established administrative practices and arrangements responded, through the people who constituted them, to the challenges of collecting, distributing, and managing resources of all kinds. In particular, I want to answer the question, what lent these arrangements their particular effectiveness in the context of the times?

A schematic account of the late Roman administration before the conquests and the subsequent transformations will set the scene. It is important to note also that we are not dealing with a set of stable, fixed, and unvarying bureaucratic-administrative practices but rather a system of ways of doing things that consisted above all of people—individuals who worked together, who had a particular social status by virtue of their roles and functions, whose position was marked out by their functional title and their rank in a system of precedence, and who were perfectly capable of responding to changes in the conditions under which they operated.

In the later sixth century, state finances were managed through three departments, the praetorian prefectures, the "sacred largesses" *(sacrae largitiones)* and the "private finance department" *(res privata)*, of which the most important was the praetorian prefecture. It was through this that the land tax assessment was calculated, collected, and redistributed, and for the eastern empire the most significant was that of Oriens, stretching from the Balkans around to Egypt and Libya. There were also prefectures for the rest of the Balkans (Illyricum) and for Italy and Africa. Each prefecture was subdivided into dioceses *(dioecesae,* "directorates"), under a deputy *(vicarius)* of the praetorian prefect; and each diocese was divided into provinces under provincial governors. The lowest unit of administration was then the city *(civitas* or *polis)* each with its district *(territorium)* upon which the assessment and collection of taxes ultimately devolved. Taxes were raised in a variety of forms, but the most important regular tax was the land tax. This could be raised in money, but much of it could be raised in kind, as needed—grains, other foodstuffs and so forth—deposited in a vast network of state warehouses, where it could be drawn on by both soldiers and civil administrators.

The prefectures were also responsible for the administration of justice, the maintenance of the public post, the state weapons and arms factories, and provincial public works. The other finance departments, which had evolved out of earlier Roman palatine departments, had more limited functions. The department of the largesses was responsible for bullion from mines, minting coin, state-run clothing workshops, and the issue of military donatives—regular and irregular gifts of coin to the troops for particular occasions such as an imperial birthday, accession celebration, and so forth. For various reasons it had also come by the later sixth century to administer the revenues drawn from civic lands and from other income, such as the cash for the commutation of military service or the provision of horses for the army. The private fisc, or *res privata*, dealt with the rental income from imperial lands and estates, with different sections responsible for its various tasks, including a department referred to as the *patrimonium* to handle the financing of the imperial household.

By the early decades of the seventh century, however, it seems that all these fiscal departments or treasuries were coming under the general authority of a high-ranking official, the *sakellarios*, the departmental head of the imperial private purse, the *sacella* (or *sakellion*).[3] Under Heraclius, mint production was centralized—mints at Ravenna, Carthage, Alexandria, and Constantinople continued to function while the rest were closed down. In practice, of course, these arrangements varied considerably in their daily operations from region to region of the empire, and these variations were especially obvious in the way the land tax was assessed and collected. But basically there was a common pattern, and the result was that the central government could be assured that each year sufficient income was generated to maintain the expenses of maintaining itself and the army and administration.[4]

The disruption brought about by the warfare of the seventh century may have been one reason underlying Heraclius's reform of the imperial mints, and it must surely have contributed to the increasing level of palatine control over the three fiscal sections noted earlier.[5] Indeed, it should be remembered that the empire was in financial trouble long before the Arabs appeared on the scene as invaders. The emperor Heraclius had inherited a fragile economic situation himself and, apart from his centralizing the minting system, seems to have introduced several measures to try to tackle the lack of revenue. Two papyri from Egypt for the period ca. 628–641 would suggest that he introduced a new tax in kind on peasant producers in Egypt, known by the older name as the *collatio lustralis* or *chrysargyron*.[6] He certainly felt obliged to borrow money from the church and then, when that proved insufficient for his military expenditure, to seize a large quantity of church plate and have it melted down for coinage.[7] According to a much later report, but one certainly based on an earlier and now lost source, in the last years of his reign and after the initial Arab conquests, he ordered a massive empire-wide census and reassessment of tax burdens, no doubt a response to the loss of the rich provinces of the east.[8] While the aim must have been to determine the fiscal potential of the territory still under direct imperial control with the aim of mobilizing as effectively as possible the available resources for the war against the Arabs, nothing is known about the success or failure of this measure. A number of ad hoc fiscal administrative measures were certainly introduced during the reign of Heraclius, some probably with a limited regional or provincial application, others with empire-wide implications. These measures frame the changes that were to follow.

The Arab invasions in Anatolia and the gradual loss of imperial control over much of the Balkans from the 630s and 640s worsened the situation considerably. In spite of the dramatic loss of revenue consequent on the loss of territory, the state still had to maintain itself, its armies, and its administrative apparatus. Crucially, it also had to continue to pay its leading officials the substantial gold incomes that they had come to expect within the context of the highly monetized late Roman system, in which it is clear that regardless of any government effort to maintain control over the coinage it issued vast quantities of gold remained in circulation or hoarded for decades, and sometimes much longer, after their issue.[9] It was this gold that secured, at least to a degree, their continued loyalty. By the later ninth century the long-term results of these changes become apparent and reveal a very different system in which the older arrangements can still be glimpsed, but much transformed. Two sets of indications exist as to how the government dealt with the increasing problems it had to face after the 650s. The first concerns the monetary policy of the central government and how it responded through its coinage to the situation it faced; the second relates to the management of resources and how they were collected and distributed to where they were needed. I will deal with each in order.

As numismatists deepen their understanding of the coinage put into circulation by the imperial government in the seventh and eighth centuries, some remarkable and significant trends become apparent. First, the evidence indicates a considerable degree of fluctuation in emissions and value of the bronze coinage from the last decades of the sixth century, particularly in the Balkans, a reflection of both the economic situation in those provinces as well as the different needs of the army and the fiscal administration at different times.[10] This highly erratic pattern continued through the reign of Heraclius. Second, the numismatic data suggest a deliberate curtailment of issues of the bronze petty coinage, beginning slowly from 658 and picking up pace until 668, possibly to be associated with a hypothesized restructuring of tax collecting mechanisms and a revaluation of the bronze coinage in relation to the gold.[11] Bronze coins of Constantine IV are much rarer than those of the preceding reigns, and bronze coinage from archaeological sites across the surviving territories of the empire in the Balkans and Anatolia remains rare until the early ninth century. In contrast, the situation in southern Italy and Sicily is quite different, the region remaining comparatively untouched by raiding and economic disruption apart from attacks that took place probably in 651 and shortly after the murder of Constans II in 668.[12] This suggests that, under duress, the government was concerned primarily with the fiscal functions of its coinage rather than its role in the normal day-to-day exchange activity of the market. The dramatic fall in the numbers of bronze issues recovered from archaeological sites across Asia Minor for the period from the later 660s until the early ninth century, corroborated by the incidence of such issues in collections, illustrates the pattern. The same pattern is evident also in Constantinopolitan contexts where, although there can be no doubt of the availability of bronze issues throughout the period, issues for the emperors from Constantine IV through to Theophilus are sparse and follow the same contours.[13] But the state continued to produce bronze petty coinage to service its requirements in terms of the military and fiscal apparatus, as can be seen in (1) the dispatch of consignments of bronze to particular locations associated with known political or military events, (2) the amount of bronze coinage recovered from excavation at settlement sites associated with state military activities (such as Amorium in central Anatolia or cities along the western littoral of Asia Minor such as Pergamum), (3) the relatively greater number of issues minted for Constantinople itself, and (4) a reform of the bronze coinage undertaken by Constantine IV.[14]

This last issue remains debated, for here was a coin that returned to the weight it had held under Justinian I a century earlier. But its emission coincided with the sudden reduction in the amount of bronze coinage produced already noted and is rarely found outside Constantinople. One suggestion is that it had a primarily ideological function, as one facet of the imperial propaganda of Constantine's early reign; another is that it reflected an attempt to substitute a more impressive and valuable bronze coin as a major medium of payment of state salaries in the aftermath of the Arab siege of the city in 668–669 and in the face of a lack of gold with which to pay for both military and administrative expenses. Neither of these is especially persuasive. There is little reason to doubt the ideological significance of the reformed coinage although the possibility that it was intended to serve as a more acceptable mode of paying soldiers, for example (even if troops had on earlier occasion been paid in bronze) is to be doubted.[15] In any case, the new coins are rarely found archaeologically outside the capital, which suggests that their value as a means of paying soldiers was somewhat limited. It would seem, rather, that this emission is closely connected with and follows from (rather than caused) the reduction in production and distribution of bronze that took place in 668–669 and that it should be associated with other significant changes in the way the state managed its resources. Particularly significant, however, is the fact that while absolute numbers of emissions of bronze declined, the government was able at some point, perhaps during the reign of Constans II and possibly in direct association with this curtailment in production, to reimpose the standard Justinianic rate of 288 bronze *folles* to a gold *nomisma*, and to enforce this fiduciary value across the board, regardless of the fluctuating weight of the bronze coin itself. Thus while the number of emissions may have been considerably reduced, the nominal value of the mass of bronze in circulation was affected to a lesser degree. Substantial quantities of bronze coins from earlier reigns remained in circulation, often for well over a century from their date of striking.[16] If, as has been argued, the cut in emissions also reflected a reduction in population (and thus a reduction in transactions), these changes may have impacted on the monetary economy of the empire less dramatically than has often been thought.

Yet the remarkable absence of bronze coins from archaeological contexts of the period from the later 660s well into the ninth century across Anatolia and much of the South Balkans cannot be ignored. Whatever the longevity of earlier issues—which, as noted above, can extend to over a century—there took place a real shift in the dynamics of coin use and circulation across the provinces over many decades that included periods of relative economic stability and security as well as periods of disruption and economic dislocation. Indeed, the fact that major urban centers associated with state administrative or military activities demonstrate throughout a different pattern underlines this point and highlights the absence, or dearth of, petty currency in rural and semirural contexts. At the very least it suggests changes in the degree and nature of day-to-day market exchange relationships and thus of the nature of economic activity more broadly.[17]

Whereas the purity of the *nomisma* was also slightly reduced during the second half of the seventh century, to be restored only quite slowly, this was a minor fluctuation compared with that in the form and quantity of the bronze coinage. On the other hand, while the reduction in issues of bronze is paralleled by clear but short-term fluctuations in emissions of the gold *nomisma* during the later seventh century, over the longer term, from the later years of the seventh century through to the tenth century, the actual rhythm of production of gold did not suffer significantly. Such swings seem most likely to have reflected peaks and troughs in fiscal demand rather than lack of bullion, especially in light of the equally long-lived circulatory life of the gold, with an average estimated life of sixty to eighty years. The degree of variation parallels the economic trends of the period as they can be extrapolated from textual and archaeological evidence. Given the loss of territory and the reduction in population, it is hardly surprising that emissions during much of the eighth century attained less than 20–30 percent of the emissions under Anastasius or Justinian in the early and middle years of the sixth century (although they were higher than those of other sixth-century emperors), and similar results apply to the later seventh century.[18]

In view of the generally agreed demographic decline of the later seventh century, therefore, such a reduction may not have had the economic consequences—both on the liquidity of the social elite of the empire, for example, and for the way the government could remunerate its officials and armies—that has generally been thought. The effects of the inflow of gold to the empire under the treaty made by Justinian II with ʿAbd al-Malik in 685–686, by which it is likely that a little under 2 million gold *nomismata* were paid into the imperial treasury, illustrate the point very well: while it was likely such funds that financed Justinian's aggressive stance in the years thereafter, the overall situation remained in balance as the empire lost equivalent amounts through subsidies in the other direction.[19]

Nevertheless, in considering the huge loss of income following the Arab conquest of the rich eastern provinces as well as the continuing drain on resources through payments of subsidies to foreign rulers,[20] it is hardly surprising—even taking into account the substantial tributes paid by the caliphs following the peace agreements of the late 670s and 685–686—that the state budget contracted and that the drop in the use of bronze coinage across the provinces is in some measure associated with this. Fiscal measures that are hinted at in the sources and in the numismatic and sigillographic records likewise reflect this. The relatively flexible trimetallic system of the previous century was simplified to a more rigid structure with a single denomination for each metal, although with important regional variations, especially in Italy, Sicily and southern Italy, and North Africa, reflecting long-observed custom and practice. The gold content and weight of the *semissis* or half *nomisma* was reduced from the year 680 and more or less disappears from the early 740s. A reformed silver coin, the *miliarēsion*, was introduced by Leo III, valued at 1/12 of a gold *nomisma*, promoting a decline in the emissions of fractional issues of the *nomisma* during the eighth century, but serving as an important intermediary between the bronze fiduciary coinage and the gold. By the end of the century the bronze coinage, especially as represented by the *follis* had been reduced to less than half the weight it had been under Heraclius. And while the short-lived reform in the metrics of this coin that took place under Constantine IV in 669[21] did not last long, the fact that the government could enforce its fiduciary value made such fluctuations less damaging to the continuing role of the bronze in the system as a whole.[22]

The government was, therefore, able to manipulate its coinage very effectively in response to specific challenges. For example, the numismatic evidence shows that in the period 619 or 620–641 a considerable number of older bronze coins were countermarked with new values (two older coins being equivalent to one current issue) in Constantinople and then dispatched to Sicily as recompense to the estate owners who supplied the grain for a dramatically increased Constantinopolitan demand following the loss of Egypt to the Persians. The appearance of countermarked *folles* of Constantine IV, dating to a period when the capital was no longer directly threatened by major Arab military operations, has similarly been associated with a sudden increase in the minting of bronze in Sicily, showing again how the central government operated a closely coordinated fiscal and minting policy.[23] Similarly, the government of Constans II issued a bronze coin in 643–644 that seems to have been designated specifically for use in Cyprus (although from there it also reached Syria) and most probably reflects military and strategic concerns.[24] And during the period in which Constans II was based in Sicily and conducting or directing military operations against the Lombards and in the northwest Balkans, considerable numbers of coins from the mints of Sicily and Carthage have been recovered from archaeological contexts illustrative of the close association between mint output and military activity.[25] By the same token, substantial amounts of bronze from Athens (issues of Constans II, Philippicus, and Leo III) and Corinth (Phocas, Heraclius, Constans II, and Constantine IV) have been explained as connected with the presence of the military. Bronze coin of seventh-century emperors from sites stretching from the Dobrudja southward along the coast of Bulgaria, especially at Mesembria (where the empire maintained a naval and military presence), contrasts with the absence of coin from inland, implying the movement of coin by sea for state purposes from which inland regions were excluded—because the government and its apparatus were absent. A final case demonstrative of the technical and fiscal sophistication with which the Constantinopolitan regime managed its coinage is that of the monetary reform undertaken by Leo III in the 720s with regard to Sicily and Calabria. According to Theophanes, writing from a hostile perspective in the early ninth century, this entailed a rise in taxes across the province and was simply a reflection of Leo's iconoclast impiety and avarice. It has recently been demonstrated, however, that the supposed increase of the tax on those provinces involved primarily the recalculation of the taxes following the introduction of a reformed precious-metal coinage, giving the appearance of an increase but in fact leaving the prereform fiscal burden itself unchanged. Again, the government was able to intervene directly in the mechanisms of its fiscality to adjust the structures of tax management as necessary.[26]

The imperial coinage was exploited also in connection with political relations with both friendly or neutral as well as hostile neighbors. Hoards of precious metal coins, mostly silver but gold also, have been identified in territories associated with "barbarian" rulers. The evidence suggests the dispatch of such coinage to foreign rulers for a variety of reasons and, in light of the different composition of the Balkan

material from that found on the Ukrainian steppe, indicates specifically
targeted payments for diplomatic and military support.[27] Measures
such as these were applied not only in the north, however. The numismatic evidence shows that metropolitan copper from Constantinople
continued to reach Syria in large quantities until the eighteenth year of
Constans II (i.e., 657/658) or a few years thereafter. Local authorities—
whether Muslim or Christian operating on an official or semiofficial
basis—appear to have continued to use this Byzantine coinage concur-
rently with imitative Byzantine coins struck locally until the 680s,
when a major reform of coinage was undertaken. One reason for this
phenomenon may be that it was assumed that the region would eventually be recovered. There is a marked regional pattern to the distribution of the coins, with, for example, clear differences between northern
Syria and Palestine, possibly a reflection of coin-use as well as market
structures and orientation. While this indicates on the one hand the
highly monetized economy of the region, it also reflects the importance
of imperial coinage as propaganda as well as the recognition by Constantinople that coinage could work to undermine the evolution of
any non- or even anti-imperial attitudes in the lost provinces. And it
should not be forgotten that this coin was active in regions that remained largely pro-monothelete, a fact the significance of which would
not have been lost on Constantinople.[28] It was also useful, of course, in
the event of Byzantine military activities in the region, where imperial
coin would have a ready practical as well as political value.

In general terms, therefore, it seems that the eastern Roman government continued to dispose of substantial resources in gold, silver and
bronze coinage. Yet while it was thus able to pay for many of its basic
requirements in manpower and resources, it had nevertheless suffered
a very substantial loss of tax revenue over a relatively short period, and
would of necessity have been forced to respond to the new structural
pressures and stresses in respect of the ways in which it supported its
fiscal administration and its military.

Crisis Management?

A good deal more can be said about the coinage of this period, but what
is absolutely clear is that the government was fully capable both of rec-
ognizing the nature of the challenges it faced in respect of fiscal and

monetary resources, and of responding to them in a coherent and managed way—even if it is also the case that such changes had to be implemented rapidly and were a response to the constantly shifting fiscal and political situation. As we saw previously, the empire suffered a major blow when it lost Egypt and access to the vast quantities of grain required both for Constantinople and for the military. Replacing this source was possible, but it took some time to achieve this, and in the meantime the emperors faced a real crisis. Egypt was in fact lost twice— first in 618 to the Sasanian Persians, and in that same year we know that the civic *annona* or bread ration for the population of Constantinople was cancelled.[29] But, just when Egyptian grain was no longer available to Constantinople, and following the termination of the civic bread ration, the lead seals of officials known as *kommerkiarioi,* in this case associated on their seals with Africa and Carthage, major producers of grain, make their appearance.[30] It has reasonably been assumed that these officials were associated with the measures taken to supply Constantinople with grain from North Africa during the years after the Persian occupation of Egypt. The last issue for several decades is dated to 642–647 or 648, coinciding with the rebellion of the exarch of Africa Gregory in the latter year.[31] In apparent confirmation of this, there are also seals for the *kommerkion* of Sicily, dateable in at least one example to a period—the early 650s—when it is likely that North African grain was not available.[32]

But why should what seems like a commercial customs levy and the officials responsible for it be associated with grain supplies in this way? *Kommerkiarioi* or *comites commerciorum* were originally subordinates of the *sacrae largitiones,* one of the government's fiscal departments. In the middle of the sixth century they were under the authority of the praetorian prefecture, and until the early years of the seventh century their chief role lay in supervising the production and sale of silk, which was a state monopoly, and probably other luxury imports and exports. But by the middle of the seventh century it is quite clear that the role of these *comites commerciorum* had undergone a radical change.[33] The main source for their history are the departmental lead seals already mentioned.[34] By the 670s we find seals bearing the names of individual *kommerkiarioi* along with the names of the *apothēkai* or storehouses for the provinces in which the storehouses were located; more than this, from the year 672/673 we find that the seals are dated by indiction, and that their issue on occasion coincides with or precedes specific military undertakings or with other particular occasions or events where the government required the delivery of supplies, either to the armies or to Constantinople.[35] This may be coincidence, but it seems clear that the most likely explanation is that their original duties (which there is no reason to believe did not continue) became vastly expanded so that the *kommerkiarioi* and their *apothēkai* encompassed both the supply of Constantinople with grain as well as the army with grain and other supplies, possibly even including military equipment also, although this remains hypothetical.[36] We also find them associated with the settlement of captured Slavs in Anatolia—less as managers of slave markets (although this is not be excluded from their range of activities), but more likely as suppliers of produce and equipment to the new settlers, who had military service for the empire imposed upon them.[37] This arrangement for managing resources for the capital and for the army underwent a substantial reform or development in the early 730s during the reign of Leo III, but the structures that evolved operated well into the eighth century until they were integrated into the developing provincial fiscal administration and, during the reign of Nicephorus I, the new "thematic" fiscal structures. That the *kommerkiarioi* were responsible for the collection of regular taxes as well seems inherently unlikely because the evidence shows that their duties were not concerned with regular annual tasks.[38]

Two interesting developments would appear to confirm this newly extended role for the *kommerkiarioi*. First, the term *"coemptio"* (Greek, *synōnē*), which until the early or middle seventh century referred to a compulsory purchase of military supplies, had come by the later seventh century—by the early 680s at the latest—to mean regular, annual levies of grain in kind (*coemptum frumenti . . . annue minima exurgebat persolvere*, as the *Liber Pontificalis* puts it; in the *Nomos georgikos*, or "Farmer's law," the *synōnē* is *ta extraordina tou dēmosiou*).[39] There is additionally the possibility that by about 650 the term *"commercium,"* customs tax or duty, could have the additional meaning of *coemptio* or *synōnē*, as indicated by a Latin–Greek lexicon of the mid-seventh century.[40] On this basis, the term *"commerciarii"* could be understood as referring to officials who might also be responsible for levies in grain. Whether this was the case or not, however, the group of anonymous seals of the *kommerkion Sikelias* (the *commercium* of Sicily), already mentioned, tentatively dated to the years from 652–672/673, have been plausibly associated with a levy of grain from Sicily. They date to the years after grain from Africa became temporarily unavailable (following the defeat of the exarch Gregory by Muslim raiders in 647–648 and the subsequent imposition of a heavy tribute on the landowners of the province), and suggest the alternative source from which the government attempted to supply Constantinople.[41] The wealthy grain-producing estates of Sicily had served before as a source of grain, for Thessaloniki at the end of the sixth and beginning of the seventh century, for other eastern cities at a slightly later date, and for Constantinople, as we have seen, in the 620s–630s, so there would be nothing unusual in this.[42]

Second, as we have noted, the general *kommerkiarioi* are frequently associated on the lead seals they or their office or department issued with a storehouse or *apothēkē*. Now the term *"apothēkē"* in its generic sense means simply a storehouse. But several texts of the period, both Greek and Latin, make it quite clear that it also had the more specific or technical meaning of granary: the glossaries—the Greek–Latin word lists of the Middle Ages—consistently translated *"apothēkē"* with *"horreum,"* for example.[43] And in the New Testament *"apothēkē"* always is used with the meaning "barn," that is, a building where provisions, especially grain, are kept in storage.[44] Numerous examples of this usage can also be found in the Old Testament.[45] Consequently, it is hardly a surprise that in the Latin translation of c. 700 of the emperor Constantine IV's letter to the synod of Rome of 681, an allusion to the *apothēkē* in Matthew 3:12 is translated as *horreum*.[46] Many other texts confirm the use of the term *"apothēkē"* to mean a storehouse or barn, and in particular a storehouse for grain.[47]

It has taken historians some time to fathom exactly what is going on here. But in spite of some contentious issues that remain to be elucidated, when this evidence is brought together it indicates intelligent and considered attempts to exploit and manage sources of grain for the capital city of the empire under difficult circumstances. These efforts then led directly to the expansion of the system of general *kommerkiarioi* and their storehouses to supply both the capital and perhaps also the armies (not regularly, but for specific occasions), alongside their original functions. One of the most important aspects of this is the fact that from 672/673, seals of general *kommerkiarioi* and the storehouses with which their names were associated were issued with indictional dates

on them. Many, although by no means all, of these dated seals have
been associated with specific events or military undertakings, but this
new step suggests that they reflected a set of activities that had a fiscal
aspect to them as well as formally representing imperial authority. The
kommerkiarioi themselves were probably based in Constantinople, with
regional officials responsible to them in the provinces. By way of example, two seals for officials with responsibility for granaries or storehouses for Africa and the province of Honorias—between Bithynia and
Paphlagonia—are dated to 673–674, the year in which a major seaborne
attack was launched against the western Anatolian littoral. Honorias
and Africa were both provinces that could supply Constantinople with
grain, and the suspicion arises as to whether the activities of these two
officials reflect imperial preparations to supply Constantinople and its
forces with the necessary provisions to resist another attack.[48] By the
same token, an exceptionally large group of bronze coins of the second
regnal year of Philippicus (711–713) was excavated in Athens and appears to have made up a specific consignment issued at precisely the
point at which a dated seal of an anonymous general *kommerkiarios*
and of the *apothēkē* of the Aegean was issued. We have already noted
that there is a clear pattern across the later seventh and into the eighth
century of groups of coins found in specific contexts associated with the
military. While the circumstances of these two events remain obscure
and the link hypothetical, the coincidence is highly suggestive of the sort
of relationship described in the foregoing.[49] How exactly these officials
provided the supplies required by the government remains debated.
One argument is that they were responsible for raising occasional resources in kind. An alternative, and perhaps more plausible explanation is that, given the evidence for the continued monetized nature of
the state's fiscal economy, they were provided with substantial sums of
cash with which to purchase the state's needs, probably through compulsory purchase, or *coemptio (Greek synōnē)*. In light of the equivalence
already noted of *coemptio* with *commercium* this may seem very likely,
and would also contribute to understanding how a word for irregular
compulsory purchases eventually came to be used of regular, annual
fiscal demands. In practice, it is likely that both compulsory purchase
and requisition were deployed, according to circumstances. And in
either case, the aim of the exercise was to raise appropriate quantities
of goods—in the case of the military, and when required beyond the

usual annual needs for maintaining the soldiers—of grain and live-stock. The added advantage for the government of doing this through compulsory purchase would be to release occasional but substantial amounts of coin onto the market, although we should also bear in mind the patchy and irregular nature of such consignments.[50]

As I have argued elsewhere, this is not by any means to suggest that the raising of various types of resource, whether through compulsory purchase or direct extraction of goods and services, excludes the con-tinued exercise by the *kommerkiarioi* of their traditional functions as cus-toms officers, responsible for collecting duties on sales and purchases. Nor is it to argue that they were responsible for managing regular fiscal impositions—on the contrary, the irregular combinations of provincial storehouses and provinces for which they were responsible, the very short periods of their tenure of office, and the irregularity, so far as the evidence of the lead seals throws light on this, shows that the *kommerki-arioi* were not directly connected with the regular collection of taxes. This took place under an evolved and evolving fiscal structure descended from the old prefectural administration.[51] What this model of the ac-tivities of *kommerkiarioi* does is to see them as responsible for raising a wide range of goods, from grain, livestock and other produce for the supply of cities and probably also for the military. There is no tension between these different facets of their role.[52]

There is, of course, an alternative explanation for the significance of these officials and the lead seals of the storehouses with which they were associated, for it has also been argued that a link between them and sup-plying the army or the state with anything should be rejected. Instead, the suggestion is that the increasing activity of the *apothēkai* in the course of the seventh century reflected an attempt by the government to ex-tract a greater revenue from the trade of luxury goods, including silk, as one means of compensating for the loss of revenue from Egypt and the Levant.[53] Now no one would deny that *kommerkiarioi* and *apothēkai* were associated with levying dues on commercial activity.[54] But while it is evident that commercial life certainly did not cease at this period,[55] the suggestion that internal trade could generate the sort of resources from luxury goods that the state required seems inherently unlikely; indeed, this flies in the face of everything else that we know, from ar-chaeology or texts, for the period.[56] When we examine the longer-term evolution of these arrangements from the sixth into the ninth century, placing the *kommerkiarioi*, the imperial *kommerkia*, and the *apothēkai* in the context of the evolution of the fate of the praetorian prefecture, the system of supplying the military, and the beginnings of the provincial "thematic" fiscal administration under the *prōtonotarioi* (senior fiscal managers) in the early ninth century, the more likely interpretation remains the first one.[57] Of course, the imperial portrait on these seals signified a relation with the imperial fisc.[58] But this tells us nothing about what these imperially ratified activities might have been; indeed, supplying the imperial armies might just as well have been one, intimately connected as it was with the state's fiscal operation.

Given the need to maximize revenues from trade and the production of goods for exchange, we might expect a clearer sequence of annual, or at least more regular, issues of seals across all the provinces of the empire, whereas, in fact, even taking into account the lacunose nature of the sigillographic record, neither the pattern of distribution nor the chronology of issues is in the least consistent, although it could readily reflect the year-on-year fluctuations in a combination of commercial, grain-supply, and military-related movements of cash, agrarian produce, goods, and other products (including silks and luxuries, where appropriate).[59] Equally, while by no means all such seals coincide with military activities in the provinces in which they were issued (and as we have seen, this is not essential for the first interpretation), several do, and it would seem counterintuitive to argue for a flourishing trade in luxury goods in such regions in the middle of a period of military activity and economic dislocation. In the final analysis, while neither of these two positions can be proved beyond doubt for want of absolutely clear indications in our sources, I believe the first argument makes much more sense.[60]

It is not necessary to pursue the question in greater detail now. But it is worth pointing out that a further change took place from 730 to 731, when the immediate crisis of survival was over. From this time a gradual reduction in the importance of individual *kommerkiarioi* is evident: instead of high-ranking general *kommerkiarioi* at Constantinople associated with provincial warehouses *(apothēkai)* there appear instead institutions called imperial *kommerkia* that appear to have fulfilled a related but more limited function, while the *kommerkiarioi* themselves now occur in association with both groups of provinces or, more usually, specific ports or entrepôts, underlining their reversion to the role of customs officials controlling trade and exchange activities with regions outside the empire.[61] One notable aspect in the pattern of distribution of seals of the imperial *kommerkia* is that there is a clear reduction in the coverage of their activities in comparison with those of the earlier *kommerkiarioi*. In Anatolia they are restricted almost entirely to the three commands of Thrakesion, Opsikion, and Anatolikon, and limited areas of the Armeniakon, other regions being entirely unmentioned. At the same time, the Balkan regions of the empire begin to predominate, with a large proportion of seals of imperial *kommerkia* for the period from 730 representing this institution in Hellas and Thrace (and later from towns such as Mesembria, Thessaloniki, Debeltus, and Adrianople). This shift in the focus of attention suggests that some at least of the activities they had formerly carried out in the southern and eastern regions of Anatolia were now carried out by other officials.

Whatever the explanation, and excluding the unlikely possibility that every single seal of any such officials in these latter areas has been lost, it would seem on the face of it improbable that a revenue-collecting agency that had operated throughout the latter part of the seventh century and that was based entirely on internal commerce would simply stop operating at precisely the point—from the 730s—when the empire was beginning to stabilize the military situation in the east, or that it would expand into areas—the Balkans—in which military operations were beginning to pick up.[62] Indeed, the transfer of attention to the Balkans might equally support an argument for supplying the military, even if not exclusively. In fact, it can plausibly be argued that the functions of general *kommerkiarioi* and *apothēkai* not related to customs dues had already been transferred into the hands of provincial tax officials known as *dioikētai* from the 730s, as the fiscal administration of the empire was rationalized under Leo III and the emergency measures that had briefly given the general *kommerkiarioi* their enhanced role were phased out.[63]

Together the numismatic evidence and the extensive sigillographic documentation for the evolution of the institution of imperial *kommerkiarioi* and their *apothēkai* demonstrate that the government had both the insight and the ability to implement sophisticated emergency measures to deal with the situation it faced, even when confronted with particularly acute situations demanding a rapid response. But such measures were not restricted to the sphere of coinage or management of grain and supplies alone. There is also good evidence for the government responding to specific regional demands and differences, notably in the case of its Italian and Sicilian lands, by adjusting taxation levels or by exploiting specific local resources, whether in manpower or in produce.[64]

Armies and Manpower

Managing fiscal resources was one aspect of the state's operations. Managing the imperial armies, especially after the disastrous series of defeats in greater Syria in the 630s, followed by the loss of Egypt by 641–642, must have thrown up a whole new set of problems. Furthermore the constant harassment of both frequent small-scale raiding across the frontier combined with much larger-scale undertakings that pushed deep into imperial territory must have contributed both to economic dislocation and the decline in morale that imperial troops appear to have suffered. Clearly, emperors such as Constans II, Constantine IV and Justinian II were able on occasion to assemble substantial field armies and mount effective campaigns against their enemies. They were likewise able to maintain a substantial naval force. And so the question arises: how was this managed? The topic has received a good deal of treatment in recent years, and I briefly summarize what is now believed to have happened.

The evidence suggests, first, that after the end of Heraclius's campaign against the Sasanians in 628, the basic fabric of the late Roman strategic system was reestablished, with some important differences. Recent work on the state of the army in Egypt in the period preceding the Arab conquest shows that much of the pre-Sasanian occupation establishment was still in place—that is to say, was reintroduced under Heraclius. In the East, the armies of the *magistri militum per Orientem* and *per Armeniam* continued to exist (although during the Persian wars they may have partially dissolved), and in the Balkans the army of the *magister militum per Thracias* was certainly restored—all three were later involved in fighting the Arabs in the 630s.[65] The forces of the *magister militum per Illyricum* disappear from the record, probably a reflection of the occupation in the period 610–630 of much of the central and north Balkan region by Slav settlers under Avar hegemony. The traditional regional command structure reemerges in the 630s and continues to appear in the sources well into the 640s,[66] although in southern Syria and Palestine greater reliance on Arab allies and federates seems to have been the order of the day; indeed, it is possible that Arab units were employed specifically to control the fractious and sometimes rebellious Samaritan and Jewish population of Palestine, for example.[67]

These arrangements completely collapsed under the Arab onslaught, and the result, by the period immediately following the battle of the Yarmuk River in 636, was the withdrawal of the major field armies that had been active against the Arabs into Asia Minor. At least three armies under their late Roman commanders, the *magistri militum*, were involved—not only the armies one might expect to find in this theater, those of the East and of Armenia, but we also find evidence for the presence of the field army of Thrace.[68] But how was the government, with its dramatically reduced income and in the pressured circumstances I have described, to support and maintain these armies, maintain recruitment, and equip them? In the 1930s George Ostrogorsky, building on some of the work of an earlier generation of German and Russian scholars, suggested that it was probably under Heraclius that a new system of farmer-soldiers was introduced, whereby soldiers would be supported by farms or agricultural properties and, in return for exemption from some fiscal impositions and protection from others, would provide military service to the state, furnishing also their own mounts and equipment. Such soldiers, so Ostrogorsky argued, were organized in military divisions called themes, or *themata* (the etymology of which was unclear), under the command of a general, or *stratēgos*, who, according to the theory, held both civil and military power in his region. The evidence for this theory, in particular for the names of the units and their officers, was based on information drawn largely from ninth-century and especially tenth-century sources, when an arrangement of this sort was in place. A further frequently cited source of evidence is the early ninth-century chronography of the monk Theophanes, which makes a few references to the term *"thema"* in a context apparently indicating military provinces and armies during the reign of Heraclius.[69] It is a very neat theory and, given the considerable achievement of Heraclius, it was for a long time accepted that he was the founder of this "theme system," supposed to have been the result of a great reform introduced in the 620s.

A great deal of research has since been invested in this discussion, and it is now very clear, first, that Theophanes's account is anachronistic in its usage of this term for the period in question and, second, that there is not a jot of evidence to support the notion of military lands and farmer-soldiers at this time; indeed, such a system as Ostrogorsky described never seems to have existed, although by the tenth century there were such things as tax-protected military properties associated with military service. Indeed, the whole notion of "farmer-soldiers" is, in practical terms and in the context of the period, absurd and has generally been recognized as such.[70] Third, it is clear that the military commanders or *stratēgoi* of these armies only achieved their position as holders of both civil and military authority in the early ninth century, long after the events with which we are concerned.

What seems to have happened is this. First, the government had to withdraw its armies to a defensible frontier, and it was able to exploit the natural barrier represented by the Taurus and Anti-Taurus ranges. Defending the Aegean coastal regions and islands was a little more problematic, but that was also a pressing need. Second, it had to ensure that they could be adequately supplied with provisions, animals, and equipment. Now, while it was recognized for many years that the field armies were withdrawn or relocated in this way, it was assumed for the most part that the areas in which these forces are later to be found reflected purely strategic considerations. While it is true that such questions must have contributed to the pattern of distribution of troops, it has now become clear that there was a much more important factor underlying it, for the way the distribution appears to have been carried out was to allocate territory to each field army according to its productive potential and fiscal capacity, proportional to the numbers of soldiers in the army in question.

Moreover, the boundaries of these areas appear to conform with a few exceptions to specific groups of late Roman provinces. The forces that had been attached to the palace and emperor remained where they had been previously based, in the provinces of northwest Asia Minor and Thrace; but the army of the *magister militum per Orientem*, henceforth known under its Greek name, the Anatolikon division, occupied southern and central Asia Minor; that of the *magister militum per Armeniam*, now known as the Armeniakon (Lat., Armeniacum), occupied the remaining eastern and northern districts of Asia Minor, again remaining in some regions where previously based but with a resource area that appears, in the end, to have been extended westward. The army of the *magister militum per Thracias,* which had been employed unsuccessfully to defend Egypt and much of which may have been among the troops evacuated under treaty and in an orderly manner from Alexandria in 642, was allocated the rich provinces of central western Anatolia and known thenceforth as the Thrakesion army. By the later seventh century, the provinces across which these different divisions were established had come to be known collectively by the name of the army based there. It can be seen from Map 7.1, first, how the areas attributed to each military command, or *stratēgis,* conform to clearly demarcated groups of provinces and, second, how the relationship between size of army and territory worked, with the substantial Thracian forces occupying a relatively small but very rich area, and the smaller Armenian divisions stretched across a much larger but very much less wealthy region, as discussed in the preceding chapter. In other words, the withdrawal, relocation, or expansion of the area across which the field armies came to be based reflects a well-thought-out plan through which the empire could continue to maintain and support substantial numbers of troops under arms in extraordinarily difficult circumstances.[71]

But a word of caution is necessary on the areas allocated to these divisional forces. While it is the case that the later evidence (ninth and tenth century) indicates the late Roman provinces that were included within these military districts, it is not at all clear what their original extent may have been. Thus, the Anatolikon force may well have occupied territory extending further to the east, into northern Mesopotamia, part of the region it had originally been allocated to defend against the Persians, while for several decades after the 630s the Armeniakon force probably moved very little from its Justinianic dispositions, as the accounts of the campaigns conducted by Constans II, Constantine IV, and Justinian II might suggest. As the Roman frontier in this region began to move northward and westward from the early 700s, however, and as Cilicia was abandoned shortly thereafter, the provinces allocated for supply purposes and occupied by the field armies must also have contracted, with the result being by the middle of the eighth century similar to that shown on Map 7.1.[72]

One final development that should not go unremarked here is the establishment of an imperial naval presence during the reign of

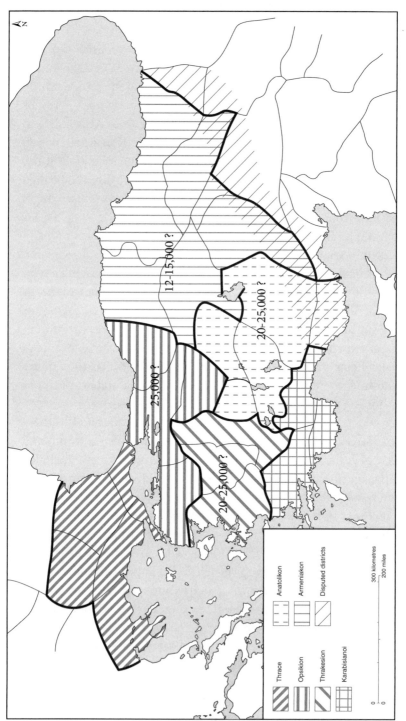

Map 7.1. Seventh-century military commands and notional divisional strengths, overlain on late Roman provinces. (Reprinted from *The Palgrave Atlas of Byzantine History* by John Haldon, Map 6.1, numbers added. Basingstoke and New York: Palgrave Macmillan. © 2005 by John Haldon.)

Constans II. The imperial fleet based at Constantinople played a key role in the defense of the city in the Arab siege and campaign of the years 668–669 and again in 717–718, was in action offensively in the late 640s against Arab-held coastal places in the Levant, and appears explicitly for the first time in action in the so-called battle of the masts off the Lycian coast in 653, led by the emperor himself (when it was heavily defeated). There is some discussion as to whether or not this naval force was a new development, given that until this time there had been no need of such a fleet in the Roman-controlled eastern Mediterranean, but in any case it played thenceforth a significant strategic role and seems also to have encouraged the construction by the caliphate of its own fleet. Constans was certainly responsible for the maintenance and repair of naval installations in southern Italy, at Vibona (certainly already a naval base) and at Reggio, as well as for the construction of a naval force to maintain East Roman control of Italian coastal waters, if not beyond. To Leo III can similarly be ascribed the strengthening and renewal of this force after a fiscal reform in the early 730s.[73]

Without pursuing the matter of Constans' fleets in further detail, it is clear that soldiers continued to be paid by the government, and largely in gold, even if their cash remuneration was rationalized into a periodic rotation with payments arriving every three or four years. Legal texts refer to the payment of soldiers by both *annonai* and by a *rhoga*.[74] Changes there were, of course, and as noted in Chapter 3, legal texts of the 740s suggest strongly that soldiers who did in fact provide some of their own equipment and were dependent on their own property had become a well-established feature. This has nothing to do with any supposed "farmer-soldiers." It will be worth dwelling on this evidence for a moment, especially since it suggests a picture of developments in Anatolia, or at least within the core lands of the empire, remarkably similar to those that appear to have taken place in the Ravenna exarchate over a century earlier. The first text, dated to the middle of the eighth century, is a decision regarding outstanding obligations on the part of a soldier and his wife's father. The issue revolves around the level of compensation the latter is to receive in respect of the soldier's earnings from his military service. The ruling is based on the recognition that, should the soldier opt to leave, thus effectively terminating the arrangement through which the son-in-law contributed to the household income, then his father-in-law should be compensated in respect of his investment in the soldier's military gear.[75]

Chapter xvi, 2 of the *Ecloga*, issued in 741, treats a comparable situation. Here the text concerns brothers who inherit a parental estate and household with joint ownership.[76] It is worth quoting the text in full:

> If brothers are left after the decease of their parents and one of them is in military service while the other remains active in the household, then, if they have made an agreement, that which was agreed should remain in force. But if they make no agreement but live together for up to ten years from the beginning of the military service of the said brother, then everything that they have acquired, whether from the pay *[rhoga]* or the exertions and the hard work of the brother or brothers remaining on the estate should be divided in equal parts. But if they live for a further three years together after these ten years and then separate, then the soldier shall keep his horse with its harness and his weapons, and also his armor, should he have acquired one; but everything else should be apportioned between them in a brotherly fashion. And if they live together longer than these thirteen years and the soldier still has after this time something from his pay, then he should retain this also.

It seems apparent that the military income was included as part of the common income, and that the soldier was by the same token understood to be supported by the household.[77] The soldier's mount and military gear are excluded from the division of property, but only after a certain period, which assumes that the other brother(s) had a claim on them. The equipment necessary to military service was thus exempted in the interests of the state. But there is no reason to think that the household had been obliged to support the soldier. The lawyers who designed the ruling clearly recognized the necessity of compensating the estate for its loss of income and its contribution up to a period of ten years. After this point, the soldier's income was taken to have recompensed the household for his maintenance, and he retained horse and other gear, until, after a period of thirteen years, his debt to his household was extinguished.

These two texts indicate that households could support soldiers but that this contribution had been formally recognized in the right of the contributing parties to make a claim on the hitherto untouchable military *peculium* for recompense. This in turn shows that the traditional regulations pertaining to military *peculium* had been modified and suggests a significant shift in assumptions about how the military was financed.[78] The decisions probably reflect cases that had come to the attention of the imperial court at some point, and they demonstrate that the soldier's family or household supported his military service in a way that could be quantified, and thus could be compensated when the arrangement changed. It implies a rather different arrangement for maintaining and supporting soldiers in field armies than had hitherto been in force[79] and reflects one aspect of the slow transformation of a large part of these armies into a more militia-like force, still capable of participating in major expeditions and in effective military action but increasingly provincialized—perhaps resembling the older *limitanei* units of the period before the Arab invasions (about whose fate, incidentally, we know virtually nothing).

To what extent this shift reflected a less regularly salaried provincial military, a less monetized provincial economy, or a planned policy on the part of the government to reduce the costs falling directly on the fisc remains unclear. Soldiers continued to be paid in gold, but at intervals that reflected a more straitened fiscal economy. A tenth-century text, for example, describes the traditional method of paying the provincial armies as based on a four-yearly cycle (or a three-yearly cycle, as described by some ninth-century Arabic accounts), and it has been suggested that this was how the government dealt with the temporarily reduced availability of gold coinage put into circulation—a real reduction, as evidenced now by the analysis of coinage-emissions for the second half of the seventh century.[80] But this rotational system can hardly have helped with the normal maintenance costs of the armies, especially when, from the 640s, the field armies seem to have been distributed across the provinces according to the pattern already discussed, and the less frequent payments to provincial forces may well over time have encouraged some—perhaps many—to place a greater degree of dependence upon their families for some aspects of their support and equipment.

Regardless of this increasing association between the service of military personnel and their households, the armies still had to rely largely on the established pattern of support, by which provincials delivered certain quantities of grain and other produce as well as livestock to key points for collection, whether following requisitions or compulsory purchase. And regardless of the amount of bronze petty coinage in circulation, supplies, provisions, and matériel had to be provided on a regular basis. At the level of micromanagement we can detect somewhat dimly and largely through the evidence of lead seals of the relevant officials some important shifts in the ways resources were purchased, collected and redistributed. By the same token, we can see how some of these shifts might fit into the emerging pattern of activities of the *kommerkiarioi* and the declining importance of the old prefectural administration, although we do not need to pursue those issues now. The bare bones of the established infrastructure for maintaining and supplying armies in the provinces continued to function, although we have little direct evidence for how this worked apart from the names of some of the officials associated with it. When a campaign was planned, however, or a defensive counterattack organized, a much greater quantity of matériel was required, and often very quickly, and the hypothesis that it was the *kommerkiarioi* who may have facilitated this seems to fit, the more so if we accept that this was achieved at first through compulsory purchases, following the established late Roman pattern. Building on an ad hoc basis upon the gradual shifts in arrangements for supplying Constantinople in the period after 618, in which the *kommerkiarioi* had come to play a key role, we can see how the government at Constantinople cleverly exploited these developing arrangements to support its activities, including its armies, in a time of reduced cash and other revenues by expanding an established framework into new areas of activity. Paying the provincial armies on a cyclical basis would have contributed to a reduction in annual costs, if not to the overall total cost of maintaining them; while this might also have encouraged a tendency—a need—for many to become more dependent on their immediate households for support, thus similarly lightening the burden on the fisc.[81] It was crisis management, but it was crisis management that worked remarkably well.

This is an appropriate point at which to reintroduce some of the issues broached in Chapter 6 regarding the environmental evidence. We have seen that the palynological data suggest that a simplified agrarian regime was representative of many regions of Anatolia from the middle and later seventh century but that it is not always clear whether this was the result of environmental pressure or reflects human agency— economic pressure reflecting market demand, for example; insecurity and warfare; or other causes. The process does not coincide with any obvious environmental shift and indeed seems to take place over different periods, at different times, and in different regions. In some parts of Anatolia, such as Paphlagonia-Pontus or Bithynia, the traditional mixed agriculture continues and coexists with the new simplified regime so that, although the record is patchy, this picture is not just a reflection of a lacunose dataset. Importantly, it also suggests that we have to do here with an element of choice: some farmers within the same environmental zone chose to adopt a different regime from the established system; others did not. We will discuss the possible motives behind these choices below.

Feeding Mars

A possible explanation for some of these changes may be sought by bringing together the developments I have now sketched out. First, let us consider the desperate financial straits in which the government found itself from the 650s onward. Resources to supply the armies were a priority because it is quite clear that the armies remained active in the provinces throughout this period, reoccupying and refortifying strongpoints, fortresses, and cities seized by the Arabs, dogging and harassing enemy detachments, and maintaining the presence of the imperial state. The changes in the fiscal system that can be detected across the same period, both in respect of the management of the basic land tax as well as in respect of raising supplies and equipment for the imperial armies, reflect these concerns, just as the changes in fiscal terminology can be shown to reflect a shift from raising tax in cash to raising a much greater proportion of the resources required for the armies in kind, predominantly in the form of grain, grain that was intended to support the operations of armies widely dispersed across the provinces of the empire, grain that was stored in imperial depositories or *apothēkai,* and grain that was collected in a way that meant that the traditional term for a compulsory purchase came to have the meaning of a regular and annual imposition.

Second, there was a dramatically changed situation with regard to trade and commerce in the east Roman world from the middle of the seventh century. Neither entirely ceased, of course, and it is clear from the archaeological data, in particular from the movement of ceramics, that exchange across political borders continued throughout the period of warfare from the 630s into the ninth century and beyond. The patterns of exchange evolved to match the new circumstances, however—fewer international products reached inland regions than before, and short- and medium-distance coastal trade and cabotage continued, but the types of goods and ceramics that were carried changed as the centers of production changed. Some long-distance trade also continued, but it was certainly affected by the changed political circumstances of the second half of the seventh century, with the establishment of new routes, the diversion of older ones, and the probable closure of many. Market demand for some commodities changed, the options for moving goods around changed, and the transport of goods by sea must on occasion have been more hazardous than usual. We have little direct information from this period, but some travel certainly continued, as we know from the accounts of pilgrims to the Holy Land, for example. Nevertheless, such dramatic shifts combined with the impact of almost constant warfare in some regions must have impacted market-orientated agricultural production considerably. Landowners, farmers, and peasant producers who grew crops for a market would have responded in the way that they have always done by ceasing to grow those items no longer in demand and turning to those that were. Such a response may well have been given added stimulus by the activities of the *kommerkiarioi* in the period up to 730, if it was indeed the case that they were responsible for substantial cash purchases, whether at fixed prices or the market rate, to support the state's activities.[82]

Third, it is precisely from the early 670s that the lead seals of *kommerkiarioi* bearing an indictional date (a year within a given fifteen-year cycle) begin to appear in quantity, a change that has been plausibly associated with an important change in some aspects of fiscal management (even if the details thereof remain obscure) and hence with the ways in which military supplies were managed.[83] And, finally, while a statistically useful quantification is not possible owing to the absence of appropriate data, it is clear that the eastern Roman state was suffering a substantial demographic decline from the second half of the sixth century onward, an effect of endemic plague as well as of the warfare and dislocation that affected different regions of the empire on and off across the period and that can be glimpsed in the archaeological evidence for shifts in the settlement pattern. Epidemics generally impacted on coastal regions, urban concentrations, and village communities to a greater extent than less well-populated inland districts, although this is not invariably so. But it might well have meant a higher demographic cost in coastal regions, such as Paphlagonia and the Pontus, than inland, and it may well be this that is reflected in the palynological data for Paphlagonia, with a clear reduction in the intensity of grain production on the one hand, yet a proportional increase in cerealiculture compared with the suite of traditional crops.[84] Manpower shortages affected the army, that much is clear; but they must also have affected the availability of labor, and it is generally—and reasonably—assumed that this meant a reduction in agrarian output.[85]

In light of these points, we must ask whether it can be a coincidence that at very roughly the same time as these developments—the second half of the seventh century—we see a change in emphasis across Anatolia from the established mixed crop of cereals, nuts, vines, and olives to the "simplified" crop just described. The traditional crops were still "essentials" in an eastern Mediterranean cultural context, but even along the coastal regions, products such as olive oil and wine probably no longer enjoyed the expansive market of the years before the earlier seventh century. A clear reduction in the proportion of crops such as vines and olives as against cereals is observable in the pollen records from several of the areas noted in Chapter 6, at a time when no obvious climatic factor or shift in conditions was present.

Olive cultivation is in any case determined largely by climatic factors and by winter temperatures in particular. Severe winter temperatures, in the order of −10°C to −13°C, will wither and kill the tree. Olive tree cultivation in Anatolia cannot usually take place above ~1000 masl, so that successful olive cultivation is restricted to lower elevations and coastal regions.[86] In general, the extensive cultivation of the olive does seem to have regressed after the late Roman period,[87] and by the tenth and eleventh centuries olive oil production in Anatolia was restricted to coastal regions and Bithynia, for example, while an eleventh-century commentator notes that olives are not cultivated further than 60 km/ 37 miles (300 *stadia*) from the sea.[88] It remains unclear to what extent this reflected market demand, a demographic collapse of the producing population, or was a response to shifts in the climatic conditions required for olive production. For the Sinope region, as noted in Chapter 6, the second factor is more likely, at least in the current state of our knowledge.[89] By the same token, it is clear that by the ninth and tenth centuries

Anatolia, and particularly the Pontic coastal plains and immediate hinterland on the northern edge of the plateau, were seen as major suppliers of grain.[90] The shifts in both medium- and longer-distance markets, especially for produce such as olive oil and wine, will have affected
those engaged in those areas of production as well as those on or near
the coasts more directly than inland producers who, with some few
exceptions, were producing almost entirely for subsistence needs and
the provisioning of local settlements, both urban and rural, in their immediate hinterland.[91]

Now cereal crops offer in general a considerably lower return (except in unusual circumstances, such as famine shortage, for example)
than those such as olives and vines, so it is not surprising that where
the conditions were appropriate and a market was available farmers preferred the latter.[92] To promote the (relative) expansion of cerealiculture
instead of other marketable produce (assuming that the land itself was
suitable for cereal production) required, therefore, some pressure, either
from the market in terms of demand, or from another source. In addition to the appropriate soils and surfaces, wheat requires some 300 mm
annual precipitation. These are conditions that are readily found in
many regions of Anatolia, and after the onset of the wetter phase from
the sixth century, as indicated very clearly in the data for the region,
were likely also present in areas hitherto less well-endowed (see Map 6.1
for modern Anatolian rainfall patterns). These were precisely the conditions that would have facilitated the relative increase in grain production that the pollen data appear to suggest.

The demands from the government, exerted through its armies in
the provinces, for grain, livestock, and other resources will have been
felt throughout the empire. More significantly, and as we have now
seen, it is clear that from sometime around the middle of the seventh
century the field armies had been distributed across Anatolia, the better
to accommodate their requirements, as well as to facilitate an effective
defensive response to the Arab raids and invasions. Such a move will
have considerably increased the burden on many regions to provide
supplies for these troops, while at the same time creating an expanded
market for the sale of the foodstuffs and other supplies they required.
The additional burden on the producing population of an area where
soldiers are based can be very heavy, and it will be worth examining
briefly some examples to demonstrate the nature of this and to consider

its implications. A good deal of work has now been done on the basic supplies required for armies in the ancient and medieval world, and some average figures for the daily rations of a soldier are generally agreed, although there is always a small margin of error. Thus, the daily grain requirements for a Roman soldier and for his late Roman and Byzantine counterpart ranges from 700 g to 1.2 kg (1.54–2.6 lbs.), with about 1 kg (2.2 lbs.) as a low estimated average. In addition to the grain or bread, of course, soldiers might also receive a portion of oil, wine, and some cheese or salted meat, depending on location and context.[93] Seventh-century evidence supports this—newly installed Muslim soldiers in Syria, Palestine, and Egypt in the 630s and 640s received a daily ration of between 2–3 lbs. of wheat (rather than baked bread) in Egypt, and somewhat less in Syria, in addition to an allowance of oil, vinegar, and honey.[94] In the tenth century a Byzantine military treatise describes the basic soldier's ration as consisting of bread with either cheese or dried salted meat.[95] Regardless of the minor variations, however, these figures permit some more general calculations about the grain requirements of soldiers. A unit of some three hundred soldiers, for example, would need an annual supply of some 110,000 kg of bread, requiring something in the order of 120,000–130,000 kg of wheat before grinding.[96]

It is possible to make some very approximate calculations of how much land was required to generate this return and thus offer some idea of what the overall cost to the landscape and to the producing population was in respect of maintaining a military force in its area. Calculations based on a range of ancient and medieval sources for Italy, Greece, the Balkans, and the Near East suggest that a low average return on seed sown to yield would have been in the region of 1:4 or 1:5 for wheat, with a per hectare production of approximately 520 kg (i.e., 208 kg per acre) and a sowing rate of 130 kg/ha (52 kg/acre). For barley rates of 770kg/ha (i.e., 308 kg/acre) have been proposed. These are indeed comparatively low yields, and while a conservative estimate is justified by the very limited evidence currently available (from texts) for the late Roman and Byzantine periods, a return of less than 1:4 would barely generate a marketable surplus.[97] Documents relating to crop yields for Anatolia as well as the Balkans indicate returns on sowing of some 1:3.5 to 1:5 on soils of medium quality and in non-irrigation agriculture conditions, with higher rates in wet or irrigated areas—as much as 1:8–9.[98] Since the variations for Italy in the later medieval and early modern periods

range from yields of 1:3–4 to 1:8–10, and in pre-1940s Turkey from
1:5–9, depending on zone (wet or dry), we may take them as averages
across a wider terrain with an assumed range of variable subareas.[99]

We do need to be cautious, however. In view of the fact that there
appears to have been remarkably little technological change between
the medieval and Ottoman periods—the wooden plow was still the chief
instrument of arable tillage into the 1960s—it is significant that, while
the evidence from late Ottoman and early Turkish Republic sources indicates considerable variability in average yields, nevertheless in most
years the yields for wheat and barley are greater than those offered by
the ancient and medieval inscriptional and textual sources.[100] Thus,
yields of wheat within the province of Çorum for the years from 1909–
1914, for example, were often three or four times expected values based
on medieval sources. A very rough estimate based on the available evidence would suggest that, at a rate of return of just 1:5, 130,000 kg of wheat
represents some 250 hectares (617.7 acres) of arable. In a good year with
a much higher yield—perhaps 1:10—the same acreage would have produced twice this amount, so the three hundred soldiers would have
needed the harvest from some 125 hectares (309 acres). Assuming these
were also cavalry soldiers, then similar amounts of hard fodder such as
barley, plus grazing, would be required—three hundred horses would
need something in the order of four to five hours per day or its equivalent in hay around the year, which amounts to some 2,225 hectares
(5,500 acres) per annum. And of course a unit of three hundred soldiers
would probably have up to one thousand horses at their disposal, to include spare mounts and replacements, for example.[101]

On the basis of a similarly crude calculation, therefore, the military
forces based in the Armeniakon region in the 660s—assuming a total
manpower of fifteen thousand—would have required some 5,475,000 kg
of bread per annum, representing up to 6 million kgs of wheat,[102] in turn
representing the product of a consolidated area of some 5,200–5,300
hectares (12,800–13,100 acres)[103] of arable, in addition to the requirement in hard and dry fodder—barley and hay—for the horses. The
amount of land actually required would in fact have been several times
greater than this, in light of the impact of losses incurred through seasonal diseases and pests as well as unusually heavy rainfall or frosts.[104]
Additionally, it should be recalled that demographic decline would have
reduced the overall total of cultivated arable. Nevertheless, such a quan-

tity is well within the wheat-growing capacity of the provinces that made up that region, providing that the soldiers were appropriately distributed to minimize the burden on any particular locality[105]—as we have now seen they were.

Agricultural output can, under the right circumstances, respond fairly rapidly to shifts in the market, and in particular to demand from the military, as examples from both the ancient and late Roman worlds as well as more recent history amply demonstrate,[106] or as illustrated by the market-orientated cash crop in olives and wine as well as mixed farming that drove the agrarian commerce of North Africa and the limestone massif in northern Syria in the fifth and first half of the sixth century.[107] In Apulia in the course of the later fourth and fifth centuries, for example, landowners and producers progressively turned over an ever greater proportion of their output to cereals in response both to market demand and the possibilities for greater profits as well as state fiscal pressure.[108] In the late third century BCE, the Roman Republic was able to increase grain production over a very short period through fiscal pressure, increasing rents in kind and exploiting the market opportunities offered to private landowners through higher prices; while in the second and third centuries CE the demands of the state for supplies for the army as well as other consumers impacted directly on levels of production of both private landlords and peasant tax payers as well as imperial estates.[109] There are many examples from the ancient world for peasant farmers, whether tenants or not, and landowners responding to both market opportunities generated by the presence of military forces as well as to fiscal pressure to meet state demands for grain, livestock, and similar produce for local military units.[110] Indeed, where a guaranteed market was accessible, landowners could increase production of the crops in demand in order to ensure their income as well as to make a profit.[111]

Armies require above all grain and livestock, the latter both for transport (horses, mules, and donkeys) as well as for food (cattle, sheep, goats, dairy, produce), along with other staples—wine, oil, and cheese, for example. Given the increased demand from military units on the Anatolian provinces from the 640s and 650s, therefore, it is perhaps not surprising to find that the palynological data indicates the expansion across this period of the simplified mixed cereal-pastoral regime that we have described in the preceding chapter. Several factors coincide to suggest an explanation. On the one hand, we have a situation clearly indicated in the archaeological record in which those areas that had formerly depended on a fairly international market for their specialized produce—wine, olives, and oil in particular—were faced with a considerably reduced demand. Minor shifts in climate may have made continuation of the traditional agriculture difficult or impossible, although as we have seen the proxy data discussed in the preceding chapter do not indicate such a shift in Anatolia at this point. At the same time, the arrival of larger than usual numbers of soldiers in many districts and on a more or less permanent basis meant an increased demand for produce such as wheat as well as livestock. Fiscal pressure exerted by the government to support these troops, together with new market opportunities, may thus have combined to generate new patterns of production to meet the new patterns of demand. The pollen data need to be understood within this broader context, especially for northern Anatolia and the Pontic region where, in a situation of real demographic down-turn (compare once again the dramatic later sixth- to seventh-century collapse of settlement numbers in the hinterland of Sinope, for example),[112] what may appear to be a reduction in relative levels of production might in fact conceal a proportionate response by producers to meet the needs of a much smaller population.

And this is what the shifting fiscal terminology of the period—as words originally signifying compulsory purchase came to have the meaning of regular imposition—may well reflect. While it is not an entirely straightforward matter for farmers already growing cereals to pull land hitherto exploited for other crops into cereal production, a state demand for certain products, or a fiscal incentive—maintaining tariffs on cereals at existing levels, for example, while increasing tax-rates on some other types of crop—are effective forcing agents.[113] Given the effectiveness of the imperial fiscal reach and the penetrative capacities of the government's provincial representatives described in earlier chapters, we should not doubt that such a deliberate intervention was possible and that it could impact on the agricultural strategies employed by landowners and farmers. The coincidence of all these developments over approximately the period ca. 650 to ca. 700 is, at the very least, suggestive of some of the measures taken by the Constantinopolitan government to address the difficult situation it faced.

A Conclusion

Now this is not the end. It is not even the beginning of the end. But it is, perhaps, the end of the beginning.[1]

We are in a much better position today to understand how the empire came through this century of crises and near catastrophe to create the basis for a renewed period of growth, prosperity, and political-military power in the ninth to eleventh centuries. Careful studies of the politics of the empire, both religious and secular and how they were intertwined; of the numismatic, fiscal, and administrative developments of the period; of the warfare and the military history of the east Roman state and its enemies, all these together offer the possibility to see behind the surface of events, wars, and religious disputes that have often been seen to characterize the seventh century.

Yet, as I remarked in the Introduction, there have been no attempts fully to integrate all the available material to generate a holistic picture, and this is what I have set out to do, or at least to inaugurate, in the present volume. We should not forget that the political and military successes that the emperors of the second half of the seventh century were able to chalk up reflect more than just effective imperial leadership—successful armies had to draw their recruits from somewhere, they needed to be trained, equipped, and properly led as well as regularly supplied and provisioned; successful provisioning depended upon the rural populations of the empire producing the right crops in appropriate quantities as well as an appropriate means of collecting and transporting what was produced to where it was needed. All this depended on an adequate communications infrastructure and a fiscal administration that could manage the resources in men and material in question. And it all has to make sense in the context of what people thought about the world they lived in and how their values and beliefs affected the way they could act. These fundamental issues have been for the most part marginalized, ignored, or taken for granted. In addition, it remains the case that in spite of the effectiveness of the strategy employed by emperors such as Constans II, Constantine IV, and Justinian II in exploiting the civil wars and internecine conflict with the caliphate— greatly to the advantage of the empire, no doubt—the empire continued to lose territory, people, and fortresses well into the reign of Leo III. Whatever the advantages it possessed in organizational respects or strategic geography, there is no doubt that it continued to be outnumbered, outresourced, and isolated.

Long before the seventh century, the need for the government at Constantinople to ensure its resource-base as well as to maintain its political authority required efforts both to impose imperially defined orthodoxy on heterodox and potentially dissident populations, notably in Egypt, Syria, and Armenia, and to control expenditure while at the same time resisting attacks on its territory and physical resources on several fronts. In the late sixth-century Balkans, these policies led indirectly to military mutiny and political revolution, events that in turn set off the Persian war in the east that lasted until 628. By the late 620s the victories of Heraclius had stabilized the eastern frontier (it seemed), but at the cost of much of the empire's Balkan territories. Heraclius had, according to a later account, permitted the migration of peoples later known as Serbs and Croats into the western Balkans as one means of maintaining imperial authority and influence, nominally at the price of conversion to Christianity. Whatever the truth of the matter, by the middle of the seventh century these areas, apart from some of the Adriatic coastline and fortified centers, were out of imperial control, along with most of the central Balkan region, including much of what is now Greece, again, apart from substantial stretches of coastline and the fortified ports or other settlements that situated there. In the east the Persian wars had if not exhausted then certainly set up a massive challenge to the government's ability to resource its armies—a rationalization of coin production under Heraclius reflects one aspect of this, as does the appearance of *kommerkiarioi* for Sicily and for North Africa at this time, whose seals, it has been argued, suggest that they had to contend with supplying Constantinople and possibly other cities with grain. Renewed tensions over Christological issues followed from attempts to find a compromise doctrine that would bring the miaphysite communities of the eastern provinces more firmly under imperial ecclesiastical as well as political authority. The Arab invasions and conquests put an end to the religious compromise, although it is important to remember that, certainly until the time of Justinian II in the 680s, the evidence suggests that the conquests continued to be seen as temporary—substantial, but still temporary—setbacks and that the lost provinces might still be recovered. Indeed, the precedent set by Heraclius' victorious war with the Persians was likely the key factor in deciding the imperial strategic response during Constans's reign.

So from the late 630s, and in a situation of relatively unfavorable climatic and demographic conditions, the government had to deal with a massively reduced income, and one result seems to have been (on a piecemeal basis from the 650s at least, and then on a permanent basis for a half century from the 670s) the expansion of the activities of the *kommerkiarioi,* which henceforth seem to have been involved with managing both the supply of the capital and of the armies with grain and perhaps other goods, alongside their traditional functions. Imperial monotheletism became under Constans II a hallmark of imperial authority and credibility, which in part (but only in part) explains the emperor's and his government's stubborn commitment to it, while its abandonment by Constantine IV in 680–681 reflected both an improved political–military situation vis-a-vis the caliphate as well as an attempt to end the empire's political ecclesiastical isolation. Unfortunately, this turn toward the west had as a major consequence the relative alienation of the patriarchates of the east and especially that of Antioch, where the great majority of the Melkite Christian population remained monothelete, at least until the arrival in the 720s of substantial numbers of dyothelete Christian captives.[2] It also cost the emperor some support in Constantinople and at Ravenna, although opposition was suppressed very quickly. In terms of broader strategy, Constans and his advisors pursued an aggressive-defensive policy, a policy aimed at retaining imperial control over as much territory as possible, of defending the frontiers, especially in the Caucasus, through client and allied rulers, whose loyalty the emperor tried to secure through gifts, court titles, and offices as well as military commands, although with only limited success, as we saw in the historical survey in Chapter 1.

This approach was based on the fundamental assumption that the Arab invasions would eventually be thrown back, just as the Persian conquests of the early part of the century had been. The propagandistic motifs on the copper coinage of Constans II suggest that this was the approach from the beginning—the conquering cross, on the one hand (the True Cross having been restored to Jerusalem before being taken to Constantinople) and the notion of renewal, on the other. But the empire had neither the resources nor the support it needed from the elites in the more distant provinces to make this policy work—the failure of imperial counterattacks in both North Africa and Italy, quite apart from the difficulties faced nearer to home in Anatolia, together with the need to introduce substantial and quite radical fiscal changes in the late 660s suggest that the government had begun to realize the nature of the problems it faced and had begun to respond accordingly.

The government's response to the unfolding difficulties it faced can be observed in several stages. From the late 630s and early 640s the field armies had to be withdrawn into Anatolia and eventually distributed across several provinces in order to provide them with the appropriate supplies and materials to continue to oppose the invaders. While this certainly facilitated the continued maintenance of substantial numbers of soldiers sufficient to defend the imperial heartlands, it must also have considerably increased the demand for grain in the affected districts. Efforts to import grain from far afield can have offered only limited support except for coastal cities such as Constantinople or, on occasion, Thessaloniki. The difficulties of relying on grain from Sicily, combined with the ultimate loss of North Africa, meant that this became extremely problematic, particularly in light of growing Arab sea power. The dramatic loss of revenues showed itself in the changes in coin production and in particular the radical cut in production of copper petty coinage from 668 indicates the fiscal problems the government faced. Groups of copper found at a number of locations in both the Balkans and Anatolia indicate that soldiers continued to be paid, at least when a particular campaign or expedition was undertaken, but how regular such payments were, how often copper rather than gold was the medium, and how much of this coinage percolated down—and at what pace—into local economic exchange economies remains unclear.

The sigillographic evidence nevertheless suggests that a fiscal machinery continued to operate throughout the provinces of the empire, far and near, and to operate efficiently enough to extract the resources necessary to maintain the armies and the apparatus of the east Roman state in effective working order and to provide the government at Constantinople with the resources through which it could retain the loyalty, support, and effective collaboration of its elites, most especially in what had by now become its core territory, Anatolia. Elites in Ravenna, Sicily, and southern Italy retained their loyalty to the emperor at Constantinople, if somewhat lukewarm on occasion and depending on the pressures exerted by the Lombards, for example. In North Africa the evidence suggest that loyalties were more readily compromised. Distance and the inability of the government to provide more than occasional and often token military support while at the same time demanding that the elite continue to make very substantial contributions to the fisc for such a limited return can hardly have promoted much enthusiasm, even if fear of the invading Arab forces promoted an implicit assumption that the empire, a known quantity, might be better than the less well-known invader.

With the death of Constans II and the failure of the Arab attack on Constantinople the empire went through a short period of reorientation, aided by the problems within the caliphate. The defeat of the attack of 668–669 meant a respite for the empire, which was able to go onto the offensive in the early 670s and defeat another major attack launched in 672–673, crushing an invading army in Lycia and destroying a large fleet off the coast at Syllaion/Pamphylia. In the late 670s the launch of maritime attacks against the Levantine coast and the deployment of the Mardaites threatened both Damascus and Jerusalem, forcing Muʿāwiya to sue for peace in 678. Whether it was at this point or earlier in his reign, it seems that Constantine IV decided on a radical shift in policy, abandoning monotheletism and reestablishing communion with Rome. Was this a result of a realization that Constans's grand strategy simply could not be made to work? Very probably, although the change was a gamble and certainly caused potentially fatal opposition from highly placed members of the palatine establishment as well as in the army. In the end, Constantine snuffed out the opposition and introduced a less expansive strategic policy. While not abandoning Italy, its defense could safely be left—as far as anything could be safely left at this time—in the hands of local commanders and the exarchs in collaboration with the papacy. Imperial efforts were refocused on Anatolia, the Caucasus, and the Balkans; in the last case, with the appearance of the Bulgars as a potential challenger to imperial power in the region, this was probably the right decision.

While the empire continued to be able to mount counterattacks by land and by sea at times, the basic strategic pattern that was emerging by the 660s was clear enough. The empire could hold onto most of Anatolia, although its eastern and Caucasian front depended heavily on the cooperation and collaboration of Armenian and other indigenous elites—hence the efforts put into this by all the emperors from Constans II onward. It could try to maintain a degree of parity at sea, if only to render seaborne invasions at the least an enterprise fraught with risk for the Arab leadership and its armies. And it could continue to maintain connections and communications with its Italian and Sicilian territories to bolster their morale and offer incentives to their elites, for which, of course, the maintenance of a reasonable naval presence was essential.

Justinian II's policies in the east were no more successful than those of his predecessors, nor were those of his successors; indeed, the empire continued to lose ground until by the end of Justinian II's second reign Roman control over Cilicia had been effectively extinguished and the Taurus mountains now became not just a barrier to invasion but effectively marked the frontier that was to divide the empire from its former provinces until the tenth century. Yet in spite of this, together with the final loss of Carthage and North Africa, the empire weathered the storm and had the resources and the strength to cling onto its remaining territory and defeat the great invasion and attack on Constantinople in 717–718. What enabled the east Roman state to survive this far has been the focus of the foregoing chapters.

In the first chapter, I noted five sets of factors that, when taken together, might explain the empire's continued existence: the role of beliefs and identity, the nature of the empire's elites, strategic geography, climate and environment, and organizational factors. To pursue the answer to the question of Byzantine survival through just two or three of these is insufficient. We might be inclined to think that, however successful imperial military action may have been and however adroitly the government was able to manage its fiscal resources and particularly its coinage, it must have been the ideological solidarity represented by the imperial church in the provinces and in the capital, rooted in the mass of the ordinary rural populace and the army, that ensured that the state could survive. There was clearly a shared Christian identity, along with a clearly understood difference between "them" and "us." Together with a vision of a God-protected Roman Empire ruled by a Christ-loving emperor, such beliefs served to reinforce an east Roman community identity and lent eastern Roman society a degree of cultural cohesion.

But I would argue strongly that the positive role of beliefs and identities, the existence of a notion of Roman versus Other, of "them" and "us," the existence of an ideological community that was both independent of the Roman state and yet contiguous with it, was only one element in a more complex picture. In spite of the clear existence of such an identity, and while it is also true that the church offered structural support to notions of Christian Romanness that permeated all levels of social being, this inquiry has also shown that the notion of a Roman "patriotism" that bolstered morale and stiffened resistance across the board remains problematic, at least as far as the evidence can take us.

Perhaps as important, then, and until recently largely overlooked, is the environmental aspect. A longer-term pattern of climatic changes that, combined with natural disasters such as the 530s–540s dust veil events, the century-long cooling that ensued, and the subsequent outbreak of plague (which remained endemic in the region until the middle of the eighth century), rendered the agrarian economy of parts of the empire more marginal than in the previous century or so. At the same time, the archaeological data, in particular the ceramic evidence (limited though it is) indicates a narrowing of commercial and exchange horizons and an intensification of highly localized patterns of consumption and distribution of goods. To some extent such a pattern had always underlain the wider pan-Mediterranean commercial networks of the late Roman period. With the gradual dissolution of most of these networks there remained the substrate of localized exchange systems. Such localized, semiautonomous but interconnecting and overlapping networks offered greater flexibility than the large-scale, "globalized" international system that had dominated into the early seventh century (although the latter was already changing by then too), the individual elements were less vulnerable to the pressures placed upon any single sector. These factors together contributed to a transformation of the economic environment of the seventh century and, in the context of the political developments of the period, produced a more resilient set of economic subregions as well as the simplified agrarian regime across much of Anatolia indicated by the palynological and related proxy data, a regime in which cereal production and stock raising played a key role.

That this simplification can only have been in part an unreflective response of farmers and landlords to climatic changes must be clear: in many areas the traditional modes of agriculture were maintained. It is equally likely that it reflected, for some areas and for some producers at least, a response to changed market demands. Given the loss of the Egyptian and then the North African sources of grain for Constantinople in particular, and the increased demand for grain and other produce on many regions of Anatolia to support the newly installed field armies, this was especially significant, because it was at precisely this point that sources of grain far closer to home came on stream. I want to emphasize, therefore, that this was not a planned response (not that we have any evidence either way). Rather, the shift in the patterns of agricultural production coincided with a greater need for grain in Anatolia and for sources of grain nearer to the military mouths they had to feed, a need that no doubt acted further to stimulate the grain and livestock regime that had been evolving. The cumulative result was to positively reinforce a hard-pressed government's attempts to reorganize its resources and support itself through these difficult times. We can thus see a dialectical relationship between climatic conditions that encouraged shifts in patterns of agrarian production and the needs of a state under pressure impacting to promote these same responses. If more influence should be ascribed to the sort of climatic shifts I have described, then it might almost be said that it was the very conditions that led to the economic weakness and political breakdown of the Roman Empire over the longer term (from the third century onward) that ultimately permitted the early medieval eastern Roman state to survive.

Yet neither can these factors alone explain the empire's continued survival unless we also take into account the substantial degree of internal cohesion and collaboration that prevailed, with conditions guaranteed less by ideological unity so much as by the fact that the vested interests of the elite in the widest sense—all those who held state or church positions at whatever level—coincided with the survival of the late Roman state, its apparatus, and, crucially, its ideological raison d'être. A combination of the coercive power of the east Roman state and its all-pervasive military across the provinces, the incorporation of the vested interests of the provincial elites of Anatolia into the ideological and political concerns of the imperial court, the reciprocity of rewards and advantages that this arrangement guaranteed to both parties, along with the absence of a viable alternative political authority, made non-cooperation, opposition, or even collaboration with the enemy, risky if not doomed to failure. There was popular as well as elite political opposition at times. Apathy, either real or potential, to the greater cause of empire may have existed among rural and urban populations most directly affected by warfare (even if we have very little evidence for such). There was certainly hostility to the fiscal officials of the government and to the oppressive appropriations of landlords although it is almost impossible to measure. But as long as the provincial ruling elites—the "rural gentry" who led the armies and who staffed the fiscal apparatus of the center—remained loyal, the state stood a good chance of surviving.

Nor was this just a reflection of material vested interests. As I have tried to show, both in the Introduction as well as in Chapters 2, 3, and 4, the acceptance by and integration of provincial, metropolitan, and ecclesiastical elites into an imperial political theology—a coherent ideological system—that bound empire, court, and provinces together through a set of common identities and social mores was a crucial part of this convergence of vested interests. The vast majority of the rural and urban population accepted this world and were bound up in reproducing it both ideologically as well as in practical, day-to-day life, except on those occasions when they were confronted with particular challenges to their versions of the way the world should be—as exemplified on occasion in the oppositional or rebellious activities of soldiers from time to time. As we noted also in Chapters 2 and 3, the Roman state in the east compromised with the church and the Christian community so that the two in effect blended in what we could describe as a sacralization of the east Roman state, its law, and its whole ideological apparatus. This did not happen overnight, nor was it straightforward. On the contrary, its roots lie in a process of sacralization of imperial rulership stretching back beyond the fifth century, one phase of which culminated in the concept of divinely elected emperor as presented in the *Codex Justinianus;* and in a liturgification of court and ceremonial that evolved in the second half of the sixth century and that further hieraticized imperial rule and sacral kingship.[3] Regardless of the inherent tensions within this system—and they were many—neither could there be any doubt that the Christian community and all that it represented and symbolized was headed by the Roman emperor, rather than by the patriarch. The Christian community, embodied in one sense in the formal equivalence of secular and canon law, was the Roman Empire.[4] This development contrasts very markedly with what happened in the west. Here, the ideas expressed in the works of Sophronius of Jerusalem and of Maximus the Confessor became the political and ecclesiastical reality—a thriving Christian community that did not require the existence of the Roman state.[5] But this was not the mainstream understanding of the world of most Christian Roman thinkers in the seventh- and eighth-century east. Had this not been the case, it would be difficult to envisage the iconoclast policies of Leo III or Constantine V having the hold that they did in the imaginary of the post-iconoclast world.

Finally, the empire enjoyed two further advantages. First, it benefited from the particular strategic geography of Anatolia, an advantage that minimized the threat of a permanent occupation of key centers and nodal points and maximized the potential for imperial counterstrikes. Second, it was endowed with remarkably flexible and effective fiscal arrangements and mechanisms for the appropriation and redistribution of essential military resources in men and provisions. The best example is the ways in which the efforts of the *kommerkiarioi* and their network of warehouses and the infrastructure that supported them were redirected to bail the government out in the period ca. 673–732. But there are other indications, as we saw in Chapters 4 and 7—in particular, in the ways in which fiscal administration was focused on the department of the *sakellion* and the *sakellarios* and the ways in which the whole administrative management of the empire was concentrated in the imperial palace—what might almost be called a "palatinization" of the state apparatus and, to a degree, the state elite.

Of course, it would be absurd to ignore the political story—whether a tale of effective leadership or incompetence, internal factionalism or civil war, competent management of limited resources or profligate waste of manpower, foolish or inappropriate handling of sensitive issues of belief and conviction. The empire benefited, or suffered, from all of these at certain moments, and this, too, must be another element in the picture. Yet had good, bad, or indifferent political leadership been the only element in this story, the eastern Roman Empire might well have succumbed by the early eighth century, to be replaced by an even more expansive Umayyad polity that could rapidly have swallowed up the Balkans and reached central Europe almost a thousand years before the Ottomans. There were as many ineffective policies or strategies, military defeats, and crushing financial losses as there were successes. But leadership and the ability and foresight of individual rulers and their advisors were just one element, and an element that needs to be firmly situated in the context that made it possible for them to believe, plan, and act with the outcomes that they had.

The other set of issues addressed at the outset of this project concerned the question of the formation of states and empires and their collapse. Historians will no doubt take issue with some of my interpretation, and that is, of course, to the good: there can be no expansion in our understanding of the period and processes with which this book is concerned if there is no debate, no discussion and challenging of views and interpretations. But I hope I have been able to suggest how the processes and mechanisms of resilience and adaptation can be observed in the minutiae of one particular example of social, cultural, and institutional history, and to demonstrate the importance of looking at every aspect of such processes rather than making assumptions based on simple correlations between the most obvious factors. Just as importantly, I have tried to show how we must put the various elements in question— beliefs, social praxis, economic structures and relationships, material conditions and environment—in their historical context in order to historicize change while at the same time retaining a degree of analytical flexibility and developing a sense of what is heuristically coherent in our efforts to generate knowledge of the subject in hand. Resilience in the case of the seventh- and eighth-century eastern Roman Empire inhered in the particular articulation of political, ideological, material cultural and organizational structures or practices, "ways of doing." This combination was unique, but the elements that comprised it were not, and can be found in any human social entity at one level or another. In trying to see more exactly how the various elements that contributed to the survival, or not, of a political, social, and cultural system such as the medieval East Roman Empire were articulated, I hope also to have suggested to those interested in large-scale comparative historical work that the answer lies as much in the detail as in the big picture. Both go hand in hand.

To conclude, we have a situation in which political will, social and cultural ambition, and calculation; the sacralization of the state, law, and imperial rule within a single, ideologically coherent bundle; organizational and logistical efficiency and flexibility; an extraordinarily fluctuating political situation at both domestic and international levels; together with longer-term changes in the physical environment of the east Roman world all converge across a period of a few decades to generate a specific and quite unpredictable outcome. Crucially, the binding of the elites of Anatolia to the imperial cause and, for a while at least, a near complete overlap of vested interests, gave the imperial state the political, structural, and institutional cohesion that was required to survive the external pressures it faced. These are—to return to the final paragraphs of the Introduction—the Goldilocks parameters for east Roman survival. Their existence meant an absolute check to the greatest series of conquests in the shortest period of time that the world had ever seen, more rapid and more wide-ranging than those of Alexander the Great, more long-lasting than those of the Huns in the fourth and fifth centuries or the Mongol empire in the twelfth and thirteenth centuries. In the period between 640 and 718, it looked as though nothing could stop the expansion of the caliphate westward. Yet what was left of the Roman Empire in the east, a rump state with what must have seemed the puniest of resources, succeeded. An early eighth-century (CE) Arabic apocalyptic tradition ascribed to the Prophet by ʿAbdullāh b. Muhayrīz put it thus: "The Romans . . . are people of sea and rock, whenever a generation goes, another replaces it. Alas, they are your associates to the end of time."[6] The eastern Roman Empire simply would not die.

ABBREVIATIONS

NOTES

GLOSSARY

BIBLIOGRAPHY

INDEX

Abbreviations

AB	*Analecta Bollandiana*
ACO II, 1	*Acta Conciliorum Oecumenicorum* II, 1: *Concilium Lateranense a. 649 celebratum,* ed. R. Riedinger (Berlin, 1984)
ACO II, 2.1–2	*Acta Conciliorum Oecumenicorum* II, 2.1–2: *Concilium universale Constantinopolitanum tertium,* ed. R. Riedinger (Berlin, 1990–1992)
ACO II, 3.1–2	*Acta Conciliorum Oecumenicorum* II, 3.1: *Concilium universale Nicaenum secundum, Concilii actiones* I–III, ed. E. Lamberz (Berlin, 2008); II, 3. 2: *Concilii actiones* IV–V (Berlin 2012)
AHC	*Annuarium Historiae Conciliorum*
AS	*Acta Sanctorum* (Antwerp, 1643ff.)
B	*Byzantion*
BBA	Berliner Byzantinistische Arbeiten
BBS	Berliner Byzantinistische Studien
BHG	F. Halkin, *Bibliotheca Hagiographica Graeca* (Subsidia hagiographica 8a. 3rd ed. Brussels 1957)
BF	*Byzantinische Forschungen*
BSl	*Byzantinoslavica*
BSOAS	*Bulletin of the School of Oriental and African Studies*
BZ	*Byzantinische Zeitschrift*
CCSG	*Corpus christianorum, Series graeca*
CFHB	*Corpus Fontium Historiae Byzantinae*
CJC	*Corpus Juris Civilis,* I: *Institutiones,* ed. P. Krüger; *Digesta,* ed. Th. Mommsen; II: *Codex Iustinianus,* ed. P. Krüger; III: *Novellae,* edd. R. Schöll, W. Kroll (Berlin, 1892–1895, repr. 1945–1963)
CP	Constantinople
CPG	M. Geerard, *Clavis Patrum Graecorum,* I–IV (Turnhout 1983, 1974, 1979, 1980); M. Geerard, F. Glorie, V (Turnhout 1987)
CSCO	*Corpus Scriptorum Christianorum Orientalium*

CSHB	*Corpus Scriptorum Historiae Byzantinae*
CTh.	*(Codex Theodosianus) Theodosiani libri xvi cum constitutionibus Sirmondianis*, ed. Th. Mommsen, P. Meyer et al. (Berlin 1905)
Dölger-Müller 2009	F. Dölger, *Regesten der Kaiserurkunden des oströmischen Reiches 565–1453* [Corpus der griechischen Urkunden des Mittelalters und der neueren Zeit, Reihe A, Abt. I] i; 2nd revised ed. A. Müller, i, 1: 565–867 (Munich 2009)
DOS	J. Nesbitt, N. Oikonomidès, *Catalogue of Byzantine seals at Dumbarton Oaks and in the Fogg Museum of Art*, I: *Italy, North of the Balkans, North of the Black Sea* (Washington, DC, 1991); II: *South of the Balkans, the Islands, South of Asia Minor* (Washington, DC, 1994); III: *West, Northwest and Central Asia Minor and the Orient* (Washington, DC, 1996); IV: *The East*, ed. E. McGeer, J. Nesbitt and N. Oikonomidès (Washington, DC, 2001); V: *The East (continued), Constantinople and environs, unknown locations, addenda, uncertain readings*, ed. E. McGeer, J. Nesbitt and N. Oikonomidès (Washington, DC, 2005)
DOT	Dumbarton Oaks Texts
EHR	*English Historical Review*
JGR	*Jus Graecoromanum*, ed. I. and P. Zepos, 8 vols. (Athens 1931/ Aalen, 1962)
JHS	*Journal of Hellenic Studies*
JÖB	*Jahrbuch der österreichischen Byzantinistik*
JRS	*Journal of Roman Studies*
LP	*Liber Pontificalis*. Texte, introduction et commentaire, ed. L. Duchesne, 2 vols. (Bibliothèque des Écoles Françaises d'Athènes et de Rome, II sér., 3. Paris, 1886/1892; repr. 1955); vol. 3: *Additions et corrections*, ed. C. Vogel (Paris 1957). Eng. trans. R. Davis, *The Book of Pontiffs (Liber Pontificalis)* (Liverpool, 1989); idem, *The Lives of the Eighth-Century Popes (Liber Pontificalis)* (Liverpool, 1992)
Mansi	*Sacrorum Conciliorum nova et amplissima Collectio*, ed. J. D. Mansi (Florence, 1759ff.)
MGH	*Monumenta Germaniae Historica*
PBE	*Prosopography of the Byzantine Empire 641–886*, ed. J. R. Martindale. CD-ROM/online version (London, 2000)
PG	*Patrologiae Cursus completus*, series Graeco-Latina, ed. J.-P. Migne (Paris, 1857–1866, 1880–1903)
PmbZ	R.-J. Lilie, C. Ludwig, T. Pratsch, I. Rochow et al., *Prosopographie der mittelbyzantinischen Zeit. Erste Abteilung (641–867)*, 6 vols. (Berlin-New York, 1999–2002)
P.Oxy.	*The Oxyrhynchus Papyri*, ed. B. P. Grenfell, A. S. Hunt et al. (London 1898f.)
REB	*Revue des Études Byzantines*

Rhalles-Potles K. Rhalles, M. Potles, Σύνταγμα τῶν θείων καὶ ἱερῶν κανόνων,
6 vols. (Athens, 1852–1859)
SRM *Scriptores rerum Merovingarum*
TIB *Tabula Imperii Byzantini*

J. Koder and F. Hild, *Tabula Imperii Byzantini* 1: *Hellas und Thessalia* (Denkschr. d. Österr. Akad. d Wiss., phil.-hist. Kl. 125. Vienna 1976)

F. Hild and M. Restlé, *Tabula Imperii Byzantini* 2: *Kappadokien (Kappadokia, Charsianon, Sebasteia und Lykandos)* (Denkschr. d. Österr. Akad. d Wiss., phil.-hist. Kl. 149. Vienna 1981)

P. Soustal, with J. Koder, *Tabula Imperii Byzantini* 3: *Nikopolis und Kephallenia* (Denkschr. d. Österr. Akad. d Wiss., phil.-hist. Kl. 150. Vienna 1981)

K. Belke (with M. Restlé), *Tabula Imperii Byzantini* 4: *Galatien und Lykaonien* (Denkschr. d. Österr. Akad. d Wiss., phil.-hist. Kl. 172. Vienna 1984)

F. Hild and H. Hellenkamper, *Tabula Imperii Byzantini* 5, 1/2: *Kilikien und Isaurien* (Denkschr. d. Österr. Akad. d Wiss., phil.-hist. Kl. 215. Vienna 1990)

P. Soustal, *Tabula Imperii Byzantini* 6: *Thrakien (Thrakê, Rodopê und Haimimontos)* (Denkschr. d. Österr. Akad. d Wiss., phil.-hist. Kl. 221. Vienna 1991)

K. Belke and N. Mersich, *Tabula Imperii Byzantini* 7: *Phrygien und Pisidien* (Denkschr. d. Österr. Akad. d Wiss., phil.-hist. Kl. 211. Vienna 1990)

H. Hellenkamper and F. Hild, *Tabula Imperii Byzantini* 8: *Lykien und Pamphylien* (Denkschr. d. Österr. Akad. d Wiss., phil.-hist. Kl. 320. Vienna 2004)

K. Belke, *Tabula Imperii Byzantini* 9: *Paphlagonien und Honorias* (Denkschr. d. Österr. Akad. d Wiss., phil.-hist. Kl. 249. Vienna 1996)
TM *Travaux et Mémoires*
ZV G. Zacos and A. Veglery, *Byzantine Lead Seals,* vol. I, parts 1–3 (Basel 1972)

Notes

Introduction

1. Theoph., 411 (transl. Mango-Scott 571).
2. See the pointed remarks of Hendy 1985: 2–3.
3. See Schreiner 2008: 17; Lilie 1993. The older view of the seventh and eighth centuries as a "Dark Age," for which the lack of sources made worthwhile research and investigation difficult if not impossible, has been under challenge since the 1960s, of course—see Maier 1968: 10–12; note Haldon 1997a: 1–2; Meier 2012: 242 with further literature.
4. There is a debate around the use of this term, too, of course. See the discussion and survey of the debate in Stouraitis 2014.
5. Mango 2002: 13. For a recent restatement of such an approach, see Brownworth 2009.
6. Gibbon 1776–1789, ch. lii, pp. 375ff. and ch. xlviii, pp. 12–15.
7. See the essays in Clucas 1988; and Obolensky 1971.
8. Theoph., 339 (transl. Mango-Scott, 471).
9. *Vita. Andrei Cret.*, §4 (173).
10. See Griffith 1987.
11. For the *atheoi Sarakēnoi: ACO* II, 2. 2: 614. 3.
12. Hoyland 1997: 294–307, 454–518; Griffith 2010: 23–74. I leave to one side, for the purposes of this discussion, the continuities in the conversation between theologians and philosophically minded intellectuals representing the three "Abrahamic" faiths that existed from the seventh century into the late medieval period: see Fowden 2015 with literature.
13. Byzantine views of early Islam in the historical tradition: Brandes 2009; Meyendorff 1964; Magdalino 1998; Argyriou 2005; for Islam: Hoyland 1997: 454–519, esp. 480–501. See also Khoury 1972.
14. See the discussion in Meier 2012, introducing the notion of "threatened order" to describe the inner workings of such processes.

15. See Bonnell 1988; the introductory survey by Scheidel 2013; and Scheidel 2009 with literature.
16. See, for example, Burbank and Cooper 2010; Alcock et al. 2001; Sanderson 1995, 1999; 2000; Chase-Dunn and Hall 1997; Denemark 2000; Yoffee and Cowgill 1988; Tainter 1988; Mann 1986; Claessen and Skalnik 1981. The quotation is part of the title of Diamond 2005.
17. As illustrated in Ward-Perkins 2005 and Heather 2005, in reaction and in contrast to the oeuvre of P. Brown, for example. Excellent and detailed review of this issue with extensive further literature: Meier 2012: 187–196.
18. See, e.g., Dark 1998.
19. For example: Sherratt 2003: 53–54; Bell 2006: esp. 15, regarding ancient trading systems.
20. See, e.g. Rosen 2007. Resilience is now a key theme in contemporary environmental planning, for example: see the webpages of the Resilience Alliance: http://www.resalliance.org/.
21. See Johnson 2007: 3–17; also Middleton 2012; see Lewin 1999 and Byrne 1998.
22. See, e.g., Gunderson and Holling 2002; Gunderson and Pritchard 2002.
23. As in Tainter 1988.
24. See, e.g., Haldon 1993d.
25. See Turchin 2003; Turchin and Nefedov 2009. I place "external" in quotes since no relatively complex sociopolitical system of the sort we are considering exists in a vacuum, and the causal connections between the internal structure of a given culture or polity and the wider conditions of its existence, shared with its neighbors, are generally such that "external" and "internal" elements are closely linked. Thus, foreign policy reflects both the needs of a ruling dynasty, an elite establishment, or a state in maintaining or enhancing its international position as well as the vested interests of the same groups within their own society. "External" pressures, perhaps leading to warfare, may not necessarily be directly associated with this nexus of relationships, but they frequently have been.
26. All these interpretative models are neatly described and evaluated in Scheidel 2013: 33–41.
27. Mann 1986.
28. See discussion in Goldstone and Haldon 2009: 11–15.
29. See Callinicos 2004: xxii–xxxii, 85–102.
30. There are many ways of using, or misusing, such conceptual terms, of course, and we must be careful to define what we mean in deploying each of them. I use "ideology" (and sometimes a more descriptively exact equivalent for the East Roman case, "political theology") to refer to a specific set of concepts and ideas extrapolated from the values and beliefs that make up the symbolic universe and employed largely in justifying and legitimating the dominant power-relationships and set of socioeconomic relations. For discussion of this and related concepts in the East Roman con-

text, see Haldon 1986b, 1997a: 324–326; Haldon 2015a. Broader reflections
and analysis in Haldon 1993d.

31. On choice and rationale: Stark 1996: esp. 163–189. For the medieval west:
Le Goff 1985 and for the Byzantine world the essays in Maguire 1995.

32. Magdalino 1999; Kazhdan 1995; Haldon 1986a.

33. See Dégh 2001 and the essays in Whitehouse and Laidlaw 2007, for some
approaches.

34. Haldon 2009: 205; Mango 2002: 10. There is a debate around the use of
the term "empire" to describe the eastern Roman polity after the seventh
century—both because of a supposed increasing cultural-linguistic ho-
mogenization of identities (e.g., Kaldellis 2012, 2009) and because of the
Constantinopolitanocentric nature of the state, which leads Magdalino
(2007) to liken the empire to a city-state. Regardless of this discussion,
for the seventh to eighth centuries I would continue to see the empire as
such, in light of its still multicultural and multiethnic composition,
even if the march toward a more unified élite Hellenic culture is clear
enough.

35. For issues of periodization and questions of understanding the interrela-
tionships between short-term and long-term change, see Meier: 2012. For
a full and up-to-date survey of the history of the empire, see the various
chapters in Shepard 2008.

36. See Kazhdan 1992.

37. The Roman and Byzantine Empires are best described, from the point of
view of their political economy, as "compromised autocracies" rather than
through terms such as "authoritarian" or "dictatorial," terms that make
better sense in the context of more recent regimes; see, for example, Chehabi and Linz 1998. Nor do I think "republican monarchy" (see below)
really fits since, while correctly drawing attention to some key elements in
both attitudes to and arrangements of government, it is hard to escape
the commonly held connotations of the term "republic" for the modern
reader.

38. See the perceptive analysis of Beck 1966.

39. Kaldellis 2015, in many respects taking his cue from Beck 1966, but going
substantially further in several respects. As an account of how the vocabulary and concept of republican government was wielded and manipulated, and of how those who understood it could deploy it; and as a theory
of the imperial system as it was historically understood and imagined by
such people, this is an important account that sets up a number of effective challenges to modern misperceptions of the attitudes and values prev-
alent in the medieval East Roman world, even if in several key respects I
find myself in disagreement with the argument, especially from a social-
or economic-history perspective. For a sensible review see Stouraitis 2016.

40. See esp. Flaig 1997; with Lilie 1984b; Winkelmann 1987; Gizewski 1988;
Meier 2012; Bjornlie 2013; as well as the essays in Angelov and Saxby

2013. One of the problems of some specialist literature is the often casual use of terms such as "the Romans/Byzantines," "the people," and so forth, thus ignoring the fact that we cannot possibly speak of any single unitary body without extreme caution, at least not at all levels of social and political action, as the analyses of Flaig 1997 and Meier 2012 have demonstrated through the deployment of the concept of "acceptance-groups." As we shall see in the chapters that follow, there are many subtypes of "Roman": the population of the empire was divided horizontally by economic and social divisions as much as it was divided geographically by local identities, vertically by lines of patronage, affiliation and community, as well as by ties of blood and kinship, real or imagined. Generalization is always possible, but the level and context for such generalizations must be very carefully determined to lend them any heuristic or analytical value.

41. For a discussion of the structure and situation of the later Roman Empire in the east in comparative perspective, see Haldon 2012b.

42. I have sketched out some approaches to understanding and analyzing Byzantine society in Haldon 2009. For Marx's comment: Marx 1968 [1852]: 96.

43. See the classic study of Patlagean 1977; and on charity and philanthropy, Constantelos 1968; the essays in Stathakopoulos 2007; and note also Herrin 2013b and 2013c.

44. For a more detailed discussion of this terminology and the issues it raises: Haldon 1993d, chapters 1 and 2.

45. For a survey of the social order of the late Roman world, see Haldon 1997a: 9–140, 92–102; Sarris 2009; and the essays in Maas 2005a.

46. See, for example, the extensive reviews of literature on these topics in Bowden, Lavan, and Machado 2004; Bowden, Gutteridge, and Machado 2006.

47. See Uthemann 1997; the essays in Heinzer and Schönborn 1982; Jankowiak 2009, 2013c; Lange 2012; Booth 2014; Price et al. 2014.

48. Settipani 2013; Howard-Johnston 2010b; Jankowiak 2009.

49. Brandes 2002; Montinaro 2013; Brubaker and Haldon 2011: 665–771; Robinson 2010; Schubert and Sijpestejn 2015; Sijpestein 2007.

50. Brubaker and Haldon 2011: 453–572; Curta 2001; Henning 2007; Walmsley 2000.

51. Material summarized in Curta 2006, for example, for the Balkans; and see the relevant chapters in Shepard 2008 for the empire's western, eastern, and northern neighbors.

52. See, e.g., the essays in Hoyland 2004, and the useful review by Papaconstantinou 2005.

53. On these and many other facets of the period from ca. 400–600: McEvoy 2013; Pfeilschifter 2013; Meier 2012 and 2004a; Sarris 2009; the literature cited in Schachner 2006 and Lavan 2006; Brandes 2002; the contributions to Cameron et al. 2000; and the summary in Haldon 1997a: 9–40.

54. For some applications of the Goldilocks Principle and a broader discussion: Davies 2006; Spier 2011: 36–39.

1. The Challenge

1. Nikeph., cap. 52. 1–11 (transl. Mango 121).
2. Jones 1964: 463; Banaji 2001: 228. The figures include the value of that part of the annual fiscal burden levied in grain. This figure is broadly supported by the report in Baladhuri that ʿAmr ibn al-ʿAs raised an annual income in Egypt of some 2 million *nomismata* in the middle of the seventh century: Hitti 1916–1924: I, 340. Calculations are based on the post-Anastasian reform coinage, where 72 gold *solidi*/*nomismata* = 1 lb., and 100 lbs. = 1 *kentēnarion* (or 7,200 *solidi*).
3. The African prefecture included Corsica and Sardinia, so rounding the total to some 400,000 would not be unreasonable. One figure from Islamic sources for later eighth-century Africa (Ifrīqiya) gives an annual revenue of 13 million silver dirhams, which converts to some 558,000 *nomismata* (Cahen 1971: 310), so it is likely that the figure of 390,000–400,000 *nomismata* is a very low estimate.
4. Hendy 1985: 164–167, 616–618.
5. Prigent 2014.
6. Hendy 1985: 168–172. Estimates of the global income from Egypt vary considerably. Jones 1964: 463 calculated it at approximately 200 *kentenaria* or 1, 440,000 *nomismata*, whereas Banaji 2001: 228, as noted already, allowing for a greater degree of fluidity within the Egyptian economy, suggested a higher figure of 2,628,000 or 365 *kentenaria* in gold. Both figures include the grain tax converted into gold equivalents at contemporary rates. Such calculations may, at least in the most general terms, be supported by later figures from Egypt in the eighth century.
7. Inalcik 1994: 77–83; Hendy 1985: 616–618. The sixteenth-century Ottoman figures are exact but do not include as central fiscal revenues a wide range of other "fiscal" resources, including local expenditures within self-supporting provinces such as Egypt and Syria; while it is also difficult to calculate the fiscal value of the thousands of timars in the "home" provinces of Rumeli (Balkans) and Anadolu, Rum, and Karaman (Anatolia).
8. Hendy 1985: 171.
9. Lybyer 1913: 179–181; Hendy 1985: 617–618, with further discussion and references; but see also Inalcik 1994: 77–83 for a more differentiated account.
10. The point was first given the emphasis it deserved by Hendy 1985: 619. On imperial resources and revenues, see the relevant chapters in Laiou et al. 2002a; Hendy 1985.
11. Hendy 1985: 618; Lilie 1987; Morrisson 2002: 940–941, with cautionary remarks on the interpretation of the data; Füeg 1997.

12. For a survey of these and related issues: Kennedy 1995; Haldon and Kennedy 2012: 341–352; Simonsen 1988; and esp. Foss 2010. On the difficulties of accessing resources from Egypt: Humphreys 2013: 239–241.

13. Ditten 1993: 45–65, with details of the evidence for the movement of refugees in the war-torn regions of both the Balkans and Asia Minor, with the most recent literature on the subject; see also the older work of Charanis 1961b, 1972. On the history or urbanism in this period: Brandes 1989; Haldon 1997: 99–117; contributions to Krause and Witschel 2006 and to Henning 2007; Brubaker and Haldon 2011: 531–563.

14. See Crow et al. 2008; Mango 1995: 17; Haldon 1997a: 116 with literature.

15. See the survey of Ahrweiler 1962; also Haldon 1997a: 114–117, 143–145. For references to devastation see, for example, the *Life* of Philaretos, whose home was in Paphlagonia and whose herds had been driven off by raiders: *Vita Philareti*: 115–117, 137 (and on this text see Brubaker and Haldon 2001: 225); or the *Life* of the tenth-century magnate Michael Maleinos, whose properties in the devastated regions of Charsianon in east-central Anatolia he improved by careful investment: *Vita Mich. Maleini*: 550.20–21. Although many of these *Lives* are full of literary topoi and rhetorical artifice and not to be taken at face value, they nevertheless reflected a recognizable reality for their listeners or readers, and there is no reason to doubt that the general situations they describe are more or less accurate.

16. See *Vita et Miracula Theodori (tironis)*: 198–199 (miracles 7, 9).

17. See the survey in Brubaker and Haldon 2011: 453–771; and especially the contributions of Koder 2012; 1986; also the essays in Henning 2007.

18. For a detailed catalog of official imperial and related documents for the period under review here, together with an analytical catalog and discussion of Byzantine-Islamic diplomatic exchanges from 639 on, see Dölger-Müller 2009 and Kaplony 1996.

19. *PmbZ*, #3691 for a summary biography with sources and literature; *PBE* Konstans 1.

20. Grierson 1968: 409, 411; Bates 1971.

21. For Constantine III: *PmbZ*, #3701 / *PLRE* III, 349–351; for Heraklonas, Martina, and Valentinus: *PmbZ*, #2565; #4842; #8545 (*PLRE* III, 587–588; 837–838; *PBE* Valentinus 1); see Dölger-Müller 2009: #218.

22. As I have noted, this brief narrative résumé of the political events of the period up to the 720s is intended primarily as a context for what follows. I will therefore limit references to modern scholarship, except where absolutely necessary. For further reading and the literature upon which this account is based, see Auzépy 2008; Booth 2014; Brown 2008; Curta 2006; Haldon 1997a; Howard-Johnston 2010b; Hussey 1986; Kaegi 2010, 2008, 1995; Kennedy 2007, 1986; Louth 2008; Sarris 2011a; Stratos 1968–1980.

23. See Lilie 1976: 63–64. Further information on Muʿāwiya, *PmbZ*, #5185 / *PBE* Muʿāwiya 1. For Theodore Rštuni: *PmbZ*, #7293 (*PBE* Pasagnathes 1) and cf. *PmbZ*, #7298; Procopius: *PmbZ*, #6353.

24. Lilie 1976: 66–67; Dölger-Müller 2009: #227–227c; and for a useful summary of events in Armenia and the Caucasus at this time, see Greenwood 2008: 341–342 and the discussion in *PmbZ*, #7293, #7298, and #10772. For Marianus: *PmbZ*, #4876; Hamazasp Mamikonian: *PmbZ*, #2538. For the caliph ʿUthmān: *PmbZ*, #8559 / *PBE* Othman 1.
25. Lilie 1976: 67–68; Greenwood 2008: 342.
26. Kennedy 1986: 69–81; Dölger-Müller 2009: 228b; Kaplony 1996: 1, 1. A4–A5.
27. Greenwood 2008: 342–343; Dölger-Müller 2009: #230a.
28. Lilie 1976: 68–83, but bearing in mind the revised chronology for the blockade and siege of Constantinople in 667–669 (rather than the traditional 674–678): Jankowiak 2013a.
29. See Howard-Johnston 2010b: 483–484; Sarris 2011a: 282.
30. See Hovorun 2015: 113–114; Tannous 2014; Lange 2012; Booth 2014: 186–208; Jankowiak 2009: 15–24, 49–95; Brandes 1998b: 147–148. For a review of the documentary evidence for the evolution of the debate, see Winkelmann 2001 and Jankowiak and Booth 2015.
31. Allen 2009; Booth 2014: 209–24; Jankowiak 2009: 133–49.
32. Hovorun 2015: 115–117; and for the development of Maximus's thought in this respect see Jankowiak and Booth 2015: #35–#39; for a treatment of the life, works and impact of Maximus, see now Allen 2015 and other essays in Allen and Neil 2015; with *PmbZ*, #4921 / *PBE* Maximos 10.
33. Dölger-Müller 2009: #211, #215; Allen 2015: 5–6; Jankowiak 2013c. The council of 636 is reported only in the Syriac *Life* of Maximus: *Vita Syr. Max. conf.*, 8–15; see Booth 2013: 239–241. Recent scholarship has, rightly, insisted on distinguishing between both the aims and originating theological contexts for the doctrines of the single operation and the single will, noting in particular that the latter was almost certainly not aimed at the miaphysite churches of the eastern provinces in the way that the doctrine of the single operation had been. Note that in a letter written in 634/635 in response to a patriarchal decision of August 633 to prohibit discussion of one or two operations, initially accepted by all the parties involved, Pope Honorius himself confessed a single will in Christ. Whether we should then conclude that the doctrine of the single will was an accidental outcome of imperial/patriarchal attempts to re-establish doctrinal order within the imperial church (see Jankowiak 2013c) remains moot: see esp. Tannous 2014: 31–32; 64–67; Allen 2009: 204–209. Monotheletism was the last in the series of Christological controversies over the nature of the Trinity and the relationship between its constituent elements. From the early fourth century the debate over the nature of Christ—divine, human, a mixture of both—had been carried on in the language of Greek philosophy, the chief dividing line evolving in the fifth century between those who believed that Christ was of two natures, human and divine, indivisible in a single divine essence (the "dyophysite" position that eventually

became the orthodoxy of the imperial church), and those who thought
that he was of one nature with the divinity ("miaphysite"), the creed that
came to dominate in much of Syria, Egypt, and Armenia. The debate was
carried on through a series of local and ecumenical church councils, and
a first resolution was achieved at the Council of Chalcedon in 451 at which
the dyophysite position prevailed (hence, "Chalcedonian"). But the debate rumbled on increasingly sharply through the later fifth and sixth
centuries. See the summary of the theological issues in Hovorun 2015:
117–122; detailed analyses in Jankowiak 2009; Booth 2014; documents and
texts: Winkelmann 2001; also Brandes 1998b; Uthemann 1997; Dagron
1993: 40–92; and the discussion in Chapter 2 of this volume.

34. The date of the *Ekthesis*: Jankowiak 2009: 150–60; Brock 1973: 323–24.
For the text of the *Ekthesis*: *ACO* II, 1. 156–62 (trans. Price et al. 2014:
226–30); and for the possibility that the patriarch Sergius had already
raised the issue of a single will in a previous dogmatic statement: Booth
2014: 213 n. 104; 240n58. Palestinian opposition moving westward:
Jankowiak 2009: 170–175.

35. Booth 2014: 151–154; 307; Brandes 1998b: 183–184.

36. Brock 1973: 67–71; Winkelmann 2001: 164 (no. 163) and 169. Although
there is some evidence to suggest that during his initial years as sole ruler
Constans and his advisers were not yet irrevocably attached to a monoen-
ergite or monothelete position (see Schacht 1936; and Eutychius, *Annales*,
335–339), the events surrounding the council of 680–681 might suggest
that by that time there existed a good deal of genuine monothelete sympathy across the empire.

37. For these see in detail *PmbZ*, #6386 / *PBE* Pyrrhos 1; *PmbZ*, # 2345 / *PBE*
Gregorios 1; *PmbZ*, # 5763 / *PBE* Paulos 2; *PmbZ*, # 4851 / *PBE* Martinos 6.
For the truce and the celebratory coin issue: Grierson 1968: 475–476
(#132.1—133).

38. Mansi x, 789D-797B (trans. Price et al. 2014: 412–417).

39. The documents are assembled and discussed in Winkelmann 2001; see
Dölger-Müller 2009: #225. Riedinger argued that the acts were in fact
prepared beforehand by Maximus and his group, but while the structure
and much of the process of the council was certainly carefully planned
and carried out, this is unlikely. See Conte 1989; Cubitt 2009; and the
detailed discussion with further literature in Price et al. 2014: 59–68.

40. Kaegi 1981: 163–64; for a slightly different position: Jankowiak 2009: 278–
79. Olympius: *PmbZ*, # 5650 / *PBE* Olympios 1.

41. For the council: *ACO* II, 2.1: 228–230, with Brandes 1998b: 207–208;
Tannous 2014: 48–49; Price et al. 2014; Booth 2014; Winkelmann 2001:
150–152 (nos. 148 and 149). The suggestion that the various accusations of
treasonous activity made at the trials of both Martin and Maximus were
spurious and served merely as fronts to cover the actual theological issues
at stake (e.g. Howard-Johnson 2010: 157–162) is to be rejected, as the anal-

yses of Brandes 1998b, Jankowiak 2009, Booth 2014 and Boudignon 2007 make quite clear.

42. Van Dieten 1972: 106–110; Herrin 1987: 255–259; Price et al. 2014: 77–83. Eugenius: *PmbZ*, # 1660 / *PBE* Eugenios 5; Peter: *PmbZ*, # 5941 / *PBE* Petros 2.

43. Summary of these events: Haldon 1997: 304–312.

44. See Brandes 1998b: 207.Constantine (IV): *PmbZ*, # 3702 / *PBE* Konstantinos 2; Heraclius: *PmbZ*, # 2556 / *PBE* Herakleios 1; Tiberius: *PmbZ*, # 8484 / *PBE* Tiberios 1; Theodosius: *PmbZ*, # 7797 / *PBE* Theodosios 1.

45. Theoph., 348 (trans. Mango-Scott, 486). On Arab raiding into Anatolia, see Kaegi 2006.

46. Haldon 1997a: 58–59, 309–312; Dölger-Müller 2009: #231. For the pope, Vitalian: *PmbZ*, #8582; *PBE* Bitalianos 3.

47. *LP* i, 344 (trans. Davis 1989: 72).

48. Andreas: *PmbZ* #354 / *PBE* Andreas 2; Troilos: *PmbZ* #8524 / *PBE* Troilos 1; Mizizios / Mzez: *PmbZ* #5163 / *PBE* Mizizios 1.

49. See esp. Jankowiak 2013a: 305–309.

50. Saborius: *PmbZ*, #6476 / *PBE* Saborios 1 (see also Saburrus 1); Dölger-Müller 2009: #235–235a; Kaplony 1996: 1, 1. A6.

51. Jankowiak 2013a; Kaegi 2010: 220–226.

52. Howard-Johnston 2010b: 490–491; Prigent 2011: 176–178; Jankowiak 2009: 600–602; 2013a: 310–314; Corsi 1983: 196–206. For Mizizius's son: *PmbZ* #2706 / *PBE* Ioannes 524; and see *LP* i, 346 (trans. Davis 1989: 70–1) for the Arab attack.

53. See Chapter 7 in this volume; Haldon 1993c; Brubaker and Haldon 2011: 723–755; Cosentino 2007; Zuckerman 2005: 109–125.

54. The new weapon was basically a type of flame-thrower based on the Roman double-action force pump and using crude petroleum as the combustible. See Haldon 2006b.

55. Their identity remains debated, although an Armenian origin—monothelete Armenians from the region of Mardali—seems most likely. *Mardoi,* soldiers from Mardali, had served under the Arsacids in Armenia IV, for example: see Bartikian 1986; Ditten 1993: 138–158. Their Armenian derivation or identity would be supported by the presence of coins bearing a Pahlavi inscription, minted probably in North Syria and based on Sicilian *folles* of Constantine IV, produced probably in the 670s: Schindel and Hahn 2010; see also Howard-Johnston 2012: 37 (unaware of Bartikian 1986 and with a less probable Persian origin).

56. Kennedy 1986: 89–91. Dölger-Müller 2009: # 228b, #240–241; Kaplony 1996: 1, 1.A7-A8. On Yazīd I: *PmbZ*, #8595 / *PBE* Yezid 1. The notion that the empire would one day recover its lost territories was a long-term aspect of imperial ideology and identity and lived on into the ninth and tenth centuries: Kazhdan 1989: 8.

57. Haldon 1997a: 313–317.

58. On forced migration from the Balkans, see Ditten 1993: 209–234.

59. Curta 2006: 77–81; Lilie 1976: 99–100; Ditten 1993: 132–136; Dölger-Müller 2009: #244a. The dating of the Bulgar campaign and the reason for Constantine IV's absence during the council (lasting from the twelfth session, which began on March 22, 681, until the seventeenth session from September 11, 681) are disputed. There is no doubt that the emperor was absent for the sessions in question, and the generally-held view is that this was because he left to lead the expedition against the Bulgars. But in a carefully-argued and well-documented analysis of all the relevant sources De Gregorio and Kresten (2007) have argued, first that this expedition in fact took place in 680, and second, that the emperor's absence in 681 was motivated by other internal political concerns, possibly in order to avoid dealing in person with the detailed condemnation of monotheletism (which would touch negatively upon past members of the imperial family, its supporters, and several former patriarchs of Constantinople), and to permit the emperor to adopt the role of neutral observer in the proceedings and their result. Jankowiak 2009: 474, note 136 dismisses this argument on the grounds that Theophanes' text is not to be relied upon. In spite of this (generally accepted) comment on Theophanes' text, the position adopted by De Gregorio and Kresten is persuasive. The issue awaits a final resolution.

60. Brandes 2014: 277; Dölger-Müller 2009: #244, #245, #247 (and see #248–250). Cyrus of Alexandria: *PmbZ*, #4213 / *PBE* Kyros 2; Macarius of Antioch: *PmbZ*, #4670 / *PBE* Makarios 1.

61. De Gregorio and Kresten 2007: 54–55; Brock 1973b; Brooks 1915; Tannous (2014) argues for a longer-term monoenergite/monothelete interest in Syria, beginning already under Heraclius.

62. Guillou 1969: 208–208; Brown 1979: 22–23.

63. Kaegi 220–265; Brett 1978: 503–513.

64. See Dölger-Müller 2009: #253; Kaplony 1996: 1, 1. A9-A11; *PmbZ*, # 3556 (Justinian II); Greenwood 2008: 344; Kennedy 1986: 90–98.

65. Kennedy 1986: 93–98; Lilie 1976: 101–107; Greenwood 2008: 344; Dölger 2009: 113 (no. 239); Kaplony 1996: 1, 1. A9-A11. For Justinian II: *PmbZ*, #3556 / *PBE* Ioustinianos 1; Leontius: *PmbZ*, #4547 / *PBE* Leontios 2 (and cf. Leontios 1); for ʿAbd al-Malik: *PmbZ*, #18 / *PBE* Abdulmalik 1; Marwān: 4864 / *PBE* Marwan 1.

66. Ditten 1993: 216–234; Lilie 1976: 237–238; Köpstein 1979; Charanis 1961b; Greenwood 2008: 344–345.

67. In response to Justinian's resettlement of Cypriots in north-west Anatolia ʿAbd al-Malik had seized many Cypriots and moved them to Syria. In ca. 698 the emperor Tiberius Apsimar opened negotiations with the caliph to return the transported groups to their homeland: Dölger-Müller 2009: #261; Kaplony 1996: 1, 1, A17.

68. Greenwood 2008: 345. There is some disagreement about this campaign since the sources offer different accounts. The battle took place well within

Roman territory and thus may have followed from an Arab invasion. On the other hand, it may have occurred after Roman troops had been chased back into imperial territory after an attack on Arab forces in Iraq, only recently pacified by ʿAbd al-Malik, and thus seen as a weak link in the caliph's defenses.

69. Dölger-Müller 2009: #258c, #258e; Kaplony 1996: 1, 1. A11; A15-A16; Haldon 1997a: 71–72; Lilie 1976: 110–111.

70. This was a serious concern for both sides, and must be taken also in the context of a revised Islamic protocol on papyri exported from Egypt to the eastern Roman capital and at a more general level an Islamization of the caliphate's administrative and institutional apparatus: Dölger-Müller 2009: #259a–#260c; Kaplony 1996: 1, 1. A13-A15; Treadwell 2012; Humphreys 2011.

71. *Iussio* of 687: Dölger-Müller 2009: #256a; on Justinian II's coinage, see Morrisson and Prigent 2013, esp. 582–583, 587–588 with further discussion: Humphreys 2015: 37–80, and Chapters 2 and 3 of this volume.

72. Ohme 1990: 35–54.

73. Dölger-Müller 2009: #259; papal opposition: Ohme 1990: 55–61; 1995; Dură 1995; Justinian's fall: Haldon 1997a: 74. Leontius had formerly commanded forces under Justinian but already in the 680s had been suspected of plotting against the emperor and was imprisoned for a while (see note 65 above). For Zacharias: *PmbZ*, #8606 / *PBE* Zacharias 15.

74. Kaegi 2010: 247–256.

75. Brett 1978: 505–507; Lilie 1976: 112–115. For the naval commander John: *PmbZ*, #2766 / PBE Ioannes 7; Tiberius Apsimar: *PmbZ*, #8483 / *PBE* Tiberios 2.

76. Greenwood 2008: 345–346.

77. Curta 2006: 82–83; Haldon 1997a: 76–77; *PmbZ*, # 8490 (Tiberios); Dölger-Müller 2009: #265. Tervel: *PmbZ*, #7250 / *PBE* Tervel 1.

78. *LP* i, 385–386 (trans. Davis 1992: 89); Dölger-Müller 2009: #264; Ohme 1990: 63 suggests the pope's response reflected his anxieties about Justinian's behavior in Constantinople since the former patriarch Kallinikos (*PmbZ*, #3587 / *PBE* Kallinikos 2), deposed and blinded by Justinian after his coup, had been banished to Rome. For John VII: *PmbZ*, #2951 / *PBE* Ioannes 228.

79. Dölger-Müller 2009: #268-#269; Ohme 1990: 68–75; Hussey 1986; for Pope Constantine: *PmbZ*, #1170 / *PBE* Konstantinos 136.

80. Dölger-Müller 2009: #266-#267; Brown 1995; Guillou 1969: 216–218; Head 1970.

81. Theoph., 382 (trans. Mango-Scott, 532); see also Haldon 1997a: 78–80; *PmbZ*, #6150 / *PBE* Philippikos 1. Agathon's account: *ACO* II, 2, 898.6–901.12.

82. Dölger-Müller 2009: #271; Beck 1959: 474, 500; Grumel 1972: nos. 320–321. For Germanus: *PmbZ*, #2298 / *PBE* Germanos 8 and for Andrew of Crete: *PmbZ*, # 362 / *PBE* Andreas 3. For the papal response, *LP* i, 391 (trans.

Davis 1989: 91–92): as well as returning Philippicus's portrait, sent to Rome in the usual way, the emperor's name was excluded from the church prayers and from the dating formulae of papal documents; in addition, images of all six ecumenical councils were put up in St. Peter's.

83. Curta 2006: 81–84; Lilie 1976: 116–121, 137–139; Tyana: Brandes 1989: 63, and for the annual targets of Arab raids and the names of settlements affected at this time: 77.

84. On Anastasius / Artemius: *PmbZ*, #236 / *PBE* Anastasios 6.

85. Dölger-Müller 2009: #273-#275; Kaplony 1996: 1, 1, A25.

86. Dölger-Müller 2009: #275b; on Maslama: *PmbZ*, #4868 / *PBE* Maslama 1.

87. Haldon 1997a: 80–82; *PmbZ*, #7793 / *PBE* Theodosios 2.

88. Dölger-Müller 2009: #276; Curta 2006: 83–84; Obolensky 1971: 65–66.

89. Dölger-Müller 2009: #277; Speck 2002: 62–102, 415–441; Haldon 1997a: 81–82; Kaegi 1981: 192–194. Leo and Artavasdos: *PmbZ*, #4242 / *PBE* Leo 3 and #632 / *PBE* Artabasdos 1.

90. Lilie 1976: 125–133; Guilland 1959; Brooks 1899; Dölger-Müller 2009: #280b. For ʿUmar II: *PmbZ*, #8550 / *PBE* Omar 2; the commander Suleymān: *PmbZ*, #7158, #7160 / *PBE* Sulayman 1; and the caliph Suleymān: *PmbZ*, #7159 / *PBE* Sulayman 4.

91. See Eger 2015.

92. See Kennedy 1986: 112–122.

93. Dölger-Müller 2009: #282; Brubaker and Haldon 2011: 70–89; and for a detailed, if at times idiosyncratic study of Leo III's reign based upon a careful analysis of the accounts in Theophanes's *Chronographia* and the patriarch Nicephorus's *Brief History:* Speck 2003. For Sergius, Tiberius (Tiberius was his adopted imperial name, his real name was Basil Onomagoulus), the *chartoularios* Paul, and Nicetas Xylinites, see also *PmbZ*, #6594 / *PBE* Sergios 3; *PmbZ*, #849 / *PBE* Tiberios 3; *PmbZ*, #5815 / *PBE* Paulos 7; *PmbZ*, #5372 / *PBE* Niketas 3.

94. Brubaker and Haldon 2011: 69–155.

95. See the analytical catalogs in Dölger-Müller 2009 and Kaplony 1996, for example; and by way of example from the considerable wider literature on the subject Treadwell 2012; Kennedy 1992: 134–136; and the essays in Hoyland 2004.

96. Summaries of these patterns as they appear through an analysis of the attacks in Lilie 1976: 83–96, 133–142, 155–162.

97. Detailed analysis in Lilie 1976; see also Howard-Johnston 2010b: 474–510.

98. On narrative in this sense: Haldon 1997a: 325–326; 2015; and see the Introduction to this volume.

99. See, for example, Jankowiak 2013b.

100. See the survey with literature and sources in Haldon 1997a: 281–323; and esp. Winkelmann 1980: 131–135; note also the useful remarks in Rotman 2005; Maas 2005b: 14–16; Gray 2005: 235–236.

101. See for some discussion of these terms and challenges to the ways in which they have been understood, Guran 2006; Kaldellis 2015; Dagron 2003: 295–312 with further literature and sources. Terms such as "state" require careful definition if they are to be deployed effectively as heuristic referents. See Goldstone and Haldon 2009; Haldon 2012b and in detail 1993d.
102. See Haldon 2004; revised and expanded in Brubaker and Haldon 2011: 575–616.
103. See esp. Jones 1964: 371; Heather 1994: 19–20; Kelly 2004: 186 and 190.
104. See Theoph., 348–350 (Mango and Scott: 488–490).
105. See the summary of the course of the warfare ca. 680–720 in Lilie 1976: 133–142, with map facing 132.
106. See Kennedy 2001: 4–5, 9–11, 23–26, with sources and older literature.
107. By far the best and most useful account of the course and pace of the early Arab invasions and raids into Asia Minor is still Lilie 1976, although some updating and minor correction is required following recent work on the Islamic sources in particular. See also Métivier 2008: 444–445; Bonner 1996: 56–61; Haldon and Kennedy 1980: 106–110.
108. Leo, *Takt.* XVIII: 118–119; and see Haldon 2014: 356, 362–366.
109. Theoph., 351 (Mango and Scott 490). On the first wintering raids: Kaegi 2006: 83–86 (reviewing the Arab sources).
110. Lilie 1976: 69–71, with sources.
111. For a detailed register, see Lilie 1976: 69–82 for the period c. 663–680; 114–133 for the period 695–717; and 144–155 for the period 720–750 (although subject to revision in several cases in the light of more recent research); see also Brandes 1989: 44–75 for a survey, with the table and map at 75–80.
112. Qudāma b. Jaʿfar: 199. The length of time an expedition could remain in the field was very dependent on the season, particularly where the soldiers were unable to live off the land. See Haldon 2006c.
113. Haldon and Kennedy 1980: 106–109, 113–116; Kennedy 2001: 105–107.
114. See ch. 3. for details of this strategy.
115. Lilie 1976: 114–155.
116. See, e.g., Trigger 2003: 279.
117. For recent survey and discussion of the material: Haldon et al. 2014: 121–127; Izdebski 2013b; McCormick et al. 2012; and see discussion in Chapter 4 of this volume. For the cold period ca. 536–660: Büntgen et al. 2016.
118. See, for example, Hendy 1985: 619–662.
119. See Haldon 2005: Figs. 3.1; 3.2; 6.1.
120. The literature on administrative and bureaucratic structures is vast. For some ways into the problem, see Arnasson 2010; White 2008; Gizewski 1988; Haldon 2009; and with a focus on later periods: Tilly 2002.
121. See Kennedy 1986: 69–103.

122. Foss 2010; Sijpesteijn 2007; Humphreys 2013; 239–241.
123. Howard-Johnston 2010b: 480–481.
124. See esp. Tritton 1954; Simonsen 1988; Puin 1970; and Hinds 1972.
125. Donner 1986.
126. See Bonner 2005: xviii. For some indicative statistical evidence, see the essays in Haldon 2006a and Pryor 2006.

2. Beliefs, Narratives, and the Moral Universe

1. *Miracula Artemii,* Mir. 34: sections from 182: 6–27.
2. See the summary of Meier 2012; Haldon 1986b.
3. Wilken 1992: 220, 325–326; Suermann 1985; Kaegi 1969; also Hoyland 1997: 524–526.
4. *ACO* II, 2, 492: 1–5.
5. See, e.g., Stoyanov 2011.
6. Looking at the narratives that individuals and groups construct and maintain in order to situate themselves and to make sense of the world around them is a useful way of approaching the connections between what people think and how they act.
7. *ACO* II, 2: 898.30–35 (see Winkelmann 2001, # 180c).
8. See Haldon 1986b: 165–166 and nn. 68–71; Jankowiak 2009; Booth 2014; Winkelmann 2001; Brandes 1998b; Dagron 1993: 40–92.
9. Theoph., 359 (Mango-Scott, 499).
10. See Theoph., 352. 15 (Mango and Scott: 491–492); Brock 1973b:64- 65; Theoph. of Edessa, *Chronicle,* 173–174; and the discussion in Brooks 1915; Brock 1973b: 66; Kaegi 1981: 184; *PmbZ* #4246. Slightly different versions of the story are found in the Syriac tradition, but it is clear that hostility to the change in religious policy was present within senior military circles, including, for example, the former commander of the *Opsikion* division, Philippos: *PmbZ* # 6153; Brandes 2001b; Haldon 2015b. One of the key supporters of the emperor was Theodore of Koloneia: see Chapter 4 of this volume. For Heraclius and Tiberius, see *PmbZ* #2556; #8484.
11. *ACO* II, 2: 832–856.
12. Modern historians have generally accepted the picture painted by the contemporary and later Byzantine sources of Phocas as evil and incompetent, but as has been persuasively demonstrated, this perspective is in need of substantial revision in light of the propaganda produced by the dynasty of Heraclius. See Meier 2014. On Anastasius: *PmbZ,* #268 (with #268 and #270).
13. Thus, after the disaster of Adrianople in 378, it was the supposed Arianism of the emperor Valens that was to blame for bringing down God's wrath upon the Romans. Similar explanations—laxness in observing God's laws, seduction by wealth and power—were offered for the fifth-century defeats

of Roman forces by those perceived as barbarians. Perhaps the best, if sometimes also idiosyncratic, exponent of such explanations was Salvian of Marseilles, whose views are beautifully described in Brown 2012a; see also Lambert 1999.

14. Anast. Sin., Qu. 65. 2; and cf. Qu. 101. 1.
15. Anast. Sin., Qu. 65. 4; Qu. 101 1; 5.
16. Leppin 2012: 252–254; Lee 2007: 21–37; McCormick 1986. Cf. Goffart 1971: 416–418 for the way in which the pagan historian Zosimus considers that the health and success of the Roman state is associated with adherence to and respect for traditional forms of religious belief and observance.
17. For the two collections of miracles, see Haldon 1997b; 2007a; the original text of the Apocalypse was composed, in Syriac, ca. 690–692 in Sinjar (Singara) in northeastern Mesopotamia, and Greek and Latin translations had been made by ca. 700–710: Reinink, ed. 1993: v–xxix; Aerts and Kortekaas, eds. 1998: 1:16, 30. For comments on the accuracy of the author's geographical knowledge, see Kaegi 2000.
18. *Mir. Therapon* §6. 5–7. In another composition Andrew employs equally dramatic language, describing the Arabs as "the shameless abortions of Hagar" who "rage against Christ": *Laudatio martyrum Cretensium,* ed. Laourdas 1949: 11, 3. See Auzépy 1995a; Haldon 2007b.
19. On the *Narrationes*: see, for example, story C4 (partly edited, but without its preface, by Nau 1903: 87.14–15; and Flusin 1991: 382 and n. 3).
20. Detailed discussion of this tendency is in Haldon 1997: 348–355. It is the case that such concerns were to be found in the preceding centuries too. But in the more ideologically and politically pressured and territorially restrictive context of the later seventh century, when survival was the order of the day, a much greater focus seems to have been the response and was clearly thought to be the key.
21. See Haldon 1997a: 345–348; and especially the discussions of Dagron 1991; Dagron and Déroche 1991; Déroche 1991. Whether such compulsory conversions were actually enforced and took place remains debated: see this chapter, p. 118.
22. Note in particular the *Trullo* canons 18, 37, 41, 42, dealing with clerical garb, itinerant hermits and preachers, the abandonment of their flocks by some of the clergy, and related issues (and see the twelfth-century commentaries to the texts in (Rhalles-Potles II: 344–345; 388–391; 402–405; 406–407). Some of these are repeated from earlier collections of canons, but their reappearance in the Quinisext is no mere antiquarian exercise—the selection of canons is quite specific and intended to reflect the requirements of the times. See Ohme 1990.
23. See Rhalles-Potles, *Syntagma,* II, comm. to *Trullo* canons 24, 51, 60–62 (pp. 356–360, 425–426, 441–452).
24. See, for example, Halkin 1944: 195, and cf. *Trullo* canon 68 (and twelfth-century commentary, Rhalles-Potles, II: 464–465) (writing holy incan-

tations on parchment from a holy book to effect a cure); or *Vita S. Ioannicii:* 390B-C, 412C-413B, and cf. *Trullo* canon 61 (using trained animals to impress the gullible believer).

25. Useful commentary on this: Brandes 2014: 271–272.

26. Anast. Sin., *Sermo iii:* 1. 84–92; see also 93–112; and Anast. Sin., Qu. 65, where Anastasius explicitly links God's punishment for sin to military and civil disaster.

27. Booth 2014: 225–328.

28. *Maximi Confessoris relatio motionis,* §9 (trans. Allen and Neil 2002: 67).

29. Mansi x, 789D–797B (Price et al. 2014: 412–417), 796D 12–14 (Price et al. 2014: 416–417); see 793C, 796E–797A. In fact, the letters of Pope Martin are extant only in Greek form and may likewise be a product of the influence of the same Greek-speaking group, under the leadership of Maximus the Confessor. See esp. Price 2014: 59–68; but note also Riedinger, in *ACO* II, 1: x; Winkelmann 2001: no. 114.

30. *ACO* II, 2: 490.14–492.11.

31. "Following the wicked Maximus, the wrath of God punished every place that had accepted his errors." *Vita Syr. Max. conf.,* §23 (312–313).

32. For a useful survey, see Kaegi 1969; Hoyland 1997: 524–526.

33. Mansi x, 850D–E, 855D–E, 856A; Martin's defense: see *Ep.* xiv *ad Theodorum* (Mansi x, 849D–850E); for comment on the trial and exiles of Maximus and his supporters: see Brandes 1998b; Allen and Neil 1999: xi–xxiii; 2002.

34. *Maximi Confessoris relatio motionis,* §1-§3 (trans. Allen and Neil 2002: 49–54): see esp. §1.

35. *Vita Martini* (ed. Peeters), 259.

36. See Potestà 2011.

37. *ACO* II, 2: 2–10 (*sacra* to the Pope); II, 1: 10–13 (addressed to the patriarch of Constantinople, George) at 10. 21–24. See also the opening paragraph of Constantine IV's edict issued after the council of 680–681 (*ACO* II, 2: 832. 8–20). Constantine IV had more than simply religious issues in mind when introducing this reversal of imperial policy, as we will see in a later chapter.

38. *ACO* II, 2. i: 53–121, at 58.11–18; 62.25–64.5, 118.3–13.

39. *ACO* II, 2. ii: 694. 24–27; see discussion in Brandes 2001b: 28–29; and *PmbZ*, #3710.

40. See Brock 1982.

41. See the remarks of Beck 1959: 474, 500 and this chapter, p. 93.

42. See Cameron 2014, for example, with further literature.

43. Déroche 2002: 172.

44. See esp. Déroche 2002, and on the role of the eucharist in the canons of the Quinisext: Humphreys 2015: 69–72, 78.

45. Eloquently expressed and discussed through the example of the *Ecclesiastical History* of Evagrius in Leppin 2012, esp. 258.

46. On the Syriac version, see also Greisiger 2009. More generally on the Byzantine apocalyptic tradition: Brandes 1990, 1991, and 2007.

47. E.g. Ps.-Methodius, Apocalypse, 13.13.

48. John of Nikiû, CXX, 56; 60 (trans. Charles 1916: 198). I thank Cecilia Palombo for drawing this important difference to my attention.

49. Drake 1979.

50. Booth 2014: 329–342; also Jankowiak 2009.

51. See Uthemann 1997; and esp. Lange 2012. A useful summary of these developments is to be found in Price 2014: 17–27; see also Tannous 2014.

52. Mansi x, 796A; (trans. Price et al. 2014: 415).

53. See esp. Ohme 2008; Price et al. 2014: 1–58 for a good survey. The detailed exposition and analysis of the key theological issues in Booth 2014.

54. Several of the canons of the Quinisext council are particularly concerned with this issue, and seek to reinforce the proper, orthodox practices and proscribe those which appeared to be heterodox: see, for example, canons 50, 61, 62, 65, 68, 94 (proscribing a range of Hellenic—i.e. pagan—practices which, it was said, prevailed in certain provincial areas), and discussion in Haldon 1997a: 334ff.

55. See the quotation from Pope Martin's letter to Constans II, above; Ohme 2008; Dagron 1990.

56. See Chapter 5 of this volume, and Brandes 1998b.

57. Discussion in Ohme 1990: 39–54; Humphreys 2015: 62–73.

58. See, e.g., Rhalles-Potless II: 448–449.

59. *Vita et miracula Theod.*, Mir. 4: 196. 15–21. There is some debate about the date of composition of the collection, with three scholars (Abrahamse 1967: 347–354; Trombley 1985a, 1989; Artun 2008) arguing for a seventh-century date (probably 663–664) and one (Zuckerman 1988) for the middle of the eighth century. The seventh-century date is to be preferred.

60. Michael the Syrian, in Theophilus of Edessa, *Chronicle,* 108.

61. Theophilus of Edessa, *Chronicle,* 192.

62. Haldon 1997a: 320–322. It is interesting that Bardanes (later the emperor Philippicus, 711–713), the son of the Armenian general Nicephorus (*PmbZ* #5258), was as a young man mentored by the monk Stephen, a close supporter of the patriarch Macarius of Antioch and staunch defender of monothelete doctrine at the council of 680–681 (*PmbZ* #6920).

63. See, e.g., Yasin 2005.

64. For an insightful approach to the relationship between "micro-Christendoms' and Christianity: Brown 2003: introduction.

65. Imperial cult, political orthodoxy, and the imperial church: Dagron 2003; Alexander 1962; Winkelmann 1980; Barnes 1981: 245–60; and Baynes 1955. See also Dvornik 1966), 2: 614–15, 652–53.

66. See Just., *Nov.* 6 (a. 535): preface.

67. Imperial ideology and the role of the emperor: Dvornik 1966; Hussey 1986: 297–310; and for the elision of notions of Roman with Christian identity, see Chrysos 1996. Important revision and challenge to the standard views: Kaldellis 2015: 165–198.

68. See in particular the important discussion in Brown 1995; also Flaig 1997 and Kaldellis 2015: 173–198.

69. See in particular Meier 2012: 206–222; further on the role and position of the emperor: Dagron 2003; 1993: 198–216; Enßlin 1943; and related essays in the same volume; also Simon 1984.

70. Meier 2012: 232–233.

71. See esp. and in detail on the sixth-century context for these developments Meier 2012: 229–236; Meier 2004a; Brandes 1990: 305–322; 1997; and cf. Haldon 1986b.

72. Cameron 1978, 1979; Nelson 1976; Meier 2004b.

73. On the evolution of an "imperial" church: Winkelmann 1980; Dagron 2003; Herrin 1987.

74. Brown 2012b: 528–30.

75. *Trullo:* 49.13–51.12.

76. Haldon 1997a: 327–337.

77. John of Ephesus, *HE*, iii, 33f; comment: Rochow 1976: 120–122.

78. As in the ninth-century History of Dionysius of Tell-Mahré, for example.

79. John of Nikiû, CXXI, 2 (trans. Charles 1916: 200). John wrote in the last decades of the seventh century. The Chronicle was originally compiled in Greek but possibly with some Coptic passages. Later translated into Arabic, it survives only in an early seventeenth-century Ge'ez translation.

80. Haldon 1997a: 338–339.

81. This council is known only indirectly through references in the acts of the council of 680–681; see Jankowiak 2010: 446–448.

82. See esp. canon 39.

83. *Oratio* II, *PG* 97: 829D.

84. Ps. Methodius, *Apocalypse*, 10: 2–4.

85. See Hoyland 1997: 297–299.

86. *Trullo,* 46.20–47. 10; 49.13–50.7 (trans. Featherstone and Nedungatt).

87. Krueger 2005: 292–297.

88. Martin 1937; Ehrhard 1937: 25–35.

89. See esp. Maxwell 2006.

90. *Trullo,* canon 19 (Nedungatt and Featherstone 1995: 95–96). See the important, brief, but useful discussion in Cunningham 1986, with sources. As we have already noted, these canons are often repeated from earlier councils; but in the context this does not make them any the less valid as a reflection of the situation as it was perceived by the assembled bishops in 691/692.

91. *Oratio de sacra synaxi,* 829A–832A. Anastasius's complaint is not new: Gregory of Nyssa likewise complains about the inattention, bad temper, constant interruptions, and general restlessness during a panegyric on the forty martyrs of Sebaste that he delivered in March 383 (in Leemans 2003: 93; 97).

92. For the structure of the collection of canons and the issues the different subgroups address, see Humphreys 2015: 62–73. It is not clear how the destruction and cutting up of codices of the Old and New Testaments played a role in the production of perfumes, see *ODB* 3:1628.

93. See esp. Cameron 1978 and 1979, with Allen 2011; and other essays in Brubaker and Cunningham 2011; also Cunningham 2008: 13–51, with literature.

94. For a detailed account see the catalogue in Janin 1969.

95. See Brown 1981: 88.

96. See Boesch-Gajano 1991.

97. For oil and related substances: see Paxton 1990: 27ff.

98. Delehaye 1933; Rordorf 1975.

99. *Miracula S. Theodori tironis,* 198.9–21 (mir. 6).

100. *Vita Nic. Sion,* 26; *Vita Theod. Syk.* 43 (trans. Dawes and Baynes 120); *Vita Ioannicii* 51 (412C–413B) (trans. Sullivan 1998: 309–310).

101. See esp. the survey in Hatlie 2007: 83–253.

102. See for further discussion Haldon 1997a: 327–337.

103. See Hatlie 2007: 216–252 for a detailed survey.

104. Humphreys 2015: 63, 66–70.

105. Background and context into the early seventh century: Kaplan 1976. For Nicaea II (787): Rhalles-Potles II: 615.

106. Herman 1967: 123–125. See *Trullo,* canons 14, 17–19, 21–27.

107. Kaplan 1992: 202–203.

108. Discussion of late Roman society and social relations in the eastern part of the empire: Sarris 2009, 2006, with further literature.

109. The subject has received a more detailed treatment for the late Roman and early medieval west in Brown 2015.

110. Anastasius Sin., qu. 19. 8; 20. 1; 21. 4.

111. Ed. Van Deun 2006. Further on this debate: Constas 2002; Déroche 2000; Dagron 1992; on the sixth- and seventh-century debate: Haldon 1997b: 44–56; note also Dal Santo 2011: 129–138.

112. Ed. Marcos 1975.

113. See the introduction to Rupprecht 1935; also Deubner 1907.

114. Ed. Lemerle 1979.

115. Ed. Delehaye 1909.

116. Ed. Papadopoulos-Kerameus 1909.

117. Ed. Deubner 1900.

118. Dagron 1992: 64.

119. See Dal Santo 2012: 273–299.
120. See Lemerle 1979: 72f.; Isaac: ed. Stiernon 1977.
121. *Trullo,* can. 63.
122. *Vita Theod. Syk.,* §61.
123. See in particular Dagron 1992; Déroche 1993: 105–107; further elaborated for the later Roman period by Dal Santo 2011 and for the Byzantine period more generally in Kaldellis 2014.
124. Theoph. Sim. iii, 1. 10–12; iii, 2. 8; trans. Whitby 73, 74–75.
125. Theoph. Sim. iii, 2. 2; 7; 9; Evagrius, *HE* 6, 4–5. For this event and the bishop of Antioch, Gregory's role in the events: Leppin 2012: 249–250.
126. Theoph., 405 (Mango and Scott 152).
127. See Auzépy 1995b.
128. See in particular Pohl 2013 for a useful approach and discussion to the hermeneutic and heuristic issues associated with the term "identity."
129. Although, as Morrisson 2013: 80 points out, people could frequently mistake the ruler's portrait for Constantine I or another emperor than the one actually represented. Note also the remarks on the impact of coinage in Phillips 2015: 58–62.
130. Stouraitis 2014; Haldon 1999: 18–27. The issue of how eastern Romans identified themselves is a topic for current discussion: see in particular Kaldellis 2009 and 2012, with the critical remarks and heuristically helpful position outlined in Stouraitis 2014. See Leppin 2012: 243 and n. 12; Rapp 2008; Greatrex 2000. For "orthodoxy" as the hallmark of Byzantine culture, see the carefully nuanced discussion in Cameron 2012; for a different approach: Magdalino 2010. More generally on approaches to identity from a sociological/social-anthropological standpoint: Brubaker and Cooper 2000; and the older but still very relevant discussion in Berger and Luckmann 1971: esp. 194–204. For elite identities, see Chapter 4 of this volume.
131. See discussion in Chapter 4 of this volume.
132. See again Magdalino 2010 and Cameron 2012; and for the West, but with much wider implications, Brown 2012b; 2003. Older literature on Christianity and the evolution of Orthodoxy: Winkelmann 1980; Dagron 1993: 9–371; Hussey 1986; Dvornik 1966.
133. On heresy and heresiology, see Gouillard 1965; Cameron 2003; Brandes 2003.
134. See Winkelmann 2001: no. 45; Engl. translation Allen 2009; John of Damascus, *De haeresibus* (*PG* 94, 677–780; cf. *CPG* III, 8044), in Kotter 1973: 7–239, with discussion in Brubaker and Haldon 2001: 248–250; see Knorr 1998; Anastasus of Sinai, *Synopsis de haeresibus:* Uthemann 1982.
135. *PG* 98: 39–88. See discussion in Brubaker and Haldon 2001: 247–248.
136. Brandes 2013: 78–81.
137. Excellent discussion for the West in Brown 2012b, for example.
138. Cameron 2007. For imperial politics and heresy/heterodoxy: Tougher 2008: 292ff.; Dagron 1993: 167ff.

139. This is repeated from the canons of the second ecumenical council at Constantinople in 381, but with additions relating to more recent heresies.

140. See Chapter 1 above for the Christological debates and monotheletism, with Tannous 2014. For general surveys and further literature, see Haldon 1997a; Brubaker and Haldon 2011; Price 2014: 1–58; and Winkelmann 1980.

141. Brandes 2003: 109–110.

142. See p. 82 above, and Tannous 2014.

143. See Speyer 1981: 155–157; Brandes 2014: 274–276; see also Herrin 2013d.

144. See, e.g., Brubaker and Haldon 2011: 375–384, 392–399.

145. See *PmbZ*, #7301 and #1721 / *PBE* Theodoros 345 and Euprepios 1.

146. For Stephen of Dor, whose "report" was incorporated into the acts of the Lateran synod of 649, see *ACO* II, 1: 42.12–14. The fact that pope Martin was known to have sent letters to Palestine attracted the attention of the imperial authorities, and with it accusations of collaborating with the Saracens (Mansi x, 849D–850E, 855D–E, 856A; cf. *PL* 129: 587C–D; see Brandes 1998b: 159–173); see also Jankowiak 2012: 18–20. In the summer of 731 imperial officials keeping a watch on Italian ports detained, on orders, a papal emissary to Constantinople. He was reportedly held in Sicily for almost a year before his release: *LP* i, 416. 13; 21ff. (trans. Davis 1992: 20).

147. See Chapter 7 of this volume and Phillips 2012.

148. On occasion extraordinary measures could be introduced to effectively seal certain border regions, as in the early fifth-century border controls introduced by Stilicho in Italy—abrogated in 408 because of the adverse impact on trade and commerce but reinstated shortly afterward: *CTh.* vii, 16. 1–2. These measures were not taken up in the Justinianic code, but they demonstrate the potential effectiveness of imperial frontier controls.

149. See Just., *Nov.* 123. 9; *Trullo,* canon 17; Jones 1964: 889; for the early medieval west, see Wood 1995: 15–16.

150. See Dölger-Müller 2009: 224d.

151. *Vita Greg. Decap.* 58. 1–12 (ch. 13). See the sources and examples collected in Dimitroukas 1997: 1, 108–111, ranging from the fifth to the eleventh century.

152. The regulations are set out in *CTh.* viii, 5, repeated in summary at *CJ* xii, 50.

153. Exactly how such regulations were enforced or effected remains obscure, especially in light of late Roman and Byzantine prescriptions on the coercion of women both within and without marriage: see Laiou 1993: 177–197. Nor is it clear when the first such edict was issued. St. Athanasia of Aegina's husband died fighting Moorish raiders, and the edict to which she was subject was issued at some point in the first half of the ninth century: *Vita Athanasiae,* 181; trans. Sherry 1996: 143. The tenth-century *De Ceremoniis* appears to refer to the results of such legislation when noting

the fiscal exemptions for "Saracen prisoners" who have received baptism and marry into a provincial household: De Cer. 694. 22–695.9.

154. For Maximus: Brandes 1998b: 177–199.

155. See the surveys and evidence in Ditten 1993: 123–305; Lilie 1976: 227–254, 301–315; Dagron 1993: 228–234; and discussion in Chapter 3 of this volume.

156. See Rochow 1978: 265–288, esp. 275–286; 1991: 307–308 with literature and sources; Pratsch 1988: 184–191; and Turner 1990b: 176–180. It is possible that the Athingani were not even Christian—the few reliable sources give very little information about their beliefs: see Speck 1997 with older literature; a slightly different account: Crone 1980: 74–79. Quite probably they are to be identified with the Tsigganoi, the Jats, or Zutt of the eighth- and ninth-century Arabic sources, and thus with the "Gypsies" who had migrated westward from the Indian subcontinent after the seventh century. See Soulis 1961. For the Paulicians: Yuzbashian 1972; Lemerle 1973, with literature: Brubaker and Haldon 2001: 271–272.

157. Crone (1980), for example, wishes to connect the introduction of imperial iconoclasm more explicitly to the challenge from Islam and to the existence of these marginal Judeo-Christian beliefs.

158. For the Jewish critique in the sixth to seventh centuries: De Lange 1992; Zellentin 2011: 137–171; see also Van Bekkum 2002. Further literature: Brubaker and Haldon 2001: 268–271.

159. See Hoyland 1997: 78–87; Déroche 1986; 1999; Cameron 1996.

160. Crone 1980: 74–78.

161. The question of the conversion of the Jews was not confined to the eastern empire alone, of course, and the issue was also discussed in western ecclesiastical and political circles: see in particular Esders 2009a. Scholars disagree on whether forced conversions were in fact carried out, see in particular Olster 1994: 84–92; and in detail Speck 1997 for plausible arguments against their historicity; and the short but useful survey of the state of the question in Brandes 2002b: 36–39. If they were, it seems that it was only in the eastern empire, with many misgivings from a number of quarters about their theological and spiritual efficacy: Booth 2014: 170–171; Dagron 1993: 72–77. Further discussion in Haldon 1997a: 345–348; Sharf 1955; Dagron 1991; Dagron and Déroche 1991. On the longer-term philosophical relationship between Judaism, Islam, and Christianity, see Fowden 2015.

3. Identities, Divisions, and Solidarities

1. Extracts from Ps.-Methodios, *Apocalypse*, 13. 5–10.

2. *Trullo*, canon 1 (Nedungatt and Featherstone 52. 8; 20); Humphreys 2015: esp. 77–80; also the discussion in Ohme 1995.

3. *ACO* II, 2: 886–887 (Justinian), on which see Ohme 1990: 21–26; *ACO* II, 2: 832–856 (Constantine IV). See Ostrogorsky 1936; Koder 1996.

4. *Adv. Iudaeos Disputatio:* esp. 1220D-122B. For date and structure, see Thümmel 1992: 253–268.
5. Ps.-Meth., *Apocalypse:* 13. 11–18 (and 19–21).
6. *Trophées de Damas,* ed. Bardy, 3. 4 (222). See especially Dagron and Déroche 1991; also Déroche 1999; and Cameron 1996.
7. Humphreys 2015: 79–80; Stolte 2002: 192–201.
8. *Ecloga,* preface, 21–31.
9. See in detail Haldon 1997a: 254–264; Humphreys 2015: 26–36, 253–261. The expression *eis ton philanthrōpoteron* (towards a more humane approach) of the proem to the *Ecloga* has been generally taken literally, to signify the production by the imperial authorities of a less draconian, more humane penal law. In contrast, Schminck 2015 has argued plausibly that this refers in fact to the production of a more comprehensible law book, a reinterpretation which fits the language of the proem and the context well.
10. Stolte 2003–2004.
11. *Ecloga,* preface, 36–51.
12. As suggested by Sarris 2011a: 56, for example.
13. See in particular the collection of important contributions in Laiou and Simon 1994; and Fögen 1994; with Fögen 1987; Simon 1973.
14. See Laiou 2009.
15. *Ecloga,* preface, 32–51, 96–109.
16. See Burgmann, in *Ecloga,* 2–19; and *Ecloga,* preface, lines 52–109. For provincial judges/courts: *Ecloga* IV, 4; VIII, 1.6; VIII, 3; XIV, 1; 4; 7; XVII, 5; XIV, 7, for example. Note also Stolte 2002: 201–203 with evidence in postconquest Egypt for continuity of legal practice.
17. The literature on the *Nomos geōrgikos* is vast. See in the last instance Humphreys 2015: 195–232, and for the date: 223–231.
18. Humphreys 2015: 203–223. Humphreys (2015: 212–213) highlights the activities of provincial *akroatai* mentioned in both the *Ecloga* and the *Nomos geōrgikos,* perhaps comparable to the later traveling justices, the "circuit judges" of the middle Byzantine period, discussed by Morris 2013, who shows both how deeply the practice of imperial justice penetrated the provinces and that the central government was not just concerned with the metropolis or the major provincial towns, but the more distant regions also.
19. See Just., *Nov.* LXXX, 2–3 (pp. 391–392).
20. For the little that can be said concerning the administration of law and justice in the seventh to early eighth centuries: Haldon 1997a: 254–280.
21. See esp. Stolte 2002: and Wagschal 2015 for a detailed structural analysis of the development of canon law from the fourth to ninth century; and Humphreys 2015 for secular law in the seventh-ninth centuries.
22. See Humphreys 2015: 94–105, with earlier literature.
23. Dagron 1993: 232–234; Sharf 1971; Starr 1939.

24. See Troianos 1988.
25. Just., *Nov.* 6. preface (trans. Barker 1957: 75–76).
26. Troianos 1991; 1994–1995. See Just., *Nov.*, 6 and 31; on the *Nomokanon in fourteen titles:* Wagschal 2015: 42, 101–102, 225, Troianos 2011: 198–202; *ODB* 1491.
27. See esp. Simon 1973.
28. Laiou 2009: esp. 56–62, 72; Beaucamp 1990–1992; 2000.
29. Humphreys 2015: 39–80, whose discussion situates the council and its canons in their longer-term cultural, historical and canon law context; also Wagschal 2015: 108–112.
30. See Ohme 1990: 28–35, and esp. 31–32; and note *Trullo* 46: "For everywhere has reasonable worship been ordained," where the verb for "ordain" is the same as that employed in secular legal contexts, *nomothetein*, an activity technically belonging to the emperor alone.
31. *Trullo* 49–50, 54.
32. Narrative and analysis: Humphreys 2015: 73–80, 93–129.
33. See the important discussion in Wagschal 2015: 80–83. As we noted in the Introduction to this volume, belief systems have a material and functional impact on social action in many ways: see Haldon 1993d: 242ff.; 2012; and for early medieval western Europe see especially the valuable discussion of Wood 1979; also Heinzelmann 1975.
34. As Kazhdan 1989: 8 noted, the *Basilika* retains from the Justinianic legislation references to long-lost territories (Africa, Syria, Egypt).
35. *Trullo* canon 42. See also discussion in Trombley 1985b: esp. 341ff.; Abrahamse 1982; more generally Maguire 1995.
36. *Trullo* canons 42, 61–62, 65; and see Haldon 1997a: 334ff. for a range of practices condemned for similar reasons; Anastasius Sin., Qu. 62, found also in other collections (see Munitiz ed.: 112, note).
37. Canon 18; see above and Haldon 1997a: 128–129. Compared with the Western church, however, the Byzantine corpus remained fairly limited (some 770 canons). See Wagschal 2015: 50–62 for a more detailed discussion.
38. Haldon 1997a: 327–337, esp. 333ff.
39. See sources and literature in Haldon 1997a: 334–335. Peter Brown's classic work on the holy men of the Syrian rural and urban world in the fifth and sixth centuries is ample testimony to this. See Brown 1971; Drijvers 1981; Rapp 1999.
40. For the extent to which the canons of Trullo were recognized outside the remaining territories under the patriarchate of Constantinople, see Landau 1995; Ohme 2005; 1990: 55–75; Dură 2005.
41. See *Trullo*, canon 1, and note 31 above. This process of "resacralization" has been described as one that followed upon what has been termed the "desacralization of the ruler in the field of religion" following upon Con-

stantine's conversion to Christianity: see Hahn 2015: 403–404; Drake 2015; Diefenbach 2015: 364–378.

42. Beck 1966: 22–29; Pfeilschifter 2013: 21–24, 41–75.

43. Pfeilschifter 2013: 357–422; Dagron 2003: 79–83 (coronation), 181–184, 223–226.

44. And regardless of the short-lived existence of an Ostrogothic kingdom with a royal court at Ravenna.

45. Humphries 2007: 21–26; see also Marazzi 2007.

46. See esp. Humphries 2007: 53–56, and for background Sotinel 2005.

47. *Maximi Confessoris relatio motionis,* 443–444; transl. Allen and Neil 2002: 71; detailed discussion in Carile 2002.

48. Larchet 1998: 125–201; Louth 2004. For Pope Vitalian's compromise: Jankowiak 2009: 327–331.

49. Well established in a number of studies: useful survey in Herrin 1987: 250–259, 265–274, 289–290; more traditional approach in Lewellyn 1993: 149–172.

50. Herrin 1987: 250–251; and for the evolution of a papal conceptualization of those it had to deal with as "other," including the eastern emperor and the empire, see Gantner 2015.

51. Van Dieten 1972: xviii. For Constantine IV: Humphries 2015: 40–41.

52. See the persuasive account in McEvoy 2013: esp. 103–131.

53. Dagron 2003: 158–181, 190–191, 295–312. The preface to Novel 6 is quoted at p. 303; for Valentinian's law: *CTh.* i, 6. 9.

54. Note in particular Dagron 2003; Meier 2012: 230–236; 2004b.

55. Dagron 2003: 184 with literature, and *Ecloga,* preface 21–24; Haldon 1993b: 104–106; Rapp 2010.

56. For the sacralization of the imperial role, a process through which the emperor was presented in parallel with Christ: Meier 2012: 230–231. On the revival of the Constantinian myth under Heraclius: Brandes 2001a.

57. Niceph., 1. 1–6; 65. 14–17; Theoph., 418. 7–11 (Mango and Scott 578); Humphreys 2015: 254–255. On the issue of identities, see Chapter 2 of this volume.

58. Good short survey in Jankowiak 2012.

59. See Dölger 2009: 104–105 (no. 228b) and 113 (no. 239); Kaplony 1996: 33–36 and 77–97 for the peace treaties. As Kaplony notes, however (1996: 96–97), while the treaties were observed formally, some raiding and warfare along the frontier did continue, so that even in such periods travel was a risky venture and communications cannot have been very secure.

60. Analysis of those present from the eastern ecclesiastical provinces: Ohme 307–315. For travelers and the movement of individual churchmen and others, see Trombley 1983; Riedinger 1979; Jankowiak 2012.

61. Haldon 1992: 113–114.

62. The archaeological evidence seems to support this: the evidence for the movement of ceramics, for example, is that it was by sea, from one coastal port to another, sometimes from major centers of production to centers of consumption—between the Levant and Cyprus, for example, or between the Aegean and the Levant. But there is to date very little evidence to suggest any extensive commercial connection at all across the land frontier. See Haldon 2012a.

63. *Vita. Andrei Cret.*, §4 (173).

64. Dimitroukas 1997: 1, 108–112.

65. The *Chronographia* of Theophanes refers for 667/668 to a *kleisourophylax,* or guard of the pass, and again for 694/695 to a *kleisourarchēs:* Theoph., 350; 368 (Mango and Scott, 490 and 514), although whether this is an official term or an anachronistic usage on Theophanes's part remains unclear: see Métivier 2008: 438–439. While the exact title of this official may or not be reliably transmitted, the fact that Theophanes's source refers to such an official at all is the material point. For Heraclius: Theophilus of Edessa, 106–108; with discussion in Kaegi 1992: 240–244; Jankowiak 2012.

66. See discussion on the nature of this frontier and its evolution in Eger 2015.

67. Meyendorff 1964; Hoyland 1997: esp. 55–103.

68. Griffith 1987; Hoyland 1997: 93–95, 480–489. For the date of the *Hodegos:* Richard 1958; Uthemann 1981: ccvi–ccxvii, ccxviii and n. 72.

69. See Hoyland 1997: 55ff. for some examples; see also 24–25; 535–544; more broadly and focusing largely on the period from 700: Rotman 2005.

70. See Brandes 2009.

71. Hoyland 2015: 197–198; Sahner 2015: 327–329. See also the discussion and survey of the Melkite patriarchs of Antioch in the seventh century in Brandes 1998a.

72. *Mir. S. Theod. Tiro,* Mir. 9, 199. 23–24.

73. Lilie 1976: 119–120; Brandes 1989: 65 with sources.

74. General and detailed accounts of the raids and attacks: Lilie 1976; Brandes 1989; Kaegi 2006; Ahrweiler 1962.

75. See Kennedy 2001: xiv; Bashear 1991; Tor 2007: 40–42.

76. A year-by-year breakdown of Arab raids and attacks in this period can be found in Lilie 1976: 69–82; see also Brooks 1898. While the list can be modified somewhat in the light of more recent research, especially in respect of the early Arab-Islamic historiography, it offers a reliable description of the nature of the warfare. For the overwintering raids of 707–708 and 713–714, see Lilie 1976: 116–117 and 121 with sources.

77. See Kennedy 2004: 88–103; Robinson 2010: 215–218 for brief accounts with sources and further literature.

78. Lilie 1976: 82.

79. The events surrounding these developments are complex and need not be pursued in detail here, but it is important to note that the empire was still

in a position to mount offensive operations. See the summary of events in Chapter 1 of this volume. In conjunction with the disruption caused by the Lebanese Mardaites, this caused serious problems for ʿAbd al-Malik in North Syria. In addition, the agreement of 685 appears also to have entailed the Caliph's acceptance of an imperial presence in Armenia and Caucasian Iberia, probably because these were areas outside his control anyway (they were nominally under that of his enemy Ibn al-Zubayr), with the possibility of a substantial additional tributary income falling to the empire as a consequence. See Kennedy 2004: 93–97; Robinson 2010: 216–217; 2005: 25ff.; Hawting 1986: 46–57. For the treaties and their terms and context: Lilie 1976: 100–105.

80. Historians disagree over the exact causes. Theophanes, following his source, claims it was the emperor's fault for moving the population of Cyprus to Kyzikos, and for refusing to accept the tribute for 691 because it was delivered in the form of a newly minted Islamic coinage with no cross or obvious Christian symbolism (see Theoph., 365; Mango and Scott 509); discussion in Lilie 1976: 106–110, and on the coinage issue: Treadwell 2012 (with earlier literature and detailed discussion of the chronology); Robinson 2010: 220; Kennedy 2004: 98–99. It is on the face of it unlikely that Justinian in fact rejected the tribute—a sum of some 365,000 gold coins would represent a substantial percentage of the surviving annual imperial fiscal revenue.

81. Lilie 1976: 117.

82. Lilie 1976: 119.

83. Ikonion: Brooks 1898: 198 (Ibn al-Athir); Caesarea: Brooks 1898: 199 (Ibn Wadih, al-Tabari, Ibn al-Athir); Theoph., 404 (Scott and Mango 559).

84. See esp. Blankinship 1994: esp. 118; Bosworth 1996: 56; events summarized in Lilie 1976: 155–162.

85. Sebeos, 170 (Howard-Johnston and Thomson 144); Theoph., 389 (Mango and Scott 539).

86. See Haldon 1997a: 104–107 and the useful survey with gazeteer in Brandes 1989: 81–141 (on the differing fate of various urban settlements); also 44–80 (the influence of warfare on urban development in the seventh and eighth centuries). See also Lilie 1976: 121 on the fate of the fortress of Gazelon, taken, retaken and taken again on several occasions, but never abandoned by the imperial forces.

87. See Ohme 1990, for Galatia II: nos. 153 (Orkistos), 154 (Synodia), 155 (Therma Hagiou Agapiou); for Lycia: 160 (Pinara); for Phrygia Pakatiane: 169 (Trapezoupolis), 170 (?Eueragapa), 175 (Akmonia), 177 (Kolassai), 179 (?Sombros); for Pisidia: 199 (Bindaios), 201 (?Manopolis), 207 (Siniandos), 208 (Tityassos); and for Armenia I: 227 (?Kitharizon). While the settlements themselves are not new, this is the first time they are ranked as episcopal sees.

88. See, e.g., Howard-Johnston 2010a: 5.

89. See Chapter 4, pp. 177–178 in this volume.
90. See the catalog of cities taken in Brandes 1989.
91. See discussion in Hoyland 1997: 23–24; and for the Syrian response to Sasanian invasion or attack, see Kennedy 2000: 593; Mitchell 2007: 390–396; also Whittow 2010: 95, with n. 63.
92. For Caesarea in Palestine: Balādhurī, 216–219; Theoph., 341 (Mango and Scott 475); Theophilus of Edessa, 123–125; for Aradus (Arwad): Theoph., 344; Theophilus of Edessa, 134–136, with Conrad 1992.
93. Brooks 1898: 192 (al-Tabarī, Kitab al-Uyūn); Balādhurī 248–249; Theoph., 376–377 (Mango and Scott 525–526); Theophilus of Edessa, 201; commentary in Lilie 1976: 117–118.
94. Michael the Syrian, in Theophilus of Edessa, 106–108, with parallel texts and the editor's notes. The order to not engage with Arab forces is found only in the Syriac tradition and seems to reflect an imperial policy that assumed that the Arabs would not stay in the conquered regions but levy tribute and eventually withdraw. Thus, it is not entirely clear that these texts should be interpreted as the inception of a policy of avoidance. On the other hand, the record of engagements from all sources does indeed suggest that imperial forces generally avoided pitched battles where they could.
95. Al-Tabarī notes a Byzantine defeat in 662, but this is not mentioned by any other source (Brooks 1898: 184). Theoph., 348 (Mango and Scott 486) mentions only a raid with many captives and much booty. Some sources also mention a battle ca. 669–670 (Brooks 1898: 186: Ibn al-Athir; Elias of Nisibis, 115; Chronicon Maroniticum, 72), but Theophanes, al-Tabarī and other Arab historians make no reference to it. Regardless of this, the relative absence of land-battles across this period, given the high number of Arab invasions and raids into Anatolia, is still remarkable. For the Byzantine defeat of the Arab forces in Cappadocia in 654: Sebeos, §171 (p. 146).
96. Indeed, the surviving accounts make it clear that several Roman armies, including a force under imperial command, might be operating at any one time, as in the campaigns of 652–654, for example.
97. Among the events that moved Constans II to avoid further offensive operations in Armenia was the failure of imperial forces there in 653 (including the betrayal of a Byzantine army by Vard, the son of Theodore Rštuni): for discussion of the chronology and sources for military and political affairs in Armenia at this time, see *PmbZ*, #10772, with #7293.
98. See, e.g., Brown 1984: 42–45.
99. Useful list and discussion in Brandes 1989: 120–124. Tyana is in fact the only substantial urban center to suffer this fate.
100. Admittedly we have few direct indications of just where military units were based, but this seems a reasonable working assumption.
101. Sermon on the dormition: *PG* 98: 352–356; *Homilia de acathisto,* §9; while there is some doubt as to the authenticity of the extant version, it never-

theless nicely represents the general sentiment of the times. See Brubaker and Haldon 2001: 24 with n. 15.

102. Bashear 1991: 177. A second element in such prophecies is that the Muslims would build mosques in Constantinople, although according to one tradition, transmitted in the tenth-century treatise *De administrando imperio*, this had indeed been fulfilled by the eighth century CE. But for some doubts about this tradition, see Woods 2013. For the Byzantine apocalyptic tradition on Constantinople and the siege of 717–718: Brandes 2007 with further literature and analysis.

103. Detailed analysis and discussion in Brandes 1989; Brandes and Haldon 2000; Haldon 1997a: 92–124; Brubaker and Haldon 2011: 531–563, the last with further literature. Literature and discussion of specific cases: Henning 2007. The implications of these changes for literacy and urban culture: Mango 1981: 49–54.

104. See Haldon 1997a: 425–428.

105. On the factions, see Cameron 1979: esp. 6–15; Cameron 1976 (and for a survey of earlier views: Winkelmann 1976, who stresses the continued importance of the Blue and Green factions in Constantinople during the seventh century; also Beck 1965: 35–41). But in Constantinople, as Alan Cameron showed, the continued "political" activity of these organizations was constrained by an increasingly circumscribing imperial ceremonial function. For monks: Hatlie 2007: 38–39, 50–52; although as Hatlie notes (2007: 150–153) such involvement by monks in urban violence seems already by the middle of the sixth century to have been greatly reduced. Still, the complete absence of any reference to such monastic activity in towns in the Quinisext certainly reflects the changing character of urbanism by the later seventh century.

106. For the role of soldiers and the armies during the later seventh and early eighth centuries, for example, see Haldon 1986b: 172, 187ff.

107. For Italy: Brown 1984: 82–108; Egypt: Jones 1964: 660–663; Kaplan 1992: 231–53 for the Anatolian rural situation.

108. Haldon 1979: 54 n. 94; 60 n. 104; 1993: 42 n. 104; 54–56.

109. Brown 1984: 85–88; Whitby 2000b: 302–303; Lee 2007: 80–81.

110. *Ecloga* XVI, 2. See Haldon 1979 and 1993c for detailed analysis; with Chapter 7 of this volume.

111. For the evidence for this localization see Haldon 1993c.

112. Brown 1984: 87; see also Hendy 1985: 646–651; Ahrweiler 1960: 7–8. Further discussion in Chapter 7.

113. *Ecloga* XVI, 1–2; 12, 6. 618–622, repeating *CJ* iv, 65.31; xii, 35. 15 (a. 458). For the tenth century: see Chapter 4 of this volume, n. 113.

114. See in particular Kaegi 1966; 1981: esp. 232ff., 270ff.

115. See Drinkwater 2013; Kulikowski 2012; Esders 2009b; Halsall 2007.

116. For some examples from a slightly later period (ninth and early tenth centuries), see Haldon 1984: 331 and note 1021; for government efforts

to maintain control over appointments to all provincial positions and to limit the length of service in a given position as well as to avoid local provincial commanders-in-chief *(stratēgoi)*: Winkelmann 1985: 137–142; 1987: 113–120.

117. See Winkelmann 1978: 205ff. and Kaegi 1981: 186ff. for the events in question.

118. *Disp. Biz.* ll. 759–777 (trans. Allen and Neil 2002: 115–117); also Max. Conf., *Gesta,* 168C-169B; the charges against Maximus (and the pope, Martin): *Relatio motionis,* ll. 19–111 (trans. Allen and Neil 2002: 49–54); Martin, *Epist.,* xiv (Mansi x: 850D–851E); *PL* 129: 587D. For Anastasios' comment: Anast. Sin., *Sermo iii:* 2, 12–19.

119. *ACO* II, 2. i: 14. 20ff.

120. Vegetius, *Epitoma,* ii, 5; Lee 2007: 52–53, 184; for the period after the sixth century: Kaegi 1981: 312–313.

121. Hendy 1985: 187–192, 625–626; Lee 2007: 57–60; Whitby 2000b: 291.

122. *Ecloga* XVIII.1.

123. McEvoy 2013: esp. 103–131; Lee 2007: 30–50, 52–66; Greatrex 2000: 268 and 274; Whitby 2000a: 470–471.

124. *ACO* II, 2. ii: 886. 19–25.

125. Ps.-Methodius, *Apocalypse,* 13.13.

126. For canon 82, see *Trullo:* 162–64. Further discussion in Vogt 1988; Ohme 1999; Thümmel 2005: 27f. The coinage reform: Grierson 1968: 568ff., who notes that the change of design on the coins may precede the decision of the council. In either case, both reflect contemporary views. See Morrisson and Prigent 2013, with summary of the discussion to date and literature; Humphreys 2013; Treadwell 2012.

127. John of Nikiû, CXVI, 3 (transl. Charles 1916: 185); *Chronicon Maroniticum,* 71 (trans. Palmer 1993: 32).

128. E.g., Trullo, 40–46. See Hatlie 2007:232–238, who also calculates (2007: 219) that whereas there had been some one hundred fifty—two hundred monastic houses in the capital ca. 600 CE, the evidence suggests that only about fifty may still have been functioning ca. 700—although the evidential basis for this is problematic, and such figures likely conceal the actual situation.

129. Good analysis and discussion in Hatlie 2007: 222–226, 242–251. Note also Chapter 2 of this volume.

130. Detailed discussion of the evidence: Hatlie 2007: 226–227. Polychronius: *PmbZ,* #6318 / *PBE* Polychronios 3; Menas: *PmbZ,* #4963 / *PBE* Menas 7; Theodotus: *PmbZ,* #6945 / *PBE* Theodotos 3.

131. See the classic interpretation of Patlagean 1977; for a western comparison: Brown 2013.

132. For discussion of the relationship between ideology, belief system, symbolic universe, and related concepts, and of the ways in which they relate to eco-

nomic and social relationships—the social relations of production—see Haldon 1997a: 324–326, and the Introduction to this volume.

133. Although even in situations of extreme perceived external threat to "the nation" ordinary working people have frequently found their conditions such that resistance to government or establishment values and leadership results—strikes of industrial workers in Britain and the United States during the Second World War, or mutinies of individual soldiers as well as of whole units or brigades during the First World War on the Western Front, to name but two examples from more recent history.

134. See Rapp 2005: 274–289; Hohlweg 1972; Jones 1964: 923–929.

135. A point emphasized and clearly demonstrated in Humphreys 2015: 255.

136. For Germanus: *ACO* II, 3. 452. 23–478.20, see 474. 13–26. For discussion of Germanus's letters and their wider context in the opening stages of the icon controversy: Brubaker and Haldon 2011: 94–105. For Thomas: *PmbZ*, #8431 / *PBE* Thomas 14.

137. *Contra Imaginum calumniatores orationes tres,* in: Kotter 1975: II, xii.1–43. See Brubaker and Haldon 2001: 248–249; Krannich et al. 2002: 26–27. To what extent acceptance of the imperial position and the teaching of the official church reflected a passive acceptance and any real grasp of the issues remains unknown. As Theodore the Studite notes much later, there was a great lack of understanding of the discussion over sacred imagery among the wider population and even among many of the clergy: Theod. Stud., *Ep,* 393, and cf. *Epp.* 162, 500 and 549.

138. Germanus—see note 101 above; Anastasius: Qu. 68 and 69, and see Haldon 1992: 134. Constantine of Nakoleia: *PmbZ*, #3779 / *PBE* Konstantinos 73.

4. Elites and Interests

1. Theoph., 383 (trans. Mango and Scott 533).

2. Schachner 2006: 41–46.

3. For definitions and analytical categories through which to approach "elites," see detailed discussion in Haldon 2004: 179–182.

4. These points hardly need to be elaborated here. See the detailed and persuasive analyses in Brown 1984: 25–66, for Italy in the sixth and seventh centuries; and Conant 2012: 200–231, for North Africa for the same period.

5. Good discussion on the evidence for this is in Brown 1984: 68–69 and Conant 2012: 240–251.

6. For discussion of the structure, mores and identity of late Roman elites, both senatorial and provincial: Beck 1965; Patlagean 1977; Haldon 2004: 183–198, with older literature.

7. On their administration and history, see Delmaire 1989 for detailed discussion, analysis, and older literature; also Delmaire 1995, I: 140ff. See

also Jones 1964: 412–27; Stein 1949: 423–425, 472–473, 748–750; Kaplan 1986; 1992: 137–138, 140–42, 151.

8. See esp. Kaplan 1986; 1981; Feissel 1985.

9. Delmaire 1989 for discussion and older literature; Jones 1964: 412–27; Stein 1949: 423–425, 472f., 748–750; Kaplan 1986; 1992: 137–138, 140–42, 151.

10. See Karayannopulos 1958: 80ff., and Delmaire 1989; and on the *vindices* (who were officials of the praetorian prefecture) see Stein 1949: 211–14, and Enßlin 1961. See Just., *Nov.* 149 (723–725) (Dölger-Müller 2009: 12). Analysis in Kaplan 1986; Köpstein 1978: 4–14.

11. See discussion in Sarris 2006: 200–227, esp. 222–226.

12. Brown 1984: 61–81; Conant 2012: 239–251.

13. See, e.g., Brown 2000; Mathisen 1993; Harries 1992; Matthews 1975.

14. Trombley 2001.

15. Brown 1984: 21–37.

16. *Ecloga* XII. 6.

17. Brown 1984: 61–81.

18. Bjornlie 2013: 124–162. Survey of literature: Schachner 2006: 41–46; Lavan 2006: 10–15.

19. See Bjornlie 2013: 34–59; Barnish et al. 2000: 181–203.

20. Pfeilschifter 2013: 76–122; Bjornlie 2013: 60–81. See also Gizewski 1988.

21. There were traditionally three grades of senator: *clarissimus,* which was a heritable rank and title, *spectabilis,* and *illustris.* In the sixth century Justinian reformed and redefined the role and membership of the senate, so senators were to sit with the consistory in judicial appeal hearings, for example, but were differentiated in status according to whether they held an office or not (Jones 1964: 333–335; Stein 1949: 432). The grade of *spectabilis* came to be associated mainly with lower administrative and military positions and so was reduced in status, while the active senate at Constantinople consisted almost entirely of middling and higher administrative and military positions with the grade of *illustris.* From the later 530s a further distinction within the order of *illustres* (increasingly awarded to those holding provincial offices, or to *curiales,* leading to a loss of status and value) appeared, with a distinction between the majority, and those with the grade of *magnificus,* on the one hand and, at the top, those with the rank of *gloriosus* or *gloriossisimus*): Arsac 1969; Stein 1949: 429–32; Jones 1964: 529–35.

22. See Nichanian 2013 for a tabulation of the changes from the sixth into the ninth century; Haldon 2004.

23. For social mobility through the military: Whitby 2000a: 473–474; Marcone 1998: 364–366; see also Browning 1971: 73–79. Cf. also Metcalfe 2013.

24. Winkelmann 1987.

25. For examples from the Mughal Empire, see Haldon 1993d: 228–231.

26. Analysis of such relationships should begin with Weber's classic discussion of patrimonial power structures, and the tension between centralized, "despotic" power and decentralized "aristocratic" particularism: see Weber 1968, 3: 1006–1069. For modern discussions, see Kautsky 1982; and the discussion in Mann 1986: 167–174; and Runciman 1989: 155–156, 190–197.

27. The rank and title of *patricius* had precedence over all others, the status of the individual being determined by which consular rank the holder possessed. A ceremony of the year 638 preserved in the tenth-century *Book of Ceremonies* confirms the order of precedence for the period: *De Cer.*, 628.10–14 (Moffatt and Tall 2012: 628), with Just., *Nov.*, 62.2 for Justinian.

28. See Brandes 2002a: 427–479.

29. Theodore Spoudaios, *Hypomnestikon* §8 (trans. Allen and Neil 2002: 158–159), an account of Pope Martin's tribulations at the hands of the imperial government (cf. Winkelmann 2001: no. 138; Brandes 1998b: 154, 159ff.). The *sacellarius* similarly plays a key role throughout the trial of Maximus Confessor in 655, along with the prefect of the City: *Maximi Confessoris relatio motionis* (and cf. Winkelmann 2001: no. 132; Brandes 1998b: 155, 180–182). On the structure of the central apparatus and the complex relationship between office-holding, titles, personal association with the emperor and imperial family, and the bestowal of posts, see Winkelmann 1985 and 1987; Beck 1974.

30. Detailed discussion: Brubaker and Haldon 2011: 584–606.

31. See *PmbZ*, #6124, #8545 / *PBE* Valentinos 1, #353 / *PBE* Andreas 1 and #7312 / *PBE* Theodoros 3, respectively. References to the *PmbZ* and *PBE* for characters named in earlier chapters will not be repeated in this chapter.

32. See especially the detailed analysis of the history of the senate in Beck 1966; for a summary of the events listed here: Haldon 1997a: 167–168.

33. Nikeph. §31.

34. See Paulinus, *Eucharisticus,* and comments and discussion of Brown 2012b: 390–392.

35. Theoph., 383 (trans. Mango and Scott, 533).

36. *PmbZ*, #2707 / *PBE* Ioannes 3. For Justinian II's demands: Theoph., 367 (trans. Mango and Scott, 513); Niceph., §39 (see *PmbZ*, #7904 / *PBE* I, Theodotos 3). Justinian II is associated in the Syriac historiography also with action directed against "the nobility and great men:" Mich. Syr. ii, 473; see Palmer 1993: 206–207.

37. See *PmbZ*, #6150, #5258 and #5254 (and the caution expressed by the editors regarding the problem of making such identifications too readily); *PBE* I, Philippikos 1, Nikephoros 1.

38. *PmbZ*, #3557 / *PBE* Justinian 3; *PmbZ*, #2298 / *PBE* Germanus 8. See also *PLRE* III: 529 (Germanus 5).

39. *PmbZ*, #8524 / *PBE* Troilos 1; *PmbZ*, #7301, #1721 and #6305 / *PBE* Theodoros 345, Euprepios 1, Ploutinos 8.
40. See *ACO* II, ii. 2. 778–796; and *PmbZ*, #6525 / *PBE* Segermas 1. The total of bishops from all patriarchates at each council was 166 and 227, respectively; see also Ohme 1990: 145–170.
41. Cameron 1992.
42. Kaplan 1992: 310–326; and 1981.
43. See Balādhurī: 231f., who describes the local elite and their followers fleeing Barbalissos for imperial territory.
44. See Ditten 1993: 64 and n. 126; Jankowiak and Booth 2015: 51–57 and nos. 46–52; Booth 2014: 254–258.
45. *PmbZ*, #7320 / *PBE* Theodoros 50.
46. *PmbZ*, #6689 / *PBE* Sergios 30 and Tiberios 9.
47. *PmbZ*, # 3414 / *PBE* Ioannes 31; for his father, Kyriakos, see *PBE* Kyriakos 6.
48. *PmbZ*, #6819 / *PBE* Sisinnios 35.
49. *PmbZ*, #1170 / *PBE* Konstantinos 136.
50. *PmbZ*, #2523 / *PBE* Gregorios 7.
51. St Saba: Sansterre 1983; 1988.
52. See Lilie 1976: 102, 106f. with n. 15; Sansterre 1983, 1: 9–31; Rotter 1982: 179; general discussion: Ekonomou 2007.
53. *PmbZ*, #285 / *PBE* Anastasios 2.
54. *PmbZ*, #2105 / *PBE* Georgios 3. See Theoph., 378.27 (trans. Mango and Scott, 528).
55. *DOS* III, 39.30; *PmbZ*, #3518 / *PBE* Isoes 1.
56. *PmbZ*, #3519 with references / *PBE* Isoes 3. There are only two other persons of this name known from the eighth and ninth centuries: see *PmbZ*, #3520 / *PBE* Isoes 2 (a priest who attended Nicaea II in 787); and *PmbZ*, # 3522 / *PBE* Isoes 4 (an imperial *mandatōr* of the ninth century). The quaestor was instrumental in framing imperial legislation and in managing judicial matters at court. See Oikonomidès 1972: 321–322; Bury 1911: 73–77; *Ecloga*, preface, 40ff., 102ff. See also Gkoutzioukostas 2001: 119ff.
57. Garsoïan 1998.
58. See Haldon 2004: 214–215; Charanis 1961a; 1959; Winkelmann 1987: 203–207; Gero 1985;also Ditten 1983; 1993: 72–82; and Cheynet 2006: 12.
59. See esp. Ditten 1983: 104–109 (sources, literature and an etymology of the name); also Malingoudis 1994: 13–20; *PmbZ* #6752 / *PBE* Sisinnios 2.
60. See Theoph., 354. 11–13 (Mango-Scott 494); Theophilus of Edessa, *Chronicle*, 167–168; *PmbZ*, #4173 / *PBE* Kyprianos 1; *PmbZ*, #5909 / *PBE* Petronas 1, and *PmbZ*, #6206 / *PBE* Phloros 1.
61. See Haldon 1997a: 140–141; and esp. Kaplan 1992: 164–169 on emphyteutic leases; and 169ff. on the provincial landed elites and their characteristics.

62. Haldon 2004: 216–219, 229–231; Cheynet 2006: 10, 21ff.
63. See Brown 2012b: 392–400; Harrison 2002; Brown 1972: 233 and Brown 1984: 107–108.
64. A post that was abolished or renamed (as *domestikos*) during the reign of Constantine V and at some point before 765: Haldon 1984: 228–235, 355.
65. *PmbZ* #7235 with references / *PBE*, Tarasios 1; with Sisinnios 85, Tarasios 6, Georgios 122. Detailed discussion in Efthymiadis 1998: 6–11.
66. He was probably the same as the Theodore who acted for the emperor's brother as commander of military forces in Thrace in 656 (*PmbZ* #10698), and the Theodore mentioned as *komes* of the Opsikion in 680: *PmbZ* #7345. Theodore was instrumental in preventing the wife and children of Constans II from leaving Constantinople to join the emperor in Sicily, and later served Constantine IV in his negotiations and subsequent crushing of the rebellious Anatolikon soldiers in September 681: see *PmbZ* #7312; *PBE* I, Theodoros 3.
67. *PmbZ* #1218 / *PBE* Daniel 1.
68. For full details: *PmbZ* #4242 / *PBE* Leo 3; Speck 2003. We know very little of the processes through which such transfers were carried out, nor whether they entailed grants of land from the state, the compulsory sale of property in the regions of origin, and so forth: see Ditten 1993: 158–161.
69. V. *Philareti*, 117. See *PmbZ* #6136 for literature and discussion; with Ludwig 1997.
70. The best analyses of this corpus of material remain Winkelmann 1987; 1985, together with the often detailed studies for individuals in *PmbZ*.
71. Haldon 2004: 211–216; cautionary comments on names and naming traditions: Brown 1984: 67–68.
72. Theoph., 367 (trans. Mango and Scott, 513); Niceph., *Short History*, §39 (*PmbZ* #7904; *PBE* I, Theodotos 3).
73. Kazhdan and McCormick 1997: 176–185, 189–195.
74. Dölger-Müller 2009: #282; *PmbZ*, #5815 / *PBE* Paulos 7; *PmbZ*, #849 / *PBE* Tiberios 3.
75. General survey of stability and instability at court and in the imperial administrative establishment more widely in the later seventh-ninth centuries: Winkelmann 1987: 98–142.
76. Conant 2012: 196–241; Brown 1984: 61–79. Egypt before its conquest in the early 640s appears to have presented yet another variant, with both senior and junior officials and commanders being Egyptian, with a sprinkling of outsiders at the highest level only: Palme 2007.
77. Theoph., 377. 2–5 (transl. Mango and Scott 526); cf. Nikeph., §44. 9–11.
78. *Miracula S. Demetrii*, 136. 17–21; discussion in Makrypoulias 2012: 116, n. 57. The interpretation of the passage in this sense is not certain, however.
79. *Miracula S. Theodori tironis*, passim.
80. Makrypoulias 2012: esp. 111–115.

81. Sarris 2011a: 128–131; 2006: 222–226.
82. Just., *Nov.* 24 (Pisidia); 25 (Lycaonia); 27 (Isauria); 28 (Helenopontus); 29 (Paphlagonia), all issued in 535; 30 (a. 536, Cappadocia); see Jones 1964: 280–281, 294; Whitby 2000a: 478–479.
83. *Vita Philareti,* 125.34ff. Philaretus died in 792; the *Life* was written by his grandson, the monk Niketas, in 821–822. See Brubaker and Haldon 2001: 225.
84. *Vita Antonii iun,* 199. The incident is evaluated and discussed in detail in Stouraitis 2014: 194–195; see *PmbZ,* #534 / *PBE* Antonios 12.
85. See the valuable discussion in Karlin-Hayter 2003.
86. Detailed discussion in Haldon 1986b.
87. See Kaegi 1981: 254–292; Brown 1984: 82–108.
88. *Ecloga* VIII. 2–4; 18.
89. For the nature of Roman fiscal oppression and its impacts: Hopkins 2009: 183–184; Jones 1964: 810–811; Wickham 2005: 62–80.
90. Edict of Justin II of 566: in Just., *Nov.* 148; novel of Tiberius Constantine of 575: in Just., *Nov.* 163); for the papyrus evidence: *P. Oxy.* 1907, and cf. Jones 1964: 307 with note 9.
91. Novel of 572 on the Samaritans: *JGR* i, 11–13, see 12. B; novel of 566 (Osrhoene, Mesopotamia, Euphratensis): *JGR* i, 5–6; novels of 570 and 582 (N. Africa): *JGR* i, 10–11 and 24.
92. *JGR* i, 1–3; 7–10; 15–16; and 19–23, see §a, §d.
93. See Just., *Nov.* 24 (a. 535: Pisidia); *Nov.* 25 (a. 535: Lycaonia); *Nov.* 30 (536: Cappadocia); *Edict.* 8 (a. 548: Pontus)
94. See Rochow 1978: 265–288.
95. See Sarris 2006 and 2011c with older literature and sources.
96. See *CJ* x, 27. 10 (for the reign of Anastasius); Just., *Nov.* 17 and *Nov.* 32, 33 and 34 (a. 535); *Nov.* 65 (a. 538). For the duty of the military to eradicate such bands and protect the tax-paying population: *JGR* i, 7–10, at §b (a. 569); i, 15–16, at §b (a. 574).
97. See Th. Sim., vii, 3; Whitby 2000a: 482. According to Theophylact the militia was recognized by the government and exempt from duties other than the defense of the town.
98. See Speck 1997 with sources and older literature.
99. Montanists: see Theoph., 401. 22–27 and *Ecloga* XVII. 52; detailed account and discussion of the evidence in Rochow 1978: 271–274. Paulicians: see Rochow 1978: 282–283 with sources and literature. For the Quinisext: *Trullo* canon 95.
100. See Just., *Nov.* 32 and *Nov.* 34 (a. 535).
101. *De mag.,* 161.7–162.8.
102. Survey of evidence with further literature: Haldon 1999: 234–239.
103. Theoph., 371.4–6 (Mango and Scott 517); 386. 5–7 (Mango and Scott 536). Note that when Constantine V recaptured Constantinople after the collapse of the rebellion of Artavasdus, he permitted "external commanders"

(exotikoi archontes) to plunder the citizens of the city—again, this may suggest the tension between rural and urban populations: Theoph., 420.24–27 (Mango and Scott 581).

104. *Strat.*, i, 6. 9.32–35; i, 9. 47–54. While it should be noted that this is a *topos* in both Roman and Hellenistic military handbooks, there is no reason to doubt that it was meant to be taken very seriously; see Haldon 1999: 145–147, 234–247; Erdkamp 1998: 84–140.

105. *Ecloga* VIII. 2–4.

106. Theoph., 351. 16–24; 367–368 (Mango and Scott 490, 513–514), and bearing in mind the bias against both emperors, esp. Constans II, in Theophanes's own sources.

107. Such as that associated with the cult of St. Artemius in Constantinople: Nesbitt and Crisafulli 1997: 253 (comm. to Mir. 18, p. 116.6–9).

108. Evident in recent studies devoted to him: Allen and Neil 2002; also Booth 2014; Jankowiak 2009.

109. See *CJ* ix, 12. 10 (a. 468); Just., *Nov.* 30 (a. 536) and *Nov.* 116 (a. 542); McGeer 2000: 76 (and cf. 70); cf. Leo, *Takt.*, Const. viii, 26.

110. For some approaches to the study of east Roman / Byzantine society and social relationships, see Haldon 2009.

111. To a degree this also reflects a perceived cultural and linguistic identity: it is notable that the earliest Arabic accounts of the course of the conquest of Syria frequently refer to the "Greek" populations fleeing the invaders, whereas the non-Greek—Syriac or Arabic-speaking—populations remained. There are many such references: see, e.g., Balādhurī: 189 (citizens of Damascus flee to the emperor at Antioch); 194 (inhabitants of coastal cities expelled by Arab commander; inhabitants of Tripoli evacuate the city and flee to Byzantine territory), 227 (some of inhabitants of Antioch leave after it is taken by the Arab forces), 231f. (local leaders and their followers abandon Barbalissos and depart for imperial territory), 253 (flight of inhabitants of Cilician and Syrian frontier settlements from Arab raiders), and it seems largely to have been the Hellenized strata of the cities that fled or later emigrated; see Ditten 1993: 55–61. But this issue is complicated by the issue of the role of Miaphysite opposition to Constantinople, on the one hand, and the ways in which the invaders themselves offered attractive terms to those who would surrender without fighting, on the other: Winkelmann 1979; Kaegi 1992: 265–268. While there is no evidence that the majority of the Christian populations of the conquered provinces were anything other than passively hostile to the invaders, at least in the first half-century or so after the initial conquests (see Hoyland 1997: 17–26; 526–535), the response of some groups was certainly ambivalent: cf. Baladhuri 211.

112. Summarized by Bashear 1991: 200–204; Lilie 1976: 99–109, 133–136, 158–159; see also Cook 1996: 83–84.

113. Bashear 1991: 191.

5. Regional Variation and Resistance

1. Theoph., 343 (trans. Mango and Scott, 477–478).
2. See Cameron 1998; Morgan 1998.
3. Cameron 1992; Brandes 1999; Brandes and Haldon 200l; Laiou and Morrisson 2007: 38–42, all with further literature.
4. See Haldon 2004: 220–221.
5. Theoph., 455. 24–25 (Mango and Scott, 628). As the imperial administration became predominantly Hellenophone from the time of Heraclius on, so the term "Greek"—*graikos*—came to define Roman speakers of the Greek language, as opposed to the term "Hellenes," which continued to mean "pagan" until the thirteenth century. See Koder 2012; 2003.
6. See Goldstone and Haldon 2009: 15–17; and other essays in Morris and Scheidel 2009, for example, and discussion in the Introduction to this volume. For detailed discussion of the ways in which elites are formed and function within a number of premodern state formations: Haldon 1993d.
7. See, in general, Hopkins 2009: 185–186; and Mann 1986: 267–272, contra the views of Ando 2000.
8. Brown 2012b: 401; Conant 2012: 130–195. For example, and from a rather different context and period, many members of the Byzantine elite on the island of Limnos in the north Aegean who had fled the island after the initial Ottoman occupation had returned by ca. 1510–1520 and were in possession of some of their original estates: see Haldon 1986c: 167–168 and n. 11.
9. Brown 2012b: 392–394.
10. See Sidonius Apollinaris, *Ep.* I, vii. 5; Teitler 1992; Harries 1994: 158–166; Harries 1992. Yet this case is interesting because it shows that, in arresting Arvandus and sending him to be tried for high treason in Rome, the Gallic senatorial establishment were still unable to think outside of an imperial system, however attenuated. See Brown 2003: introduction.
11. See Drinkwater 2013; Halsall 2007; the essays in Drinkwater and Elton 1992; Matthews 1975; also Wickham 1984: 18–19, 24–25.
12. Cf. the case of Theodore Rštuni in the 640s and 650s (*PmbZ*, #7293; Dölger-Müller 2009: #227a-c), or Smbat Bagratuni in 698 (*PmbZ* #6828; Dölger-Müller 2009: 261a and 262), where in both cases imperial forces were dispatched at short notice to deal with the situation. On the latter, see Settipani 2013. Other examples: Dölger-Müller 2009: #228a, #230a, #258c, #267a-b.
13. See *PmbZ*, #5254 (Nicephorus, the general send to deal with the rebellion) and #6476 (Saborius); see also Dölger-Müller 2009: 235 and 235a).
14. See *PmbZ* #2969. For the flight of Syrian "Greeks" from the conquerors, see Ditten 1993: 55–61 and Chapter 4, n. 111, in this volume.

15. See now the painstaking analyses of Jankowiak 2009; and Booth 2014.
16. See, e.g., Brandes 1998b: 212.
17. Booth 2014: 7–185, 305–328.
18. Anast. Sin., Qu. 64.
19. Dölger-Müller 2009: #222; Brock 1973: 310–11; Booth 2014: 254–258; Boudignon 2007: 247–256. For the matter of the imprisoned nuns see the analysis in Jankowiak and Booth 2015: 51–57 and nos. 46–52.
20. The text is edited and published as *Disputatio cum Pyrrho* in *PG* 91: 287–353. For Gregory: *PmbZ*, # 2345 / *PBE* Gregorios 1.
21. Rebellions and attempted coups plagued the reigns of Heraclius Constantine and Constans II—the Armenian general Valentinus, the exarchs of Italy and Africa, Olympius and Gregory, respectively, as well as those of the generals Saborius and Mizizius (one Armenian, the other Persarmenian): Kaegi 1981: 154–69.
22. See, e.g., McEvoy 2013: 29–30, 109–113; more generally and with the longer-term Roman context: Lee 2007: 21–37; McCormick 1986.
23. Conant 2012: 355–357; Jankowiak 2009: 221–22, 227; Booth 2014: 287.
24. See Kaegi 2010: 116–44.
25. Dölger-Müller 2009: #224e.
26. Van Dieten 1972: 84 (n. 32) argues for an attempt to establish an autonomous Roman state under the banner of an antimonothelete orthodoxy; see also Price et al. 2014: 15; Howard-Johnston 2010b: 477; Jankowiak 2009: 220–223.
27. Kaegi 2010: 120–44.
28. *Relatio motionis:* 16–17; see discussion with further literature and sources in Brandes 1998b: 185–192.
29. Durliat 1990: 271–272.
30. Detailed discussion in Prigent 2006: 293–294; see Brandes 2002a: 309–312; Morrisson and Seibt 1982. For Sicily, see Prigent 2004, 2010. Further discussion on the role of *kommerkiarioi* in Chapters 6 and 7 of this volume.
31. For Philagrios: Nikeph., *Short history,* cap. 30 (p. 80) with Brandes 2002a: 459–460; *PmbZ*, #6124. Seals from Carthage of *chartoularioi* (clerical officials) of the Constantinopolitan department of the *sitōnikon* (grain supply) indicate the imperial concern with grain from Africa: see Durliat 1990: 214–217; and Cheynet 1999: 5. Detailed account and analysis of the sources for Gregory's rebellion and his defeat at Sbeitla: Kaegi 2010: 120–143; also Modéran 1999.
32. Noyé 2006a: 461; Morrisson and Seibt 1982; Prigent 2006: 293–294.
33. See Conant 2012: 203, 243.
34. Conant 2012: 196.
35. See in particular the important contribution of Boudignon 2007.
36. Booth 2014: 287–289, 307–309; Conant 2012: 306–353; Hovorun 2008: 81–84.

37. Prigent 2006; Morrisson 1982: 239; Kennedy 2007: 206–207; Slim 1982. On the structure and composition of the North African elite, see Conant 2012: 196–251; and for Italy, see Brown 1984: 39–81.
38. Slim 1982: 81; Ben Abbès 2013: 1163; Kaegi 2010: 143, 146.
39. Discussion of the sources in Kaegi 2010: 190–191.
40. Dölger-Müller 2009: #231c; *LP* i, 344 (trans. Davis 1989: 72): "tales afflictiones posuit populo seu habitatoribus vel possessoribus provinciarum Calabriae, Siciliae, Africae vel Sardiniae per diagrafa seu capita atque nauticatione per annos plurimos, quales a saeculo numque fuerunt." ("He imposed such afflictions on the people, inhabitants and proprietors of the provinces of Calabria, Sicily, Africa and Sardinia for many years by tributes, poll-taxes and ship-money, such as had never before been seen"). See discussion in Noyé 2015: 364–367. For a somewhat different version retailed by later Arabic sources but emphasizing the fiscal oppression of the imperial government and the disaffection of the North African élite: Kaegi 2010: 190–193.
41. Zuckerman 2002; Kaegi 2010: 179–182. Forces sent in 665–666 (according to a later Arab report, although not otherwise corroborated): Dölger-Müller 2009: 231d.
42. Conant 2012: 330–361.
43. Kaegi 1992: 159–169.
44. Brandes 1998b; also Jankowiak 2009 and Boudignon 2007.
45. Kaegi 2010: 220–229. Imperial fiscal officials, as evidenced in their lead seals, appear prominently again in the years 673–674 (Morrisson and Seibt, no. 17; Brandes 2002a: 310–311). The *Liber pontificalis* records for the year 685 that "the province of Africa was subdued and restored to the Roman Empire" (*LP* i, 366; trans. Davis 1989: 80).
46. Kaegi 2010: 146–152.
47. Discussed in detail in Kaegi 2010: 154–165.
48. As claimed in a mid-eighth-century Spanish chronicle (*Continuationes Isidorianae Byzantina Arabica et Hispana,* 344), and as implied in the chronicle of Fredegar, 81.
49. Conant 2012: 357–361; Kaegi 2010: 226–257.
50. Booth 2014: 290–1; for the context, see also Bertolini 1958.
51. Booth 2014: 259; *LP* i, 331 (Davis 1989: 68). See *PmbZ*, #7769 / *PBE* Theodoros 49; *PMBZ*, #2689 / *PBE* Ioannes 533.
52. *LP* i, 332–333 (Davis 1989: 70–1); *PmbZ*, #5763.
53. For the Lateran synod see Price et al. 2014; *ACO* II, I, and the editor's introduction: ix–xxviii.
54. See Gantner 2015 for an exemplary analysis of the eighth and ninth century material, which is relevant to the earlier material as well.
55. *LP* i, 331 (Davis 1989: 69); *PmbZ*, #3466 / *PBE* Isaakios 2; *PmbZ*, #4894 / *PBE* Maurikios 7.
56. See *PmbZ*, #6266 / *PBE* Platon 12.

57. See Brown 1984: 82–108; Guillou 1969; and *LP* i, 337 (Davis 1989: 71–72). For Olympius: *PmbZ*, #5650 / *PBE* Olympios 1.
58. Theod. Spudaeus, *Narrationes*, 194–99. Detailed discussion in Brandes 1998b: 168–173, followed by Booth 2013: 300–305.
59. Brown 1984: 87; Booth 2014: 293–300. For the Arab attack: Jankowiak 2009: 278–279; Howard-Johnston 2010b: 478; although Stratos 1976 does not believe that it ever took place.
60. Calliopas had held the office before Plato, in 643–645. *LP* i, 338 (Davis 1989: 68); Brandes 1998b: 182.
61. *LP* i, 341 (Davis 1989: 69).
62. Dölger and Müller 2009: #228b; Howard-Johnston 2010b: 486.
63. See the detailed account of Constans II's achievements in Noyé 2015: esp. 340–343, 345–346; Dölger and Müller 2009: #231d (Nikephoros); #229; #231 (peace with Romuald of Beneventum); Corsi 1983: 117–57; 1988; Kaegi 2010: 191.
64. *LP* i, 343 (Davis 1989: 70).
65. *LP* i, 344.2–4 (Davis 1989: 71); Dölger and Müller 2009: 231c. The exact nature of these measures remains debated: see Zuckerman 2004; Cosentino 2008.
66. Howard-Johnston 2010b: 490–92.
67. See Jankowiak 2013a. The Arabic source tradition brings with it its own complexities in terms of transmission and method, and the accounts of the various Arab raids against Sicily are especially problematic in this respect: see Amari 1933–1939: 71–72, 194–214; Stratos 1976; in general Conrad 1992.
68. See Prigent 2011: 180, 202–203.
69. Dölger-Müller 2009: #232, #233and #251 (Ravenna); developments discussed in detail in Jankowiak 2009: 427–87.
70. Dölger-Müller 2009: #256a, #259, #264, #266–267, #268–269; see Brown 1995: 32–33.
71. See *LP* i, 392 (Davis 1989: 94); Dölger-Müller 2009: #271.
72. Brown 1984: 147–148.
73. Brown 1984: 64–81.
74. Falconieri 2012; Brown 1984: 144–163, with a more nuanced interpretation of local separatism or anti-imperial sentiment than Guillou 1969. Revenues: Brown 1984: 113–115.
75. Brown 1984: 71–75.
76. Falconieri 2012: 571–583; Brown 1984: 145–146, 149–155.
77. Noyé 2002: 592–593; see also Guillou 1974; Brown 1984: 66.
78. Brown 1984: 65.
79. Dölger-Müller 2009: #231c, #250; *LP* i, 344.2–4 (Davis 1989: 71).
80. Sadori et al. 2015.
81. Martin 1993: 146–169; see also Arthur 2006.

82. *LP* i, 366.9–10 (Dölger-Müller 2009: 250). For grain production in Apulia: Volpe 1996: 258–270, 321–322, 369–372; in Calabria: Noyé 2006a: 446–449; 2002; 2015: 363.
83. Noyé 2015: 326.
84. *LP* i, 368.19–369.2; Dölger-Müller 2009: #255. For the wealth of Calabria: Noyé 2015: 346–361; for further fiscal measures in the year 685/686: Noyé 2015: 366–367.
85. Noyé 2015: 346–348, 354–358 with sources and further literature.
86. Until a peace was arranged at some point in the period 678–680: Dölger-Müller 2009: #240; Noyé 2015: 343–344.
87. Noyé 2006a: 463–469; Raimondo 2006: 427–431; Di Gangi and Lebole 2006: 474–475. For disaffection from the imperial cause: Martin 1993: 158–160.
88. Brown 1984: 56, 148–155; Morrisson 2002: 958; Noyé 2006b.
89. McCormick 2001: 627ff.; Jankowiak 2009: 278–279; Booth 2014: 300–314. For the grain supply and provisioning of Ravenna see Cosentino 2005.
90. Winkelmann 1985: 84–90; more specifically on Sicily: Prigent 2006; and esp. 2010: 226–230; Morrisson 1998.
91. See the discussion in Schuller 1975; and that in Gizewski 1988.
92. See discussion in Brandes 2003: 112–113, 117–118; Winkelmann 2001: 43–44, and for iconoclasm: Brubaker and Haldon 2011: 642–661.

6. Some Environmental Factors

1. Theoph., 351, 353 (trans. Mango and Scott, 490, 492) for the years 666/667 and 669/670.
2. Geyer 2002: 35; Sarış, Hannah and Eastwood 2010.
3. For accounts of the eastern Mediterranean landscape, its major long-term climatic characteristics and the products and activities the land supports, see Hendy 1985: 21–68; Geyer 2002: 32–37 (for the Byzantine Balkans and Anatolia); with Horden and Purcell 2000: 175–400; Wagstaff 1985; and Braudel 1972–1973: I.
4. Named for the site at which it was first identified, Beyşehir Gölü, in southwest Turkey: see Bottema et al. 1986; Bottema and Woldring 1990; Eastwood et al. 1998.
5. Eastwood et al., 1998, 1999; Kaniewski et al., 2007.
6. Bottema et al., 1986; Sullivan, 1989; Eastwood et al., 1998, 1999; Vermoere et al., 2000, 2002, 2003; Vermoere, 2004.
7. Bottema 1979; Bottema and Woldring, 1990; van Zeist and Bottema, 1991; Bottema et al., 1993.
8. Good general surveys in Hendy 1985: 21–145; Geyer 2002.
9. See Hendy 1985: 58–68; Geyer 2002: 36–40.
10. See Garnsey 1988; Gallant 1991; Geyer 2002: 41–42.
11. See, e.g., Lockwood 2006; Bond et al. 2001; Neff et al. 2001.

12. Perry and Hsu 2000.
13. For example Stuiver and Quay 1980; Stuiver and Braziunas 1988; 1991; 1993.
14. Beer et al. 2006; Beer 2000; Muscheler et al. 2007.
15. For a useful broad survey of the issues, see Luterbacher et al. 2012.
16. See, in particular, Manning 2013; Rosen 2007; Bakker et al. 2013; Dominguez-Castro et al. 2012; Nichol and Küçükuysal 2012 for overviews of both approaches to climate history as well as of the range of types of data that can be employed.
17. See, e.g., Gordon Childe 1928; and the overview in Roberts 1998. Note also the pioneering volume edited by Rabb and Rotberg 1981.
18. See in particular McCormick et al. 2007; 2012; with Luterbacher et al. 2012.
19. McCormick et al. 2012; Manning 2013; Haldon et al. 2014 for surveys.
20. Izdebski, Roberts, and Waliszewski 2015: sections 3.2.1–2, revising substantially earlier views that the period of relative humidity in the Levant ends in the mid-sixth century; also Decker, 2009: 189–192. The implications for our understanding of the apparent fairly gradual demographic and economic decline on the limestone massif of north Syria after the middle years of the sixth century, indicated by the archaeological data, require further interrogation, for which Izdebski, Roberts, and Waliszewski 2015: sections 4–5 offer some pointers.
21. Gogou et al. 2007; Triantaphyllou et al. 2014.
22. Baillie 2010; Larson et al. 2008; discussion of other sources and impacts: Stathakopoulos 2004: 265–267.
23. McMichael 2012; Gunn 2000; Little 2006; Stathakopoulos 2000; Keys 1999.
24. Izdebski 2011; Izdebski, Roberts and Waliszewski 2015.
25. Izdebski et al. 2015; Izdebski and Słoczyński 2015.
26. Butzer 2012; O'Connor and Kiker 2004; Alley et al. 2003; Weiss 1982.
27. Fei, Zhou and Hou 2007; Stothers and Rampino 1983; and cf. Rogers et al. 2012; Büntgen et al. 2016.
28. See, e.g. Fischer-Kowalski et al. 2014.
29. See Haldon et al. 2014: 127–131.
30. See McCormick 2007; 2012.
31. Türkeş, Koç, and Sarış 2009.
32. See, e.g., Luterbacher et al. 2012: 138–139.
33. For the LALIA: Büntgen et al. 2016. The results of a range of analyses across Asia Minor are briefly summarized in Izdebski 2013b: conclusions at 201–214; see also his shorter account: Izdebski 2012.
34. Evidence summarized in tabular form in Telelis 2004; Stathakopoulos 2004; Haldon et al. 2014: 153–160. Methodological issues regarding the written sources in this respect: Telelis 2005, 2008; Stathakopoulos 2003.
35. Izdebski 2011; Izdebski 2013b; Izdebski et al. 2015.

36. See Izdebski, Koloch and Słoczyński 2015.
37. Knipping et al. 2008; Izdebski 2016.
38. The material is summarized in Izdebski 2012 and in detail 2013a: 145–200; 2013b.
39. See detailed analysis of the evidence and discussion in Izdebski 2012; Izdebski, Koloch, and Słoczyński 2015.
40. Discussion and evidence: Haldon et al. 2014: 133–147. See, for example, for the Konya plain region, where a hitherto relatively dense settlement pattern, dependent in part on extensive seasonal irrigation, retreats fairly radically at some point in the later seventh century or shortly thereafter: Baird 2004.
41. See Brubaker and Haldon 2011: 531–563.
42. Izdebski 2012 and 2013b.
43. Beyşehir: Bottema et al. 1990; Eastwood et al. 1998; Van Zeist 1975; Sagalassos: Bakker et al. 2013; Lycia and the southern Aegean coast: Eastwood et al. 1998; Bottema and Woldring 1990; Van Zeist et al. 1975; Knipping et al. 2008; Bithynia: Argant 2003; Leroy et al. 2002; Paphlagonia/Pontus: Roberts, Eastwood, and Carolan 2009; Izdebski 2011; 2013a; Cappadocia: England et al. 2009; Eastwood et al. 2009.
44. Bakker et al., 2012; Kaniewski et al., 2012, 2013 classified pollen taxa in groups according to their climatic preferences and on this basis made claims about temperature and climate more broadly. But there are a number of methodological problems associated with this approach (e.g., Luterbacher et al., 2012: 134–139), not the least of which is that in this case the change they detect coincides with the mid-seventh century. The only other proxy that suggests the mid-seventh century as a turning point in temperature in the Anatolia region is the data from Lake Gölhisar, which has very unreliable chronological definition. See for a critique with further literature Izdebski, Roberts and Waliszewski 2015.
45. Doonan 2004; Izdebski 2013b: 182–186; on olive susceptibility: Tous and Ferguson 1996.
46. Akçer Ön 2011.
47. England et al. 2009; Eastwood et al. 2009.
48. The material is summarized in Izdebski 2012 and in detail 2013a: 145–200.
49. Magny et al. 2011.
50. Further discussion: Haldon et al. 2014.
51. Izdebski, Roberts, and Waliszewski 2015.
52. See Meier 2005: 94–95; in detail: Koder 1984: 151–154; Stathakopoulos 2008: 310–312. For other estimates, and older literature, although all broadly following the same pattern: Laiou 2002b: 47–51.
53. For the effects of plague and pandemics in the eastern Mediterranean in the late ancient and early medieval period: Stathakopoulos 2004, and more specifically for the Justinianic plague Meier 2005; Stathakopoulos

2000 with a review of literature; see also Leven 1987; and for the Levant, Conrad 1994 and Stathakopoulos 2003.

54. The following account follows England et al. 2008, and for a broader historical context and discussion Haldon 2007a; Eastwood et al. 2009. See also Bottema et al. 1986; Eastwood et al. 1998.

55. Woldring and Bottema 2003.

56. England et al. 2009.

57. Grove and Rackham 2001.

58. England et al., 2008: 1238. For example, pine trees are not found in Cappadocia today, except where planted, whereas relatively high levels of pine pollen are recorded for the last two millennia at Nar. This can only be the product of long distance aerial transport, probably chiefly from the Taurus Mountains some seventy kilometers distant to the south and southeast.

59. *TIB* 2: 207f.; Lilie 1976: 69 (not Koloneia in Pontus).

60. Hild 1977: 41–63, 65–76 with maps.

61. Lilie 1976: 69–80 with sources. *TIB* 2: 261f., 258f., 298f., 243f., 142. For the history of the region(s) of Kappadokia between the seventh and ninth centuries, see *TIB* 2, 70–84; and for the arrangements along the frontier, Haldon and Kennedy 1980; Métivier 2008. For the archaeology of the frontier region as well as sensible analysis of socioeconomic evolution on both sides of the divide: Eger 2015.

62. Ps.-Methodios, *Apocalypse,* 11. 9–11; 17 (pp. 144–145 and 152–153). The reference to Cappadocia does not appear in the Syriac version, but Aerts and Kortekaas 1998: II, 36, note to 11, 9. 3–4, argue that the Greek and Latin versions preserve the original where these names have dropped out of the Syriac tradition. For comments on the accuracy of the author's geographical knowledge, see Kaegi 2000.

63. Although the Syriac version treats much of this as having already occurred and preparatory to the events still to come. While mostly of later date, the chronicle writers drew on earlier, lost accounts of the period: see discussion on the various traditions (Roman, Syriac, Armenian, and Arabic) in Howard-Johnston 2010b.

64. Ditten 1993: esp. 45–65, with details of the evidence for the movement of refugees in the war-torn regions of both the Balkans and Asia Minor, with the most recent literature on the subject; see also the older work of Charanis 1959, 1961b.

65. See the survey of Ahrweiler 1962; Haldon 1997a: 114–7, 143–5; note also the summary in Drauschke 2013. For references to devastation, see, for example, the *Life* of Philaretos, whose home was in Paphlagonia and whose herds had been driven off by raiders: *Vita Philareti,* at 115–117, 137; for literature, see Brubaker and Haldon 2001: 225; or the *Life* of the tenth-century magnate Michael Maleinos, whose properties in the devastated regions of Charsianon in east-central Anatolia he improved by careful investment: *Vita Mich. Maleini,* 550.20–21. Although many of these *Lives* are

full of literary *topoi* and rhetorical artifice and are not to be taken at face value, they nevertheless reflect a recognizable reality for their listeners or readers, and there is no reason to doubt that the general situations they describe are more or less accurate.

66. See *Vita et miracula Theodori,* 198–199.

67. See Xoplaki et al. 2015; England et al. 2008: 1243–1244; Eastwood et al. 2009: 57–59.

68. Izdebski 2012: 55–57.

69. See McCormick 1998: 31–32; Sansterre 1983: 9–31; Van Dieten 1972: 109.

70. Charanis 1959: n. 25. See the list with sources and discussion in Lilie 1976: 231–234.

71. Sision: Lilie 1976, 119; Euchaïta: *Vita et Miracula Theodori,* 198–9 (miracles 7, 9). Canon 8 of the Quinisext council in 691–692 calls for the reestablishment of yearly provincial synods, which had been abandoned due to barbarian raids; and canon 18 notes that many clergy had left their provincial sees for the same reason, along with the local populace in many cases: see also the twelfth-century commentaries by Balsaman and Zonaras in Rhalles-Potles II: 325–326; 344–346.

72. See Ohme 1990: 252–315 and 316–320; Jankowiak 2013b: 448–461, with maps 2 and 3 (451) and 4 (457). There may, of course, have been other reasons for a bishop's absence, but as Ohme, followed by Jankowiak, showed, the pattern is especially marked in the case of these two councils.

73. Canon 38, with twelfth-century comm. in Rhalles-Potles II: 392–394; canon 39 (see Rhalles-Potles II: 395–396, and Brandes 1989: 117–119); canon 95 with Rhalles-Potles II: 531–533; and see esp. Ditten 1993: 45–65; Lilie 1976: 230–236; Charanis 1961b.

74. See Garsoïan 1967: 114ff. with sources; Garsoïan 1970.

75. See Theoph., 347; 364 (Mango and Scott: 484, 508); Lilie 1976: 237–238; Ditten 1993: 209–234 (and 234–237). For the lead seals see Seibt and Theodoridis 1999; Brandes 2002a: 351–365; 2005; Brubaker and Haldon 2011: 685 n. 67. After both transfers many of the Slavs deserted to the Arabs, although others remained and are referred to on seals of the later 690s, for example, while evidence for the descendants of these immigrants is found from the early ninth century in Bithynia: see Haldon 1997a: 247 and n. 118; Anagnostakes 2001; Vryonis 1961.

76. In Palmer 1993: 62 (AG 1028:157).

77. On the bread dole, reduced in 619 and then stopped in 626 (*Chron. Pasch.,* 711. 11–15): see Teall 1959: 89; Jones 1964: 696–697. For a comparable case in respect of grain supply, Ravenna: see Cosentino 2005.

78. For a detailed discussion of the role of these *kommerkiarioi* (who are not entirely unproblematic) and their storehouses, which also served as granaries, see Chapter 7 of this volume, with Brubaker and Haldon 2011: 683–695, esp. 686–687.

79. See also Guzzetta 2000 on Sicilian fiscal revenues.

80. See esp. Prigent 2008, 2010 and 2011; the evidence summarized in Winkelmann 1985: 84–90; McCormick 2001: 627ff. For the coinage, see Prigent 2006. For a summary of the evidence, see Brubaker and Haldon 2011: 489–493.

81. Morrisson 1982: 239: a seal of Sergius, *commerciarius,* dateable to 642–647 or 648; the next seal is dated to 673–674, a seal of Mikinnas and Gregory, general *kommerkiarioi* (of) the warehouse of Africa. Prigent 2006 has directly linked the African *kommerkiarioi* with the grain supply of Constantinople. The lacuna in the sigillographic record may simply reflect loss of evidence, of course, but is at least indicative.

82. See Teall 1959: 117–132; Lilie 1976: 201–227; Hendy 1985: 44–54, 561–564; Koder 1995.

83. See Teall 1959: 125; and for grain after the siege of 717–718: Theoph., 397 (trans. Mango and Scott: 546).

84. Brubaker and Haldon 2011: 514–515.

85. For grain ships delivering to Cherson, see *Vita S. Martini Papae,* 261; and discussion in Brubaker and Haldon 2011: 513–515, 520.

86. Crow and Hill 1995: 251, 261; *TIB* 9, 142.

87. See Brandes 2002a: 565 and *TIB* 9: 162 and n. 28; and the catalogue in Brandes 2002a: 601, 603, 605–606, 608–610.

88. Nicephorus I's measures: Theoph., 487 (Mango and Scott, 668; comm. 670). The letter was written by Ignatius the deacon in the 820s: Ignatius diac., *Ep.* 21 (67–68; comm. 178–181). See also *PBE,* Anonymi 34; *PmbZ,* #10602 with further literature.

89. *DAI,* §53. 532–5. For Aminsos as a port (for which there are a number of seals of *kommerkiarioi*), see Bryer and Winfield 1985, 92ff.

90. Strabo, *Geography,* xii, 3. 38. Phazemon is modern Merzifon; for Diakopene: Strabo, *Geography,* xii, 3.39; Mauropous, *Letters,* no. 64. 55–62 (see also Hendy 1985: 140–141).

91. See Brubaker and Haldon 2011: 695–705.

92. Lefort 2002: 248–260 provides a good summary of the evidence and the relevant literature.

93. See esp. Kondov 1974 for detailed discussion. There is a large literature on this topic. See Patlagean 1977: 246–248 (with very pessimistic estimates); Kaplan 1992: 80–82; Jardé 1925/1979); Garnsey 1998; Halstead 1987; Isager and Skygaard 1992. On seed:yield ratios see Spurr 1986; Garnsey 1992: 147–155.

94. Kraemer 1958: 237–240. Kraemer notes that documents from Egypt suggest yields of between 1: 4.5 and 1:10, and from Roman Sicily of 1:8: 1958: 238–239.

95. The text: Lefort et al. 1991: §51; discussed in Lefort 2002: 299–300.

96. The *modios* was the standard measure of quantity for grains and pulses, as well as being employed as a measure of area. The exact volume of the

modios remains disputed, the more so since there are several different *modioi* employed for functionally and contextually diverse purposes. See Haldon 1999: 281–283 for the *modios;* the tenth-century figures: Haldon 1999: 285–286; 2000: 296–298 for sources, literature and discussion. The larger *thalassios modios* (28.2 lbs / 12.8 kg) may be meant, however, which would increase these figures by well over a third.

97. The *modios* as a measure of area was also variable but amounted to ⅒ of a hectare, or just under ¼ of an acre: see Schilbach 1970: s.v. *modios.*

98. Lefort 2002: 259–260.

99. Roberts, Eastwood, and Carolan 2009.

100. See Teall 1971.

101. Izdebski 2015; Knipping et al. 2008.

102. On the general situation in respect of trade and commerce at this time: Haldon 2012a.

103. For a detailed discussion see Haldon 1997a: 215–51; Brubaker and Haldon 2011: 724–728.

104. This beneficial climate ended ca. 750 CE, and has been seen as one possible contributory factor in the decline of the island economy and its conquest by the Arabs from the 820s. See Sadori et al. 2015.

7. Organization, Cohesion, and Survival

1. Leo, *Taktika,* preface §5. 37–40.

2. Robinson 2010: 212–215; Sijpesteijn 2007; Donner 1981: 94–111; Haldon 1995.

3. See Brandes 2002a: 449–479; Haldon 1997a: 183–194; also Delmaire 1989.

4. A more detailed survey, with older literature and sources: Haldon 1997a: 173–180.

5. See Hendy 1985: 417–420; Haldon 1997a: 186–187.

6. McCoull 1994; see Brandes and Haldon 2000: 160; Brandes 2002a: 23.

7. Dölger 1924: no. 176; Hendy 1984: 231; Van Dieten 1972: 10–11; Grierson 1968: 17–18; see Theoph., 302, 34–303.3 (Mango and Scott: 435).

8. Reported by Theodorus Scutariotes, a historian of the thirteenth-century employing much older and now lost material, often ignored by modern scholarship. See Scutariotes, *Synopsis Chronike,* 110. 5–8. The measure is discussed in Kaegi 1992: 256–258; Brandes 2002a: 459–460.

9. Banaji 2006.

10. See Gândilă 2009.

11. See Haldon 1997a: 226–227, 232–244, with earlier literature; Phillips and Goodwin 1997: 75ff.; the reduction in emissions appears to be associated with the production of a large reformed copper *follis* by Constantine IV, which is found only very rarely outside Constantinople: Phillips 2012, with further literature.

12. Kislinger 1995b; Morrisson 1998, 307–334; McCormick 2001, 627–629; Morrisson 2002, 915, 957–958. For the Arab raids on Sicily in 651 (the date is debated): Jankowiak 2009: 277; and in ca. 671–672: see *LP* i, 346.8–11 (Davis 1989: 72) and Jankowiak 2013a: 313–314.

13. Good summary of developments in Prigent 2014: 184–185 with literature; and the useful summary in Phillips 2012; with Hendy 2007: 179ff., and fig. 79; 181; Metcalf 2001.

14. See Morrisson 1986: 156ff.; Grierson 1960: 436, with table 2; 1968, 1: 6f.; Hendy 1985: 496–499; 640f.; Brandes 1989: 226–227. The pattern is demonstrated across both the Balkan and Anatolian regions of the empire: Morrisson 2001: esp. 383. For the consigning of bronze, see the evidence summarized by Hendy 1985: 641–642, 659–662.

15. See Hendy 1985: 415–416, 642–643, for example. While it is true that paying troops regularly in bronze would have entailed the striking of impossibly large quantities (see Prigent 2014: 186 and n. 11), occasional "emergency" demands in highly localized contexts may have made it sometimes unavoidable, if only as a "stop-gap" measure (Brubaker and Haldon 2011: 470).

16. The question of "residuality" is an important one: see Prigent 2014: 189–190.

17. See in particular Prigent 2014: 188–191; Brandes 2002a: 324–329; Hahn 1981, III: 157–159; Grierson 1968, II/2: 514, 517–518; Jankowiak 2013a: 315.

18. See Füeg 2007:153, 166–171; Morrisson 2002: 936–942, with tables and further literature. The fiscal reforms under Leo III in the early 730s reflect some of these difficulties. See Prigent 2015; Brandes 2002a: 368–384; Brubaker and Haldon 2011: 695–705.

19. For a broad-ranging discussion of these developments with further literature, see Prigent 2014: 192–195. For Justinian's windfall: Theoph., 364 (trans. Mango and Scott, 506).

20. Curta 2005; Morrisson et al. 2006, 41–73; Ivanišević 2006.

21. See Hahn 1981: III, 17. For the Sicilian coinage and regional variations in general, see esp. Prigent 2006b; Morrisson and Callegher 2014 (on Ravenna); and Morrisson 1998.

22. See Oddy 1988; and Morrisson 1985; Morrisson 2002: 928–930.

23. Prigent 2006, 2008; Noyé 2015: 361–362.

24. Philipps 2012: 44 and 50–51, with literature.

25. Curta 2005: 118–124.

26. Detailed and persuasive analysis: Prigent 2015.

27. The evidence, with earlier literature, is presented in detail by Curta 2005. See Morrisson et al. 2006, 41–73; and the summary in Brubaker and Haldon 2011: 467–468.

28. See now Phillips 2012 with earlier literature; Phillips and Goodwin 1997. For the strength of monothelete sentiment in Syria, see the Introduction to this volume, and Brock 1973: 69–71.

29. Durliat 1990, 271f.
30. See Morrisson and Seibt 1982; Prigent 2006: 293–294.
31. Morrisson and Seibt 1982; in detail Prigent 2006, 293–294.
32. Prigent 2006: 290–293; Noyé 2015: 364–365.
33. Oikonomides 1986 and 1993: 638–640 argues that *kommerkiarioi* were still principally occupied with the production and sale of silk in the seventh and eighth centuries. But this has been shown to be implausible, given the climatic conditions of Asia Minor, which permit the breeding of silk worms in only a small number of areas as well as the military and political circumstances of the times: see Haldon 1997a: 232ff.; Muthesius 1989; Jacobi 1932: 51–53; note also Jacoby 1991/1992: 454 n. 7.
34. Presented in great detail in Brandes 2002a: 511–610.
35. This was the second year of a new cycle (incorrectly described as the first year in Brubaker and Haldon 2011: 689). It has been objected that not all can be thus associated, that indeed many are issued before such military undertakings took place, and that, for the year(s) during which the military operations actually occurred, there are few or no seals of such officials (see, e.g., Montinaro 2013: 414–415, following Oikonomidès 1986b). While this is certainly the case, not all preparations for supplying a city such as Constantinople or a military force need take place in the year of the actual conflict but rather in advance, possibly by more than a year, depending on the situation and what is known or expected of the enemy
36. For the evolution of their role from the fifth into the seventh and eighth centuries: Brandes 2002a: esp. 329–351 for the period from 672; Dunn 1993; Hendy 1985: 654–60, 667–9; and for their functions Brubaker and Haldon 2011: 682–705; and with an alternative interpretation Montinaro 2013.
37. Brandes 2002a: 351–365; Seibt and Theodoridis 1999.
38. Brandes 2002a: 322–323; but see Brubaker and Haldon 2011: 690–693. Nor is it clear that they managed the supply of military equipment, as opposed to food and provisions, although the former cannot be excluded: see Hendy 1985: 619–620.
39. *LP* I, 366 (a. 685, but referring to imperial edicts issued in 681); see Haldon 1994; Brandes 2002a: 316; *Nomos geōrgikos,* cap. 19 (Zepos 1931: 66); Noyé 2015: 363–364. The Farmers' Law makes no reference at all to *synone/coemptio* in the traditional sense (see Lemerle 1979: 40, 41 n. 1), whereas these *extraordina* clearly refer to a regular—annual—imposition: see Haldon 1994.
40. See Brandes 2002a: 319. Montinaro 2013: 392–393 notes, however, that this interpretation remains problematic, reflecting probably a mechanical rather than a technical translation by the glossator.
41. See Prigent 2006: 290–295, who also notes that the need to protect the grain supply of Constantinople may have been a prime motive in the decision of Constans II to establish his base of operations in the island.
42. See Teall 1959: 137–138; Durliat 1990: 390–404; also Noyé 2015: 364–365.

43. Goetz 1888: 69, 17; 237, 1; 503, 67; 1892: 192, 45; 306, 22; 450, 42; 489, 9; material and discussion summarized in Brandes 2002a: 291–296. Montinaro 2013: 353–354 showed that the seals should be understood as having been issued by (local officials of) the storehouse or *apothēkē* rather than by the individual high-ranking general *kommerkiarios* under whose authority they were placed.

44. Matt. 3:12; 6:26; 13:30; cf. Luke 3:17.

45. References collected in Brandes 2002a: 294–295.

46. Ed. Riedinger 1992: 864.18 (Greek text) and 865.18 (Latin translation).

47. For discussion see Brandes and Haldon 2000: 163–168; Noyé 2015: 359 reminds us that in Italy during the fifth and sixth centuries, imperial *horrea* (granaries) were used to store all the different types of produce raised for the *annona*, the supply of Rome and the army.

48. For seals see Brandes 2002a: 522–523 and 583 (nos. 61, 62, 64).

49. Brubaker and Haldon 2011: 689–690; Curta 2005: 119–120; Hendy 1985: 656–661.

50. For the raising of resources in kind: Brubaker and Haldon 2011: 686–689; for the compulsory purchase via the *kommerkiarioi* of such resources: Prigent 2014: 195–198. Following Prigent the beginnings of this development should be dated in the reign of Heraclius, beginning in Africa in the 620s, before being applied in Sicily; and by the 670s it had become entrenched across the whole empire. I would now tend to agree with Prigent that the role of the *kommerkiaroi* as managers of compulsory purchases of resources in the provinces was a highly monetized one, rather than, as I have previously argued, based entirely on the levying of resources as tax. In neither case, however, is there a suggestion that *kommerkiarioi* were responsible for the movement of the goods thus acquired to their delivery locations (whether the *apothēkai* or other consumers such as officials or soldiers). On the contrary (and *pace* Prigent 2014: 197 and n. 70), and following standard late Roman practice, the delivery of the resources in question was always, as far as the sources permit us to say, the responsibility of the producers, up to a certain distance from their point of origin, and in the case of soldiers, the military units themselves. The *kommerkiarioi* merely purchased or requisitioned the resources.

51. Brubaker and Haldon 2011: 690–693 (and *pace* Prigent 2014: 196 and n. 64: there is thus no conflict between these activities and those of the regular fiscal officials in the provinces).

52. Emphasized in Brubaker and Haldon 2011: 687–688, 693–695.

53. Montinaro 2013: 408–419.

54. Brubaker and Haldon 2011: 687, 689, 693–695.

55. See the relevant essays in Morrisson 2012 and in Mundell-Mango 2009; with the survey in Brubaker and Haldon 2011: 482–530.

56. The omission of the archaeological data available for most of the areas in which seals of *kommerkiarioi* are attested is a major weakness of this perspective.
57. Detailed discussion in Brubaker and Haldon 2011: 709–717.
58. See Brandes 2002a: 281–291; Montinaro 2013: 375–378.
59. Montinaro 2013: 414–415, with the chart at 419; Brubaker and Haldon 2011: 693.
60. Further cogent reasons for rejecting the notion of general *kommerkiarioi* and *apothēkai* being associated with commerce alone in Prigent 2006: 290–294.
61. See Brandes 2002a: 365–394; detailed analysis Brubaker and Haldon 2011: 695–705.
62. Evidence summarized by Oikonomidès 1986b: 44 and maps 3 and 4; Brandes 2002a: 384–388.
63. Detailed discussion: Brubaker and Haldon 2011: 695–717.
64. See Prigent 2015; Brandes 2002a: 316–318; Zuckerman 2005: 95–104; Guzzetta 2000.
65. See Schmitt 2001; 2007; Kaiser 2012.
66. See Schmitt 2001; Haldon 1995; Isaac 1995: 144–145.
67. See Haldon 1995; Kaegi 1992: 52–56.
68. See in detail Haldon 1993a.
69. For a detailed survey of the discussion and its history, with the relevant earlier literature, see Haldon 1993c, where the relevant works by Ostrogorsky will be found.
70. It should be noted that the notion of farmer-soldiers was challenged almost from the beginning by scholars such as Pertusi and Karayannopoulos, although it has had a peculiarly romantic attraction for many. Hendy 1985: 640ff. reasserted the idea on the basis of what he saw as a deliberate reduction in coin emissions, which he believed could only have been compensated for by grants of land. The exact mechanisms of such a process were, of course, never examined. Ostrogorsky's farmer-soldier still survives, even in quite recent literature: see, e.g., Sarris 2011a: 288.
71. The relationship between military commands and groupings of provinces was originally noted by Gelzer 1897: 127–130, and discussed by Hendy 1985: 623–625, with comments in Zuckerman 2005: 129–131. For this and for the relationship between military forces and the ability of the regions across which they were based to support them: Haldon 1997a: 217–229.
72. See discussion in Hendy 1985: 623–624.
73. Zuckerman 2005: 122ff.; a different position argued by Cosentino 2007; see also Cosentino 2004. For the South Italian fleet: Noyé 2015: 352–354, 368–370; Prigent, 2004: 567.
74. See *Ecloga* xvi, 4; also xvi, 1 and 2; see also Simon 1977: 94 (A)2, 7; (B)4 (an eighth-century text, probably of Leo III and Constantine V, appended in its older form to manuscripts of the *Ecloga* as article 19).

75. Humphreys 2015: 126 and 135–138; discussed also in Lilie 1984a: 196–197; Oikonomidès 1988: 130–132.
76. *Ecloga,* xvi, 4; also xvi, 1 and 2; cf. Karayannopoulos 1956: 498–99; Antoniadis-Bibicou 1966: 105–106.
77. A soldier's property earned through military service was defined as *idiok-tēton* (*Ecloga,* xvi, 1, with Haldon 1979: 54, n. 94; 71 n. 126), distinguished from property derived through inheritance or other sources.
78. A significant change that conflicted with the traditional legal statutes: Simon 1977: 99; Haldon 1993c: 22–23.
79. Although we should be careful not to ascribe too modern an appearance to the late Roman army or to exaggerate the difference between it and the eastern Roman armies of the later seventh century: sons of cavalry veterans already in the early fourth century were permitted to enroll into a cavalry unit if they provided a horse; if they provided two, they were enrolled in a junior officer grade: Jones 1964: 617.
80. Whether this was connected with an evolved version of the quinquennial donatives (Hendy 1985: 645–651) or the traditional *rhoga,* issued according to payment cycle for provincial troops called up for campaigns away from their home province (Oikonomidès 1988: 122–128). In either case, it is clear that the payment cycle mentioned in the tenth-century text (*De Cer.,* I, 493–494; Const. Porph., *Three Treatises* [C] 647–652) represents a much older structure than those of Constantine's own time.
81. Detailed analysis of the relevant sources and evidence for all these developments in Haldon 1997a and 1999. In respect of the development of the fiscal system and the role of *kommerkiarioi* and *apothēkai,* it is important to fit them into the broader context of developments from the sixth into the ninth century and not isolate them from the wider pattern of which they were but a part: see Brubaker and Haldon 2011: 679–717.
82. See for an overview: Haldon 2012a; McCormick 2012; for the economic stimulus lent to provincial economies by the injections of cash through the activities of *kommerkiarioi,* see Prigent 2014: 197.
83. Brandes 2002a: 312–329; Brubaker and Haldon 2011: 682–695.
84. See Chapter 6 of this volume; Izdebski 2012; Izdebski, Koloch, and Słoczyński 2014.
85. Laiou and Morrisson 2007: 38–42; Stathakopoulos 2012; 2004: 155–165, 166–169; Morrisson and Sodini 2002: 193–195; Laiou 2002b: esp. 49–50.
86. See Geyer 2002: Map 2; Bottema and Woldring, 1990; Grove and Rackham, 2001.
87. For Late Roman production: Mitchell 2005; also Izdebski 2013a.
88. Hendy 1985: 52–53; 139; Lefort 2002: 248.
89. Doonan 2003; Haldon et al. 2014:145–146.
90. See the discussion in chapter 6 of this volume; Lefort 2002: 250–251; Teall 1959: 118, 136; Hendy 1985: 49–50, 52. Grain exporting areas were all within reasonable transport distance of coasts or rivers, due to the high

cost of overland transport as against transport by sea: cf. Braudel 1972: I, 576–579.

91. See Koder 2012 for networks of trade and communication.

92. Duncan-Jones 1982: 35; Morrisson and Cheynet 2002: 836. Detailed discussion of the impact of famine on prices and markets: Stathakopoulos 2004: 35–87.

93. A figure of 1 Roman lb. (11.28 oz. / 327 g) of meat and/or 2–3 Roman lbs. (1.41 lbs. / 654 g to 2.1 lbs. / 981 g) of bread per diem per man given in one document for stationary troops seems to have been standard into the seventh century in Egypt: *P. Oxy.* 2013–4; and Gascou 1989: 290–292. For the Byzantine army: Haldon 1999: 166–167, 287; 2006: 148. Calculations vary according to the reliability of the ancient sources: see Haldon 1999: 281–283 and Foxhall and Forbes 1982. For Roman and Hellenistic figures: Roth 1999: 24; Goldsworthy 1996: 291; Engels 1978: 124.

94. Mayerson 1995. The consumption of bread per soldier per day while on campaign was still assessed at 2 lbs. per head in the European wars of the seventeenth and eighteenth century: Van Creveld 1977: 24, 34; for the Ottoman army in the same period: Aksan 1995: 1–14.

95. *Skirmishing,* 8. 9–14 (trans. Dennis 164).

96. A late Roman papyrus document dealing with military supplies notes that 80 (Roman) lbs. of "dry" bread (i.e., 25.6 kg / 56.3 lbs.) could be baked from 1 *artaba* (87.78 Roman pounds (28.7kg / 63.2 lbs.) of wheat: *P.Oxy.* 1920; Johnson and West 1949: 183. Since premodern milling was less efficient than industrial techniques, the result was a less refined flour, with an average return in flour after grinding of between 75–90 percent on weight of grain: Kent-Jones 1995: Smith 1945. Ancient documents show that 26–27 Roman lbs. of grain would produce between 20 and 24 Roman lbs of flour. In ancient and medieval bread-making, although fine white bread (using only some 75 percent of the product of grinding and milling) was baked for the luxury market, the degree of water absorption was much less, especially in the case of "military bread"—*bucellatum/paximadin* or biscuit—thus, the return on flour per weight of dough produced was lower, varying from 1:1 to 1:1.75, depending on type of grain milled, the degrees of refinement of the milling process, and other variables: Matz 1959; Kent-Jones 1995: 350–352.

97. See esp. Kondov 1974 for detailed discussion; also Jardé 1925/1979; Garnsey 1998; Halstead 1987; Isager and Skygaard 1992. On seed yield ratios, see Spurr 1986; Garnsey 1992: 147–155; 1988: 95–96.

98. Patlagean 1977: 246–248; Kaplan 1992: 80–82.

99. Aymard 1973; Hillman 1973.

100. Karpat 1960.

101. Figures and sources in Haldon 2006c: 144–146.

102. That is, 6,500 metric, or 6, 397.4 long tons (UK), or 7,165 short tons (US).

103. Or 52–53 km^2 (20.5 miles^2).

104. See, for example, *Turkey* II, 1943: 130–131.
105. Cf. the figures in Whittaker 1983: 118 for Roman forces on the Danube.
106. See, e.g., Whittaker 2002: 224–227, 232; Wierschowski 2002: see 291.
107. Decker 2009: 147, 204–227.
108. See Volpe 1996: 265–270; see also Vera 2008.
109. Garnsey 1988: 197; Erdkamp 1998: 283; 2002.
110. See the examples offered in Morizot 2002; Roth 2002; Whittaker 2002.
111. See Erdkamp's comments, 1998: 283, for example.
112. Doonan 2004; 2003.
113. To take but one example, it was market forces encouraged by Venetian government and commercial interests that promoted the immensely wealthy viticulture of fifteenth- and sixteenth-century Crete; it was Venetian government policy that forced changes in this near-monocultural régime before the Ottoman conquest, and it was market forces again that, under Ottoman rule, saw Crete develop an equally lucrative oleoculture: Greene 2000:110–140.

A Conclusion

1. W. S. Churchill, Speech in the Mansion House, London, November 10th 1942.
2. See Brock 1973b: 68–71.
3. Meier 2012: 220–222, 229–236.
4. Chapter 3.
5. Brown 2012b: 528–30; and Chapter 2.
6. See Ibn Hajar 1987: 4, 26 (quoting the Musnad of al-Harith b. Abi Usama). See Bashear 1991: 191.

Glossary

acheiropoiēton Lit., "not made by human hand"; usually of a sacred image.

akribeia Exactitude.

Anatolikon District in central and eastern Anatolia named after the army billeted there; originally that under the *magister militum per Orientem*.

annona Grain supply for Constantinople; Military rations issued from taxation collected in kind; Gr., *synonē*.

annonikos modios A measure of volume: 18.6 pounds or 8.5 kilograms.

anthypatos Proconsul, a high-ranking grade in the palatine hierarchy.

apo hypatōn Ex-consul, also high ranking.

apothēkē A state depository for various goods and materials; in the seventh to ninth centuries, the warehouse, and the district to which it pertained, under the control of a *kommerkiarios*.

archontes Holders of imperial titles or offices.

Armeniakon District in eastern Anatolia/Armenia named after the army billeted there; originally that under the *magister militum per Armeniam*.

artaba An Egyptian measure of volume: 87.78 Roman pounds or 28.7 kilograms / 63.2 pounds.

'atā' Monthly salary drawn by those in the *dīwān*.

Athingani A probably dualist sect in Anatolia, esp. Lycaonia, possibly with origins in India or Iran.

autokratōr Greek equivalent of the Latin *imperator*, emperor, used especially after the seventh century to emphasize the emperor's autonomous and God-granted rule.

Basileus Formal title of the Byzantine emperor from the seventh century.

boulē Town or city council.

Broumalia Month-long winter solstice celebrations beginning on November 24 and lasting until the commencement of the Saturnalia in late December.

chartoularios Clerical official.

chōrepiskopoi   Country bishop.

chrysargyron   Lat., *collatio lustralis*; a tax on commercial exchange, abolished by Anastasius (491–518), possibly reintroduced (in Egypt) under Heraclius (610–641).

civitas   City; Gr. *polis*.

clarissimus   Lowest grade of senatorial rank.

Codex Justinianus   Codification of Roman law produced at the beginning of the reign of Justinian I and the basis for all later Byzantine law.

coemptio   A compulsory purchase of foodstuffs.

coemptum frumenti   Compulsory purchase of grain, but after the later seventh century possibly signifying an obligatory tax.

collatio lustralis   Latin for *chrysargyron*.

comitatenses   Soldiers/units of the field armies under their *magistri militum*, fourth to seventh centuries (cf. *limitanei*).

comites commerciorum   Senior customs officials in the later Roman period, the predecessors of the *kommerkiarioi*.

commerciarii   See *kommerkiarioi*.

commercium   Customs tax.

cubicularius   Imperial chamber attendant; rank in the imperial hierarchy.

curator   Gr., *kouratōr*. Senior manager of an estate, state, private, ecclesiastical or monastic.

curia/curiales   Town council and councilors; governing body of a city.

cursus publicus   Public postal and transport service; until the sixth or seventh century organized into a rapid mail service (*cursus velox*) and a slower transport service (*cursus clabularis*).

Demes   Chariot-racing fan clubs, sometimes acting as foci of political/religious violence or protest.

dēmosios logos   Public, that is, state fisc/treasury.

diocese   Lat. *dioecesa*, Gr., *dioikēsis*; an administrative unit consisting of several provinces; from the fourth century, the episcopal administrative unit of the Church.

dioikētēs   Fiscal administrator responsible for the land tax, usually in a group of provinces from the seventh century.

dīwān   The list of Muslims established in garrison settlements or towns who draw their incomes from the revenues of the conquered territories.

domestikos   Originally a personal assistant, but came to have many meanings, including that of senior military palatine commander.

dromos   Greek term for *cursus publicus*.

drouggarios   Provincial brigade commander of several smaller units.

dux   Senior military commander, especially in the West in the seventh to eighth centuries.

Ecloga   Selections from Roman law, interpreted in the light of its own time and codified as a handbook of Roman law during the reign of Leo III

(717–741). The basic Byzantine law book until the time of the emperor Basil I (867–886).

Ekthesis Imperial notice issued by Heraclius prohibiting discussion of imperial religious policy.

excubitores/exkoubita Small palace bodyguard recruited from Isaurian mountain people by the emperor Leo I. During the seventh century they became a show troop, but the unit was revived as a larger active elite regiment under Constantine V in the 760s as the *exkoubita*.

exōtikoi archontes Military leaders from outside Constantinople; provincial commanders.

fay' Traditional Arabic term for booty, real estate, and other immovables acquired through conquest.

fitna A complex term with many related meanings, used historically to refer to civil strife within the Caliphate. The best known are the so-called first fitna (656–661, Muʿāwiya's war against Ali for supremacy), second fitna (680–692, the succession struggles following Muʿāwiya's death), and third fitna (744–747, a succession struggle within the Marwanid family), although other, later civil conflicts are also referred to as fitna.

follis Low value copper coin worth 40 *nummi*: there were 288 to the gold *solidus* or *nomisma*.

formatae Officially endorsed pass letters confirming an individual's right to travel.

gloriosus Gr., *endoxos*; high-ranking senatorial title introduced by Justinian.

graikos Hellenized form of Lat. *graecus*, used to indicate an Easterner as opposed to someone from Italy or the West.

hexagram Silver coin introduced by Heraclius, lit., "six grams"; twelve to a *nomisma*. Although issued in large quanities under Heraclius and Constans II, its use dwindled until production ceased in the early eighth century.

horreum Granary or storehouse.

hypatos Consul.

idioktēton Property acquired through one's own labor.

illustris Until the middle of the sixth century, the highest grade of senatorial rank.

iussio A command, order, or decree; Gr., *prostagma*.

kastron Fortress, but after the seventh century, also used to mean town or city.

kleisoura Lat., *clisura*; a mountain pass.

kleisourarchēs/kleisourarchia Commander of the force controlling a *kleisoura*; the command of the force or pass.

komēs tou Opsikiou The commander of the Opsikion division, based around Constantinople and in northwest Anatolia.

kommerkiarioi   Fiscal officials responsible for state-supervised commerce and the taxes thereon. During the seventh and eighth centuries had a much expanded role in the fiscal system, probably including aspects of supplying the armies; from the middle of the eighth century, reverted to chiefly commercial functions.

kommerkion/commercium   Customs tax.

koubikoularios.   See *cubicularius.*

kuaistōr   Greek version of the Latin *quaestor*; senior legal official.

limitanei   Provincial garrison troops in the later Roman period.

logothetēs   Fiscal official; lit., accountant; from the seventh century, all the main fiscal bureaus were placed under such officials, who were often very high ranking.

magister militum   Divisional military commander, replaced by the *stratēgos* of the period after ca. 660.

magnificus   High-ranking senatorial grade introduced by Justinian.

mandatōr   Messenger; rank in the palatine hierarchy.

mandylion   The *mandylion* of Edessa, a holy relic consisting of a square or rectangle of cloth upon which a miraculous image of the face of Jesus is imprinted.

miaphysitism/monophysitism   Doctrine of the single nature; Christian tendency rejecting the two natures, both human and divine, of Christ, believing instead that the divine subsumed the human nature after the incarnation. Condemned as heretical at council of Chalcedon in 451, but remained the majority creed in large parts of Syria and Egypt, and of the Syrian and Coptic churches today.

miliarēsion   Lat., *milliarensis*, a silver coin worth one-twelfth of a *solidus/ nomisma*. Originally struck at 72 to the pound, from the seventh to eleventh centuries used of the basic silver coin, struck at varying rates from 144 to 108 to the pound, especially of the reformed silver coin introduced under Leo III.

modios   A measure of both area and volume, differing both regionally and according to function.

monoenergism   Compromise formula adopted by the patriarch Sergius aimed at reconciliation between Miaphysite and Dyophysite communities, by which the issue of the two natures was made secondary to the notion that they were united in a single divine energy. Rejected by all parties within a few years of its being proposed, and condemned as heretical at the sixth ecumenical council in 681.

monotheletism   A second attempt at compromise proposed by Sergius and supported by the emperor Heraclius, by which the key issue was acceptance of the notion of a single divine will, within which natures and energy were subsumed. Imposed during the reign of Constans II, but condemned and rejected at the council of 681.

nakharar   Hereditary title held by members of the Armenian nobility.

naukleroi   Lat., *navicularius*; masters of merchant ships, also maritime contractors to the government or church.

nomisma   Lat., *solidus*; the gold coin introduced by Constantine I which remained the basis for the Byzantine precious metal coinage until the Latin conquest in 1204. Weighing 4.5 grams, it was reckoned at 24 *keratia*, a unit of account (carat), and its fractions were 12 silver *hexagrams* or *milliaresia* and 288 copper *folleis*.

novellae constitutions   New constitutions or laws.

oikonomia   Lit., economy, but generally with the sense of "license."

oikoumenē   The inhabited world, civilized world.

Opsikion   Lat., *Obsequium*; originally an accompanying procession or retinue, from the middle of the seventh century also applied to the imperial field army based in and around Constantinople.

paterfamilias   In Roman law the head of a household with absolute authority.

patricius/patrikios   Patrician, a senior court title awarded to the most important members of the imperial court and administration.

patrimonium   Property and possessions belonging to a household; used of the imperial estates and lands.

paximadin   Lat., *bucellatum*; hard tack issued to soldiers.

peculium castrense   Goods (including cash income, legacies, and booty) acquired by an individual during service as a soldier, and distinct from other income or patrimony. The soldier held such property with no obligation to share it with dependents or other members of his family.

peculium   Property and possessions held by a person as their own exclusive possession.

polis   City; Lat., *civitas*.

politeia   Polity, the state.

praetorian prefecture   The largest administrative unit of the empire from the time of Constantine I, under a praetorian prefect (originally a commander of the praetorian guard). Each prefecture was divided into dioceses and then provinces, and each had its own fiscal administrative and judicial structure.

proskynēsis   Full prostration.

prosphōnētikos logos   Introductory address.

prōtoasēkrētis   Chief private secretary.

prōtospatharios   Senior *spatharios*, or sword bearer. Originally an active post; from the seventh century a palatine grade.

quaestor   Senior legal official.

res privata   Imperial treasury, originating in emperor's private finances. Subsumed during the seventh century into the department of imperial estates.

rhogai   Salary or wages paid to soldiers or state official.

sa'ifa   The annual summer campaign from Syria against Byzantine lands.

sacrae largitiones (sacred largesses)   Government fiscal department originating in the imperial household, responsible for bullion and coinage until the seventh century.

sakellarios/sacellarius   Senior fiscal officer with oversight over other fiscal departments after the seventh century. Originally in charge of emperor's personal treasury or purse (*sacellum/sakellion*).

scamares   Rebels or bandits in the Balkan region during the fifth and sixth centuries.

scholae   In the period from Constantine I until the later fifth century, a crack cavalry unit; by the later fifth century, a show force. The units were reformed and became once more elite regiments under Constantine V, forming until the eleventh century the core of the imperial field armies.

semissis   Half of a *solidus* or *nomisma*.

sigillia kai sphragides   Official seals and stamps.

sitōnikon   A department dealing with grain provision.

spatharios   Sword bearer, a palatine rank from the sixth and seventh centuries.

spectabilis   Second-rank senatorial grade.

stratēgos   A general; usually the governor of a provincial military force.

synōnē   Lat. *coemptio*, from the later seventh century applied to an annual tax in grain.

territorium   The territory under the jurisdiction of a city.

thema   A fiscal term describing the arrangements for supporting provincial soldiers from the early ninth century; the territory of the army thus supported.

Thrakēsion   The army of the *magister militum per Thracias*, and the territory occupied by that army in western Anatolia from the 640s.

tourmarchēs   A provincial military commander in charge of two or more brigades.

Typos   Document issued by Constans II in 648 prohibiting further discussion of the doctrine of the single will.

vicarius   Originally an assistant or second-in-command; later a senior officer with civil or military authority.

vota   Pagan offerings or dedications to a god or gods; Lat., *votum*, pl. *vota*.

Bibliography

Sources

Agathon diaconus, in: *ACO* II, 2, 898–901.

Al-Balādhurī, Kitāb futūḥ al-Buldān: The Origins of the Islamic State, trans. P. K. Hitti (London 1916; repr. Beirut 1966).

Allen P. and B. Neil 1999: *Scripta saeculi VII vitam Maximi Confessoris illustrantia,* ed. P. Allen and B. Neil (Corpus christianorum. Series Graeca 39. Turnhout-Leuven 1999).

Anast. Apocr., *ep. ad Theod.* = *Anastasii Apocrisiarii epistola ad Theodosium Gangrensem,* in Allen and Neil 1999: 171–189; trans. Allen and Neil 2002: 132–147.

Anast. Mon., *ep. ad mon. Caral.* = *Anastasii Monachi epistola ad monachos Calaritanos,* in Allen and Neil 1999: 165–169; trans. Allen and Neil 2002: 124–131.

Anastasii Sinaitae adversus iudaeos disputatio, in *PG* 89: 1203–1272.

Anastasii Sinaitae oratio de sacra synaxi, in *PG* 89: 825A–849C.

Anastasii Sinaitae Quaestiones et Responsiones, ed. M. Richard & J. Munitiz (*CCSG* 59, Turnhout, 2006); J. A. Munitiz, *Anastasios of Sinai, Questions and Answers: Introduction, Translations and Notes* (Turnhout 2011).

Anastasii Sinaitae Sermo iii adversus Monotheletas, in K.-H. Uthemann, ed., *Anastasius Sinaites, Sermones duo in constitutionem hominis secundum imaginem Dei necnon opuscula adversus Monotheletas* (*CCSG* 12, Turnhout 1985).

Anastasii Sinaitae synopsis de haeresibus et synodis, in K.-H. Uthemann, "Die dem Anastasios Sinaites zugeschriebene Synopsis de haeresibus et synodis. Einführung und Edition," *Annuarium Historiae Conciliorum* 14 (1982), 58–94.

Andrew of Crete, *Homilies,* in *PG* 97, 806–1302.

Chron. Pasch. Chronicon Paschale, ed. L. Dindorf (*CSHB,* Bonn 1832); Eng. trans. M. and M. Whitby, *Chronicon Paschale 284–628 AD* (Liverpool 1989).

Chronicon Maroniticum, ed. E. W. Brooks, tr. J. B. Chabot, in *CSCO Sciptores Syri,* ser. 3, t. 4, *Chronica minora* pars ii, 3, 35–57.

Codex Justinianus, ed. P. Krüger, in *CJC* ii (Berlin, [13]1963).

Continuationes Isidorianae Byzantina Arabica et Hispana, in *MGH* (AA) xi, 2, 334–368.

DAI Constantine Porphyrogenitus, *De Administrando Imperio*, I: Greek text ed. Gy. Moravcsik, Eng. trans. R. J. H. Jenkins. New rev. ed. (*CFHB* 1 = DOT 1, Washington, DC, 1967); II: Commentary, ed. R. J. H. Jenkins (London, 1962).

De Cer. Constantini Porphyrogeniti imperatoris *De cerimoniis aulae byzantinae libri duo*, ed. J. J. Reiske (*CSHB*, Bonn 1829); Engl. trans.: A. Moffatt and M. Tall, *Constantine Porphyrogenius: The Book of Ceremonies* (Byzantina Australiensia 18/1–2. Canberra 2012).

Disp. Biz. = *Disputatio inter Maximum et Theodosium*, in Allen and Neil 1999: 53–151; trans. Allen and Neil 2002: 75–119.

Disputatio cum Pyrrho, in *PG* 91: 287–353.

Ekloga Ecloga. *Das Gesetzbuch Leons III. und Konstantinos' V.*, ed L. Burgmann (Forschungen zur byzantinischen Rechtsgeschichte X, Frankfurt a. M. 1983).

Eliae Metropolitae Nisibeni opus chronologicum, i, ed. E. W. Brooks, in *CSCO Scriptores Syri*, ser. 3, t.7; ii, ed. J. B. Chabot, in *CSCO Scriptores Syri*, ser. 3, t.8.

Eustratii presbyteri Constantinipolitani, De statu animarum post mortem, ed. P. Van Deun (*CCSG* 60, Turnhout 2006).

Fredegarius . . . Chronicarum libri IV, ed. B. Krusch, in *MGH (SRM 2)* (1888); Engl. trans., J.-M. Wallace-Hadrill, *The Fourth Book of the Chronicle of Fredegar, with Its Continuations* (London and New York 1960).

Germanus, *De synodis et haeresibus* in *PG* 98: 39–88, originally edited by A. Mai in *Spicilegium Romanum*, 10 vols. (Rome 1839–1844), 7:3–73.

Germanus, *Homilia de acathisto vel de dormitione*, ed. V. Grumel, "Homélie de S. Germain sur la délivrance de Constantinople," *REB* 16 (1958), 183–205.

Gesta in Primo eius Exsilio, in *PG* 90: 135–172 (*BHG* 1233).

Gregory of Nyssa, "First Homily on the Forty Martyrs of Sebaste," in J. Leemans, W. Mayer, P. Allen, and B. Demandschutter, eds., *"Let us die that we may live": Greek Homilies on Christian Martyrs from Asia Minor, Palestine and Syria c. 350–450 AD* (London 2003): 67–75.

Hypomnesticon Theodori Spudaei Hypomnesticon, in Allen and Neil 1999, 191–227; trans. Allen and Neil 2002, 148–174.

I. and P. Zepos, eds., *Jus Graecoromanum*, 8 vols. (Athens 1931; repr. Aalen 1962).

Ibn Hajar, *al-Matālib al-Āliya fī Zawa'id al-Masānīd al-Thamāniya* (Beirut 1987).

Ignatius diac., *Ep.* C. Mango, *The Correspondence of Ignatios the Deacon: Text, Translation and Commentary* (with collaboration of St. Efthymiadis) (*CFHB*, ser. Washington 39, Washington, DC, 1997).

Isaac of Nicomedia D. Stiernon, "La vision d'Isaïe de Nicomédie," *REB* 35 (1977), 5–42.

John Lydus, *De mag.* R. Wuensch, ed., *De magistratibus populi Romani libri tres* (Leipzig 1903); Eng. trans. by A. C. Bandy, A. Bandy, D. J. Constanteolos, and C. J. N. de Paulo, *On Powers, or the Magistracies of the Roman State (De magistratibus reipublicae romanae)* (Lewiston 2013).

John of Damascus, *Contra Imaginum calumniatores orationes tres,* in B. Kotter, ed., *Die Schriften des Johannes von Damaskos* III (Berlin, 1975); *PG* 94, 1232–1420; Engl. trans., D. Anderson, *On the Divine Images: Three Apologies against Those Who Attack the Holy Images* (Crestwood 1980).

John of Damascus, *Fount of Knowledge* pt. 2: *De haeresibus,* in B. Kotter, *Die Schriften des Johannes von Damaskos* (Patristische Texte und Studien, Berlin 1973), 2:7–239; *PG* 94, 677–780. Engl. trans., F. H. Chase Jr., trans., *St John of Damascus, Writings (The Font of Knowledge, etc.)* (Fathers of the Church 37, New York, 1958).

John of Nikiû *The Chronicle of John, Bishop of Nikiû,* ed. with Engl. trans. R. H. Charles (London 1916); *La Chronique de Jean de Nikioû,* ed. with Fr. trans. H. Zotenberg *Notices et Extraits des manuscrits de la Bibliothèque Nationale,* XXIV, I (Paris 1883), 125–605.

Just., *Nov.* *Novellae constitutiones,* in *CJC* III.

Lateran council ed. Riedinger, in *ACO* II, 1; Eng. trans. in Price, Booth, and Cubitt 2014.

Leo diac. *Leonis diaconi Caloensis Historiae libri decem,* ed. C. B. Hase (*CSHB,* Bonn 1828); Engl. trans. A.-M. Talbot and D. Sullivan, *The History of Leo the Deacon: Byzantine Military Expansion in the Tenth Century* (Washington, DC, 2005).

Leo, *Takt.* G. Dennis, ed. and trans., *The Taktika of Leo VI. Text, translation and commentary* (*CFHB* 49 = DOT 12, Washington, DC, 2010).

Mauropous, *Letters* ed. A. Karpozilos, *The Letters of Ioannes Mauropous Metropolitan of Euchaita* (*CFHB* 34, Thessalonica 1990).

Maximi Confessoris ep. ad Anast. = *Maximi epistula ad Anastasium monachum discipulum,* in Allen and Neil 1999: 153–163; trans. Allen and Neil 2002: 120–123.

Maximi Confessoris Epistolae, in *PG* 91: 364–649.

Maximi Confessoris relatio motionis, in Allen and Neil 1999: 1–51; trans. Allen and Neil 2002: 48–74.

Mich. Syr., *Chron.* *La Chronique de Michel le Syrien, Patriarche Jacobite d'Antioche,* ed. et trad. J. B. Chabot, 4 vols. (Paris 1899, 1901, 1905, 1924).

Miracula Cosmae et Damiani E. Rupprecht, *Cosmae et Damiani sanctorum medicorum vita et miracula* (Berlin 1935) (*BHG,* nos. 372ff.).

Miracula S. Artemii in Papadopoulos-Kerameus, ed., *Varia Graeca sacra* (St. Petersburg 1909), 1–75 (*BHG,* no. 173); Eng. trans. in J. Nesbitt and V. Crisafulli 1997), 76–224.

Miracula S. Demetrii in P. Lemerle, *Les plus anciens recueils des miracles de S. Démétrius et de la pénétration des Slaves dans les Balkans* I: *le texte* (Paris, 1979), 45–241 (*BHG,* nos. 497ff.).

Miracula S. Theodori tironis in H. Delehaye, ed., *Les légendes grecques des saints militaires* (Paris, 1909), 183–201 (*BHG,* 1764).

Miracula S. Therapontis   in L. Deubner, *De Incubatione capita quattuor* (Leipzig, 1900) 120–134 (*BHG*, 1798).

Miracula Sophronii   in N. Fernandez Marcos, *Los thaumata di Sofronio, contribucion al estudio de la "incubatio" Cristiana* (Madrid 1975) (*BHG*, nos. 477–479).

Nikeph.   *Nicephorus, Patriarch of Constantinople. Short History.* Text, trans. and commentary by C. Mango (*CFHB*, ser. Washingtoniensis 13 = DOT 10. Washington, DC, 1990).

Nomos georgikos   W. Ashburner, "The Farmers' Law," *JHS* 30 (1910) 85–108; 32 (1912) 68–95 (repr. in Zepos 1931, II: 63–71).

The Oxyrhynchus Papyri, ed. B. P.Grenfell, A. S. Hunt et al. (London 1898–1916).

Palmer, A., *The Seventh Century in the West-Syrian Chronicles* (Liverpool 1993).

Paulinus, *Eucharisticus*   in H. G. Evelyn White, ed. and trans., *Ausonius* (Cambridge MA 1921), ii: 295–351.

(Ps.-) Methodios (Gr./Lat.) W. J. Aerts and G. A. A. Kortekaas, eds., *Die Apokalypse des Pseudo-Methodius. Die ältesten griechischen und lateinischen Übersetzungen* I–II (*CSCO* 569–570. Subsidia 97–98. Louvain 1998); trans. in B. Garstad, *Apocalypse. Pseudo-Methodius; an Alexandrian world chronicle* (Dumbarton Oaks Medieval Library 14, Cambridge, MA, 2012), 1–71.

(Ps.-) Methodios (Syr.)   G. Reinink, *Die syrische Apokalypse des Ps.-Methodius* (*CSCO* 540, 541. Scriptores Syri 220, 221) (Louvain, 1993).

Qudāma b. Ja'far   *Abū'l-Faraj al-Kātib al-Baghdādī Kudāma ibn Ja'far, Kitāb al-Harāj,* in: M.-J. De Goeje, ed. and Fr. trans., *Bibliotheca Geographorum Araborum* (Leiden 1870ff./rev. ed. R. Blachère, Leiden 1938ff.), 196–9.

S. Martini papae (Encyclical letter)   *ACO* II, 1: 404.2–420.10.

S. Martini papae epistolae   Mansi, x, 682–853.

S. Sophronii . . .epistola synodica ad Sergium patr. CP, in *ACO* II. 2, 410. 13–494.9.

Sebeos   J. D. Howard-Johnston and F. Thomson, *The Armenian History Attributed to Sebeos,* 2 vols. (Liverpool, 1999).

Sidonius Apollinaris, *Ep.   Sidonius. Poems, Letters 1–2,* trans. W. B. Anderson (Cambridge, MA, 1936).

Skirmishing   ed. G. Dagron, H. Mihaescu, in *Le traité sur la Guérilla (De velitatione) de l'empereur Nicéphore Phocas (963–969).* Texte établi par Gilbert Dagron et Haralambie Mihaescu, trad. et comm. par G. Dagron (Paris 1986); also ed. and trans. G. T. Dennis, in *Three Byzantine Military Treatises: Text, Translation and Notes* (*CFHB* 25 = DOT 9, Washington, DC, 1985), 137–239.

Skylitzes   *Ioannis Scylitzae synopsis historiarum,* ed. J. Thurn (*CFHB* 5, Berlin and New York 1973).

Strabo, *Geography   The Geography of Strabo,* trans. H. L. Jones (Loeb Classical Library, London and New York, 1928), 8 vols.

Theod. Spudaeus, *Narrationes de exilio sancti papae Matini,* ed. and trans. Brown Neil, *Seventh-Century Popes and Martyrs: The Political Hagiography of Anastasius Bibliothecarius* (Turnhout 2006).

Theod. Stud., *Ep.* ed. A. Fatouros, *Theodori Studitae Epistulae,* 2 vols. (*CFHB* 31, no. 1–2, Vienna, 1992).

Theodorus Scutariotes, *Synopsis Chronikê,* in C. N. Sathas, ed. *Bibliotheca Graeca Medii aevi,* vol. 7 (Venedig and Paris 1894; repr. Hildesheim and New York 1972).

Theoph. Sim., *Historia Theophylacti Simocattae Historia,* ed. C. de Boor (Leipzig, 1887; rev. and emend. ed., P. Wirth, Stuttgart, 1972); Eng. trans. M. and M. Whitby, *The History of Theophylact Simocatta* (Oxford, 1986).

Theoph. *Theophanis Chronographia,* ed. C. de Boor, 2 vols. (Leipzig, 1883, 1885); Engl. trans. *The Chronicle of Theophanes Confessor,* trans. C. Mango and R. Scott (Oxford, 1997).

Theophilus of Edessa, *Chronicle* R. G. Hoyland, *Theophilus of Edessa's Chronicle and the Circulation of Historical Knowledge in Late Antiquity and Early Islam* (Liverpool, 2011).

Trullo (Quinisext council) G. Nednungatt and M. Featherstone, "The Canons of the Council in Trullo," in *The Council in Trullo Revisited* (*Kanonika* 6, Rome 1995): 41–186 (repr. of the text of P.-P. Joannou, *Les canons des conciles oecuméniques* [Discipline génerale antique I, 1. Grottaferrata 1962], 101–241, with English translation).

Vegetius, *Epitoma rei militaris,* ed. M. D. Reeve (Oxford, 2004); Engl. trans. N. P. Milner, Vegetius, *Epitome of Military Science* (Liverpool, 1993).

Vita Andreae Cretensis ed. A. Papadopoulos-Kerameus, in *Analekta* v, 169–180, 422–444.

Vita Antonii Iunioris, ed. A. Papadopoulos-Kerameus, in *Pravoslav. Palestinskij Sbornik* 19/3 (57) (St. Petersburg 1907) 186–216; suppl. F. Halkin, in *AB* 62 (1944) 187–225 (*BHG* 142).

Vita Athanasiae Aeginae ed. F. Halkin, "Vie de sainte Athanasie d'Égine," in F. Halkin, *Six inédits d'hagiologie byzantine* (Subsid, Hag. 74. Brussels 1987), 179–195; Eng. trans. L. Sherry, "St. Athanasia of Aegina," in Talbot 1996, 137–158.

Vita et Miracula Theodori (tironis), in H. Delehaye, *Les légendes grecques des saints militaires* (Paris 1909), 183–201 (*BHG* 1764).

Vita Gregorii Agrigentini ed. A. Berger, *Leontios presbyteros von Rom, Das Leben des Heiligen Gregorios von Agrigent. Kritische Ausgabe, Übersetzung und Kommentar,* ed. A. Berger (BBA 60, Berlin, 1994) (BHG 707) older ed., *Vita Gregorii Agrigentini,* in *PG* 98, 549–716.

Vita Gregorii Decapolitae ed. F. Dvornik, *La vie de St. Grégoire le Décapolite et les Sl;aves macédoniens au IXe siècle* (Paris 1926).

Vita Martini P. Peeters, "Une vie grecque du pape S. Martin I," *AB* 51 (1933) 225–262 (*BHG* 2259).

Vita Maximi confessoris, in *PG* 90, 68–109 (*BHG* 1234).

Vita Mich. Maleini   L. Petit, "Vie de S. Michel Maleinos," *Revue de l'Orient Chrétien* 7 (1902): 543–603.

Vita Nicolai Sionitae, in I. Sevcenko and N. P. Sevcenko, trans., *The Life of St. Nicholas of Sion* (Brookline 1984).

Vita Philareti   ed. M.-H.Fourmy and M.Leroy, "La vie de S.Philarète," *Byzantion* 9 (1934), 85–170 (*BHG* 1511z); L. Rydén, *The Life of St Philaretos the Merciful Written by His Grandson Niketas: A Critical Edition with Introduction, Translation, Notes and Indices* (Acta Universitatis Upsaliensis. Studia Byzantina Upsaliensia 8. Uppsala 2002).

Vita S. Ioannicii   in *AS,* Nov. II/1 (Vita a Petro), 384–434; trans. D. Sullivan in Talbot 1998, 243–351.

Vita Syr. Max. conf. in S. Brock, "An Early Syriac Life of Maximos the Confessor," *AB* 91 (1973), 299–346, at 302–319.

Vita Theod. Syk.   *Vie de Théodore de Sykéon,* ed. et trad. A. Festugière, 2 vols. (Subsid. Hag. 48, Brussels 1970) (cf. BHG 1748); Eng. trans. E. Dawes and N. H. Baynes, *Three Byzantine Saints: Contemporary Biographies of St. Daniel the Stylite, St. Theodore of Sykeon and St. John the Almsgiver* (Oxford, 1948), 87–192.

Literature

Abrahamse, D. 1967. *Hagiographic Sources for Byzantine Cities 500–900 AD* (Ann Arbor).

———. 1982. "Magic and sorcery in hagiography of the middle Byzantine period." *BF* 8: 3–17.

Ahrweiler, H. 1960. "Recherches sur l'dministration byzantine aux IXe–XIe siècles." *Bulletin de Correspondance Hellenique* 84: 1–111.

———. 1962. "L'Asie Mineure et les invasions arabes." *Revue Historique* 227: 1–32.

Akçer Ön, S. 2011. "Late Holocene Climatic Records of Küçükçekmece Lagoon, Yeniçağa, Uludağ Glacial and Bafa Lakes (Western Turkey)." Diss., Istanbul Technical University / Eurasia Institute of Earth Sciences (Istanbul).

Aksan, V. 1995. "Feeding the Ottoman troops on the Danube, 1768–1774." *War and Society* 13, no. 1: 1–14.

Alcock, S. E., T. N. D'Altroy, K. D. Morrison, and C. M. Sinopoli, eds., *Empires* (Cambridge).

Alexander, P. 1962. "The strength of empire and capital as seen through Byzantine eyes." *Speculum* 37: 339–357.

Allen, P. 2009. *Sophronius of Jerusalem and Seventh-Century Heresy: The Synodical Letter and Other Documents* (Oxford).

———. 2011. "Portrayals of Mary in Greek Homiletic Literature (6th–7th Centuries)," in Brubaker and Cunningham 2011: 69–88.

Allen, P., and B. Neil. 2002. *Maximus the Confessor and His Companions: Documents from Exile* (Oxford 2002).

———, eds. 2015. *The Oxford Handbook of Maximus the Confessor* (Oxford).

Alley, R. B., J. Marotzke, W. D. Nordhaus, J. T. Overpeck, D. M. Peteet, R. A. Pielke Jr., R. T. Pierrehumbert, P. B. Rhines, T. F. Stocker, L. D. Talley, and J. M. Wallace. 2003. "Abrupt climatic change." *Science* 299: 2005–2010.

Amari, M. 1933–1939. *Storia dei musulmani di Sicilia. Seconda edizione modificata e accresciuta dall'autore. Pubblicata con note a cura di Carlo Alfonso Nallino,* 3 vols. (Catania).

Anagnostakes, E. 2001. "Περιούσιος λαός," in E. Kountoura-Galake, ed., *The Dark Centuries of Byzantium* (Athens), 325–345.

Ando, C. 2000. *Imperial Ideology and Provincial Loyalty in the Roman Empire* (Berkeley, Los Angeles, and London).

Angelov, D. and M. Saxby, eds. 2013. *Power and Subversion in Byzantium* (Farnham).

Antoniadis-Bibicou, H. 1966. *Études d'histoire maritime à Byzance, à propos du Thème des Caravisiens* (Bibliothèque Générale de l'École Pratique des Hautes Études, VIe section. Paris).

Argant, J. 2003. "Données palynologiques," in B. Geyer and J. Lefort, eds., *La Bithynie au moyen âge* (*Réalités byzantines* 9, Paris), 175–200.

Argyriou, A. 2005. "Perception de l'Islam et traductions du Coran dans le monde byzantin grec," *B* 75: 25–69.

Arikan, R. 1983. "Agricultural statistics and data administration in Turkey." *Agricultural Administration* 14, no. 2: 95–103.

Arnason, J. P. 2010. "Byzantium and Historical Sociology," in P. Stephenson, ed., *The Byzantine World* (London and New York), 491–504.

Arsac, P. 1969. "La dignité sénatoriale au Bas-Empire." *Revue historique de droit français et étranger* 47: 198–243.

Arthur, A. 2006. "Economic Expansion in Byzantine Apulia," in Jacob et al. 2006, 389–405.

Artun, T. 2008. "The Miracles of St. Theodore Tērōn: An eighth-century source?" *JöB* 5: 1–11.

Auzépy, M.-F. 1995a. "La carrière d'André de Crète." *BZ* 88: 1–12.

———. 1995b. "L'évolution de l'attitude face au miracle à Byzance (VIIe–IXe siècle)," in *Miracles, prodiges et merveilles au Moyen Age* (Paris), 31–46.

———. 2008. "State of Emergency (700–850)," in Shepard, ed. 2008, 251–291.

Aymard, M. 1973. "Rendements et productivité agricole dans l'Italie moderne." *Annales. Économies, Sociétés, Civilisations* 28: 456–492.

Baillie, M. G. L. 2010. "Volcanoes, ice-cores and tree-rings: One story or two?" *Antiquity* 84: 202–215.

Baird, D. 2004. "Settlement Expansion on the Konya Plain, Anatolia: 5th–7th Centuries AD," in Bowden, Lavan, and Machado 2004, 219–246.

Bakker, J., E. Paulissen, D. Kaniewski, J. Poblome, V. De Laet, G. Verstraeten, and M. Waelkens. 2013. "Climate, people, fire and vegetation: new insights into vegetation dynamics in the Eastern Mediterranean since the 1st century AD." *Climate of the Past* 9: 57–87.

Bakker, J., D. Kaniewski, G. Verstraeten, V. De Laet, and M. Waelkens. 2012. "Numerically derived evidence for late-Holocene climate change and its impact on human presence in the southwest Taurus Mountains, Turkey." *Holocene* 22: 425–438.

Bang, P. F. 2003. "Rome and the comparative study of tributary empires." *Medieval History Journal* 6, no. 2: 189–216.

Bang, P. F., and C. Bayly. 2003. "Introduction: Comparing pre-modern empires," *Medieval History Journal* 6, no. 2: 169–187.

Bang, P. F., and W. Scheidel, eds. 2013. *The Oxford Handbook of the Ancient State in the Ancient Near East and the Mediterranean* (Oxford).

Barnes, T. D. 1981. *Constantine and Eusebius* (Cambridge, MA, and London), 245–60.

Barnish, S., A. D. Lee, and M. Whitby. 2000. "Government and Administration," in Cameron et al. 2000, 164–206.

Bartikian, H. 1986. "Ἡ λύση τοῦ αἰνίγματος τῶν Μαρδαϊτῶν," in *Byzantion, Tribute to Andreas N. Stratos* I (Athens), 17–39.

Bashear, S. 1991. "Apocalyptic and other materials on early Muslim-Byzantine wars: A review of Arabic sources." *Journal of the Royal Asiatic Siciety,* 3rd ser., 1: 173–207 (repr. in M. Bonner, ed., *Arab-Byzantine Relations in Early Islamic Times* [Aldershot 2004], 181–207).

Bates, M. 1971. "Constans II or Heraclonas? An analysis of the Constantinopolitan folles of Constans II." *American Numismatic Society Museum Notes* 17: 141–161.

———. 1986. "History, geography and numismatics in the first century of Islamic coins." *Revue Suisse de Numismatique* 65: 231–262.

Baynes, N. H. 1955. "Eusebius and the Christian Empire," in N. H. Baynes, *Byzantine Studies and other Eassays* (London): 168–72.

Beaucamp, J. 1990–1992. *Le statut de la femme (4e–7e siècle).* 2 vols. (Paris).

———. 2000. "Exclues et aliénées: Les femmes dans la tradition canonique byzantine," in D. C. Smythe, ed., *The Byzantine Outsider* (Aldershot), 87–103.

Beck, H.-G. 1959. *Kirche und theologische Literatur im byzantinischen Reich* (Handbuch der Altertumswissenschaft xii, 2.1 = Byzantinisches Handbuch 2.1, Munich).

———. 1965. "Konstantinopel. Zur Sozialgeschichte einer frühmittelalterlichen Hauptstadt." *BZ* 58: 11–45.

———. 1966. *Senat und Volk von Konstantinopel. Probleme der byzantinischen Verfassungsgeschichte,* Sitzungsber. d. Bayer. Akad. d. Wiss., phil.-hist. Kl., Heft 6 (repr. in H.-G. Beck, *Ideen und realitäten in Byzanz* [London 1972], XII).

————. 1974. *Theorie und Praxis im Aufbau der byzantinischen Zentralverwaltung.* Sitzungsberichte der Bayerischen Akademie der Wissenschaften, philosophisch-historische Klasse, Heft 8.

Beer, J. 2000. "Long-term indirect indices of solar variability." *Space Science Reviews* 94: 53–66.

Beer, J., Vonmoos, M. and R. Muscheler. 2006. "Solar variability over the past several millennia." *Space Science Reviews* 125: 67–79.

Ben Slimène Ben Abbès, H. 2013. "La production de la monnaie d'or en Afrique byzantine au VIIe siècle," in J. Gonzalez et al., eds., *Africa Romana XVII* (Rome), ii, 1151–64.

Berger, P. L., and Th. Luckmann. 1966. *The Social Construction of Reality* (New York).

Bertolini, O. 1958. "Riflessi politici nelle controversie religiose con Bisanzio nelle vicende del sec. VII in Italia," in *Caratteri del secolo VII in occidente* (Settimane di studio del centro italiano sull'alto medioevo, XX. Spoleto), 733–810.

Bjornlie, M. S. 2013. *Politics and Tradition Between Rome, Ravenna and Constantinople: A Study of Cassiodorus and the Variae 527–554* (Cambridge, MA, and New York).

Blankinship, K. Y. 1994. *The End of the Jihād State: The Reign of Hishām B. ʿAbd Al-Malik and the Collapse of the Umayyads* (Albany).

Boesch-Gajano, S. 1991. "Uso e abuso del miraculo nella cultura altomedievale," in *Les fonctions des saints dans le monde occidental (IIIe–XIIIe siècle)* (Collection de l"école française de Rome, 149, Rome), 109–122.

Bond, G., B. Kromer, J. Beer, R. Muscheler, M. Evans, W. Showers, S. Hoffman, R. Lotti-Bond, I. Hajdas, and G. Bonani. 2001. "Persistent solar influence on North Atlantic surface circulation during the Holocene." *Science* 294: 2130–2136.

Bonnell, V. E. 1988. "The uses of theory, concepts and comparison in historical sociology." *Comparative Studies in Society and History* 22: 156–173.

Bonner, M. 1996. *Aristocratic Violence and Holy War: Studies in the Jihad and the Arab-Byzantine Frontier* (New Haven).

————, ed. 2005. *Arab-Byzantine Relations in Early Islamic Times* (The Formation of the Classical Islamic World 8, Aldershot).

Booth, P. 2014. *Crisis of Empire: Doctrine and Dissent at the End of Late Antiquity* (Berkeley, Los Angeles, and London).

Bosworth, C. E. 1996. "Byzantium and the Syrian Frontier in the Early Abbasid Period," in C. E. Bosworth, *The Arabs, Byzantium and Iran: Studies in Early Islamic History and Culture* (Aldershot): XII.

Bottema, S. 1979. "Pollen analytical investigations in Thessaly, Greece." *Palaeohistory* 21: 19–40.

Bottema, S., and H. Woldring. 1990. "Anthropogenic Indicators in the Pollen Record of the Eastern Mediterranean," in S. Bottema, G. Entjes-Nieborg and W. Van Zeist, eds., *Man's Role in the Shaping of the Eastern Mediterranean Landscape* (Rotterdam), 231–264.

Bottema, S., H. Woldring, and B. Aytuğ. 1986. "Palynological Investigations on the Relations Between Prehistoric Man and Vegetation in Turkey: the Beyşehir Occupation Phase," in *Proceedings of the 5th Optima Congress, September 1986* (Istanbul), 315–328.

———. 1993. "Late Quaternary Vegetation History of Northern Turkey," *Palaeohistoria* 35–36: 13–7.

Boudignon, C. 2007. "Le pouvoir de l'anathème, ou Maxime le Confesseur et les moines palestiniens du VII⁄ siècle," in A. Camplani and G. Filoramo, eds., *Foundations of Power and Conflicts of Authority in Late-Antique Monasticism* (Leuven), 245–277.

Bowden, W., A. Gutteridge, and C. Machado, eds., 2006. *Social and Political Life in Late Antiquity* (Leiden and Boston).

Bowden, W., L. Lavan, and C. Machado, eds. 2004. *Recent Research on the Late Antique Countryside* (Leiden and Boston).

Brandes, W. 1989. *Die Städte Kleinasiens im 7. und 8. Jahrhundert* (BBA 56, Berlin).

———. 1990. "Die apokalyptische Literatur," in F. Winkelmann, W. Brandes, eds., *Quellen zur Geschichte des frühen Byzanz (4.–9. Jahrhundert). Bestand und Probleme* (BBA 55, Berlin), 305–322.

———. 1991. "Endzeitvorstellungen und Lebenstrost in mittelbyzantinischer Zeit (7.–9. Jahrhundert)," in *Poikila Byzantina* 11. *Varia* 3 (Berlin), 9–62.

———. 1997. "Anastasios *ho dikoros:* Endzeiterwartung und Kaiserkritik in Byzanz um 500." *BZ* 90: 24–63.

———. 1998a. "Die melkitischen Patriarchen von Antiocheia im 7. Jahrhundert. Anzahl und Chronoplogie." *Le Muséon* 111: 37–57.

———. 1998b. "Juristische Krisenbewältigung im 7. Jahrhundert? Die Prozesse gegen Papst Martin I. und Maximos Homologetes." *Fontes Minores* 10: 141–212.

———. 1999. "Byzantine Towns in the Seventh and Eighth Century—Different Sources, Different Histories?," in G. P. Brogiolo and B. Ward-Perkins, eds., *The Idea and Ideal of the Town between Late Antiquity and the Early Middle Ages* (Leiden), 25–57.

———. 2001a. " Konstantin der Große in den monotheletischen Streitigkeiten des 7. Jahrhunderts," in E. Kountoura-Galaki, ed., *The Dark Centuries of Byzantium* (Athens), 80–107.

———. 2001b. "Philippos ὁ στρατηγὸς τοῦ βασιλικοῦ Ὀψικίου. Anmerkungen zur Frühgeschichte des Thema Opsikion," in C. Sode and S. Takács, eds., *Novum Millennium: Studies on Byzantine History and Culture Dedicated to Paul Speck. 19 December 1999* (Aldershot), 21–39.

———. 2002a. *Finanzverwaltung in Krisenzeiten. Untersuchungen zur byzantinischen Administration im 6.–9. Jahrhundert* (Frankfurt am Main).

———. 2002b. "Heraclius Between Restoration and Reform: Some Remarks on Recent Research," in G. J. Reinink and B. H. Stolte, eds., *The Reign of Heraclius (610–641): Crisis and Confrontation* (Leuven), 17–40.

———. 2003. "Orthodoxy and Heresy in the Seventh Century: Prosopographical Observations on Monotheletism," in Av. Cameron, ed., *Fifty Years of Prosopography: The Later Roman Empire and Beyond* (Proceedings of the British Academy 118, Oxford), 103–118.

———. 2005. "Georgios ἀπὸ ὑπάτων und die Kommerkiariersiegel," in Ludwig 2005, 31–47.

———. 2007. "Die Belagerung Konstantinopels 717/718 als apokalytpisches Ereignis. Zu einer Interpolation im griechischen Text der Pseudo-Methodios-Apokalypse," in K. Belke, E. Kislinger, A. Külzer, and M. Stassinopoulou, eds., *Byzantina Mediterranea: Festschrift fü Johannes Koder zum 65. Geburtstag* (Vienna), 65–91.

———. 2009. "Der frühe Islam in der byzantinischen Historiographie. Anmerkungen zur Quellenproblematik der *Chronographia* des Theophanes," in A. Goltz, H. Leppin, and H. Schlange-Schöningen, eds., *Jenseits der Grenze. Beiträge zur spätantiken und frühmittelalterlichen Geschichtsschreibung* (Berlin and New York), 313–343.

———. 2013. "Taufe und soziale/politische Inklusion und Exklusion in Byzanz." *Rechtsgeschichte/Legal History* 21: 75–88.

———. 2014. "Damnatio für die Ewigkeit—zur Entwicklung der Anathematismen auf Konzilien des 7. Jahrhunderts," in S. Scholz, G. Schwedler and K.-M. Sprenger, eds., *Damnatio in memoria. Deformation und Gegenkonstruktionen in der Geschichte* (Köln-Weimer-Wien), 265–277.

Brandes, W., and J. F. Haldon. 2000. "Towns, Tax and Transformation: State, Cities and Their Hinterlands in the East Roman World, ca. 500–800," in N. Gauthier, ed., *Towns and Their Hinterlands between Late Antiquity and the Early Middle Ages* (Leiden), 141–172.

Braudel, F. 1972–1973. *The Mediterranean and the Mediterranean World in the Age of Philip II,* 2 vols. (New York).

Brett, M. 1978. "The Arab Conquest and the Rise of Islam in N. Africa," in *Cambridge History of Africa,* 2 (Cambridge), 490–555.

Brock, S. P. 1973a. "An early Syriac life of Maximus the Confessor," in *AB* 91: 299–346, 323–324.

———. 1973b. "A Syriac fragment on the sixth council." *Oriens Christianus* 57: 63–71.

———. 1982. "Syriac Views of Emergent Islam," in G. H. A. Juynboll, ed., *Studies on the First Century of Islamic Society* (Carbondale and Edwardsville), 9–21 and 199–203 (repr. in S. P. Brock, *Syriac Perspectives on Late Antiquity* [London 1984], VIII).

Brooks, E. W. 1898. "The Arabs in Asia Minor (641–750) from Arabic sources," *JHS* 18: 182–208.

————. 1899. "The campaign of 716–718 from Arabic sources." *JHS* 19: 19–31.

————. 1908. "The Sicilian Expedition of Constantine IV." *BZ* 17: 455–459.

————. 1915. "The Brothers of the Emperor Constantine IV", *EHR* 30: 42–51.

Brown, P. R. L. 1971. "The rise and function of the holy man in Late Antiquity." *JRS* 61: 80–101.

————. 1972. *Religion and Society in the Age of St. Augustine* (London).

————. 1981. *The Cult of the Saints: Its Rise and Function in Latin Christianity* (Chicago).

————. 1995. "Christianisation: Narratives and Process," in P. R. L. Brown, *Authority and the Sacred: Aspects of the Christianisation of the Roman World* (Cambridge and New York): 1–26.

————. 2000. "The study of élites in Late Atiquity," in C. Rapp and M. Salzman, eds., *Elites in Late Antiquity* (*Arethusa* 33, no. 3): 321–346.

————. 2003. *The Rise of Western Christendom: Triumph and Diversity, AD 200– 1000* (3rd rev. ed., Cambridge, MA).

————. 2012a. *Salvian of Marseilles: Theology and Social Criticism in the Last Century of the Western Empire* (Dacre Lecture 2010, Oxford).

————. 2012b. *Through the Eye of a Needle. Wealth, the Fall of Rome, and the Making of Christianity in the West, 350–550 AD* (Princeton).

————. 2013. "From Amator Patriae to Amator Pauperum and Back Again," in D. Rodgers, B. Raman and Helmut Reimitz, eds., *Cultures in Motion* (Princeton), 87–106.

————. 2015. *For the Ransom of the Soul: Wealth and the Afterlife in Western Christianity from Late Antiquity to the Early Middle Ages* (Cambridge, MA).

Brown, T. S. 1979. "The church of Ravenna and the imperial administration in the seventh century." *EHR* 94: 1–28.

————. 1984. *Gentlemen and Officers. Imperial Administration and Aristocratic Power in Byzantine Italy, AD 554–800* (Rome).

————. 1995. "Justinian II and Ravenna." *BSl* 61: 29–36.

————. 2008. "Byzantine Italy (680–876)." in Shepard 2008, 433–464.

Browning, R. 1971. *Justinian and Theodora* (London).

Brownworth, L. 2009. *Lost to the West. The Forgotten Byzantine Empire that rescued Western Civilization* (New York).

Brubaker, L., and M. Cunningham, eds. 2011. *The Cult of the Mother of God in Byzantium: Texts and Images* (Farnham).

Brubaker, L., and J. F. Haldon. 2001. *Byzantium in the Iconoclast Era (ca. 680–850). The Sources: An Annotated Survey* (Birmingham Byzantine & Ottoman Monographs 7, Aldershot).

————. 2011. *Byzantium in the Iconoclast Era, c. 680–850: A History* (Cambridge).

Brubaker, R., and F. Cooper. 2000. "Beyond 'identity.'" *Theory and Society* 29: 1–47.

Burbank, J. and F. Cooper. 2010. *Empires in World History: Power and the Politics of Difference* (Princeton).

Bryer, A. A. M., and D. Winfield. 1985. *The Byzantine Monuments and Topography of the Pontos,* 2 vols. (Washington, DC).

Bury, J. B. 1911. *The Imperial Administrative System in the Ninth Century, with a Revised Text of the Kletorologion of Philotheos* (British Academy Supplemental Papers, I, London).

Butzer, K. W. 2012. "Collapse, environment and society." *Papers of the National Academy of Sciences* 109, no. 10: 3632–3639.

Cahen, C. 1971. "A new version of Ibn al-Mutarrif's list of revenues in the early times of Hārūn al-Rashīd." *Journal of the Economic and Social History of the Orient* 14, no. 1: 303–320.

Callinicos, A. 2004. *Making History: Agency, Structure and Change in Social Theory* (Leiden-Boston).

Cameron, A. 1976. *Circus Factions: Blues and Greens at Rome and Constantinople* (Oxford).

Cameron, Av. 1978. "The Theotokos in Sixth-Century Constantinople: A City Finds Its Symbol." *Journal of Theological Studies* 29, no. 1: 79–108.

———. 1979. "Images of Authority: Elites and Icons in Late Sixth-Century Constantinople." *Past and Present* 84: 3–35.

———. 1982. "Byzantine Africa—the literary evidence," in *University of Michigan Excavations at Carthage*, 7:29–62.

———. 1992. "New Themes and Styles in Greek Literature: Seventh–Eighth Centuries," in Cameron and Conrad 1992, 81–105.

———. 1996. "Byzantines and Jews: Some recent work on early Byzantium." *Byzantine and Modern Greek Studies* 20: 249–274.

———. 1998. "Education and Literary Culture," in *Cambridge Ancient History* (Cambridge), 8:655–707.

———. 2003. "How to read heresiology." *Journal of Medieval and Early Modern Studies* 33, no. 3: 471–92.

———. 2007. "Enforcing Orthodoxy in Byzantium," in K. Cooper and J. Gregory, eds., *Discipline and Diversity,* Studies in Church History 43 (Woodbridge), 1–24.

———. 2012. *The Cost of Orthodoxy* (Dutch Lectures in Patristics 2, Leiden), 2–24.

———. 2014. *Dialoguing in Late Antiquity* (Cambridge, MA, and London).

Cameron, Av., and L.I. Conrad, eds. 1992. *The Byzantine and Early Islamic Near East,* vol. 1: *Problems in the Literary Source Material* (Princeton).

Cameron, Av., B. Ward-Perkins, and M. Whitby, eds. 2000. *The Cambridge Ancient History,* vol. 14: *Late Antiquity: Empire and Successors, AD 425–600* (Cambridge).

Carile, A. 2002. "Roma Vista da Costantinopoli," in *Roma fra Oriente e Occidente* (Settimane di studio sull'altro medioevo. Spoleto): 1:49–100.

Charanis, P. 1972. *Studies on the Demography of the Byzantine Empire* (London).

———. 1959. "Ethnic changes in the Byzantine empire in the seventh century." *Dumbarton Oaks Papers* 13: 23–44.

———. 1961a. "The Armenians in the Byzantine empire." *Byzantinoslavica* 22: 196–240.

———. 1961b. "The transfer of population as a policy in the Byzantine empire." *Comparative Studies in Society and History* 3, no. 2: 140–54 (repr. in Charanis 1972: III).

Chase-Dunn, C., and T. D. Hall. 1997. *Rise and Demise: Comparing World-Systems* (Boulder).

Chehabi, H. E., and J. J. Linz. 1998. *Sultanistic Regimes* (Baltimore).

Cheyet, J.-Cl. 1999. "Un aspect du ravitaillement de Constantinople aux Xe/XIe siècles d'après quelques sceaux d'hôrreiarioi," in N. Oikonomidès, ed., *Studies in Byzantine Sigillography* (Washington, DC), 6:1–26.

———. 2006. "The Byzantine aristocracy (8th–13th centuries)," in J.-Cl. Cheynet, *The Byzantine Aristocracy and Its Military Function* (Aldershot), 1:1–43.

Cheynet, J.-C., C. Morrisson, and W. Seibt. 1991. *Sceaux byzantins de la Collection Henri Seyrig* (Paris).

Childe, V. G. 1928. *The Most Ancient East: The Oriental Prelude to European Prehistory* (London).

Chrysos, E. 1996. "The Roman Political Identity in Late Antiquity and Early Byzantium," in K. Fledelius, ed., *Byzantium: Identity, Image, Influence. XIX Int. Congress of Byzantine Studies, University of Copenhagen. Major Papers* (Copenhagen), 7–16.

Claessen, H. J. M., and P. Skalník, eds. 1981. *The Study of the State* (The Hague).

Clucas, L., ed. 1988. *The Byzantine Legacy in Eastern Europe* (East European Monographs 230, New York).

Conant, J. 2012. *Staying Roman* (Cambridge).

Conrad, L. I. 1992. "The Conquest of Arwād: A Source-Critical Study in the Historiography of the Early Medieval Near East," in Cameron and Conrad 1992: 317–401.

———. 1994. "Epidemic disease in central Syria in the late sixth century: Some new insights from the verse of Hassan ibn Thabit." *Byzantine and Modern Greek Studies* 18: 12–58.

Constantelos, D. J. 1968. *Byzantine Philanthropy and Social Welfare* (New Brunswick, N.J).

Constas, N. 2002. "An apology for the cult of saints in Late Antiquity: Eustratius Presbyter of Constantinople, on the state of souls after death (CPG 7522)." *Journal of Early Christian Studies* 10, no. 2: 267–285.

Cook, D. 1996. "Muslim apocalyptic and *Jihād*." *Jerusalem Studies in Arabic and Islam* 20: 66–104.

Corsi, P. 1983. *La spedizione italiana di Costante II* (Bologna).

———. 1988. "La politica italiana di Costante II," in *Bisanzio, Roma e l'Italia nell'alto Medioevo* (Spoleto: Centro italiano di studi sull'alto Medioevo), 751–96.

Cosentino, S. 2004. "La flotte byzantine face a l'expansion musulmane: Aspects d'histoire institutionnelle et sociale (VIIe–Xe siècle)." *Byzantinische Forschungen* 28: 1–20.

———. 2005. L'approvvigionamento annonario de Ravenna dal V all'VIII secolo: L'organizzazione e i riflessi socio-economici," in *Ravenna. Da capital impeiale a capital* esarcale (Atti del XVII Congresso internazionale di studio sull'alto medioevo, Ravenna, 6–12 giugno 2004, Spoleto), 405–434.

———. 2007. "Constans II and the Byzantine navy." *BZ* 100: 577–630.

Crone, P. 1980. "Islam, Judaeo-Christianity and Byzantine iconoclasm." *Jerusalem Studies in Arabic and Islam* 2: 59–95 (repr. in M. Bonner, ed., *Arab-Byzantine Relations in Early Islamic Times* (The Formation of the Classical Islamic World 8, Aldershot 2005), 361–397.

Crow, J., J. Bardill, and R. Bayliss. 2008. *The Water Supply of Constantinople* (JRS Monographs 11, London).

Crow, J., and S. Hill. 1995. "The Byzantine fortifications of Amastris in Paphlagonia." *Anatolian Studies* 45: 251–265.

Cunningham, M. 1986. "Preaching and the Community," in R. Morris, ed., *Church and People in Byzantium* (Birmingham), 29–47.

———. 2008. *Wider Than Heaven. Eighth-Century Homilies on the Mother of God* (Crestwood).

Curta, F. 2005. "Byzantium in dark-age Greece (the numismatic evidence in its Balkan context)." *Byzantine and Modern Greek Studies* 29: 113–146.

———. 2006. *Southeastern Europe in the Middle Ages 500–1200* (Cambridge).

Dagron, G. 1990. "La règle d'exception: Analyse de la notion d'économie," in D. Simon, ed., *Religiöse Devianz: Untersuchungen zu sozialen, rechtlichen und theologischen Reaktionen auf religiöse Abweichung im westlichen und östlichen Mittelalter* (Frankfurt a. M.), 1–18.

———. 1991. "Judaïser." *TM* 11: 359–380.

———. "L'ombre d'un doute: L'hagiographie en question, VIe–XIe siècle," *Dumbarton Oaks Papers* 46:59–68.

———. 1993. "L'Église Byzantine au VIIe Siècle," in *Histoire du Christianisme,* vol. 4: *Évêques, moines et empereurs (610–1054)* (Paris).

———. 2003. *Emperor and Priest: The Imperial Office in Byzantium,* trans. J. Birrell (Cambridge).

Dagron, G., and V. Déroche. 1991. "Juifs et Chrétiens dans l'Orient du VIIe siècle," *TM* 11: 17–273.

Dal Santo, M. 2011. "The God-Protected Empire? Scepticism towards the Cult of Saints in Early Byzantium," in Sarris et al. 2011, 129–149.

———. 2012. *Debating the Saints' Cult in the Age of Gregory the Great* (Oxford).

Davies, P. 2006. *The Goldilocks Enigma* (London).

Decker, M. 2009. *Tilling the Hateful Earth: Agricultural Production and Trade in the Late Antique East* (Oxford).

Dégh, L. 2001. *Legend and Belief: Dialectics of a Folk Genre* (Bloomington).

De Lange, N. 1992. "Jews and Christians in the Byzantine Empire: Problems and Perspectives," in D. Wood, ed., *Christianity and Judaism: Studies in Church History* (Oxford), 29:15–32.

Delehaye, H. 1933. *Les origines du culte des martyrs* (Subs. Hag. 20. Brussels).

Delmaire, R. 1989. *Largesses sacrées et Res privata : L'aerarium impérial et son administration du IVe au VIe siècle* (Collection de l'École française à Rome 121, Rome).

Denemark, R.A., ed. 2000. *World System History: The Social Science of Long-Term Change* (London/New York).

Déroche, V. 1986. "L'authenticité de l'Apologie contre les juifs de Léontios de Néapolis." *Bulletin de Correspondance Hellenique* 110: 655–669.

———. 1991. "La polémique anti-judaïque au VIe et au VIIe siècle: Un mémento inédit, les *Kephalaia*." *TM* 11: 275–311.

———. 1993. "Pourquoi écrivait-on des recueils de miracles? L'exemple des miracles de Saint Artémios," in *Les saints et leur sanctuaires: textes, images et monuments* (Byzantina Sorbonensia 13, Paris), 95–116.

———. 1999. "Polémique anti-judaïque et émergence de l'Islam." *REB* 57: 141–199.

———. 2000. "Tensions et contradictions dans les recueils de miracles de la première époque byzantine," in D. Aigle, ed., *Miracle et Karama: Hagiographies médiévales comparées* (Paris), 145–166.

———. 2002. "Représentations de l'eucharistie dans la haute époque byzantine." *TM* 14 (Mélanges Gilbert Dagron): 167–180.

Deubner, L. 1907. *Kosmas und Damian* (Berlin and Leipzig).

Devréesse, R. 1935. "Le texte grec de l'Hypomnesticum de Théodore Spoudée." *AB* 53: 66–80 (*BHG* 2261).

Di Carpegno Falconieri, T. 2012. "La militia a Roma: Il formarsi di una nuova aristocrazia (secoli VII–VIII)," in J.-M. Martin, A. Peters-Custot and V. Prigent, eds., *L'héritage byzantine en Italie (VIIIe–XIIe siècle)* (Rome), 559–583.

Diefenbach, S., 2015. "A Vain Quest for Unity: Creeds and Political (Dis) Integration in the Reign of Constantius II," in Wienand 2015, 353–378.

Di Gangi, G., and C. M. Lebole. 2006. "La Calabria bizantina (VI–XIV secoloe): Un evento di lunga durata," in Jacob et al. 2006, 471–487.

Ditten, H. 1983. "Prominente Slawen und Bulgaren in byzantinischen Diensten (Ende des 7. bis Anfang des 10. Jhdts.," in Köpstein and Winkelmann 1983, 95–119.

———. 1993. *Ethnische Verschiebungen zwischen der Balkanhalbinsel und Kleinasien vom Ende des 6. bis zur zweiten Hälfte des 9. Jahrhunderts* (BBA 59, Berlin).

Dölger, F. and Müller, A. 2003. *Regesten der Kaiserurkunden des oströmischen Reiches 565–1453* (Corpus der griechischen Urkunden des Mittelalters und der neueren Zeit, Reihe A, Abt. I. i–iv, Munich-Berlin 1924–1965); ii, 2nd ed., ed. P. Wirth (Munich 1977); 2nd rev. ed., A. Müller, i, 1–2 (Munich).

Dominguez-Castro, F., J. M. Vaquero, M. Marín, M. C. Gallego, and R. Garcia-Herrera. 2012. "How useful could Arab documentary sources be for reconstructing past climate?" *Weather* 67, no. 3: 76–82.

Donner, F. M. 1981. *The Early Islamic Conquests* (Princeton).

———. 1986. "The formation of the Islamic state." *Journal of the American Oriental Society* 106: 283–295.

Doonan, O. 2003. "Production in a Pontic Landscape: The Hinterland of Greek and Roman Sinope," in M. Faudot et al., eds., *Pont-Euxin et commerce: La genèse de la 'Route de soie'* (Besançon), 185–198.

———. 2004. *Sinop Landscapes: Exploring Connection in the Hinterland of a Black Sea Port* (Philadelphia).

Drake, H. 1979. "A Coptic version of the discovery of the Holy Sepulchre." *Greek, Roman and Byzantine Studies* 20, no. 4: 381–392.

———. 2015. "Speaking of Power: Christian Redefinition of the Imperial Role in the Fourth Century," in Wienand 2015, 291–308.

Drauschke, J. 2013. "Bemerkungen zu den Auswirkungen der Perser- und Arabereinfälle des 7. Jahrhunderts in Kleinasien," in O. Heinrich-Tamaska, ed., *Rauben—Plündern—Morden. Nachweis von Zerstörung und kriegerischer Gewalt im archäologischen Befund* (Hamburg), 117–158.

Drijvers, H. W. 1981. "Hellenistic and Oriental Origins," in S. Hackel, ed., *The Byzantine Saint* (London), 25–33.

Drinkwater, J. F. 2013. "Un-Becoming Roman," in G. M. Müller and S. Diefenbach, eds., *Gallien in Spätantike und Frühmittelalter. Kulturgeschichte einer Region* (Berlin), 59–77.

Drinkwater, J. F., and H. Elton, eds. 1992. *Fifth-Century Gaul: A Crisis of Identity?* (Cambridge).

Duncan-Jones, R. 1982. *The Economy of the Roman Empire: Quantitative Studies* (Cambridge).

Dunn, A. 1993. "The Kommerkiarios, the Apotheke, the Dromos, the Vardarios, and the West." *Byzantine and Modern Greek Studies* 17: 3–24.

Dură, N. 1995. "The Ecumenicity of the Council in Trullo: Witnesses of the Canonical Tradition in the East and in the West," in Nedungatt and Featherstone 1995, 229–262.

Durliat, J. 1990. *De la ville antique à la ville byzantine: Le problème des subsistances* (Rome).

Dvornik, F. 1966. *Early Christian and Byzantine Political Philosophy* (Washington, DC).

Eastwood, W. J., O. Gümüşçü, H. Yiğitbaşioğlu, J. F. Haldon, and A. England. 2009. "Integrating Palaeoecological and Archaeo-Historical Records: Land Use and Landscape Change in Cappadocia (Central Turkey) since Late Antiquity," in T. Vorderstrasse and J. Roodenberg, eds., *Archaeology of the countryside in medieval Anatolia* (Leiden, 2009), 45–69.

Eastwood, W. J., N. Roberts, and H. F. Lamb. 1998. "Palaeoecological and archaeological evidence for human occupance in southwest Turkey: The Beyşehir Occupation Phase." *Anatolian Studies* 48: 69–86.

Eastwood, W. J., N. Roberts, H. F. Lamb, and J. C. Tibby. 1999. "Holocene environmental change in southwest Turkey: A palaeoecological record of lake and catchment-related changes." *Quaternary Science Reviews* 18: 671–695.

Efthymiadis, S., ed. 2014. *The Ashgate Research Companion to Byzantine Hagiography*, vol. 2: *Genres and Contexts* (Farnham).

Eger, A. 2015. *The Islamic-Byzantine Frontier: Interaction and Exchange among Muslim and Christian Communities* (New York).

Ekonomou, A. 2007. *Byzantine Rome and the Greek Popes: Eastern Influences on Rome and the Papacy from Gregory the Great to Zacharias, AD 590–752* (Lanham).

Enßlin, W. 1943. "Gottkaiser und Kaiser von Gottes Gnaden," in *Sitzungsberichte der Bayerischen Akademie der Weissenschaften, philosophisch-historische Abteilung* (Munich), Heft 6.

———. 1961. art. "Vindex," in *Paulys Realencyclopädie der classischen Altertums-Wissenschaft, neue Bearbeitung*, ed. G. Wissowa, IXA/1 (Stuttgart), 25–27.

Engels, D. 1978. *Alexander the Great and the Logistics of the Macedonian Army* (Berkeley).

England, A., W. J. Eastwood, C. N. Roberts, R. Turner, and J. F. Haldon. 2008. "Historical landscape change in Cappadocia (central Turkey): A paleoecological investigation of annually-laminated sediments from Nar Lake." *Holocene* 18, no. 8: 1229–1245.

Erdkamp, P. 1998. *Hunger and the Sword: Warfare and Food Supply in Roman Republican Wars (264–30 BC)* (Amsterdam).

———. 2002a. "The Corn Supply of the Roman Armies during the Principate (27 BC–235 AD)," in Erdkamp 2002b, 47–69.

———, ed. 2002b. *The Roman Army and the Economy* (Amsterdam).

Esders, S. 2009a. "Herakleios, Dagobert und die 'beschnittenen Völker': Die Umwälzungen des Mittelmeerraums im 7. Jahrhundert in der fränkischen Chronik des sog. Fredegar," in A. Goltz, H. Leppin, and H. Schlange-Schöningen, eds., *Jenseits der Grenzen. Studien zur spätantiken und frühmittelalterlichen Geschichtsschreibung* (Millennium-Studien 25, Berlin), 239–311.

———. 2009b. "Rechtliche Grundlagen frühmittelalterlicher Staatlichkeit. Der allgemeine Treueid," in W. Pohl and V. Wieser, eds., *Der frühmittelalterliche Staat—Europäische Perspektiven* (Forschungen zur Geschichte des Mittelalters, 16, Vienna), 423–432.

———. 2012a. "'Faithful Believers': Oaths of Allegiance in Post-Roman Societies As Evidence for Eastern and Western Visions of Community," in W. Pohl, C. Gantner, and R. Payne, eds., *Visions of Community in the Post-Roman World: The West, Byzantium and the Islamic World, 300–1100* (Aldershot), 357–374.

———. 2012b. "Spätantike und frühmittelalterliche Dukate: Überlegungen zum Problem historischer Kontinuität und Diskontinuität," in H. Fehr and I. Heitmeier, eds., *Die Anfänge Bayerns: Von Raetien und Noricum zur frühmittelalterlichen Baiovaria* (St. Ottilien), 425–462.

Every, G. 1947. *The Byzantine Patriarchate (451–1204)* (London).

Fei, J., J. Zhou, and Y. Hou. 2007. "Circa AD 626 volcanic eruption, climatic cooling, and the collapse of the eastern Turkic empire." *Climate Change* 81: 469–475.

Feissel, D. 1985. "Magnus, Mégas et les curateurs des 'maisons divines' de Justin II à Héraclius." *TM* 9: 465–476.

Fischer-Kowalski, M., F. Krausmann, and I. Pallua. 2014. "A sociometabolic reading of the Anthropocene: Modes of subsistence, population size and human impact on Earth." *Anthropocene Review* 1, no. 1: 8–33.

Flaig, E. 1997. "Für eine Konzeptualisierung der Usurpation im spätrömischen Reich," in F. Paschoud and J. Szidat, eds., *Usurpationen in der Spätantike* (*Historia* Einzelschriften 111. Stuttgart): 15–34.

Flogaus, R. 2009. "Das Concilium Quinisextum (691–692). Neue Erkenntnisse über ein umstrittenes Konzil und seine Teilnehmer." *BZ* 102: 25–64.

Flusin, B. 1991. "Démons et Sarrasins: L'auteur et le propos des *Diègèmata stèriktika* d'Anastase le Sinaïte." *TM* 11: 380–409.

Fögen, M.-Th. 1987. "Gesetz und Gesetzgebung in Byzanz: Versuch einer Funktionsanalyse." *Ius Commune* 14: 137–158.

———. 1994. "Legislation in Byzantium: A Political and a Bureaucratic Technique," in Laiou and Simon 1994, 53–70.

Fowden, G. 2015. *Abraham or Aristotle? First Millennium Empires and Exegetical Traditions* (Cambridge).

Foxhall, L., and H. A. Forbes. 1982. "Σιτομετρεία: The role of grain as a staple food in Classical Antiquity." *Chiron* 12: 41–90.

Füeg, F. 1997. "Vom Umgang mit Zufall und Wahrscheinlichkeit in der numismatischen Forschung." *Schweizerische Numismatische Rundschau* 76: 135–160.

———. 2007. *Corpus of the Nomismata from Anastasius II to John I in Constantinople 717–976: Structure of the Issues, Corpus of Coin Finds, Contribution to the Iconographic and Monetary History* (Lancaster).

Gallant, T. W. 1991. *Risk and Survival in Ancient Greece* (Cambridge).

Gândilă, A. 2009. "Early Byzantine Coin Circulation in the Eastern Provinces: a Comparative Statistical Approach," *American Journal of Numismatics* 21: 151–226.

Gantner, C. 2015. *Freunde Roms und Völker der Finsternis: Die päpstliche Konstruktion von Anderen im 8. und 9. Jarhundert* (Vienna).

Garnsey, P. 1988. *Famine and Food Supply in the Graeco-Roman World: Responses to Risk and Crisis* (Cambridge).

———. 1992. "Yield of the Land," in B. Wells, ed., *Agriculture in ancient Greece* (Stockholm), 147–155.

———. 1998. *Cities, Peasants and Food in Classical Antiquity. Essays in Social and Economic History* (Cambridge).

Garsoian, N. 1967. *The Paulician Heresy: A Study of the Origin and Development of Paulicianism in Armenia and the Eastern Provinces of the Roman Empire* (The Hague and Paris).

———. 1970. "Les sources grecques pour l'histoire des Pauliciens d'Asie Mineure: Texte critique et traduction." *TM* 4: 1–227.

————. 1998. "The Problem of Armenian Integration into the Byzantine Empire," in H. Ahrweiler and A. Laiou, eds., *Studies on the Internal Diaspora of the Byzantine Empire* (Washington, DC), 61–66.

Gascou, J. 1989. "La table budgétaire d'Antaeopolis *(P. Freer 08.45 c-d),*" in *Hommes et richesses dans l'empire byzantin,* vol. 1: *IVe–VIIe siècle* (Paris), 279–313.

Gero, S. 1985. "Armenians in Byzantium: Some reconsiderations." *Journal of Armenian Studies* 2: 13–26.

Geyer, B. 2002. "Physical Factors in the Evolution of the Landscape and Land Use," in Laiou 2002a, 31–45.

Gibbon, E. 1776–1789. *The History of the Decline and Fall of the Roman Empire* (London).

Gizewski, C. 1988. *Zur Normativität und Struktur der Verfassungsverhältnisse in der späteren römischen Kaiserzeit* (Munich).

Gkoutzioukostas, A. 2001. Ο θεσμός του κοιαίστωρα του ιερού παλατίου: Η γένεση, οι αρμοδιότητες και η εξέλιξή του (Thessaloniki).

Goetz, G. ed. 1888, 1892. *Corpus glossariorum Latinorum* II, III (Leipzig).

Gogou, A., I. Bouloubassi, V. Lykousis, M. Arnaboldi, P. Gaitani, and P. A. Meyers. 2007. "Organic geochemical evidence of Late Glacial-Holocene climate instability in the North Aegean Sea." *Palaeogeography, Palaeoclimatology, Palaeoecology* 256: 1–20.

Goldstone, J., and J. F. Haldon. 2009. "Ancient States, Empires and Exploitation: Problems and Perspectives," in Morris and Scheidel 2009, 3–29.

Goldsworthy, A. 1996. *The Roman Army at War: 100 BC–AD 200* (Oxford).

Gouillard, J. 1965. "L'Hérésie dans l'empire byzantin des origines au XIIe siècle. " *TM* 1: 299–324.

Gray, P. 2005. "The Legacy of Chalcedon: Christological Problems and Their Significance," in M. Maas, ed., *The Cambridge Companion to the Age of Justinian* (Cambridge), 215–238.

Greatrex, G. 2000. "Roman Identity in the Sixth Century," in G. Greatrex and S. Mitchell, eds., *Ethnicity and Culture in Late Antiquity* (London), 267–292.

Greene, M. 2000. *A Shared World: Christians and Muslims in the Early Modern Mediterranean* (Princeton).

Greenwood, T. 2008. "Armenian Neigbours (600–1045)," in Shepard 2008, 333–364.

Greisiger, L. 2009. "Pseudo-Methodius (Syriac)," in D. Thomas and B. Roggema, eds., *Christian–Muslim Relations: A Bibliographical History,* vol. 1: *(600–900)* (Boston), 163–171.

Grierson, P. 1968. *Catalogue of the Byzantine Coins in the Dumbarton Oaks Collection and in the Whittemore Collection,* vol. 2: *Phocas to Theodosius III, 602–717* (Washington, DC).

————. 1973. *Catalogue of the Byzantine Coins in the Dumbarton Oaks Collection and in the Whittemore Collection,* vol. 3: *Leo III to Nicephorus III, 717–1081* (Washington, DC).

Griffith, S. 1987. "Anastasios of Sinai, the *Hodegos* and the Muslims." *Greek Orthodox Theological Review* 32: 341–358.

———. 1998. "What Has Constantinople to Do with Jerusalem? Palestine in the Ninth Century: Byzantine Orthodoxy in the World of Islam," in L. Brubaker, ed., *Byzantium in the Ninth Century: Dead or Alive?* (Aldershot), 181–194.

———. 2010. *The Church in the Shadow of the Mosque: Christians and Muslims in the World of Islam* (Princeton).

Grove. A. T., and O. Rackham. 2001. *The Nature of Mediterranean Europe: an Ecological History* (New Haven).

Gunderson, L. H., and C. S. Holling, eds. 2002. *Panarchy: Understanding Transformations in Human and Natural Systems* (Washington, DC).

Gunderson, L. H., and L. Pritchard, eds. 2002. *Resilience and the Behavior of Large Scale Systems* (Washington, DC).

Gunn, J. D., ed. 2000. *The Years without Summer: Tracing AD 536 and Its Aftermath* (BAR International Series 872, Oxford).

Guilland, R. 1959. "L'Expedition de Maslama contre Constantinople (717–718)," in *Études byzantines* (Paris), 109–133.

Guillou, A. 1969. *Régionalisme et indépendance dans l'empire byzantin au VIIe siècle: L'exemple de l'Exarchat et de la Pentapole d'Italie* (Rome).

———. 1974. "Italie méridionale byzantine ou Byzantins en Italie méridionale? " *Byzantion* 44: 152–190 (repr. in A. Guillou, *Culture et société en Italie byzantine* [London 1978], XV).

Guran, P. 2006. "From Empire to Church, and Back. In the Aftermath of 1204." *Revue des Etudes Sud-Est Européennes* 44: 59–69.

Guzzetta, G. 2000. "Sull'imposta del thema di Sicilia nell'epoca di Leone III." *Bollettino della Badia greca di Grottaferrata* n.s. 54: 89–95.

Hahn, J. 2015. "The Challenge of Religious Violence: Imperial Ideology and Policy in the Fourth Century," in Wienand 2015, 379–404.

Hahn, W. 1981. *Moneta imperii Byzantini: Von Heraclius bis Leo III. Alleinregierung (610–720)* III (Vienna).

Haldon, J. F. 1979. *Recruitment and Conscription in the Byzantine Army c. 550–950: A Study on the Origins of the Stratiotika Ktemata*. Sitzungsberichte der Österreichischen Akademie der Wissenschaften, philosophisch-historische Klasse, Band 357 (Vienna)

———. 1984. *Byzantine Praetorians: An Administrative, Institutional and Social Survey of the Opsikion and Tagmata, c. 580–900* (Poikila Byzantina 3, Bonn).

———. 1986a. "Everyday life in Byzantium: Some problems of approach." *Byzantine and Modern Greek Studies* 10: 51–72.

———. 1986b. "Ideology and social change in the seventh century: Military discontent as a barometer." *Klio* 68: 139–190.

———. 1986c. "Limnos, Monastic Holdings and the Byzantine State c.1261–1453," in A. A. M. Bryer and H. W. Lowry, eds., *Continuity and Change in Late Byzantine and Early Ottoman Society* (Birmingham), 161–215.

———. 1992. "The Writings of Anastasius of Sinai: A Key Source for Seventh-Century East Mediterranean History," in Averil Cameron, L. Conrad, eds., *The Early Medieval East: Problems in the Literary Source Materials* (Princeton), 107–147.

———. 1993a. "Administrative Continuities and Structural Transformations in East Roman Military Organisation c. 580–640," in M. Kazanski, ed., *L'Armée romaine et les barbares du 4e au 7e siècle* (Colloque du CNRS. Paris), 45–53 (repr. in J. F. Haldon, *State, Army and Society in Byzantium: Approaches to Military, Social and Administrative History, 6th–12th Centuries* [Aldershot 1995], V).

———. 1993b. "Constantine or Justinian? Crisis and Identity in Imperial Propaganda in the Seventh Century," in P. Magdalino, ed., *New Constantines: The Theme of Imperial Renewal in Byzantium* (London), 95–107.

———. 1993c. "Military service, military lands and the status of soldiers: Current problems and interpretations," *Dumbarton Oaks Papers* 47: 1–67 (repr. in J. F. Haldon, *State, Army and Society in Byzantium: Approaches to Military, Social and Administrative History, 6th–12th Centuries* [Aldershot 1995], VI).

———. 1993d. *The State and the Tributary Mode of Production* (London).

———. 1994. "Synônê: Re-considering a problematic term of middle Byzantine fiscal administration." *Byzantine and Modern Greek Studies* 18: 116–153 (repr. in J. F. Haldon, *State, Army and Society in Byzantium: Approaches to Military, Social and Administrative History, 6th–12th Centuries* [Aldershot 1995], VIII).

———. 1995. "Seventh-Century Continuities and Transformations: the Ajnâd and the 'Thematic Myth,' " in Av. Cameron and L. A Conrad, eds., *States, Resources and Armies: Papers of the Third Workshop on Late Antiquity and Early Islam* (Princeton), 379–423.

———. 1997a. *Byzantium in the Seventh Century: the Transformation of a Culture* (Cambridge).

———. 1997b. "The Miracles of Artemios and Contemporary Attitudes: Context and Significance," in J. Nesbitt and V. Crysafulli, eds., *The Miracles of Saint Artemios: Translation, Commentary and Analysis* (Dumbarton Oaks, Washington, DC), 33–73.

———. 1999. *Warfare, State and Society in Byzantium, 550–1204* (London).

———. 2000. "Chapters II, 44 and 45 of the *Book of Ceremonies:* Theory and practice in tenth-century military administration." *Travaux et Mémoires* 13 (Paris): 201–352.

———. 2004. "The Fate of the Late Roman Elite: Extinction or Assimilation?," in L. Conrad and J. F. Haldon, eds., *Elites Old and New in the Byzantine and Early Islamic Near East.* Papers of the VIth Workshop in Late Antiquity and Early Islam (Princeton), 178–232.

———. 2005. *The Palgrave Atlas of Byzantine History* (Basingstoke and New York).

————. 2006a. *General Issues in the Study of Medieval Logistics: Sources, Problems and Methodologies* (Leiden).

————. 2006b. "Greek Fire Revisited: Recent and Current Research," in E. Jeffreys, ed., *Byzantine Style, Religion and Civilization: in Honour of Sir Steven Runciman* (Cambridge), 290–325.

————. 2006c. "Roads and Communications in Byzantine Asia Minor: Wagons, Horses, Supplies," in J. Pryor, ed., *The Logistics of the Crusades* (Aldershot), 131–158.

————. 2007a. " 'Cappadocia Will Be Given over to Ruin and Become a Desert': Environmental Evidence for Historically-Attested Events in the 7th–10th Centuries," in *Mediterranea: Festschrift Johannes Koder* (Vienna), 215–230.

————. 2007b. " 'Tortured by my conscience': The *Laudatio Therapontis*. A neglected source of the later seventh or early eighth century," in H. Amirav and B. ter h. Romeney, eds., *From Rome to Constantinople. Studies in honour of Averil Cameron* (Leiden), 263–278.

————. 2009. "Towards a Social History of Byzantium," in J. F. Haldon, ed., *A Social History of Byzantium* (Oxford), 1–30.

————. 2012a. "Commerce and Exchange in the Seventh and Eighth Centuries: Regional Trade and the Movement of Goods," in C. Morrisson, ed., *Trade and Markets in Byzantium* (Dumbarton Oaks and Washington, DC), 99–122.

————. 2012b. "Comparative State Formation: Rome and Neighboring Worlds," in S. Johnson, ed., *The Oxford Handbook of Late Antiquity* (Oxford and New York), 1111–1147.

————. 2015a. "Contribution to the symposium on Alex Callinicos," in *Making History: Agency, Structure, and Change in Social Theory*, (=*Historical Materialism* (forthcoming)

————. 2015b. "More Questions About the Origins of the Imperial *Opsikion*," in C. Ludwig, B. Zielke, B. Krönung, and A. Beihammer, eds., *Festschrift Ralph-Johannes Lilie* (Berlin) (forthcoming).

Haldon, J. F., H. Elton, and J. Newhard. 2016. *Euchaïta: A Late Roman and Byzantine City in Anatolia* (Cambridge).

Haldon, J. F., N. Roberts, A. Izedebski, D. Fleitmann, M. McCormick, M. Cassis, O. Doonan, W. Eastwood, H. Elton, S. Ladstätter, et al. 2014. "The Climate and Environment of Byzantine Anatolia: Integrating Science, History, and Archaeology," *Journal of Interdisciplinary History* 45, no. 2: 113–161.

Haldon, J. F., and H. Kennedy. 1980. "The Byzantine-Arab frontier in the eighth and ninth centuries: Military organisation and society in the borderlands." *Zbornik Radova Vizantoloskog Instituta* 19: 79–116.

————. 2012. "Regional Identities and Military Power: Byzantium and Islam ca. 600–750," in W. Pohl, C. Gantner and R. Payne, eds., *Visions of Community in the Post-Roman World. the West, Byzantium and the Islamic World, 300–1100* (Farnham), 317–353.

Halkin, F. 1944. "S. Antoine le Jeune et Petronas le vainqueur des Arabes en 863." *AB* 62: 187–225.

Halsall, G. 2007. *Barbarian Migrations and the Roman West, 376–568* (Cambridge).

Halstead, P. 1987a. *Traditional and Ancient Rural Economy in Mediterranean Europe* (London).

———. 1987b. "Traditional and ancient rural economy in Mediterranean Europe: plus ça change?" *JHS* 107: 77–87.

Hamilton, B. 1998. "Historical Introduction," in B. and J. Hamilton, eds., *Christian Dualist Heresies in the Byzantine World c. 650–c. 1450* (Manchester), 5–25.

Harries, J. 1992. "Sidonius Apollinaris, Rome and the Barbarians: A Climate of Treason?," in Drinkwater and Elton 1992, 298–308.

———. 1994. *Sidonius Apollinaris and the Fall of Rome (AD 407–485)* (Oxford).

Harrison, D. 2002. "The Development of Élites: From Roman Bureaucrats to Medieval Warlords," in W. Pohl and M. Diesenberger, eds., *Integration und Herrschaft. Ethnische Identitäten und soziale Organisation in Frühmittelalter* (Vienna), 289–300.

Hatlie, P. 2007. *The Monks and Monasteries of Constantinople, ca. 350–850* (Cambridge).

Hawting, G. 1986. *The First Dynasty of Islam: The Umayyad Caliphate AD 661–750* (London).

Head, C. 1970. "Towards a Reinterpretation of the Second Reign of Justinian II." *Byzantion* 40: 14–32.

Heather, P. 1994. "New Men for New Constantines? Creating an Imperial Élite in the Eastern Mediterranean," in P. Magdalino, ed., *New Constantines* (Aldershot), 11–33.

———. 2005. *The Fall of the Roman Empire* (London).

Heinzelmann, M. 1975. "L'Aristocratie et les évêchés entre Loire et Rhin jusqu' à la fin du VIIe siècle." *Revue d'Histoire de l'église de France* 62: 75–79.

Hendy, M. F. 1985. *Studies in the Byzantine Monetary Economy, c. 300–1450* (Cambridge).

———. 2007. "Roman, Byzantine and Latin Coins," in C. L. Striker, Y. D. Kuban, eds., *Kalenderhane in Istanbul: The Excavations* (Mainz).

Henning, J. ed. 2007. *Post-Roman Towns, Trade and Settlement in Europe and Byzantium*, vol. 2: *Byzantium, Pliska, and the Balkans*. Millennium-Studien, 5, no. 2 (Berlin and New York).

Herman, E. 1967. "The Secular Church," in J. M. Hussey, ed., *The Cambridge Medieval History*, vol. 4: *The Byzantine Empire*, part 2: *Government, Church and Civilisation* (Cambridge), 105–133.

Herrin, J. 1987. *The Formation of Christendom* (Princeton).

———. 2013a. *Margins and Metropolis: Authority across the Byzantine Empire* (Princeton),

————. 2013b. "From Bread and Circuses to Soup and Salvation: The Origins of Byzantine Charity," in Herrin 2013a: 267–298.

————. 2013c. "Ideals of Charity, Realities of Welfare: The Philanthropic Activity of the Byzantine Church," in Herrin 2013a: 299–311.

————. 2013d. "Book Burning as Purification in Early Byzantium," in Herrin 2013a: 335–355.

Hild, F. 1977. *Das byzantinische Strassensystem in Kappadokien* (Denkschriften der Österreichischen Akademie der Wissenschaften, philosophisch-historische Klasse 131, Vienna).

Hillman, G. 1973. "Agricultural productivity and past population potential at Aşvan: An exercise in calculation of carrying capacity." *AS* 23: 225–244.

Hinds, G. M. 1972. "The murder of the Caliph ʿUthmān." *International Journal of Middle East Studies* 3: 450–469 (repr. in G. M. Hinds, *Studies in Early Islamic History,* eds. J. Bacharach, L. Conrad, P. Crone [Princeton 1995], 29–55).

Hohlweg, A. 1972. "Bischof und Stadtherr im frühen Byzanz." *Jahrbuch der österreichischen Byzantinistik* 20: 51–62.

Hopkins, K. 1965. "Élite mobility in the Roman Empire." *Past and Present* 32: 12–36.

————. 2009. "The Political Economy of the Roman Empire," in Morris and Scheidel 2009, 178–204.

Horden, P., and N. Purcell. 2005. *The Corrupting Sea: A Study of Mediterranean History* (Oxford).

Hovorun, C. 2008. *Will, Action and Freedom: Christological Controversies in the Seventh Century* (Leiden).

Howard-Johnston, J. D. 2010a. "The Rise of Islam and Byzantium's Response," in A. Oddy, ed., *Coinage and History in the Seventh-Century Near East* (London), 1–9.

————. 2010b. *Witnesses to a World Crisis: Historians and Histories of the Middle East in the Seventh Century* (Oxford).

————. 2012. "The Mardaites," in T. Goodwin, ed., *Arab-Byzantine Coins and History* (London), 27–38.

Hoyland, R. G. 1997. *Seeing Islam As Others Saw It: a Survey and Evaluation of Christian, Jewish and Zoroastrian Writings on Early Islam* (Studies in Late Antiquity and Early Islam 13, Princeton).

————. ed. 2004. *Muslims and Others in Early Islamic Society* (The Formation of the Classical Islamic World 18, Aldershot).

————. 2015. *In God's Path: the Arab Conquests and the Creation of an Islamic Empire* (New York).

Humphreys, M. 2011. "Images of Authority? Imperial Patronage of Icons from Justinian II to Leo III," in Sarris et al. 2011, 150–168.

————. 2015. *Law, Power and Imperial Ideology in the Iconoclast Era, c. 680–850* (Oxford).

Humphries, M. 2007. "From Emperor to Pope? Ceremonial, Space, and Authority at Rome from Constantine to Gregory the Great," in K. Cooper and J. Hillner, eds., *Religion, Dynasty, and Patronage in Early Christian Rome, 300–900* (Cambridge), 21–58.

Hunger, H. ed. 1975. *Das byzantinische Herrscherbild* (Wege der Forschung 341, Darmstadt).

Hussey, J. M. 1986. *The Orthodox Church in the Byzantine Empire* (Oxford).

Isaac, B. 1995. "The Army in the Late Roman East: The Persian War and the Defence of the Byzantine Provinces," in Av. Cameron and L.I Conrad, eds., *States, Resources and Armies: Papers of the Third Workshop on Late Antiquity and Early Islam* (Princeton) , 125–155.

Isager, S. and J. E. Skygaard. 1992. *Ancient Greek Agriculture: An Introduction* (London).

Ivanišević, V. 2006. "Les trésors balkaniques, témoins des invasions et de leurs routes," in C. Morrisson, V. Popović and V. Ivanišević, eds., *Les trésors monétaires byzantins des Balkans et d'Asie Mineure (491–713)* (Paris), 75–93.

Izdebski, A. 2011. "Why did agriculture flourish in the late antique east? The role of climate fluctuations in the development and contraction of agriculture in Asia Minor and the Middle East from the 4th till the 7th c. AD." *Millenium* 8: 291–312.

———. 2012. "The changing landscapes of Byzantine northern Anatolia." *Archaeologia Bulgarica* 16, no. 1: 47–66.

———. 2013a. "The Economic Expansion of the Anatolian Countryside in Late Antiquity: the Coast Versus Inland Regions," in L. Lavan, ed., *Local Economies? Production and Exchange of Inland Regions in Late Antiquity* (Boston and Leiden): 343–376.

———. 2013b. *A Rural Economy in Transition: Asia Minor from Late Antiquity into the Early Middle Ages* (*Journal of Juristic Papyrology* Supplement Series, Warsaw).

———. 2015. "An environmental-economic history of Miletus's hinterland in Late Antiquity and the Middle Ages," in A. Demirel, A. Izdebski, Ph. Niewöhner, H. Sancaktar and N. Schwert, *The Byzantine Settlement History of Miletus and its Hinterland—Quantitative Aspects. Stratigraphy, Pottery, Anthropology, Coins, and Palynology* (German Archaeological Institute, Berlin).

Izdebski, A., G. Koloch, and T. Słoczyński. 2016. "Exploring Byzantine and Ottoman economic history with the use of palynological data: a quantitative approach." *JöB* 65: 67–109.

Izdebski, A., J. Pickett, N. Roberts, and T. Waliszewski. 2015. "The environmental, archaeological and historical evidence for climatic changes and their societal impacts in the Eastern Mediterranean in Late Antiquity." *Quaternary Sciences Review* 10.1016/j.quascirev.2015.07.022.

Jacob, A., J.-M. Martin, and G. Noyé, eds. 2006. *Histoire et culture dans l'Italie byzantine* (Collection de l"École française de Rome, 363, Rome).

Jacobi, G. 1932. *Die Wirtschaftsgeographie der Seide* (Berlin).

Jacoby, D. 1991–1992. "Silk in Western Byzantium before the Fourth Crusade." *BZ* 84–85: 452–500.

Jankowiak, M. 2009. *Essai d'histoire politique du monothélisme à partir de la correspondance entre les empereurs byzantins, les patriarches de Constantinople et les papes de Rome,* PhD thesis (Paris-Warsaw).

———. 2012. "Travelling Across Borders: a Church Historian's Perspective on Contacts Between Byzantium and Syria in the Second Half of the 7th Century," in A. Goodwin, ed., *Arab-Byzantine Coins and History* (Papers presented at the seventh century Syrian numismatic round table, 2011. London), 13–25.

———. 2013a. "The first Arab siege of Constantinople." *TM* 17 (C. Zuckerman, ed., *Constructing the Seventh Century*): 237–320.

———. 2013b. "The *Notitia* 1 and the impact of Arab invasions on Asia Minor." *Millennium* 10: 435–461.

Jardé, A. 1925–1979. *Les céréales dans l'antiquité grecque* (Paris).

Jones, A. H. M. 1964. *The Later Roman Empire: A Social, Economic and Administrative Survey,* 3 vols. and maps (Oxford).

Kaegi, W. E. 1966. "The Byzantine armies and iconoclasm." *BSl* 27: 48–70.

———. 1969. "Initial Byzantine reactions to the Arab conquests." *Church History* 38: 139–149.

———. 1981. *Byzantine Military Unrest 471–843: An Interpretation* (Amsterdam)

———. 1992. *Byzantium and the Early Islamic Conquests* (Cambridge).

———. 2000. "Gigthis and Olbia in the Pseudo-Methodius Apocalypse and their significance." *BF* 26: 161–167.

———. 2008. "Confronting Islam: Emperors versus Caliphs (641–c. 850)," in Shepard 2008, 365–394.

———. 2010. *Muslim Expansion and Byzantine Collapse in North Africa* (Cambridge).

Kaiser, A.-M. 2012. "Militärorganisation im spätantiken Ägypten (284–641 n. Chr.)" (Diss., Vienna).

Kaldellis, A. 2009. *Hellenism in Byzantium: The Transformations of Greek Identity and the Reception of the Classical Tradition* (Cambridge).

———. 2012. "From Rome to New Rome, from Empire to Nation-State: Reopening the Question of Byzantium's Roman Identity," in L. Grig and G. Kelly, eds., *Two Romes. Rome and Constantinople in Late Antiquity* (Oxford and New York), 387–404.

———. 2014. "The Hagiography of Doubt and Scepticism," in Efthymiadis 2014, 453–477.

———. 2015. *The Byzantine Republic. People and Power in New Rome* (Cambridge, MA-London)

Kaniewski, D., E. Paulissen, V. De Laet, K. Dossche, and M. Waelkens. 2007. "A high-resolution Late Holocene landscape ecological history inferred from an intramontane basin in the Western Taurus Mountains, Turkey." *Quaternary Science Reviews* 26: 2201–2218.

Kaplan, M. 1976. *Les propriétés de la couronne et de l'église dans l'empire byzantine (Ve–VIe siècles)* (Byz. Sorbonensia 2, Paris).

———. 1981. "Les grands propriétaires de Cappadoce (VIᵉ–XIᵉ siècles)," in *Le aree omogenee della Civiltà rupestre nell'ambito dell'Impero bizantino: La Cappadocia* (Galatina), 125–158.

———. 1986. "Quelques aspects des maisons divines du VIe siècle." Αφιέρωμα στον Νίκο Σβορωνό (Rethymno): 70–96.

———. 1992. *Les hommes et la terre à Byzance du VIᵉ au XIᵉ siècles* (Paris).

———. 2011. "L'activité pastorale dans le village byzantin du VIIe au XIIe siècle," in I. Anagnostakis, T. Kolias, and E. Papdopoulou, eds., *Animals and Environment in Byzantium (7th–12th c.)* (Athens), 407–420.

Kaplony, A. 1996. *Konstantinopel und Damaskos. Gesandtschaften und Verträge zwischen Kaisern und Kalifen 639–750. Untersuchungen zum Gewohnheits-Völkerrecht und zur interkulturellen Diplomatie* (Islamkundliche Untersuchungen 208, Berlin).

Karayannopoulos, J. 1956. "Contribution au problème des thèmes byzantins." *Hellenisme contemporain* 10: 455–502.

———. 1958. *Das Finanzwesen des frühbyzantinischen Staates* (Munich).

Karlin-Hayter, P. 2003. "Appartenir à l'empire," in C. Dendrinos, J. Harris, E. Harvalia-Crook, and J. Herrin, eds., *Porphyrogenita: Essays on the History and Literature of Byzantium and the Latin East* (Aldershot), 117–128.

Karpat, K. H. 1960. "Social effects of farm mechanization in Turkish villages." *Social Research* 27, no. 1 (1960): 83–103.

Kautsky, J. 1982. *The Politics of Aristocratic Empires* (Chapel Hill).

Kazhdan, A. 1989. "Do we need a New History of Byzantine law?" *JÖB* 39: 1–28.

Kazhdan, A. 1992. "The Notion of Byzantine Diplomacy," in J. Shepard and S. Franklin, *Byzantine Diplomacy* (Aldershot), 3–21.

———. 1995. "Holy and Unholy Miracle Workers," in Maguire 1995, 73–82.

Kelly, C. 2004. *Ruling the Later Roman Empire* (Cambridge, MA).

Kennedy, H. 1992. "Byzantine-Arab Diplomacy in the Near East from the Islamic Conquests to the Mid Eleventh Century," in J. Shepard and S. Franklin, eds., *Byzantine Diplomacy* (Aldershot), 133–143; repr. in M. Bonner, ed., *Arab-Byzantine Relations in Early Islamic Times* (The Formation of the Classical Islamic World 8, Aldershot 2004), 81–91.

———. 1995. "The Financing of the Military in the Early Islamic State," in Av. Cameron, ed., *States, Resources and Armies: Papers of the Third Workshop on Late Antiquity and Early Islam* (Princeton), 361–378.

———. 2000. "Syria, Palestine and Mesopotamia," in Av. Cameron, B. Ward-Perkins, and M. Whitby, eds., *The Cambridge Ancient History* XIV: *Late Antiquity: Empire and Successors, AD 425–600* (Cambridge), 588–611.

———. 2004. *The Prophet and the Age of the Caliphates: The Islamic Near East from the Sixth to the Eleventh Century* (London 1986; repr. Harlow).

————. 2007. *The Great Arab Conquests: How the Spread of Islam Changed the World We Live In* (London).

Kent-Jones, D. W. 1995. "Processing of Major Food Groups: Cereals and Other Starch Products," in *The New Encyclopaedia Britannica*, vol. 19: *Macropaedia* (Chicago), 346–355.

Keys, D. 1999. *Catastrophe: A Quest for the Origins of the Modern World* (New York).

Khoury, A. T. 1972. *Polémique byzantine contre l'Islam (VIIIe–XIIIe s.)* (Leiden).

Knipping, M., M. Müllenhof, and H. Brückner. 2008. "Human induced landscape changes around Bafa Gölü (western Turkey)." *Vegetation History and Archaeobotany* 17: 365–380.

Knorr, O. 1998. "Zur Überlieferungsgeschichte des 'Liber de haeresibus' des Johannes von Damaskos (um 650–vor 754)." *BZ* 91: 59–69.

Koder, J. 1986. "The urban character of the early Byzantine empire: Some reflections on a settlement geographical approach to the topic," in *17th International Byzantine Congress, Major Papers* (New Rochelle): 155–187.

————. 1995. "Fresh Vegetables for the Capital," in C. Mango and G. Dagron, eds., *Constantinople and Its Hinterland* (Aldershot), 49–56.

————. 1996. "Byzantinische Identität—einleitende Bemerkungen," in K. Fledelius, ed., *Byzantium: Identity, Image, Influence*. XIX International Congress of Byzantine Studies, University of Copenhagen. Major Papers (Copenhagen), 3–6.

————. 1998. "Παρατηρήσεις στην οικιστική διάρθρωση της κεντρικής Μικράς Ασίας μετά τον 6ο αιώνα," in S. Lampakis, ed., *Byzantine Asia Minor (6th–12th cent.)* (Athens), 245–265.

————. 2003. "Griechische Identitäten im Mittelalter—Aspekte einer Entwicklung," in A. Avramea, A. Laiou, and E. Chrysos, eds., *Byzantio—kratos kai koinonia. Mneme Nikou Oikonoimide* (Athens), 297–319.

————. 2012a. "Regional Networks in Asia Minor during the Middle Byzantine Period, Seventh-Eleventh Centuries: An Approach," in Morrisson 2012, 147–175.

————. 2012b. "Sprache als Identitätsmerkmal bei den Byzantinern (auf–isti endende sprachenbezogene Adverbien in den griechischen Quellen)." *Anzeiger der philosophisch-historischen Klasse der Österreichischen Akademie der Wissenschaften* 147, no. 2: 5–37.

Kondov, N. 1974. "Über den wahrscheinlichen Weizenertrag auf der Balkanhalbinsel im Mittelalter." *Études Balkaniques* 10: 97–109.

Köpstein, H. 1978. "Zu den Agrarverhältnissen," in Köpstein et al. 1978, 1–72.

————. 1979. "Zum Bedeutungswandel von *sklabos*/sclavus." *BF* 7: 67–88.

Köpstein, H., and F. Winkelmann, eds. 1983. *Studien zum 8. und 9. Jahrhundert in Byzanz*, eds. (BBA 51, Berlin).

Köpstein, H., F. Winkelmann, H. Ditten, and I. Rochow. 1978. *Byzanz im 7. Jahrhundert: Untersuchungen zur Herausbildung des Feudalismus* (BBA 48, Berlin).

Kraemer, C. 1958. *Excavations at Nessana,* iii: *The Non-Literary Papyri* (Princeton).

Krannich, T., C. Schubert, and C. Sode. 2002. *Die ikonoklastische Synode von Hiereia 754. Einleitung, Text, Übersetzung und Kommentar ihres Horos, nebst einem Beitrag zur Epistula ad Constantiam des Eusebius von Cäsarea,* von A. Stockhausen (Studien und Texte zu Antike und Christentum 15, Tübingen).

Krause, J.-U., and C. Witschel. 2006. *Die Stadt in der Spätantike—Niedergang oder Wandel?* (Stuttgart).

Kulikowski, M. 2012. "The Western Kingdoms," in S. Johnson, ed., *The Oxford Handbook of Late Antiquity* (Oxford and New York), 31–59.

Lackner, W. 1967. "Zu Quellen und Datierung der Maximosvita (BHG3 1234)." *AB* 85: 285–316.

Laiou, A. E. 1993. "Sex, Consent and Coercion in Byzantium," in A. E. Laiou, ed., *Consent and Coercion to Sex and Marriage in Ancient and Medieval Societies* (Washington, DC), 109–221.

———, ed. 2002a. *The Economic History of Byzantium from the Seventh through the Fifteenth Century* (Washington, DC).

———. 2002b. "The Human Resources," in Laiou 2002a, 47–55.

———. 2009. "Family Structure and Transmission of Property," in J. F. Haldon, ed., *The Social History of Byzantium* (Oxford), 51–75.

Laiou, A. E., and C. Morrisson. 2007. *The Byzantine Economy* (Cambridge).

Laiou, A. E., and D. Simon, eds. 1994. *Law and Society in Byzantium, Ninth-Twelfth Centuries* (Washington, DC).

Lambert, D. 1999. "The uses of decay: history in Salvian's *De gubernatione dei.*" *Augustinian Studies* 30: 115–130.

Landau, P. 1995. "Überlieferung und Bedeutung der Kanones des Trullanischen Konzils im westlichen kanonischen Recht," in Nedungatt and Featherstone 1995, 215–227.

Lange, C. 2012. *Mia Energeia. Untersuchungen zur Einigungspolitik des Kaisers Heraclius und des Patriarchen Sergius von Konstantinopel* (Tübingen).

Larchet, J.-Cl. 1998. *Maxime le Confesseur médiateur entre l'orient et l'occident* (Paris).

Larsen, L. B., B. M. Vinther, K. R. Briffa, T. M. Melvin, H. B. Clausen, P. D. Jones, M.-L. Siggaard-Andersen, C. U. Hammer, M. Eronen, H. Grudd, B. E., Gunnarson, R. M. Hantemirov, M. M. Naurzbaev, and K. Nicolussi. 2008. "New ice core evidence for a volcanic cause of the A.D. 536 dust veil." *Geophysical Research Letters* 35: L04708, doi:10.1029/2007GL032450.

Lavan, L. ed. 2001. *Recent Research in Late-Antique Urbanism* (*Journal of Roman Archaeology,* supplementary series 42, Portsmouth).

———. 2006. "Political Life in Late Antiquity: A Bibliographic Essay," in Bowden, Gutteridge, and Machado 2006, 3–40.

Lee, A. D. 2007. *War in Late Antiquity: A Social History* (Oxford).

Lefort, J. 2002. "The Rural Economy, Seventh-Twelfth Centuries," in Laiou et al. 2002, 231–310.

Lefort, J., R. Bondoux, J.-C. Cheynet, J.-P. Grélois, V. Kravari, and J.-M. Martin. 1991. *Géométries du fisc byzantin, édition, traduction, commentaire* (Réalités byzantines, 4, Paris).

Le Goff, J. 1985. *L'imaginaire medieval* (Paris).

Lemerle, P. 1973. "L'Histoire des Pauliciens d'Asie Mineure d'après les sources grecques." *Travaux et Mémoires* 5: 1–114.

———. 1979. *The Agrarian History of Byzantium from the Origins to the Twelfth Century: the Sources and the Problems* (Galway).

Lenski, N. ed. 2012. *The Cambridge Companion to the Age of Constantine* (Cambridge and New York).

Leppin, H. 2012. "Roman Identity in a Border Region: Evagrius and the Defence of the Roman Empire," in W. Pohl, C. Gantner, and R. Payne, eds., *Visions of Community in the Post-Roman World: The West, Byzantium and the Islamic World, 300–1000* (Farnham), 241–258.

Leroy, S., N. Kazancı, Ö. Ileri, M. Kibar, O. Emre, E. McGee, and H. I. Griffiths. 2002. "Abrupt environmental changes within a late Holocene lacustrine sequence south of the Marmara Sea (Lake Manyas, N-W Turkey): Possible links with seismic events." *Marine Geology* 190: 531–552.

Leven, K.-H. Leven. 1987. "Die 'Justinianische' Pest." *Jahrbuch des Instituts für Geschichte der Medizin der Robert-Bosch-Stiftung* 6: 137–161.

Lilie, R.-J. 1976. *Die byzantinische Reaktion auf die Ausbreitung der Araber* (Misc. Byz. Monacensia 22, Munich).

———. 1984a. "Die zweihundertjährige reform: zu den Anfängen der Themenorganisation im 7. und 8. Jahrhundert." *BSl* 45: 27–39, 190–201.

———. 1984b. "Des Kaisers Macht und Ohnmacht. Zum Zerfall der Zentralgewalt in Byzanz vor dem Vierten Kreuzzug." *Poikila Byzantina* 4. *Varia* 1 Berlin): 9–121.

———. 1987. "Die byzantinischen Staatsfinanzen im 8./9. Jahrhundert und die *stratiotika ktemata*." *BSl* 48: 49–55.

Little, L. K. ed. 2006. *Plague and the End of Antiquity: The Pandemic of 541–750* (Cambridge).

Llewellyn, P. 1993. *Rome in the Dark Ages* (London).

Lockwood, M. 2006. "What do cosmogenic isotopes tell us about past solar forcing of climate?" *Space Science Reviews* 125: 95–109.

Loos, M. 1974. *Dualist Heresy in the Middle Ages* (Prague).

Louth, A. 2007. *Greek East and Latin West: The Church AD 681–1071* (Crestwood).

———. 2008. "Byzantium Transforming (600–700)," in Shepard, ed., 2008: 221–248.

Ludwig, C. 1997. *Sonderformen byzantinischer Hagiographie und ihr literarisches Vorbild. Untersuchungen zu den Viten des Äsop, des Philaretos, des Symeon Salos und des Andreas Salos* (Berliner Byzantinistische Studien 3, Berlin): 74–166.

Luterbacher, J. et al. 2012. "A Review of 2000 Years of Paleoclimatic Evidence in the Mediterranean," in P. Lionello, ed., *The Climate of the Mediterranean Region: From the Past to the Future* (Amsterdam), 87–185.

Lybyer, A. H. 1913. *The Government of the Ottoman Empire in the Time of Suleiman the Magnificent* (Cambridge, Mass.).

Maas, M. ed. 2005a. *The Cambridge Companion to the Age of Justinian* (Cambridge).

———. 2005b. "Roman Questions, Byzantine Answers: Contours of the Age of Justinian," in M. Maas, ed., *The Cambridge Companion to the Age of Justinian* (Cambridge), 3–27.

MacCoull, L. S. B. 1994. "BM 1079, CPR IX 44, and the Chrysargyron." *Zeitschrift für Papyrologie und Epigraphik* 100: 139–143.

Magdalino, P. 1998. "The Road to Baghdad in the Thought-World of Ninth-Century Byzantium," in L. Brubaker, ed., *Byzantium in the Ninth Century: Dead or Alive?* (Aldershot), 195–213.

———. 1999. "'What We Heard in the Lives of the Saints We Have Seen with Our Own Eyes': the Holy Man As Literary Text in Tenth-Century Constantinople," in J. D. Howard-Johnston, ed., *The Cult of Saints in Late Antiquity and the Middle Ages: Essays on the Contribution of Peter Brown* (Oxford), 83–112.

———. 2007. "Constantinople and the ΕΞΩ ΧΩΡΑΙ in the Time of Balsamon," in P. Magdalino, *Studies on the History and Topography of Byzantine Constantinople* (Aldershot), 179–197.

———. 2010. "Orthodoxy and Byzantine Cultural Identity," in A. Rigo and P. Ermilov, eds., *Orthodoxy and Heresy in Byzantium: The Definition and Notion of Orthodoxy and Some Other Studies on the Heresies and the Non-Christian Religions* (Quaderni di *Nea Rome* 4, Rome), 21–46.

Magny, M., O. Peyron, L. Sadori, E. Ortu, G. Zanchetta, B. Vannière, and W. Tinner. 2011. "Contrasting patterns of precipitation seasonality during the Holocene in the south- and north-central Mediterranean." *Journal of Quaternary Science* 27, no. 3: 290–296.

Maguire H, ed. 1995. *Byzantine Magic* (Washington, DC).

Maier, F.-G. 1968. "Die Legende der 'Dark Ages'," in F.-G. Maier, ed., *Die Verwandlung der Mittelmeerwelt* (Frankfurt a. Main).

Makrypoulias, C. G. 2012. "Civilians as Combatants in Byzantium: Ideological versus Practical Considerations," in J. Koder and I. Stouraitis, eds., *Byzantine War Ideology between Roman Imperial Concept and Christian Religion* (Denkschriften der Österreichischen Akademie der Wissenschaften, philosophisch-historische Klasse 452, Vienna): 109–120.

Malingoudis, Ph. 1994. "Zur sozialen und ethnischen Assimilierung der Slawen in Byzanz: Der Fall der Rhendakioi." *Annuaire de l'Université de Sofia 'St. Kliment Ohridski'* 87, no. 6: 13–20.

Mango, C. 1981. "Discontinuity with the Classical Past in Byzantium," in M. Mullett and R. Scott, eds., *Byzantium and the Classical Tradition* (Birmingham), 48–57.

———. 2002. "Introduction," in C. Mango, ed., *The Oxford History of Byzantium* (Oxford), 1–16.

Mann, M. 1986. *The Sources of Social Power,* vol. 1: *A History of Power from the Beginnings to AD 1760* (Cambridge).

Manning, S. 2014. "The Roman World and Climate: Context, Relevance of Climate Change, and Some Issues," in W. V. Harris, ed., *The Ancient Mediterranean: Environment between Science and History* (Leiden), 103–170.

Marazzi, F. 2007. "The Last Rome: From the End of the Fifth to the End of the Sixth Century," in S. J. Barnish and F. Marazzi, eds., *The Ostrogoths from the Migration Period to the Sixth Century: An Ethnographic Perspective* (Woodbridge), 279–316.

Marcone, A. 1998. "Late Roman Social Relations," in Av. Cameron and P. Garnsey, eds., *The Cambridge Ancient History,* vol. 8: *The Late Empire, AD 337–425* (Cambridge), 338–370.

Marx, K. 1968 [1852]. "The Eighteenth Brumaire of Louis Bonaparte," in K. Marx and F. Engels, *Selected Works* (London/Moscow), 94–179.

Mathisen, R. W. 1993. *Roman Aristocrats in Barbarian Gaul: Strategies for Survival in an Age of Transition* (Austin).

Matthews, J. 1975. *Western Aristocracies and the Imperial Court, AD 364–425* (Oxford).

Matz, S. ed. 1959. *The Chemistry and Technology of Cereals as Food and Feed* (London).

Maxwell, J. 2006. *Christianization and Communication in Late Antiquity* (Cambridge).

Mayerson, P. 1995. "An additional note on rouzikon (Ar. *Rizq*)." *Zeitschrift für papyrologie und Epigraphik* 107: 279–281.

McCormick, M. 1986. *Eternal Victory: Triumphal Rulership in Late Antiquity, Byznatium and the Early Medieval West* (Cambridge).

———. 1998. "The Imperial Edge: Italo-Byzantine Identity, Movement and Integration, AD 650–950," in H. Ahrweiler and A. E. Laiou, *Studies on the Internal Diaspora of the Byzantine Empire* (Washington, DC), 17–52.

———. 2001. *Origins of the European Economy: Communications and Commerce, AD 300–900* (Cambridge).

———. 2012. "Movements and Markets in the First Millennium: Information, Containers, and Shipwrecks," in Morrisson 2012, 51–98.

McCormick, M., U. Büntgen, M. A. Cane, E. R. Cook, K. Harper, P. Huybers, T. Litt, S. W. Manning, P. A. Mayewski, A. F. M., Moore, K. Nicolussi, and W. Tegel. 2012. "Climate change during and after the Roman Empire: Reconstructing the past from scientific and historical evidence." *Journal of Interdisciplinary History* 43, no. 2: 169–220.

McCormick, M., P. E. Dutton, and P. A. Mayewski. 2007. "Volcanoes and the climate forcing of Carolingian Europe, AD 750–950." *Speculum* 82: 865–895.

McEvoy, M. 2013. *Child Emperor Rule in the Late Roman West, AD 367–455* (Oxford).

McGeer, E. 2000. *The Land Legislation of the Macedonian Emperors* (Toronto).

McMichael, A. J. 2012. "Insights from past millennia into climatic impacts on human health and survival." *Papers of the National Academy of Sciences* 109, no. 13: 473–4737.

Meier, M. 2004a. *Das andere Zeitalter Justinians. Kontingenzerfahrung und Kontingenzbewältigung im 6. Jahrhundert n. Chr.* (Göttingen).

———. 2004b. "Sind wir nicht alle heilig? Zum Konzept des 'Heiligen' *(sacrum)* in spätjustinianischer Zeit." *Millennium* 1: 133–164.

———. 2005. "'Hinzu kam auch noch die Pest . . .' Die sogennante Justinianische Pest und ihre Folgen," in M. Meier, ed., *Pest. Die Geschichte eines Menschheitstraumas* (Stuttgart), 86–107, 396–400.

———. 2012. "Ostrom-Byzanz, Spätantike-Mittelalter. Überlegung zum 'Ende' der Antike im Osten des römischen Reiches." *Millennium* 9: 187–253.

———. 2014. "Kaiser Phokas (602–610) als Erinnerungsproblem." *BZ* 107: 139–174.

Metcalf, D. M. 2001."Monetary recession in the middle Byzantine period: The numismatic evidence." *Numismatic Chronicle* 161: 111–155.

———. 2013. "An Imperial Initiative in the Time of Tiberius III (698–705): *Apo hypatōn* and *apo eparchōn*," in E. G. Papaefthymiou and I. P. Touratsoglou, eds., Ὁλοκότινον. Μελέτες Βυζαντινῆς Νομισματικῆς καὶ Σιγιλλογραφίας στη μνήμη τοῦ Πέτρου Πρωτονοταρίου. *Studies in Byzantine Numismatics and Sigillography in Memory of Petros Protonotarios* (Athens), 167–172.

Métivier, S. 2008. "L'organisation de la frontière arabo-byzantine en Cappadoce (VIIIᵉ–IXᵉ siècle)," in E. Cuozzo, V. Déroche, A. Peters-Custot, and V. Prigent, eds., *Puer Apuliae: Mélanges offerts à Jean-Marie Martin* (Paris), 433–454.

Meyendorff, J. 1964. "Byzantine views of Islam." *Dumbarton Oaks Papers* 18: 115–132 (repr. in M. Bonner, ed., *Arab-Byzantine Relations in Early Islamic Times* [Formation of the Classical Islamic World, 8, Aldershot 2004], 217–234).

Mitchell, S. 2005. "Olive Cultivation in the Economy of Roman Asia Minor," in S. Mitchell and C. Katsari, eds., *Patterns in the Economy of Roman Asia Minor* (Swansea), 83–113.

———. 2007. *A History of the Later Roman Empire, AD 284–641* (Oxford).

Modéran, Y. 1984. "Gréoire," in *Encyclopédie Berbère* (Aix-en-Provence), 21:3211–3213.

Montinaro, F. 2013. "Les premiers commerciaires bizantins," *TM* 17 (C. Zuckerman, ed., *Constructing the Seventh Century*): 351–538.

Morgan, T. 1998. *Literate Education in the Hellenistic and Roman Worlds* (Cambridge).

Morris, I. and W. Scheidel, eds. 2009. *The Dynamics of Ancient Empires: State Power from Assyria to Byzantium* (Oxford).

Morris, R. 2013. "Travelling Judges in Byzantine Macedonia (10th–11th c.)." *Zbornik Radova Vizantološkog Instituta* 50: 335–345.

Morrisson, C. 1985. "La monnaie d'or byzantine à Constantinople: purification et modes d'altérations (491–1354)," in Cl. Brenot, J.-N. Barrandon, J.-P. Callu, J. Poirier, R. Halleux, and C. Morrisson, *L'or monnayé,* vol. 1: *Purification et altérations de Rome à Byzance* (Cahiers Ernest Babelon 2, Paris), 113–187.

———. 1986. "Byzance au VIIe siècle: le témoignage de la numismatique," in Βυζάντιος. Αφιέρωμα στον Νίκο Σβορωνό (Athens), 1:149–163.

———. 1998. "La Sicile byzantine: Une lueur dans les siècles obscurs." *Quaderni ticinesi di numismatica e antichità classiche* 27: 307–334.

———. 2001. "Survivance de l''économie monétaire à Byzance (VIIe–IXe s.)," in E. Kountoura-Galaki, ed., *The Dark Centuries of Byzantium* (Athens), 377–397.

———. 2002. "Byzantine Money: Its Production and Circulation," in Laiou 2002a, 909–966.

———, ed. 2012. *Trade and Markets in Byzantium* (Washington, DC).

———. 2013. "Displaying the Emperor's Authority and Kharaktèr on the Marketplace," in P. Armstrong, ed., *Authority in Byzantium* (London), 65–82.

Morrisson, C. and B. Callegher. 2014. "Ravenne: le déclin d'un avant-poste de Constantinople à la lumière de son monnayage (V. 540–751)," in S. Cosentino, ed., *L'Italia Bizantina : una Prospettiva Economica* (*Cahiers de recherches médiévales et humanistes/Journal of Medieval and Humanistic Studies* 28. Paris), 255–278

Morrisson, C. and V. Prigent. 2013. "L'empereur et le Calife (690–695). Réflexions à propos des monnayag es de Justinien II et d'Abd al-Malik." *Topoi* Supplement 12: 571–592

Morrisson, C. and W. Seibt. 1982. "Sceaux de commerciaires byzantins du VIIe siècle trouvés à Carthage. " *Revue Numismatique* 24: 222–241.

Mundell-Mango, M. ed. 2009. *Byzantine Trade, 4th–12th Centuries: The Archaeology of Local, Regional and International Exchange* (Aldershot).

Muscheler, R., F. Joos, J. Beer, S. Müller, M. Vonmoos, and I. Snowball. 2007. "Solar activity during the last 1000 yr inferred from radionuclide records." *Quaternary Science Reviews* 26: 82–97.

Muthesius, A. 1989. "From seed to samite: Aspects of Byzantine silk production." *Textile History* 20, no. 2: 135–149.

Nau, F. 1903. "Le texte grec des récits utiles à l''âme d'Anastase (le Sinaïte)," *Oriens Christianus* 3: 56–89.

Nedungatt, G., and M. Featherstone, eds. 1995. *The Council in Trullo Revisited* (Kanonika 6, Rome).

Neff, U., S. J. Burns, A. Mangini, M. Mudelsee, D. Fleitmann, and A. Mater. 2001. "Strong coherence between solar variability and the monsoon in Oman between 9 and 6 kyr ago." *Nature* 411: 290–293.

Nichanian, M. 2013. "La distinction à Byzance: Société de cour et hiérarchie des dignités à Constantinople (VIe–IXe s.)," in *TM* 17 (C. Zuckerman, ed., *Constructing the Seventh Century*): 579–636.

Nichol, K., and C. Küçükuysal. 2012. "Emerging multi-proxy records of late Quaternary palaeoclimate dynamics in Turkey and the surrounding region." *Turlkish Journal of Earth Sciences* 21: 1–19.

Newfield, T. P. 2013. "Early Medieval Epizootics and Landscapes of Disease: the Origins and Triggers of European Livestock Pestilences," in S. Kleingärtner, T. P. Newfield, S. Rossignol, and D. Wehner, eds., *Landscapes and Societies in Medieval Europe East of the Elbe. Interactions between Environmental Settings and Cultural Transformations* (Papers in Medieval Studies 23, Toronto), 73–113.

Noyé, G. 2002. "Economia e società nella Calabria bizantina (IV–XI secolo)," in A. Placancia, ed., *Storia della Calabria medievale: I quadri generali* (Rome), 579–655.

———. 2006a. "Les premiers siècles de la domination byzantine en Calabre," in Jacob et al. 2006, 445–469.

———. 2006b. "Anéantissement et renaissance des élites dans le sud de l'Italie, Ve-IXe siècles," in F. Bougard, L. Feller and R. Le Jan, eds., *Les élites au haut Moyen Âge. Crises et renouvellements* (Rome, 6–8 mai 2004) (Turnhout), 167–205.

Noyé, G. 2015. "L'économie de la Calabre de la fin du VIe au VIIIe siècle, " in S. Cosentino, ed., *L'Italia Bizantina : una Prospettiva Economica* (*Cahiers de recherches médiévales et humanistes/Journal of Medieval and Humanistic Studies* 28. Paris), 323–388

Obolensky, D. 1971. *The Byzantine Commonwealth: Eastern Europe 500–1453* (London).

O'Connor, T. G., and G. A. Kiker. 2004. "Collapse of the Mapungubwe society: Vulnerability of pastoralism to increasing aridity." *Climate Change* 66: 49–66.

Oddy, W. A. 1988. "The Debasement of the Provincial Byzantine Gold Coinage from the Seventh to Ninth Centuries," in W. Hahn and W. E. Metcalf, eds., *Studies in Early Byzantine Gold Coinage* (New York), 135–142.

Ohme, H. 1990. *Das Concilium Quinisextum und seine Bischofsliste: Studien zum Konstantinopler Konzil von 692* (Arbeiten zur Kirchengeschichte 56, Berlin and New York).

———. 1995. "Die sogennanten "antirömischen" Kanones des Concilium Quinisextum," in Nedungatt and Featherstone 1995, 307–321.

———. 2008. "*Oikonomia* im monenergetisch-monotheletischen Streit." *Zeitschrift für antikes Christentum* 12: 308–343.

Oikonomidès, N. 1972. *Les listes de préséance byzantins des IXe–Xe siècles* (Paris).

———. 1988. "Middle Byzantine provincial recruits: salary and armament," in J. Duffy, J. Peradotto, eds., *Gonimos. Neoplatonic and Byzantine Studies presented to Leendert G. Westerink at 75* (Buffalo), 121–136.

———. 1986a. *Dated Byzantine Lead Seals* (Washington, DC).

———. 1986b. "Silk Trade and Production in Byzantium from the Sixth to the Ninth Century: the Seals of the Kommerkiarioi." *Dumbarton Oaks Papers* 40: 33–53.

———. 1993. "Le marchand byzantin des provinces (IXe–XIe s.)," in *Mercati e mercanti nell'alto medioevo: L'area euroasiatica e l'area mediterranea = Settimane di studio del centro italiano sull'alto medioevo* 40: 633–660.

Olster, D. 1994. *Roman Defeat, Christian Response, and the Literary Construction of the Jew* (Philadelphia).

Ostrogorsky, G. 1936. "Die byzantinische Staatenhierarchie." *Seminarium Kondakovianum* 8, 49–53.

Palme, B. 2007. "The Imperial Presence: Government and Army," in R. Bagnall, ed., *Egypt in the Byzantine World, 300–700* (Cambridge), 244–270.

Papaconstantinou, A. 2005. "Confrontation, interaction, and the formation of the early Islamic *oikoumene*. Review article." *REB* 63: 167–181.

Patlagean, P. 1977. *Pauvreté économique et pauvreté sociale à Byzance, 4e–7e siècles* (Paris).

Paxton, F. 1990. *Christianising Death: The Creation of a Ritual Process in Early Medieval Europe* (Ithaca).

Perry, C. A., and K. J. Hsu. 2000. "Geophysical, archaeological, and historical evidence support a solar-output model for climate change." *Proceedings of the National Academy of Sciences* 97: 12433–12438.

Pfeilschifter, R. 2013. *Der Kaiser und Konstantinopel. Kommunikation und Konfliktaustrag in einer spätantiken Metropole* (Millennium-Studien 44. Berlin-Boston).

Phillips, M. 2012. "The Import of Byzantine Coins to Syria Revisited," in T. Goodwin, ed., *Arab-Byzantine Coins and History: Papers Presented at the Seventh-Century Syrian Numismatic Round Table, Oxford 2011* (London), 39–72.

Phillips, M., and A. Goodwin. 1997. "A seventh-century Syrian hoard of Byzantine and imitative copper coins." *Numismatic Chronicle* 157: 61–87.

Pohl, W. 2010. *Archaeology of identity / Archäologie der Identität* (Vienna).

———. 2013. "Strategies of Identification: A Methodological Profile," in W. Pohl and G. Herdemann, eds., *Strategies of Identification: Ethnicity and Religion in Early Medieval Europe* (Turnhout), 1–64.

Pohl, W. and H. Reimitz, eds. 1998. *Strategies of Distinction: the Construction of Ethnic Communities, 300–800* (Leiden).

Potestà, G. L. 2011. "The *Vaticinium of Constans*. Genesis and original purposes of the legend of the Last World Emperor." *Millennium* 8: 271–289.

Pratsch, T. 1998. *Theodoros Studites (759–826)—zwischen Dogma und Pragma* (BBS 4, Frankfurt a. M.).

Price, R., P. Booth, and C. Cubitt. 2014. *The Acts of the Lateran Synod of 649* (Liverpool).

Prigent, V. 2004. "Les empereurs isauriens et la confiscation des patrimoines pontificaux d'Italie du Sud." *Mélanges de l'École française de Rome. Moyen Âge* 116: 557–94.

———. 2006. "Le rôle des provinces d'Occident dans l'approvisionnement de Constantinople (618–717). Témoignages numismatique et sigillographique." *Mélanges de l'École française de Rome. Moyen Âge* 118: 269–299.

———. 2008. "Nouvelle hypothèse à propos des monnaies de bronze à double marque de valeur de l'empereur Constantin IV," in E. Cuozzo, V. Dénoche, A. Petens-Custot and V. Prigent, eds., *Puer Apuliae. Mélanges en l'honneur de Jean-Marie Martin,* II (Centre d'histoire et de civilisation de Byzance, Monographies, 30. Paris), 637–654.

———. 2010. "La Sicile byzantine, entre papes et empereurs (6ème–8ème siècle)," in D. Engels, L. Geis and M. Kleu, eds., *Zwischen Ideal und Wirklichkeit: Herrschaft auf Sizilien von der Antike bis zur frühen Neuzeit* (Wiesbaden), 201–230.

———. 2011. "La Sicile de Constant II: l'apport des sources sigillographiques," in A. Nef and V. Prigent, eds., *La Sicile de Byzance à l'Islam* (Paris), 157–187.

———. 2014. "The Mobilisation of Fiscal Resources in the Byzantine Empire (Eighth to Eleventh Centuries)," in J. Hudson and A. Rodriguez, eds., *Diverging Paths ? The Shapes of Power and Institutions in Medieval Christendom and Islam* (Leiden-Boston), 182–229.

———. 2015. "Un confesseur de mauvaise foi. Notes sur les exactions financières de l'empereur Léon III en Italie du Sud," in S. Cosentino, ed., *L'Italia Bizantina : una Prospettiva Economica* (*Cahiers de recherches médiévales et humanistes* 28. Paris), 279–304.

Pryor, J., ed. 2006. *Logistics of Warfare in the Age of the Crusades* (Aldershot).

Puin, G.-R. 1970. *Der Dīwān von ⁽Umar ibn al-Hattāb* (Bonn).

Rabb, T. K., and R. I. Rotberg, eds. 1981. *Climate and History: Studies in Interdisciplinary History* (Princeton).

Ramsay, W. M. 1890. *The Historical Geography of Asia Minor.* Royal Geographical Society, Supplementary Papers IV (London and Amsterdam).

Rapp, C. 1999. " 'For Next to God, You Are My Salvation': Reflections on the Rise of the Holy Man in Late Antiquity," in J. Howard-Johnston and P. Hayward, eds., *The Cult of Saints in Late Antiquity and the Middle Ages: Essays on the Contribution of Peter Brown* (Oxford), 63–81.

———. 2005. *Holy Bishops in Late Antiquity: The Nature of Christian Leadership in an Age of Transition* (Berkeley, Los Angeles, and London).

———. 2008. "Hellenic Identity, *Romanitas,* and Christianity in Byzantium," in K. Zacharia, ed., *Hellenisms: Culture, Identity and Ethnicity from Antiquity to Modernity* (Aldershot), 127–147.

———. 2010. "Old Testament Models for Emperors in Early Byzantium," in P. Magdalino and R. Nelson, eds., *The Old Testament in Byzantium* (Washington, DC), 175–197.

Reinink, G. 1993. *Die syrische Apokalypse des Ps.-Methodius* (CSCO 540, 541. Scriptores Syri 220, 221. Louvain).

Richard, M. 1958. "Anastase le Sinaite, l'Hodegos et le Monothélisme," *REB* 16: 29–42 (repr. in M. Richard, *Opera minora,* III [Leuven 1976–1977]: no. 63).

Riedinger, R. 1979. "Die Präsenz- und Subskriptionslisten des VI. ökonomischen Konzils (680/1) und der Papyrus Vind. gr. 3," *Abhandlungen der Bayerischen Akademie der Wissenschaften, philosophisch-historische Klasse, neue Folge* 85 (Munich).

Roberts, N. 2014. *The Holocene: An Environmental History* (Oxford and Malden, MA).

Roberts, C. N., W. J. Eastwood, and J. Carolan. 2009. "Palaeolimnological Investigations in Paphlagonia," in C. Glatz and R. Matthews, eds., *At Empire's Edge: Project Paphlagonia: Regional Survey in North-Central Turkey* (London), 64–73.

Roberts, C. N., W. J. Eastwood, A. England, M. Waelkens, E. Paulissen, M. Vermoere, S. Six, M. Jones, P. Kerswell, P. Boyer, and A. Morris. 2005. "Late Holocene Landscape Disturbance and Recovery: An East Mediterranean Case Study," in *PAGES Second Open Science Meeting 10–12 August 2005, Beijing, China* http://www.pages-igbp.org/download/docs/meeting-products/posters/2005-osm2/Roberts-N.pdf.

Robinson, C. F. 2005. *Abd al-Malik* (Oxford).

———. 2010. "The Rise of Islam, 600–705," in C. F. Robinson, ed., *The New Cambridge History of Islam*, vol. 1: *The Formation of the Islamic World, Sixth to Eleventh Centuries* (Cambridge), 173–225.

Rochow, I. 1991. *Byzanz im 8. Jahrhundert in der Sicht des Theophanes. Quellenkritisch-historischer Kommentar zu den Jahren 715–813* (BBA 57, Berlin).

Rogers, J. D., T. Nichols, T. Emmerich, M. Latek, and C. Cioffi-Revilla, "Modeling scale and variability in human-environmental interactions in Inner Asia." *Ecological Modeling* 241: 5–14.

Romančuk, A. I. 2005. *Studien zur Geschichte und Archäologie des byzantinischen Cherson*, ed. H. Heinen (Leiden).

Rordorf, W. 1975. "Aux origines du culte des martyrs chrétiens," in *Forma futuri : Studi in onore del Cardinale Michele Pellegrino* (Turin), 445–461.

Rosen, A. M. 2007. *Civilizing Climate: Social Responses to Climate Change in the Ancient Near East* (Lanham).

Roth, J. 2002. "The Army and the Economy in Judaea and Palestine," in Erdkamp 2002b, 375–397.

Rotman, Y. 2005. "Byzance face à l'Islam arabe, VIIe—Xe siècle. D'un droit territorial à l'identité par la foi." *Annales. Histoire, Sciences Sociales* 60: 767–788.

Rotter, G. 1982. *Die Ummayaden und der zweite Bürgerkrieg (680–692). Abh. für die Kunde des Morgenlandes* 45.

Runciman, W. G. 1989. *A Treatise on Social Theory*, vol. 2: *Substantive Social Theory* (Cambridge).

Sadori, L., C. Giraudi, A. Masi, M. Magny, E. Ortu, G. Zanchetta, and A. Izdebski. 2015. "Climate, environment and society in Southern Italy during the last 2000 years: A review of the environmental, historical and archaeological evidence." *Quaternary Science Reviews* 2016 doi: 10.1016/j.quascirev.2015.09.020

Sahner, C. 2015. *Christian Martyrs and the Making of an Islamic Society in the Post-Conquest Period* (Diss., Princeton).

Sanderson, S.K. ed. 1995. *Civilizations and World Systems : Studying World-Historical Change* (Walnut Creek, CA).

Sanderson, S. K. 1999. *Social Transformations: A General Theory of Historical Development* (Lanham).

Sanderson, S.K., ed. 2000. *Sociological Worlds : Comparative and Historical Readings on Society* (Chicago/London)

Šandrovskaya, V. 1999. "Das Siegel eines *Chalkoprates* aus Sudak." *Studies in Byzantine Sigillography* 6: 43–46.

Sansterre, J.-M. 1983. *Les moines grecs et orientaux à Rome aux époques Byzantine et carolingienne (milieu du VIe siècle-fin du IXe siècle)*, 2 vols. (Brussels).

———. 1988. "Le monachisme byzantin à Rome," in *Bisanzio, Roma e l'Italia nell'alto medioevo* (Settimane di studio del centro italiano sull'alto medioevo, 34, Spoleto), 701–746.

Sariş, F., D. M. Hannah, and W. J. Eastwood. 2010. "Spatial Variability of Precipitation Regimes over Turkey." *Hydrological Sciences Journal* 55, no. 2: 234–249.

Sarris, P. 2006. *Economy and Society in the Age of Justinian* (Cambridge).

———. 2009. "Social Relations and the Land," in J. F. Haldon, ed., *A Social History of Byzantium* (Oxford), 92–111.

———. 2011a. *Empires of Faith: The Fall of Rome to the Rise of Islam, 500–700* (Oxford).

———. 2011b. "Law and Custom in the Byzantine Countryside from Justinian I to Basil II (c. 500–1000)," in A. Rio, ed., *Law, Custom, and Justice in Late Antiquity and the Early Middle Ages* (London), 49–61.

———. 2011c. "Restless Peasants and Scornful Lords: Lay Hostility to Holy Men and the Church in the Late Antiquity and the Early Middle Ages," in Sarris et al. 2011, 1–10.

Sarris, P., M. Dal Santo, and P. Booth, eds. 2011. *An Age of Saints? Power, Conflict and Dissent in Early Medieval Christianity* (Leiden-Boston).

Schachner, L. 2006. "Social Life in Late Antiquity: a Bibliographiuc Essay," in W. Bowden, A. Gutteridge, and C. Machado, eds., *Social and Political Life in Late Antiquity* (Late Antique Archaeology 3, no. 1, Leiden and Boston), 41–93.

Scheidel, W. 2009. "Introduction," in W. Scheidel, ed., *Rome and China: Comparative Perspectives on Ancient World Empires* (Oxford), 3–10.

———. 2013. "Studying the State," in Bang and Scheidel 2013, 5–57.

Schilbach, E. 1970. *Byzantinische Metrologie* (Handbuch d. Altertumswiss. xii, 4=Byzantinisches Handbuch iv, Munich).

Schminck, A. 2015. "Minima Byzantina." *Zeitschrift der Savigny-Stiftung für Rechtsgeschichte* 123: 469–483.

Schmitt, O. 2001. "Untersuchungen zur Organisation und zur militärischen Stärke oströmischer Herrschaft im Vorderen Orient zwischen 628 und 633." *BZ* 94: 211–216.

———. 2007. "From the Late Roman to the Early Byzantine Army: Two Aspects of Change," in A. S. Lewin and P. Pelegrini, eds., *The Late Roman Army in the Near East from Diocletian to the Arab Conquest* (BAR International Series 1717, Oxford), 411–419.

Schreiner, P. 2008. *Byzanz 565–1453*. Oldenbourg Grundriss der Geschichte. 3rd ed. (Munich).

Schuller, W. 1975. "Grenzen des spätrömischen Staates: Staatspolizei und Korruption." *Zeitschrift für Papyrologie und Epigraphik* 16: 1–21.

Seibt, W., and D. Theodoridis. 1990., "Das Rätsel der Andrapoda-Siegel im ausgehenden 7. Jahrhundert. Waren mehr Slawen oder mehr Armenier Opfer dieser Staatsaktion?" *BSl* 60: 404–405.

Settipani, C. 2013. "The Seventh-Century Bagratids between Armenia and Byzantium." *TM* 17 (C. Zuckerman, ed., *Constructing the Seventh Century*): 559–578.

Sharf, A. 1955. "Byzantine Jewry in the Seventh Century." *BZ* 48: 103–115.

———. 1971. *Byzantine Jewry from Justinian to the Fourth Crusade* (London).

Shepard, J., ed. 2008. *Cambridge History of the Byzantine Empire ca. 500–1492* (Cambridge).

Sijpesteijn, P. 2007. "New Rule over Old Structures: Egypt after the Muslim Conquest," in H. Crawford, ed., *Regime Change in the Ancient Near East and Egypt, from Sargon of Agade to Saddam Hussein* (Proceedings of the British Academy 136, London), 183–200.

Simelides, C. 2011. "The Byzantine understanding of the Qur'anic term *al-Samad* and the Greek translation of the Qur'an." *Speculum* 86: 887–913.

Simon, D. 1973. *Rechtsfindung am byzantinischen Reichsgericht* (Frankfurt am Main).

———. 1977. "Byzantinische Hausgemeinschaftsverträge," in *Beiträge zur europäischen Rechtsgeschichte und zum geltenden Zivilrecht. Festgabe für J. Sontis* (Munich), 91–128.

———. 1984. "Princeps legibus solutus: Die Stellung des byzantinischen Kaisers zum Gesetz," in *Gedächtnisschrift für Wolfgang Kunkel* (Frankfurt a. M.), 449–492.

Simonsen, J. B. 1988. *The Genesis and Development of the Caliphal Taxation System* (Copenhagen).

Slim, H. 1982. "Le trésor de Rougga et l'expédition musulmane en 647 en Ifrīkiya," in R. Guéry, C. Morrisson, and H. Slim, *Recherches d'archéologie franco-tunisiennes à Rougga*, vol. 3: *Le trésor de monnaies d'or byzantines* (Rome), 76–94.

Smith, L. 1945. *Flour Milling Technology* (London).

Sotinel, C. 2005. "Emperors and Popes in the Sixth Century: The Western View," in Maas 2005a, 267–287.

Soulis, G. 1961. "The Gypsies in the Byzantine Empire and the Balkans in the Late Middle Ages," *Dumbarton Oaks Papers* 15: 141–165.

Speck, P. 1997. "Die vermeintliche Häresie der Athinganoi." *JöB* 47: 37–50.

———. 2003. *Kaiser Leon III., die Geschichtswerke des Nikephoros und des Theophanes und der Liber Pontificalis* (Poikila Byzantina 19–20, Bonn).

Speyer, W. 1981. *Büchervernichtung und Zensur des Geistes bei Heiden, Juden und Christen* (Bibliothek des Buchwesens 7, Stuttgart).

Spier, F. 2011. *Big History and the History of Humanity* (Oxford).

Spurr, M. S. 1986. *Arable Cultivation in Roman Italy (c. 200 BC–100 AD)* (London).

Stark, R. 1996. *The Rise of Christianity: How the Obscure, Marginal Jesus Movement Became the Dominant Religious Force in the Western World in a Few Centuries* (San Francisco).

Starr, J. 1936. "An Eastern Christian Sect: The Athinganoi." *Harvard Theological Review* 29: 93–106.

———. 1939. *The Jews in the Byzantine Empire, 641–1204* (Athens).

Stathakopoulos, D. 2000. "The Justinianic Plague Revisited." *Byzantine and Modern Greek Studies* 24: 256–76.

———. 2003. "Reconstructing the Climate of the Byzantine World: State of the Problem and Case Studies," in J. Laszlovsky and P. Szabó, eds., *People and Nature in Historical Perspective* (Budapest), 247–261.

———. 2004. *Famine and Pestilence in the Late Roman and Early Byzantine Empire. a Systematic Survey of Subsistance Crises and Epidemics* (Aldershot).

———. ed. 2007. *The Kindness of Strangers : Charity in the Pre-modern Mediterranean* (London).

———. 2012. "Death in the Countryside: Some Thoughts on the Effects of Epidemics and Famines." *Antiquité Tardive* 20: 103–112.

Stein, E. 1949. *Histoire du Bas-Empire,* vol. 2 (Paris).

Stolte, B. H. 2002. "The Challenge of Change: Notes on the Legal History of the Reign of Heraclius," in G. J. Reinink and B. H. Stolte, eds., *The Reign of Heraclius (610–641): Crisis and Confrontation* (Leuven), 191–204.

———. 2005. "Is Byzantine Law Roman Law?" *Acta Byzantina Fennica* 2 (N. S. Helsinki).

Stothers, R. B., and M. R. Rampino. 1983. "Volcanic Eruptions in the Mediterranean Before 630 A.D. from Written and Archaeological Sources." *Journal of Geophysical Research* 88: 6357–6371.

Stouraitis, I. 2014. "Roman identity in Byzantium: A critical approach." *BZ* 107: 175–220.

———. 2016. "Review of Kaldellis 2015," *JHS* 136.

Stoyanov, Y. 2011. *Defenders and Enemies of the True Cross: the Sasanian Conquest of Jerusalem in 614 and Byzantine Ideology of Anti-Persian Warfare* (Vienna).

Stratos, A. N. 1968–1980. *Byzantium in the Seventh Century,* vol. 1: *602–634* (Amsterdam, 1968); vol. 2: *634–641* (Amsterdam, 1972); vol. 3: *642–668* (Amsterdam, 1975); vol. 4: *668–685* (Amsterdam, 1978); Vol. 5: *685–711* (Amsterdam, 1980).

———. 1976. "The exarch Olympius and the supposed Arab invasion of Sicily in AD 652." *JöB* 25: 63–73.

Stuiver, M., and T. F. Braziunas. 1988. "The Solar Component of the Atmospheric 14C Record," in F. R. Stephenson and A. W. Wolfendale, eds.,
Secular Solar and Geomagnetic Variations in the Last 10,000 Years (Dordrecht),
245–266.

———. 1991. "Climatic, solar, oceanic, and geomagnetic influences on
late-glacial and Holocene atmospheric 14C/12C change." *Quaternary
Research* 35: 1–24.

———. 1993. "Sun, ocean, climate and atmospheric 14CO2: An evaluation of
causal and spectral relationships." *Holocene* 3: 289–305.

Stuiver, M., and P. D. Quay. 1980. "Changes in atmospheric carbon-14
attributed to a variable sun." *Science* 207: 11–19.

Suermann, H. 1985. *Die geschichtstheologische Reaktion auf die einfallenden Muslime
in der edessenischen Apokalyptik des 7. Jahrhunderts* (Frankfurt am Main).

Tainter, J. A. 1988. *The Collapse of Complex Societies* (Cambridge).

Talbot, A.-M. ed. 1996. *Holy Women of Byzantium: Ten Saints' Lives in English
Translation* (Washington, DC).

———. ed. 1998. *Byzantine Defenders of Images: Eight Saints' Lives in English
Translation* (Washington, DC).

Teall, J. L. 1959. "The grain supply of the Byzantine Empire." *Dumbarton Oaks
Papers* 13: 87–139.

Teitler, H. C. 1992. "Un-Roman Activities in Late Antique Gaul: The Cases of
Arvandus and Seronatus," in Drinkwater and Elton 1992, 309–318.

Telelis, I. G. 2004. Μετεωρολογικά Φαινόμενα και κλίμα στο Βυζάντιο. 2 vols.
(Athens).

———. 2008. "Climatic fluctuations in the eastern Mediterranean and the
Middle East AD 300–1500 from Byzantine documentary and proxy
physical paleoclimatic evidence—a comparison." *Jahrbuch der österreichischen Byzantinistik* 58: 167–207.

Thümmel, H.-G. 2005. *Die Konzilien zur Bilderfrage im 8. und 9. Jahrhundert. Das
7. Ökumenische Konzil in Nikaia 787* (Paderborn-Munich-Vienna-Zurich).

Tilly, C. 2002. *Stories, Identities and Political Change* (Lanham).

Tor, D. 2007. *Violent Order: Religious Warfare, Chivalry, and the* "Ayyār *Phenomenon in the Medieval Islamic World* (Würzburg).

Tougher, S. 2008. "After Iconoclasm (850–886)," in J. Shepard, ed., *Cambridge
History of the Byzantine Empire ca. 500–1492* (Cambridge), 292–304.

Tous, J., and L. Ferguson. 1996. "Mediterranean Fruits," in J. Janick, ed.,
Progress in New Crops (Arlington), 416–430.

Treadgold, W. 1981. *The Byzantine State Finances in the Eighth and Ninth Centuries*
(New York).

Treadwell, L. 2012. "Byzantium and Islam in the Late 7th Century AD: A
'Numismatic War of Images'?," in A. Goodwin, ed., *Arab-Byzantine Coins
and History* (Papers Presented at the Seventh Century Syrian Numismatic
Round Table, 2011. London), 145–155.

Triantaphyllou, M. V., A. Gogou, I. Bouloubassi, M. Dimiza, K. Kouli, G. Rousakis, U. Kotthoff, K. C. Emeis, M. Papanikolaou, M. Athanasiou, C. Parinos, C. Ioakim, and V. Lykousis. 2014. "Evidence for a warm and humid Mid-Holocene episode in the Aegean and northern Levantine Seas (Greece, NE Mediterranean)." *Regional Environmental Change* 14: 1697–1712.

Trigger, B. G. 2003. *Understanding Early Civilizations: A Comparative Study* (Cambridge).

Tritton, A. S. 1954. "Notes on the Muslim system of pensions." *BSOAS* 16: 170–172.

Troianos, S. N. 1988. "Kirche und Staat: Die Berührungspunkte der beiden Rechtsordnungen in Byzanz." *Ostkirchliche Studien* 37: 291–296.

———. 1991. "Nomos und Kanon in Byzanz." *Kanon* 10: 37–51.

———. 1996. "Die Kanones des Trullanum in den Novellen Leons VI." *Diptycha* 6: 399–410.

———. 2011. *Oi peges tou Byzantinou dikaiou* (Athens-Komitini).

Trombley, F. 1983. "Note on the see of Jerusalem and the synodal list of the sixth oecumenical council (680–681)." *B* 53: 632–638.

———. 1985a. "The Decline of the Seventh-Century Town: The Exception of Euchaita," in S. Vryonis Jr., ed., *Byzantina kai Metabyzantina*, vol. 4 *Byzantine Studies in Honor of Milton V. Anastos* (Malibu), 65–90.

———. 1985b. "Paganism in the Greek World at the End of Antiquity." *Harvard Theological Review* 78: 327–352.

———. 1989. "The Arab Wintering Raid against Euchaita in 663/4," in *Abstracts of the Fifteenth Annual Byzantine Studies Conference 1989*. http://www.bsana.net/conference/archives/1989/abstracts_1989.html.

———. 2001. "Town and Territorium in Late Roman Anatolia (late 5th–early 7th c.)," in Lavan 2001, 217–232.

Tsorbatzoglou, P.-G. 2011. "Ένας Έλληνας απο την Τάρσο της Κιλικίας. ο Θεόδωρος αρχιεπίσκοπος Κάντερμπουρυ (Canterbury) της Αγγλίας (668–690). Όψεις του βίου του," in T. Korres, P. Katsoni, I. Leontiadis, and A. Gkoutzioukostas, eds., Φιλοτιμία. Τιμητικός τόμος για την Αλκμήνη Σταυρίδου-Ζαφρακά (Thessaloniki), 641–668.

Turchin, P. 2009. *Historical Dynamics: Why States Rise and Fall* (Princeton).

Turchin, P., and S. A. Nefedov. 2009. *Secular Cycles* (Princeton).

Türkeş, M., T. Koç, and F. Sarış. 2009. "Spatiotemporal variability of precipitation total series over Turkey." *International Journal of Climatology* 29: 1056–1074.

Turkey, vol. 2, Naval Intelligence Division, Geographical Handbook Series, B. R. 507a (Naval Intelligence Division. London 1943).

Turner, D. 1990. "The origins and accession of Leo V (813–820)." *JöB* 40: 171–203.

———. 2003. "The Trouble with the Trinity: The Context of a Slogan During the Reign of Constantine IV (668–85)." *Byzantine and Modern Greek Studies* 27: 68–119.

Uthemann, K.-H. 1981. *Anastasius of Sinai, Viae Dux* (*CCSG* 8, Leuven).

———. 1997. "Der Neuchalkedonismus als Vorbereitung des Monotheletismus: Ein Beitrag zum eigentlichen Anliegen des Neuchalkedonismus." *Studia Patristica* 29: 373–413.

Van Bekkum, W. 2002. "Jewish Messianic Expectations in the Age of Heraclius," in G. J. Reinink and B. H. Stolte, eds., *The Reign of Heraclius (610–641): Crisis and Confrontation* (Leuven), 95–112.

Van Crefeld, M. 1977. *Supplying War: Logistics from Wallerstein to Patton* (Cambridge).

Van Dieten, J. L. 1972. *Geschichte der Patriarchen von Sergios I. bis Johannes VII. (610–705)* (Amsterdam).

Van Zeist, W., H. Woldring, and D. Stapert. 1975. "Late quaternary vegetation and climate of southwestern Turkey." *Palaeohistoria* 17: 53–144.

Vera, D. 2008. "Gli horrea frumentari nell'Italia tardoantica: Tipi, funzioni, personale." *Mélanges de l'École française de Rome. Moyen Âge* 120, no. 2: 323–336.

Vermoere, M. 2004. *Holocene Vegetation History in the Territory of Sagalassos (Southwest Turkey): A Palynological Approach.* (Turnhout).

Vermoere, M., E. Smets, M. Waelkens, H. Vanhaverbeke, I. Librecht, E. Paulissen, and L. Vanhecke. 2000. "Late Holocene environmental change and the record of human impact at Gravgaz near Sagalassos, southwest Turkey." *Journal of Archaeological Science* 27: 571–595.

Vermoere, M., L. Vanhecke, M. Waelkens, and E. Smets. 2003. "Modern and ancient olive stands near Sagalassos (southwest Turkey) and reconstruction of the ancient agricultural landscape in two valleys." *Global Ecology and Biogeography* 12: 217–235.

Vermoere, M., T. Van Thuyne, S. Six, L. Vanhecke, M. Waelkens, E. Paulissen, and E. Smets. 2002. "Late Holocene local vegetation dynamics in the marsh of Gravgaz (southwest Turkey)." *Journal of Paleolimnology* 27: 429–451.

Vogt, H. J. 1988. "Der Streit um das Lamm. Das Trullanum und die Bilder." *Annuarium Historiae Conciliorum* 20: 135–149.

Volpe, G. 1996. *Contadini, pastori e mercanti nell'Apulia tardoantica* (Bari).

Vryonis, S. 1961. "St. Ioannicius the Great (754–846) and the 'Slavs' of Bithynia." *B* 31: 245–248.

Wagschal, D. 2015. *Law and Legality in the Greek East: The Byzantine Canonical Tradition, 381–883* (Oxford).

Wagstaff, J. M. 1985. *The Evolution of the Middle Eastern Landscapes* (London).

Ward-Perkins, B. 2005. *The Fall of Rome and the End of Civilization* (Oxford).

Weber, M. 1968. *Economy and Society,* Eng. ed., 3 vols. (Berkeley).

Weiss, B. 1982. "The decline of late bronze age civilization as a possible response to climatic change." *Climate Change* 4:173–198.

Whitby, L. M. 1988. *The Emperor Maurice and His Historian: Theophylact Simocatta on Persian and Balkan Warfare* (Oxford).

———. 2000a. "Armies and Society in the Later Roman World," in Av. Cameron, B. Ward-Perkins and M. Whitby, eds., *The Cambridge Ancient History,* XIV: *Late Antiquity. Empire and Successors AD 425–600* (Cambridge), 469–495.

———. 2000b. "The Army, c. 420–602," in Av. Cameron, B. Ward-Perkins, and M. Whitby, eds., *The Cambridge Ancient History,* XIV: *Late Antiquity. Empire and Successors AD 425–600* (Cambridge), 288–314.

White, H. 2008. *Identity and Control: How Social Formations Emerge,* 2nd ed. (Princeton and Oxford).

Whitehouse, H., and J. Laidlaw, eds. 2007. *Religion, Anthropology, and Cognitive Science* (Durham).

Whittaker, C. R. 1983. "Trade and Frontiers of the Roman Empire," in P. Garnsey and C. R. Whittaker, *Trade and Famine in Classical Antiquity* (Cambridge), 110–127

———. 2002. "Supplying the Army: Evidence from Vindolanda," in Erdkamp 2002b, 204–234.

Whittow, M. 2010. "The Late Roman / Early Byzantine Near East," in C. Robinson, ed., *The New Cambridge History of Islam,* vol. 1: *The Formation of the Islamic World, Sixth to Eleventh Centuries* (Cambridge), 72–97.

Wienand, J. ed., 2015. *Contested Monarchy: Integrating the Roman Empire in the Fourth century AD* (New York).

Wierschowski, L. 2002. "Das römische Heer und die ökonomische Entwicklung Germaniens in den ersten Jahrzehnten des 1. Jahrhunderts," in Erdkamp 2002b, 264–292.

Wilken, R. L. 1992. *The land called Holy: Palestine in Christian History and Thought* (New Brunswick).

Winkelmann, F. 1979. "Ägypten und Byzanz vor der arabischen Eroberung," *Byzantinoslavica* 40: 161–182 (repr. in W. Brandes and J. Haldon, eds., *Friedhelm Winkelmann, Ausgewälte Aufsätze: Studien zu Konstantin dem Grossen und zur byzantinischen Kirchengeschichte* (Birmingham, 1993), IV.

———. 1980. *Die östlichen Kirchen in der Epoche der christologischen Auseinandersetzung (5.–7. Jahrhundert)* (Kirchengeschichte in Einzeldarstellungen I/6, Berlin).

———. 1985. *Byzantinische Rang- und Ämterstruktur im 8. und 9. Jahrhundert* (BBA 53, Berlin).

———. 1987. *Quellenstudien zur herrschenden Klasse von Byzanz im 8. und 9. Jahrhundert* (BBA 54, Berlin).

———. 2001. *Der monenergetisch-monotheletische Streit* (BBS 6, Berlin).

Woldring, H., and S. Bottema. 2003. "The vegetation history of east-central Anatolia in relation to Archaeology: The Eski Acıgöl pollen evidence compared with the Near Eastern environment." *Palaeohistoria,* no. 43–44: 1–31.

Wood, I. 1979. "Kings, Kingdoms and Consent," in P. H. Sawyer, I. N. Wood, eds., *Early Medieval Kingship* (Leeds), 6–29.

———. 1995. "Northumbrians and Franks in the Age of Wilfrid." *Northern History* 31: 10–21.

Woods, D. 2013. "Maslama and the Alleged Construction of the First Mosque in Constantinople c. 718," in B. Crostini and S. La Porta, eds., *Negotiating Co-Existence: Communities, Cultures and Convivencia in Byzantine Society* (Bochumer Altertumwissenschaftliches Colloquium, Bd. 96. Trier), 19–30.

Xoplaki, E., D. Fleitmann, J. Luterbacher, S. Wagner, E. Zorita, J. Haldon, I. Telelis, A. Toreti, and A. Izdebski. 2015. "The medieval climate anomaly and Byzantium: A review of the evidence on climatic fluctuations, economic performance and societal change." *Quaternary Sciences Review* (forthcoming)

Yasin, A. M. 2005. "Funerary monuments and collective identity: From Roman family to Christian community." *Art Bulletin* 87, no. 3: 433–457.

Yoffee, N., and G. L. K. Cowgill, eds. 1988. *The Collapse of Ancient States and Civilizations* (Tucson).

Yuzbashian, K. 1972. "De l'origine du nom 'Pauliciens.'" *Revue des Études Arméniennes* 9: 355–77.

Zellentin, H. 2011. *Rabinic Parodies of Jewish and Christian Literature* (Tübingen).

Zuckerman, C. 1988. "The reign of Constantine V in the miracles of St Theodore the Recruit (*BHG* 1764)." *REB* 46: 191–210.

———. 2002. "La haute hiérarchie militaire en Afrique byzantine." *Antiquité Tardive* 10: 169–175.

———. 2006. "Learning from the enemy and more: Studies in 'Dark Centuries' Byzantium." *Millenium* 2: 79–135.

Index

'Abd al-Malik, Caliph, 46, 47, 48, 139–140, 153, 190, 255, 310n67, 311n68, 327n79
'Abdullāh b. Muhayrīz, 294
Aegean basin, 15–16
Africa, 16, 26, 30, 32, 37, 40, 42, 43, 49–50, 56, 63, 92, 131, 160, 161, 162, 170, 176, 196, 197–204, 209, 211, 212, 214, 216, 238, 240, 241, 248, 305n3; agriculture in, 183, 240, 241, 259, 290, 339n31; coinage in, 256; commerce in, 259, 261, 262, 281, 285, 290, 347n81, 351n50; invasions and occupations of, 193, 207, 216, 241, 286, 287; Justinianic prefecture of, 27, 324n34; rebellions in, 193, 259, 339nn21, 31; Roman presence in, 46, 49, 86, 120, 208, 216, 250, 286, 287, 288, 340n45; Roman taxation of, 27, 29, 183, 207, 340n40. *See also* Carthage; Egypt
Agatho, Pope, 87
Agathon, 51, 80
agriculture, 22, 29, 66, 215–221, 233–234, 244–245; climate and, 71, 216–217, 219–221, 225, 227–231, 243, 246, 278; government and, 121, 211, 246–248, 267–268, 275–282, 352n70; styles of, 66, 227–228, 229, 244–246, 279–280, 290. *See also* fruits; grain; olives and olive oil; wine
Akroinos, 1, 54
'Ali, Caliph, 34–35
'Amr ibn al-'As, 32, 305n2
Anastasius, Patriarch, 170

Anastasius of Sinai, 102, 106, 112, 121, 134, 151, 180; *Hodēgos (Viae dux)*, 135; Questions and Answers (*Erōtapokriseis*), 82–83, 105, 114, 158, 199, 319n91; religious explication, 5, 85, 87, 108, 316n26
Anastasius II, Emperor, 52–53, 54, 169, 171, 173, 255, 305n2
Anatolia, 15–16, 62, 63, 183, 185, 190–191, 216; as agricultural center, 216–217, 219, 225–231, 241, 245, 248; attacks on, 1, 32, 34, 35, 40–41, 44, 47–48, 49–50, 52, 53, 55–56, 59, 67, 68, 138–139, 140, 141, 142, 143–146, 167, 172, 177, 189, 227, 236–238, 313n107; Christianity and, 37, 93, 106, 114, 117–118, 119; climate of, 65, 66, 70–71, 221, 223–229, 231; coinage in, 253, 254–255; elites in, 73–74, 146, 162–164, 171–172, 174, 176, 194, 196–197, 209, 213; as entrance to empire, 116, 134–135; finances, 27, 29; paganism and, 98; population transfers, 35, 44, 47, 58–59, 68, 170, 236, 239; Roman forces in, 43, 148–151, 171, 177, 267–269. *See also* Asia Minor
Andrew of Crete, 51, 83, 87, 99, 101, 315n18
Apsimar. *See* Tiberius Apsimar, Emperor
Arabs: conflicts with non-Romans, 29–30, 56, 74–75, 138, 139, 267; conflicts with Romans, 1, 4, 18, 26, 29, 32–34, 37, 39, 42–43, 46, 47, 49–50, 52–56, 65, 67–70, 83, 93, 98, 110, 134–135, 137–139, 140–145, 181,